BOOKS ON FIRE

LUCIEN X. POLASTRON

Translated by Jon E. Graham

BOOKS ON FIRE

THE TUMULTUOUS STORY OF THE WORLD'S GREAT LIBRARIES

Thames & Hudson wishes to express its appreciation for assistance given by the government of France through the National Book Office of the Ministère de la Culture in the preparation of this translation.

Nous tenons à exprimer nos plus vifs remerciements au government de la France et le ministère de la Culture, Centre National du Livre, pour leur concours dans le préparation de la traduction de cet ouvrage.

Back cover image courtesy of Corbis Images

First published in the United Kingdom in 2007 by
Thames & Hudson Ltd, 181A High Holborn,
London WC1V 7QX

www.thamesandhudson.com

British Library Cataloguing-in-Publication Data
A catalogue record for this book is available from the British Library

ISBN: 978-0-500-51384-2

Printed and bound in the USA

To Michel Godard

CONTENTS

	Acknowledgments	viii
	Preface	ix
ONE	In the Cradle of Libraries	1
TWO	The Papyrus Region	6
THREE	Islam of the First Days	42
FOUR	People of the Book	73
FIVE	Asia before the Twentieth Century	80
SIX	The Christian West	112
SEVEN	The New Biblioclasts	169
EIGHT	Peace Damages	238
NINE	An Embarrassment of Modernity	267
TEN	Flameproof Knowledge	282
ELEVEN	Epilogue: Return to Alexandria	292
Appendix 1	The Great Writers Are Unanimous: *Delenda est bibliotheca!*	300
Appendix 2	A Short History of the Census of Lost Books with a Legend to Bring It to a Close—The Hidden Library	316
Appendix 3	A Selective Chronology	322
	Notes	328
	Bibliography	343
	Index	363

ACKNOWLEDGMENTS

I would like to thank all those whose erudition, patience, or the furnishing of a clue or encouragement have facilitated the writing of this book, particularly Alain Arrault, Ibrahim Ashraf, José Luis de Balle, Pierre Barroux, María-Jesús Becerril y Gonzáles-Mata, Jeremy Black, Dorothee Bores, Marc Boulet, Alexandred Bucchianti, Michela Bussotti, Julie Caporiccio, Gérard Cathaly-Prétou, Margaret Connolly, Gérard Conte, Fabrice Costa, Roger Darrobers, Jean-Marc Dreyfus, Nadia Elissa-Mondeguer, Margarete van Ess, Marie Gustalla, Hai Chen, Jean-François Foucaud, Marc Galichet, Valerie Hawkins, Hans van der Hoeven, Guissou Jahangiri, Margareta Jorpes-Friman, Jean-Pierre Lafosse, Isabelle Landry-Deron, Agnès Macquin, Annie and Pierre Mansiat, Felix de Marez Oyens, Madiha Massoud, Matsubara Hideichi, Jacques Mawas, Isy Morgensztern, Karen Muller, Sawsan Noweir, Magda El Nowieemy, Daniel and May Ortiz, Ouyang Jiaojia, Paul Otchakovsky-Laurens, Isabelle Pleskoff, Patrick Rambaud, Jean-Noël Robert, Lucien Scotti, Raymond Josué Seckel, Walter Sommerfeld, Talko, Alain Terseur, Wang Renfang, Hans Wedler, Annette Wieviorcka, Wu Jianmng, Charlotte Yu, Danqing, and Zheng Buyon. I assume full responsibility for this work, however, and for any errors that this text might reveal, which, touching on all nooks and crannies of history in the attic of every civilization, runs the risk of attracting the finicky magnifying glass of the experts. More than their indulgence, I welcome any possible light they might shed.

PREFACE

———— ✤ ————

The first staff had only one end.

Enriching a personal library is an impulse shared by the world's teachers and all those who seek to pierce the world's secrets. Every case of this enrichment consists of the infinite repetition of the preservation and juxtaposition of books to assemble "in parallel," as the poet [Jorge Luis Borges] says, the essential or whole of all that has been said, studied, and recorded—unless it is simply motivated by a desire to see just how large a collection like this could grow.

This, however, is a case where size hardly matters: A few handfuls of manuscripts could describe a great library for one community whereas a million titles would be the measuring unit in another. The monks of Patmos were just as proud of their 330 books in the thirteenth century as the Library of Congress was when its collection exceeded 100 million shelf marks at the end of the twentieth. Likewise, at different times there have even been universal libraries that have held only one book—which are the hardest to destroy, as we shall see.

Nations and crowds of amateurs alike have pompously perpetuated this obligatory collection exercise of the powerful, and even the idiots among their ranks have never let slip a word. Like a Prometheus who practices his scales with the torture of Sisyphus, however, this feat seems to hold and accept its own condemnation. Generations and fortunes can be consumed in this pursuit of possessing knowledge, whereas the further along we get, the harder it becomes to classify and preserve books—and even to read them, if necessary, because the book hides in the library as surely as the tree hides in the heart of the forest—and any collection is exposed to the risk of destruction by fire and water, worms and wars and earthquakes. And of course there is the primary threat, which comes into play much more often than we would like to imagine: the open desire to arrange matters to give the impression that they never existed.

Why? Because, as the lawmakers of ancient China and the Nazis in Czechoslovakia decided, an educated people cannot be governed; because the conquered peoples must change their history or their beliefs, like the Aztecs; because only the illiterate can save the world, a common theme of the millenarian preachers of every era; because the nature of a great collection of books is a threat to the new power, like Taoism in the eyes of the Mongols, or Shiism to the Sunnis, or the Reformation to traditional Catholicism. To these instances we can sometimes add the self-destruction of libraries to avoid getting into trouble, as was common in Imperial China and during the Cultural Revolution.

But there is yet another, more deeply buried meaning that is always present beneath all the others: The book is the double of the man, and burning it is the equivalent of killing him. And sometimes one does not occur without the other. Except for Gérard Haddad in France (who examined the role of Jewish books), Berkeley sociologist Leo Löwenthal has been the only one to give critical examination to this phenomenon of the equivalence of the book and the human and the transposable misfortunes of the two. In his book *The Legacy of Caliban,* Löwenthal lists some of the library tragedies known as of 1983 and sketches out a corresponding psychoanalysis of humanity, which he feels is an urgent necessity because of the recurrence of these tragedies (for this "calendar holds many entries"). The consequence of the continued absence of this psychoanalytical investigation would ensure "the relapse of the continuity of meaningful history into nothingness." Löwenthal, however, did not continue his examination of what followed in history after 1983, and this work remains to be done.

Not all of the thousands of large and small collections that my research mentions or allows us to visit were burned, defecated on, or tossed into the river. They were also victims of seizure or dispersal, either in one blow or one book at a time, out of stupidity, greed, or necessity. These kinds of disappearances herald the end of a chimerical entity or turn a populace of readers into orphans, an intellectual family of "erased horizons," as another poet [Victor Hugo in *Les Misérables*] puts it without even the benefit of the glory of a cruel apotheosis that would give them eternal remembrance.

Conversely, the larger an institution may be, the more it may hide an insatiable vampire or fence bloated with quickly forgotten misappropriations. A rich library implies a dead library; sometimes such an institution should simply be renamed Museum of Colonial Booty and Sordid Thefts. To pick an example at random: France has fattened itself on fabulous, free books from Hanoi, Danang, and Louvain, and from Egypt, Spain, and Italy through Napoleon, and from North Africa and even Paris itself in 1940. I won't belabor the point; things have calmed somewhat in this regard recently, but one day such books will have to be returned to their proper owners.

In all places where an erudite construction has collapsed, there are remnants betraying its presence: the inscription on a chipped stone, for example, in Timgad; four lacunary codices that represent the entire extent of Mayan literature and knowledge; two half phrases for Carthage; or a dubious line by a semi-unknown or, conversely, a plethora of pathetic, sometimes tricky commentaries that conceal what truly happened.

The concept of the radical accumulation of ideas is a primordial myth quite capable of taking the place of this or that god. The Talmud, for example, says that there was a vast library before the creation of the world. The Qur'an clearly confirms that, yes, such a library does exist and will continue to exist for all eternity. Here is an even stronger perspective, if we are to take the Vedas at their word: This library existed before the Creator created himself.

The library vibrates in the fantasies surrounding the time before the book. The collections of Brahama and of Odin are described as an alignment of goblets of milk that, once ingested, will transform a hitherto normal individual into "a poet and a man of knowledge." The Babylonians said that the sky was made to be read: The zodiac aligns the books of revelation whereas the fixed stars are the marginal commentary, unless it is the other way around. Similarly, Berosius, priest and seer who invented the sundial, wrote a history of civilization under Alexander "based on ancient sources" that declared that before the Flood, the capital of the world was called All the Books.

Furthermore, during the weeks preceding this fateful event, Noah buried all the works he owned, "the most ancient, the ancient, and the recent," because he thought their combined weight would sink the ark. Could these have subsequently become the foundation of the Babylonian libraries? This is more or less the gist of what survived as a fireside tale, but the Egyptian priests declared that, on the contrary, the Flood dissolved these books forever because they were made of unbaked earth. Thus consigned to oblivion were the volumes written by Adam after the Fall: the *De nominibus animantium,* a census of everything that stirred in the Garden of Eden, as well as a mouthwatering poem on the creation of Eve and many other marvels that centuries of enflamed erudition will have attributed to this promising author.[1] Lost as well were the essential texts of Cain, Seth, Enoch, Methuselah. . . . We know that after the Flood, Noah's descendants mounted an assault by tower on the heavens in order to reconstruct this first of the great collections, which Noah would have been well advised to install in his hold in place of so many stupid animals.

Creation deserves cremation. In this fundamental myth of the universal library that makes man heaven's equal, what is carved into memories is the tragedy of its ruin more than the scope it sought to attain or the long adventure of its enrichment.

Here, from pure wickedness to unconscious actions organized in passing by the lowest of the low, we will see, century after century, the varied face assumed by barbarism. Toward the end, however, we risk finding that this face is a little too close to our own—too close and too similar.

ONE

IN THE CRADLE
OF LIBRARIES

——————— ❦ ———————

The weather was invisible northern lights
in the waiting rooms of the dictionary.

BENJAMIN PÉRET,
TOUTE UNE VIE [AN ENTIRE LIFETIME]

WHEN EARTH COULD SPEAK

The great library that is presumed to have been the oldest in the world has tended to be better than its younger sisters at resisting time. It can be seen, weighed in one's hands, and its books can be read today in an appreciable quantity thanks to the solidity of their texts, which were entrusted to a building material. The mason of Uruk recuperated the very first writings to raise his walls more quickly, before any desire was displayed in the years around 2500 B.C.E. to preserve these writings.[1]

Sumer-Akkadian writings, popularly called cuneiform, are punched impressions on tablets made from the clay collected between the Tigris and the Euphrates and served as the means of recording a dozen languages. Each tablet was dried in the sun, which made it brittle, or in an oven after it had been worked with fine lines to prevent it from exploding. It seemed to be a useless object except as a target for the overpowering urge to smash something into pieces, as has obviously occurred.

In addition, entire shelves of such books managed to collapse over the course of time, and once the wood rotted away, nothing was left behind but the documents they once supported, which offered the first available archaeologist the discovery of a library in its entirety and with its original classification. As for fire, which was responsible for the majority of library disappearances throughout history, here it had the effect only of vitrifying the page in its natural state *ad aeternum.*

The Sumerians of this time organized their texts and archives in willow baskets, leather sacks, or wooden boxes indexed with labels, which were also manufactured from baked clay. In one Philadelphia museum there is such a clay tablet, or "label," that includes a list of sixty-two titles dating from 2000 B.C.E. Later, in Babylon, Hammurabi's dynasty exhibited its greed for the text collections from other city-states. This could be said to have been written in the stars: The first large, encyclopedic national library could have appeared only in Mesopotamia—and, as we have known for only a little while, this is indeed what happened.

In 1850, the young and dashing Henry Austen Layard stumbled upon the site of Nineveh without truly having been in search of it in the tumulus of the "little lamb," Quyundjik, facing Mosul. The French consul Paul-Émile Botta had broken his teeth and his nails there, causing Layard to mock him in his memoirs for his overly cautious manner of exploring. Financed by the British Museum and without a second thought, Layard gutted a good half of the seventy-one rooms of Sennacherib's "peerless palace," carrying off thousands of bronzes, vases, weapons, and ivories and, most significantly, the gigantic wall reliefs and the human-headed bulls.

He said he viewed as secondary the "little rectangular tablets of dark baked clay that lay on the floors of the rooms." In places his boots sank 1–1.5 feet deep in what he took for potsherds. Even specialists in Assyria are still convinced that these holes in the clay—cuneiform—"were devised only according to the whim of the artist, in order to provide a bizarre decoration for the palace walls."[2] Three years later, southwest of the tell, the teams unearthed the "chamber of the lion hunt," decorated with now world-famous bas-reliefs whose value was much more visible to British eyes than the mounds of worn clay the discoverers were again trampling through to the tune of feverish cracking. This time, in this palace of Sennacherib's son-in-law, Ashurbanipal, there were two halls full of these clay tablets. Ashurbanipal was a complete unknown at that time, for his name appeared nowhere in antiquity. He has been made famous because of his *girginakku*, which is the Sumerian word for library.

Becoming king in 669 B.C.E., he gathered in Nineveh one of the largest libraries every created by sending scribes into every region of the empire—Assur, Nippur, Akkad, and Babylon—to hunt for every ancient text that could be found so all could be collected, revised, and copied again—often by the king himself—then categorized in his palace. Because of this, he could one day sigh: "I, Ashurbanipal, have acquired the wisdom of Nabu. I have learned to write on the tablets. . . . I have solved the old mystery of division and multiplication, which had not been clear. . . . I have read the elegant texts of Sumer and the obscure words of the Akkadians and decoded the inscriptions on the stone from the time before the Deluge." He turned a pretty phrase to describe cuneiform paleography, saying that words are "hermetic, dull, and higgledy-piggledy."

The riddled waffles of twelve hundred distinct texts unveil what a royal library was twenty-five centuries ago. To our eyes it included more raw poetry than law: invocations, rituals, divinatory materials, Sumerian lexicons, epic tales such as *The Epic of Gilgamesh*, the Creation story and myth of Adapa the first man (which may have remained unknown to us if not for Ashurbanipal), scientific manuals and treatises, as well as folktales such as *The Poor Man of Nippur*, which are precursors of *The Thousand and One Nights*.

As a direct consequence of the disappearance of Ashurbanipal and the fallow fields of his intellectual legacy, the sources are silent after 631 B.C.E. on the fate of this first great book lover and the destruction of his patrimony. We know only that Nineveh was razed by a coalition of Babylonians, Scythians, and Medes in 612 B.C.E., fourteen years after his death, and it is believed that during the burning of the palace, the tablets discovered there fell from an upper story along with the floorboards. It has also been deduced that this wealth of tablets is a mere smidgen of the royal library, whose collections were divided among a number of rooms, each of which was dedicated to a specific subject. But events move swiftly at the "little lamb." The thirty thousand tablets swiped from this mound between 1849 and 1854 were collected by shovel and amounted to 328 feet cubed, or the equivalent of five hundred of each of our quarto books containing five hundred pages. They were thrown in a jumble at the bottom of chests and tins to be lugged to Basra, then on to London, where one Henry Rawlinson had to put these puzzles together again. What he discovered prompted his nomination as head of the Nineveh excavations. Vexed, Layard abandoned archaeology. Grateful for the wealthy trove its museums owed to his efforts, the nation first made him a minister, then an ambassador and nobleman.*

Esarhaddon, the father of Ashurbanipal, wrote in July 672 B.C.E.: "This palace will grow old and fall into ruin. Raise up these ruins and, just as I have put my name next to that of the father who engendered me, you who shall reign after me, keep the memory of my name, restore my inscriptions, raise up the altars, and write my name next to yours." In 1880, Joachim Menant, who cites these words of Esarhaddon, added: "It is impossible to foresee what history holds in store for us in this regard." Prediction was all too easy, though: With time would come more pillaging, more bombs, and more imbecilic destruction, as we shall see.

The girginakku of the "king of everything, king of Assyria" could, as some researchers believe, have housed a collection of half a million tablets and some five thousand titles. Given the intrinsic resistance of this kind of book, it is easy to imagine the greatest part of the library still buried in the mound of Quyundjik, at the mercy of the direct and indirect depredations brought about by repeated Gulf wars. The curators of Western museums are in despair. They are now strictly forbidden to acquire any stolen antiquities. Just what is an Assyrian-Babylonian tablet taken out of its context, separated from the other potential sections of the same book, and stripped of the historical and scientific data that accompany its archaeological discovery if not a dust magnet in the display case of some collector in Texas or anywhere else?

---

*Some claim that certain features of this interesting if not completely honorable character were the inspiration for cinema's Indiana Jones.

Six hundred miles away and three centuries later, the custom of using clay as a writing medium fell into disuse. Certain evenings, the soul of another library that this time truly vanished in smoke hovers over the terrace of the palace of Darius I and Xerxes in Persepolis. One of its dark halls was allegedly named Fortress of Writings. There were housed, it is said, the archives of the Achaemenian kings, carved in tin or lead. Furthermore, in Hall 33 of the building known as the Treasury, under three feet of debris and pieces of the calcified cedar scaffolding of the roof, archaeologists have discovered a thick layer (some seventeen to twenty-nine inches in depth) of large balls bearing seals and effigies. These balls were in fact labels created by pressing in the palm a handful of soft clay over a string tied around a valuable object. It was thus that the seal of the proprietor king was pressed into the clay.

The raging fire that ravaged this site cooked these large balls while causing the disappearance of the objects they designated: text scrolls, according to George Cameron. It seems that here there were housed the only two manuscripts of the priest Zoroaster, "the Book of Books for the Persians." Legend has most likely inflated the size of this book; it asserts that this copy consisted of twenty times one hundred thousand lines in letters of gold on fifty-two hundred cowhides. Legend also adds that it escaped this fire only to be burned a little less than three centuries later in Alexandria. A reprieve of this nature, however, would have left some trace. As in the Boeotian Thebes and Tyre, it was Alexander the Great who ordered this deplorable destruction of the palace in Persepolis in 330 B.C.E., but his ghost whispers that the crime for which all authors since Arrian have accused him with unbroken unanimity was an accident. The decision to destroy the palace and its contents corresponds so little to the image of the legendary conqueror that doubt has been able to get a foothold, primarily among his adulators.

Incantations, dreams, accounts, and tales of humanity are inseparable from the material on which they are inscribed. As the centuries passed, this humanity would go with eyes closed to ever more finesse and flimsiness. With every change—from clay to papyrus and eventually to paper—these writings would become more vulnerable.

TWO

THE PAPYRUS REGION

— ❧ —

*If Homer had been asked what heaven Sarpedon's soul
had gone to, or where that of Hercules was, Homer
would have been quite discomfited and answered
with only some harmonious verses.*

VOLTAIRE,
PHILOSOPHICAL DICTIONARY

EGYPT

A bureaucrat from the time of Neferirkara (2462–2426 B.C.E.) had carved on his tomb that he was "scribe of the house of books." Were it not for this inscription, it would be possible to doubt the very existence of ancient pharaonic libraries. The Greek philosophers, including both Pythagoras and Plato, who visited Egypt much later, starting in the sixth century B.C.E., never said a word about such libraries, although they learned much there. This silence was so extreme that a wicked rumor was birthed: A nameless Greek had found in one of them a complete version of what would subsequently be entitled the *Iliad* and the *Odyssey*.

Vestiges of what could well be libraries, with their catalog sometimes engraved upon the wall, have been unearthed in Dendara, Esneh, and the Temple of Isis of Philae, but these are sacerdotal libraries of a limited intellectual range. "May his majesty enter his libraries and may his majesty see all the sacred words," a stela to Neferhotep commands.[1]

If there is a Hall of the Book in the Temple of Horus in Edfu, it was one rebuilt under one of the Ptolemies, which is as much as saying yesterday. With respect to the Place of the Pharaoh's Documents in Amarna, this site contains only baked-clay ostraca, the support for short texts such as correspondence, which in this case was diplomatic. The words of the Egyptian scholar were not entrusted to the glebe.

There is one pile of ruins that proves to be more troubling than the others, and its silence is greater: The "sacred library" mentioned by Diodorus in the first century B.C.E. was allegedly nestled within the Ramesseum of Thebes. Its entrance bore a warning and a profession of faith: "House for care of the soul." In this mausoleum of Ramesses II (1279–1213 B.C.E.), the institution conformed to an original and ambitious plan ordered by the king: the grouping of a number of important books (in the year 325 B.C.E., Iamblicus of Syria speaks of twenty thousand scrolls)[2] for an initiatory purpose, divvied up within a planned, highly symbolic architectural structure depicting ibis-headed Thoth, the inventor of letters, as well as Saf, "mother of writings" and "president of the hall of books."

We have no testimony available on the function or the fate of this archive most likely destroyed during the Persian conquest, but for the French scholar and Egyptologist Champollion, there was nothing in Egypt "more noble or pure" than this building. He explored this edifice and found the precise spot where he believed the books had been located—where he, too, searched with bull-headed tenacity—but his conclusion was that all had been "razed." Of course, nothing—not the slightest piece of papyrus—could have remained in this pile of stones, but the substantial quantity of documents of great value that were exhibited elsewhere in Thebes did not go unnoted. Thus the lost library of the Ramesseum, the facade guarded by its piquant epigraph, was able to excite the imagination of thirty-three centuries of writers, a period of time equivalent to the blink of an eye in this place the pharaoh called his "castle of millions of years."

Herodotus came close to saying that papyrus was a gift of the Nile. The oldest fragment is fifty centuries in age and still virgin. The first vestige bearing hieroglyphs dates from 2400 B.C.E. Thanks to papyrus, administrative documents, correspondence, and other contracts were established with a clearly pettifogging obsession for detail. Religious texts and funereal *vade mecums* multiplied along with scientific and medical treatises. The *Maxims of Ptahhotep,* surrendered by the Prisse Papyrus,* testifies to a marked respect for the book and reading. "As things currently stand, no one has ever been born intelligent . . . A written act is more useful than a stone house." Even during the Old Kingdom and especially after the Middle Kingdom, folk or imaginative literature bloomed and was the subject of meticulous transcriptions. The story and the novel were the favored genres: *The Tale of Sinuhe,* of course, but also *The Shipwreck Survivor, The Two Brothers, The Eloquent Peasant,* and the highly inappropriate *Tale of Neferkare,* in which an amateur detective trails a pharaoh, who at night scales a shaky ladder into the room of his general.[3] The texts were most likely preserved in a "school of books" located in the temple; if not, a "house of life" also makes a plausible library. There the youth were instructed in the communication professions (painting, sculpture) at the same time they practiced the liturgy intended to protect the sovereign's life. In either case, we should not imagine high buildings with shelving: The scrolls were placed either in narrow wall niches or four-foot wooden chests with convex lids, like those depicted in the frescoes of the New Kingdom.

For the thirty demotic documents discovered in two jars beneath the remnants of a Theban house, or the twenty or so books of rituals and magic found in a chest decorated with a jackal from the Thirteenth dynasty in a tomb beneath the Ramesseum,† how many hundreds of thousands of manuscripts were abandoned to destruction out of pure ignorance? Such was the fate of that collection of ancient literary works from a contemporary of Ramesses II, which was passed down through the hands of five solicitous heirs until the last one, a carpenter by trade,

---

*[The Prisse Papyrus, now in the National Library in Paris, was found at Thebes in 1846 by M. Prisse d'Avennes. —*Ed.*]

†This can be seen at the British Museum.

detached the pages—notably from the valuable *Book of Dreams*—so that he could use the other side for his business correspondence,[4] and, in 1778, of the forty or fifty Greek documents accidentally excavated in Giza by the fellahin, who burned them in order to get intoxicated from their heady aroma. The last of these scrolls was wrested from the fellahin for a price hardly higher than a cake of incense and was taken to Cardinal Borgia in Rome. Long mistakenly presented as the sole Hellenic papyrus of Egypt, it includes a list of stevedores from the years 193–192 B.C.E.

If none of the pharaonic libraries survived in a better state, it was because none of them held any reason to exist once its glorious commander faded into the afterworld on his barque. Furthermore, through many regime changes, they could have been subject to the ritual of destruction ordered by Amenhotep IV for the totality of the works possessed by the priests of Amun when Amenhotep transmuted into Akhenaten and settled in Amarna. We know that the Theban clergy returned the favor upon his death: All the scrolls housed in his temples and palaces were rudely destroyed, perhaps like his own body, evidence of how true the saying is, even this early on, that "the books of my enemy are my enemies."

Whatever of the book collections of ancient Egypt was spared from internal wars was obliterated in one fell swoop by the conquest of the Persians of Cambysus in 525 B.C.E., although this was not truly expected. All at once, Herodotus says, "it became quite obvious that Cambysus was prey to a violent madness": He had the priests flogged, the statues broken, the temples razed, and all trace of the country's culture burned, sparing the gold for himself only because it was not at all offensive to memory.

This valley of books that was mythic Egypt thus beheld the birth of elitist and anonymous libraries at the same time that it witnessed the art of making them disappear, by collections either succumbing to general decay or dying with a majestic burial. This gesture of burying treasures with the corpse of His Nibs (and thereby depriving a reading community of them) became increasingly more frequent in history, the most famous example being the Chinese emperor Taizong, who, during the seventh century, spent the bulk of his reign gathering by ruse the most beautiful writings in existence, such as the *Orchid Pavilion Preface* by the monumental calligrapher Wang Xizhi, in order to carry them away with him in his tomb. Many others followed his example. For instance, the first Mongol historian, Rashid al-Din, before being executed in Tabriz in 1318, acquired rare manuscripts by the hundreds and had them neatly arranged in his sepulchre. It contained more than a thousand works by the best writers, such as Yaqut al-Mussta'simi and even Ibn Muqla, initiators of the beautiful Arabic script.[5]

To the extent that such marvels are sometimes exhumed and found to be still legible, it is certainly possible to view as a fairly honest conservation system this egotistical practice that wipes them from the face of the earth.

The Buildings of Alexandria

Alexandria is worth a detour: Do not miss its lighthouse or the tomb of Alexander or the royal buildings, which cover a good quarter of the city (you can't do it all in just one visit), the Serapeum, and the Museum with its famous library. This is close to what a contemporary tour guide would write if he was transported twenty-two centuries into the past. Unfortunately, nothing remains of the four-hundred-foot-tall lighthouse; the fifty to seventy tons of its stone blocks are beneath the water or drowned in the walls of the neat, tidy, small Mameluk fortress that has taken its place. The palace of the Ptolemies and thus the apartments of Cleopatra have left even less trace than the temple dedicated to Serapis, which many have claimed to have been magnificent. And what of the Soma in which Alexander's noseless remains lie in state in a translucent coffin? It is perhaps here, or even there, beneath that insignificant mosque that will undoubtedly forbid any excavations until the end of Islam. As for the Library—ah! The Library . . .

Never has a construction whose location or appearance is unknown been the source of so much scholarly paper and ink or incited so many otherwise serious individuals to abandon themselves to fantasy. One example out of a hundred among the nonspecialists is Chateaubriand, who, in book ten of *Les Martyrs* (The Martyrs) absconded with the epigraph of the Ramesseum in order to replace it after altering it to suit his taste: "One evening, I remained alone in the storehouse of remedies *and poisons* of the soul. From atop a marble gallery, I watched Alexandria illuminated by the final rays of the day . . ." Then, the incomparable viscount added this promotional observation in the event his reader had been dozing: "Isn't it more relevant for us with the word I added?" In less romantic eras, however, it was wondered if the great Library of Alexandria ever really existed—at least in the architectural sense.

The irresistible Macedonian founded the first and most enduring of his Alexandrias in 331 B.C.E., then left to die far away. The son of his former bodyguard inherited the satrapy of Egypt and made off with the disputed remains of the conqueror and buried them at the center of the new city, like a sacred seed. Myth immediately put down roots. Having thereby found legitimacy, this first Ptolemy proclaimed himself king and ordered the erection of the lighthouse, which would later be called the seventh wonder of the world, and, at the same time, he erected the Museum or Temple of the Muses, site of the Library, a paradise of knowledge.*

The greatest minds of the known world were invited to collaborate on the undertaking of Ptolemy II Philadelphus, son of Ptolemy I, who had finished the construction. They were fed, housed, well paid, and exempted from taxation. Even their clothes were laundered. Euclid was a member of this circle of scholars, as was the doctor Herophilus; Erosthenes calculated the circumference of the Earth; Zenodotus produced the critical edition of Homer, the comma, and the calamus; and Archimedes sent theorems there for demonstration. Their success and notoriety were enormous—so substantial, in fact, that they inspired

---

Bibliothèque [library] first meant "box," then "warehouse of books," and comes from the Greek *biblion*, the papyrus scroll that constituted the most widespread form of the book in that era, when an appreciable quantity of written texts began to exist. This *biblion* is itself taken from *büblos*, the heart of the papyrus stalk, a preeminent Egyptian product. However it came about, the word for library took birth and its first name in Alexandria.

jealousy. As Timon of Philus, who, we can suppose, would have paid dearly to be one of the group, wrote, "Populous Egypt nurtures papyrus scratchers who ceaselessly bicker with each other in the birdcage of the Muses."

Rome, however, displayed a more fearsome envy than this forgotten skeptic. Alexandria, the city of the Athenian renaissance, with its streets lit at night and properly irrigated during the day thanks to its five hundred cisterns, Alexandria, glowing with the greatest prestige and earning the admiration of the world, with the great Library as its most original jewel: How long could this last?

> All the buildings are connected to each other and the harbor, even those lying beyond the harbor. There is a *peripatus* (a covered walkway), an *exedre* (an apse supplied with benches), and a large building inside of which is a hall where the philologists of the Museum dine together. They hold property in common and they are headed by a priest who is in charge of the institution. He was formerly appointed by the kings, but today is chosen by Caesar.

At this time, the Caesar was Augustus. Geographically speaking, all has been said—and nothing more is known. Strabo's sparse description of the premises given in 24 c.e. (or in 26 or in 27, according to different experts) says not a word about the books or how they were arranged or even anything about their destruction by Caesar several years earlier. Given that his contemporaries also guarded their silence on the matter and that the sole specific document on the Library, *The Letter of Aristeus,* which comes a century after the Library's founding, is of contested authenticity, the field is left free for conjecture and vaticination—hence polemic.

The Museum (or Mouseion, as it was then called) is, as indicated by its name, the sanctuary of the Muses, who watched over this religious foundation and in principal guaranteed its literary, philosophical, and even scientific genius. It was a university without students, a research center organized by Demetrios of Phalera, a fallen Greek tyrant but proven philosopher who was rather a snob and with whom the new king was infatuated. It was a luxurious spot modeled after the Athenian schools, particularly the Lyceum, with meeting rooms and a promenade for the exchange of peripatetic views, gardens, cloisters, a refectory, and perhaps lodgings. Nothing is said about any particular building devoted to the books, documents, and archives made available to the occupants, from which it has been deduced that the Library was "plain to view everywhere."

There is a nouveau riche–like element in all this: The king was also fond of priceless legendary animals, but never before in history has financing of such largesse been put at the disposal of men of such great expertise. Furthermore, any and all means were suitable for enriching the collection. Ambassadors were given the mission to collect books, bearing the official request from one sovereign to another to send books "of all kinds"—for example, Ptolemy was in communication with the great Indian king Asoka—but also to purchase them at hallucinatory prices. Outright theft was also an option: Customs had instructions to search for even the smallest manuscript among every vessel entering the port. If found, it would be seized and examined and a copy of it returned to the original owner. From the bottom of the hold was born the "ship collections," labeling these indexed scrolls. Ptolemy III demonstrated yet another option. As recorded, this ruler convinced the Athenian state to entrust him with the original manuscripts of Sophocles, Aeschylus, and Euripides against a high security. He later returned reproductions with a note saying: "Thank you. You may keep the money." We have the learned commentary of Galen: "Even if he had not sent copies, the people of Athens would have been powerless to do anything about the exchange, for they had accepted the money on the condition that they would keep it if Ptolemy did not return the books." The avowed purpose of this confiscation was to reconstruct all Greek science and literature and crown it all with an actual segment of Aristotle's library. The current and fairly piquant hypothesis is that Ptolemy Philadelphus was indeed able to buy "the books of Aristotle." This may indeed be true, but they were not necessarily the books the philosopher had written.[6] Added to these acquisitions were the confiscations carried out in Egypt—no doubt in Thebes or Memphis—wherever anything remained, and finally what the scholars of the Museum inevitably brought in their immigrant baggage, which was doubtless far from negligible.

All of this is of little consequence compared to the immense labor of translation, analysis, and copying that animated these premises. "Sowing, if I can put it this way, the seeds for an infinity of books," as Vitruvius said, the great Library of Alexandria was primarily the largest publishing house of antiquity, and a considerable trade in books took place in the port and toward the inner lands because the city was the Hong Kong of its era, a universal emporium. Alexandrian philology "transformed into books an ancient literature, which had not been intended at its birth to be fixed in that state."[7] Thus there appeared on its shelves Buddhist texts, two million lines on Zoroastrianism, the history of Babylon by a Chaldean priest, and the translation of the Bible by the Septante: sixty-two "Hellenists" (in the original sense of the term, meaning Jews who knew Greek), who, legend claims, were confined to the island of the lighthouse in separate cells for seventy-two days before turning in the Pentateuch. When the Library burned down, logically countless original manuscripts vanished in one fell swoop—in particular, all the versions of Homer's texts carried away by Zenodotus, the body of Hippocrates' work studied and vouched for by Galen, the great Athens tragedies, the original of the Torah brought from Jerusalem, and so forth.

Ptolemy* asked: "Precisely how many thousands of books are here?" Demetrios hastened to respond: "We are at twenty thousand, my king, but I am urgently seeing to the final steps necessary to reach five hundred thousand." We must pay attention to the meaning of the words in this exchange: A scroll or *volumen* represents one "book," meaning the chapter of a work. Homer required forty-eight scrolls, Polybius forty, and Plato's *Republic* comprised a dozen total. Keeping in mind that each title requires twenty-four rolls of papyrus on average, as is the case with the *Odyssey,* we can deduce that five hundred thousand volumes would

---

*[Historians do not agree on whether this was Ptolemy I or II. —*Trans.*]

represent some twenty thousand titles as we now conceive of them.

Once this figure had been attained, it was a young instructor from the suburbs who had the merit and energy to inventory and classify the works into a dozen categories and to organize the authors by alphabetical order within each category. This Callimachus, who was also a great poet, therefore became the first of the great bibliographers, if not curators. Responsible for the exactitude of the texts produced, he sighed, *"Mega biblion, mega kakon,"* which means "Many writings equals many worries." Entitled *Tables* (pinakes) *of the Authors Who Have Distinguished Themselves in All Forms of Knowledge and the Works They Have Written,* his catalog alone took up 120 volumes, which were added to the ninety thousand scrolls consisting of isolated works and the 410,000 of those consisting of "mixed works." Because space was lacking, an annex was contrived in the Serapeum, and this "daughter" library contained 42,800 scrolls when it opened.

So why did Strabo fail to talk in more detail about such an important library? In a deliciously nebulous book that cannot fail to bring to mind the adventures of Blake and Mortimer, the Italian academic Luciano Canfora brazenly takes a stance opposite all other academics* and describes the books arranged in the walls, in particular those of the *peripatos,* rather than in an isolated building. As proof he cites two niches constructed in just this way in the Temple of Horus in Edfu, rebuilt during the same era as the Library. These niches are actually accompanied by a list of thirty-seven book titles painted on the wall. It is necessary to picture the great Library displayed along the peripatus, "a large covered promenade. Each niche welcomed a definite kind of author." This hypothesis is more than audacious: Existing as it does between the sea and Lake Mareotis, Alexandria has ferocious humidity, and scrolls stored in the open air would not have lasted two years.

Furthermore, archaeology seems to show that in the Serapeum

---

*While Mostafa El-Abbadi summed up more sensibly the commonly accepted facts in *Vie et destin de l'ancienne Bibliothèque d'Alexandrie* (Paris: UNESCO, 1992), in 1952, E. A. Parsons pulled out all the stops to prove that Caesar was not responsible, albeit with much less subtlety than Canfora and even in a way that was described in Oxford as "lamentably defective."

annex, the walls of the rooms holding books are twice as thick as the other walls in the structure, as in Pergamum and Ephesus, while braziers sent currents of hot air through baked clay pipes to offset the moldiness. In addition, all we need to do is count: Knowing that the average papyrus scroll has a diameter of 2.5 inches, one half million such books requires twenty linear miles of shelving or, in the more likely case of niches with shelves crossed to form a diamond pattern with a total of five hundred copies for every six-foot niche, we come up with an unthinkable gallery of more than a mile. Alternatively, we can accept the idea of several interconnecting rooms with walls full of papyri—perhaps one for each category, a dozen in all to reflect the divisions Callimachus noted for his classification.

When, several decades later, Pergamum founded a library rivaling the one in Alexandria, it is logical that it would have copied the architecture of Alexandria's great Library. We happen to know the plan of this construction: rooms in a line that open on to a lighted colonnade serving as a promenade for reading. This arrangement created a long air intake that provided favorable conditions for the misfortune that eventually destroyed the works housed in Alexandria.

The Destructions of Alexandria

Decked out in her finery, Cleopatra would have found it somewhat difficult to visit this great Library regularly with great pleasure. The Mouseion's glory days were already long past. Perhaps the great Library was also in a reduced state if not totally extinguished? Among other events, the return from exile of the eighth Ptolemy (Evergetes II, known as Physkon or Fat Belly) had emptied Alexandria of its Greeks (around 127 B.C.E.), especially those on the Museum's payroll. The Roman world had taken the upper hand over a fin-de-siècle Egypt by refereeing the civil war of the queen against her younger brother, the thirteenth Ptolemy. Caesar, as we know, sided with the sister, but finding himself trapped far from Rome with few forces, he decided to destroy the large enemy fleet in the port, swollen with about fifty ships that had sailed to the rescue. The fire, says Lucan, "spread to other parts of the city. . . . The buildings close to the sea caught on fire, the wind increased the force of the disaster, the flames . . . raced over the roofs with the speed of a meteor," and so on. And thus was destroyed the great Library of Alexandria in 48 B.C.E.

When personally recounting the battle, however, Caesar discards the unfavorable cards in his hand and, as justification for the fire, describes the critical position he was in. Given the unusually defensive tone of this text, it can be read as an involuntary admission of his guilt.[8] Within this hypothesis, Strabo's careful avoidance of any mention of the vanished Library would be a case of self-censorship. In fact, the matter remained a thorny one less than twenty years after the dire event. The dead Caesar was still the living Caesar. Conversely, Seneca, Plutarch, and Aulus Gellius formed a choir charging Cleopatra's lover with this catastrophe and differed only as to the number of books annihilated: forty thousand; five hundred thousand; or seven hundred thousand to a million.

The narratives closest to the actual time of the event speak only of the warehouses of books located near the docks, not of the buildings of the Museum. In fact, whether this concerns books seized from ships or the bundles of scrolls imported by royal decree, books just arrived in Alexandria were likely initially housed in "certain buildings," the *apothecae,* where they were held for a specified period of time and perhaps stamped, sorted, and distributed among the mother and daughter libraries. It is equally possible that the many copies ordered from the publishing center that Alexandria was at that time could also have been stored there awaiting export. Is it possible that there were forty thousand books in this storage zone?

Three versions of the story remain to be noted. The first recalls that Caesar clearly wished to establish a large public library in Rome. His assassination prevented him from witnessing the realization of this project, but nine years following the battle of Alexandria, the Roman library was inaugurated. Had the transfer of the Mouseion's contents already been under way with the consent of Cleopatra, whose sole intent was always to rule on both sides of the Mediterranean? Would the books Caesar had withdrawn and made ready for embarkation have been reduced to ashes with the burning of the port? This would explain the contrite sobriety of the accounts of the battles. Another notion is that almost all the books survived the battle of Alexandria only to be later destroyed during the various and quite violent events that followed. The third possibility is that, fantasy and dithyramb having fueled the literature on this topic, all the authors writing about the Library could have casually overestimated the wealth of this then aging archive, as would occur on many occasions in the years to follow. When the queen of kings is described by Aphthonius as visiting the Library dressed as Isis, he was actually speaking of the Serapeum. Had the number of books in the Library of Alexandria been reduced to forty thousand scrolls—Seneca's accepted figure—by the year 48 B.C.E.? This number brings the majority of hypotheses into the realm of the reasonable. It also represents a quantity of books that is infinitely easier to destroy . . . and to reconstruct, as we shall see.

"To study Alexandria today is to personally become an Alexandrian," says Christian Jacob. It is enough, in fact, to lean over a sun-drenched balcony of the Azarita quarter to realize how narrow is the port in front of the palace and to picture the harbor full of the burning Egyptian fleet there on the right and a handful of Roman galleys huddled far away, near the lighthouse, and to imagine heading toward you that wave of fire that would consume the shipyards, the royal warehouses, and everything that is "right after."

When clever arguments confront each other too long over details, the truth eventually returns yawning to its lair. The card deck of ancient history can sometimes be beaten and reshuffled at will, especially when it is studded, as in this case, with jokers that are interpretable ad libitum: Cicero's mysterious silence, for example, or the loss of Titus-Livy's Book 112 that specifically deals with Caesar's sojourn in Egypt, or, foremost among them, Strabo's account, as he saw exactly what happened and said nothing.

But then we have Marcus Antonius making off with the library of Pergamum and depositing two hundred thousand volumes made of parchment at the feet of Cleopatra. Established in this ephemeral city of Asia

Minor was the dynasty of the Attalids, who adorned their modest origins with an ostentatious taste for arts and letters. Eumenes II (196–160 B.C.E.) took little time to create a fabulous library and toiled so relentlessly on stocking it that people would hide their favorite books. It is said that a jealous Ptolemy V decreed an embargo on papyrus to halt this development, which would have brought about the emergence of parchment, then called *pergamene charta.* Varro, who in the same simplistic phrase swore that papyrus was invented in Alexandria (which makes it all a bit dubious), is responsible for recording this matter for history.

The books of Pergamum most likely joined the tens of thousands of scrolls in the daughter library of the Serapeum, which, according to all the hypotheses, remain intact after the fire. Although more restricted, the research activity by less prestigious scholars continued uninterrupted. Far from what we might expect, however, the reputation of Hellenic Alexandria still managed to irritate Rome. Octavius brought a final end to this love song.

The convulsions of the moribund Roman Empire now violently shook its Egyptian colony. In 213 C.E. Caracalla saw to the slitting of the throats of the young men of the city who had mocked him and he expelled all foreign researchers from the Museum, whose revenues he had eliminated, and saw to its destruction. Sixty years later, Aurelian attacked the city that had invested Zenobia, queen of Palmyra. Battles raged within the royal enclosure and supposedly caused substantial destruction to the Museum. (Those historians who seek to absolve Caesar place the destruction of the Great Library here; otherwise, they blame the humidity or the Arabs, if they are Christian.) The ravages resumed with Diocletian: In 296 C.E. the city was devastated by fire and sword following an eight-month siege, and the bulk of its inhabitants were murdered. Blood flowed again in reprisals against the thinkers who allegedly were concocting alchemical treatises. Books on manufacturing gold were burned, "apprehensive, as we are assured, lest the opulence of the Egyptians [responsible for it] should inspire them with confidence to rebel against the empire," writes John of Antioch, quoted by Edward Gibbon, who adds with the humor that was his trademark: "It is much more likely that his [Diocletian's] good sense discovered to him the folly of such magnificent pretensions and that he was desirous of preserving the reason and fortunes of his subjects from such mischievous pursuits."

These storms, however, followed by anti-Christian persecutions in which Galerius ordered all the prophets' writings cast publicly into the fire, did not come about at the end of the old Museum. A number of Christian thinkers spent much time there or visited it: Clement from Alexandria itself; Origen and Pamphila from Caesarea; another Alexander, from Jerusalem, who founded or developed a large library. All four of these were schooled in the shadow of the Muses of the Serapeum. In 315 c.e., the Syrian rhetorician Aphthonius wrote, "[T]he public library of Alexandria was at the Acropolis, next to the chambers of the former gods. There are also scholars who frequent this spot and perform great service." He described it as garnished with cases "that serve to hold the books and are open to those who enjoy working to acquire philosophy and offer the entire city an easy means of acquiring wisdom," which is, frankly, an exaggeration. But the daughter library did not fail to impress: "The wealth of these porticos was extraordinary. The ceiling was gilded, and the capitals of the columns were gilded in bronze."[9] At the end of the fourth century, Ammiansis Marcellinus could then testify: "Even now in this city, the various branches of learning make themselves heard because the masters of the arts are still alive."

But not for much longer. When Christianity became mandatory, it was the turn of paganism to be persecuted. Theodosius undertook the destruction of all the monuments. It was also his zealot, the Alexandrian bishop Theophilus, whose "hands were as stained by blood as they were by gold," who attacked the Serapeum at the head of a band of fanatics. The intellectual intrigues taking place within the "Alexandrian Acropolis" seemed alarming to even the least devoted: "Many things now found refuge in this ancient Ptolemaic sanctuary—philosophy, magic, learning, license."[10] The mob left not a stone of it standing or a single statue intact.

The library fared even less well. Paulus Orosius, the Spanish priest and author of *Stories against the Pagans,* which would hold such sway during the Middle Ages, noted when he arrived in Alexandria twenty years later: "There are at present temples, which we have seen, whose bookshelves have been emptied by the men of our time." The historians recording his remarks unfailingly add "full of rancor" or "indignation," but it can be asked if "with satisfaction" may not be more apt, for it was that year (415 C.E.) that the common people were greatly influenced by Theophilus's nephew, the patriarch Cyril, and his *parabolani,* or militiamen, displaying a frenetic enthusiasm against whomever they pleased, particularly the Jews, although they had been full Alexandrian citizens for seven centuries. Similarly, Cyril had the philosopher and algebraist Hypatia, the sole woman in the history of mathematics, murdered one day when she was on her way to give a conference at the Museum. She was quite beautiful as well as wise, it was said, and she was inordinately popular and not a Christian. Consequently, she found herself stripped naked by the mob and dragged into a church before Peter the Reader, then cut to pieces with oyster shells while still alive before being thrown along with all her works into the fire. Hypatia was the daughter of Theon, a mathematician and astronomer who had died in 380 C.E., and who had been the last scholar to be a member of the Mouseion. Cyril was canonized.

Like the phoenix, however, the intellectual predominance of Alexandria seemed to have been restored during the fifth century, and a university was founded there by Mark the Evangelist. Then, in 640, Egypt fell into the hands of Islam under the caliphate of Umar and was occupied by the famous general Amr ibn al-As. A companion of the Prophet and a member of the tribe of Quraysh, Amr founded Fustat and again became governor of Egypt under the Ummayads before dying there in 663. He was a friend of an old sage named John the Grammarian. One day John said to him: "You have stamped your seal on everything of value in this city. I ask nothing of you that is useful, but things that are useless could still be of service to us."

"What do you have in mind?" asked Amr.

"The books of wisdom that are in the royal treasury," answered John.

Amr had his friend recount the long history of the Library and, won over, answered, "I cannot dispose of these books without the authorization of the caliph. I will write him a letter telling him what you have just told me."

A report was therefore written and during five or six weeks, while they awaited a response, the Arab general and the elderly Alexandrian were able to discuss delicate points of theology at their leisure. Umar finally sent his answer: "Regarding the books of which you spoke, if what is found therein conforms to the Book of God, the Book of God allows us to do without them; if there is something therein that is contrary to the Book of God, then they are evil. Please see to their destruction." Amr ibn al-As therefore unwillingly ordered that these books be distributed among the *hammans*—of which there were some four thousand—as heating fuel. It took six months for this resource to be exhausted. "Listen to this adventure with admiration," concludes Ib al-Qifti in his *History of the Scholars*, written around 1227. Some gentlemen closer to our own time have made utterly sincere calculations that at twenty volumes a day per bath, heating the water would have required some 14 million scrolls. Not at all, retorts a colleague, some hammans were maintained at 140 degrees Fahrenheit, which would require a hundred books a day, meaning at least 72 million copies.

This shameless and late appropriation of the Alexandrian myth by the Arab imagination would lead to the somewhat tortured parable seeking to excuse Saladin,[11] who sold off the legendary Fatamid library of Cairo to pay his soldiers, which we will revisit later. Yet it is not necessarily without any foundation: Umar, the second caliph and the first to proclaim himself *amir al-mu'minin,* "commander of the believers," would also be the first great Muslim vandal—again, a topic we will revisit.

If, therefore, the great Library of Alexandria is incontestably posed as the symbol of all other libraries—*um al-maktabat,* the "mother of libraries," in Arabic—it is, first of all, because no physical reality exists either to contradict or to support the alarming exultations it inspires, and also because it provides a tangible symbol of the intellectual turning point between antiquity and our own dark world. Regardless of the length of Cleopatra's nose, its works offered the vertiginous possibility of a Greek, not Roman, future. Its durability might well have created a dam to hold back the monotheistic tidal wave and, according to some, made it possible to leap squarely over the early Middle Ages. "If this Library had survived, the dark ages, despite the preponderance of Christianity, could have been considerably lighter."*

How could a dream that has become a foundational myth of such consequence not have experienced a good half-dozen real or imagined fires to finish it off?

ATHENS

Strabo declares that Aristotle was always the greatest book collector and that he "taught the kings of Egypt how to organize a library." He did so in quite indirect fashion, as we have seen, for it was a disciple of his successor, Theophrastus, who organized the first Great Alexandrian Library necessarily modeled after the Greek Lyceum.

Aristotle (384–322 B.C.E.), son of a rich landowner and doctor, was a dandy, fingers covered with rings, who was the first to grasp the power of the book. His teacher Plato scornfully nicknamed him the Reader, a sign of just how bizarre it seemed at that time to collect writings. Plato never guessed that this disciple would soon become a rival by going far beyond reading alone: Aristotle's texts exceed 170 titles, which equals several hundred papyrus scrolls.

All that remain are thirty works, which fill some two thousand of our paper pages. They have come down to us in a fairly chaotic fashion: Bequeathed to Theophrastus, Aristotle's library then fell into possession of Neleus of Skepsis. It is reckoned[12] that the works of both Aristotle and Plato put together represent only 676,078 lines. Neleus's uneducated descendants sought to hide these books from the lustful eyes of the Pergamum library and buried them in a cave or well, in a "kind of trench full of moths," says Strabo, then sold the authentic

---

*Hugh Lloyd-Jones

books by Aristotle that had escaped Ptolemy[13] to Apellicon of Teos (who, according to some, was a philologist and, according to others, was a dealer in secondhand goods). Apellicon brought them to Athens, where Sulla stole them in 86 B.C.E. They eventually ended up in Rome with Tyrannion the Grammarian, then made their way through various hands (not always the cleanest) to Andronicus of Rhodes, who attempted the first edition of the works of the celebrated Aristotle but who was forced to work from copies of copies in which holes made by rats, moths, and worms had been filled by various scribes (depending on the different authors, not all at once) for their own financial benefit.

But we must not get sidetracked here: It is now believed that the surviving texts were not correct and were actually distorted copies by Aristotle's students, to whom the philosopher gave the task of recording his arguments. John Philoponus, among others, reports in the fourth century: "Of the forty books of his *Analytica* preserved in the ancient libraries, four alone were regarded as authored by him, and there can be no doubt that this is so." Strabo had already indicated his own suspicions: "Some booksellers employ unqualified scribes and do not collate the manuscripts, something that happens when books are copied for commercial reasons, here or in Alexandria. But enough on this topic!"* We have reached a point at which it is possible to ask if we know the true logic of Aristotle's work, if not his thought. In any case, what does emerge from it on the scientific plane, which was already lagging far behind for its time, has been subsequently rendered into a figure of ridicule by research. Because he also maintained that woman was an imperfect man, Aristotle's philosophy was widely adopted by both church and mosque to the detriment of quite a few other systems, which plunged half of the world into a forced Aristotelianism at least until the reappearance of Neoplatonism in fifteenth-century Florence.

Geographica 13.1, cited by Drossaart Lulofs, who does not give a moment's credence to this pilgrimage of the double library (copies of books made for commercial reasons) but has nothing to suggest in its stead. Furthermore, we can note what seems to be an involuntary admission on the part of Strabo: Books were still being published in Alexandria.

Legend has it that before the library of the Lyceum, there was the curious example of the tyrant Pisistratus 1, who would have collected for good reason: His ancestors were named in the works of the Homeric era,* thus he established the first written version of the *Illiad* (without which we may well have had only echoes of the epic) and installed all of it in what would be the world's first public library. On September 21, 480 B.C.E., it is said that this library was pillaged by Xerxes, the man who ordered the sea flogged when it acted contrary to his wishes, and he carried off the collection to his palace of Persepolis, where Seleucus Nicator later took possession of it, along with the rest of the Achaemenian empire, with the intention, it seems, of returning the works to Athens.[14] But to tell the truth, the collection vanished from sight.

As these myths go, the most highly preferred is the sack of Athens by the Goths in 260 C.E.: All the libraries were emptied and their contents heaped in an enormous pile. At the moment it was about to be set alight, one of the Goth leaders said: "As long as the Greeks remain slaves to reading, they will remain unskilled in the vocation of arms." The almost-thousand-year scholarly tradition of Athens was truly abolished in 529 with no need for a barbarian to flex his muscles; instead it was destroyed by Justinian, a Bulgarian peasant turned Byzantine emperor. He imposed silence on all the Athenian schools by proscribing all "philosophical inquiry so repugnant to the doctrine, or at least to the temper, of a humble believer," says Gibbon. Speed was of the essence to eradicate the danger. The last and brilliant director of Plato's Academy, Proclus, who died in 485, had established eighteen arguments that rendered unacceptable the Christian version of the world's creation.

Classical Greece had about a thousand authors, only a tenth of whose production we think we know, for papyrus is such a perishable substance. This is no doubt an essential reason for the disappearance of the literature of antiquity in humid Alexandria and everywhere else. On

---

*This has also been said about Polycrates of Samos, but with very few confirming elements, and several historians (E. Edwards, A. Hessel, and R. Pfeiffer, among others) deem the case to be little likely; others (such as Platthy) accept it.

the other hand, old texts survived beneath the dry sand, as, for example, the hundreds of fragments of scrolls and codices in papyrus or parchment discovered in Oxyrhynchos, two hours south of Cairo: personal and business letters, extracts from the Christian scriptures and ancient poets such as Sappho and Sophocles, along with a piece of an unpublished work. Had this lot of documents been piously gathered together in the archives of a former Greco-Roman colony? Not at all. Someone (but who?) had thrown it away as trash.

ROME

When Paulus Aemilius defeated Perseus in 168 B.C.E., his soldiers laid hands on everything of any possible value in the Macedonian king's palace while making a cursory attempt to respect the general's order not to touch the books. He was reserving them for the use of his sons, which, he said with his customary flair for language, would do them more good than gold. The first Roman libraries were built upon the backs of plundered foes and older cultures. It was thus with Sulla as with Lucullus, who dispossessed Mithradates, king of Pontus, and was famous at the time less for his munificent pleasures than for his wealth of reading material and welcoming shelves. Plutarch said that "his arcades, galleries, and reading rooms were open to all visitors," and that vacationing geniuses from Greece loved to frequent this spot and give dissertations in which the master of the house sometimes liked to participate.

Scipio Aemilius in Carthage reveals himself to be much more of a numbskull. Because the books in the libraries were in foreign tongues and he swore only by the Greek, he authorized the destruction of everything with the exception of a work attributed to Magon that, he had been told, touched on agriculture and from which all the Latin manuals on this subject were henceforth concocted. Here is a little squeaking of *fatum*: Scipio's father was none other than Paulus Aemilius.

Yet "according to some very learned men, there were many good things in the Punic books."[15] Pliny even claims that they were not burned: "Carthage conquered, the Senate distributed the libraries to the kinglets of Africa." But the opposite is more likely: Nothing should have remained of Carthage and especially not the *libri punici* (whose labels may well have been found, as in Persepolis, in the form of signet clay disks baked by a conflagration). Sallust could have allowed this controversy to be settled, but "for Carthage, I would prefer saying nothing rather than saying too little." As with Strabo in Alexandria, the only recourse offered historians was to raise their arms to heaven.

Varro, who died in 27 B.C.E. at a very advanced age, was the author of seventy-four titles represented by more than six hundred volumes on all manner of subjects such as grammar, agriculture, and archaeology. Limited printings, if not single copies, were the hallmark of that era. Because of Marcus Antonius, who had these titles burned for reasons that remain obscure, all that is left are fragments of these works. Most important, there is nothing of his *De bibliothecis,* which constitutes a square loss. It was in fact their reading of this work that allowed Pliny, Suetonius, and Aulus Gellius to describe so knowingly the great collections of vanished books, especially the Greek volumes, and leave us with nothing but our curiosity. Varro's expertise in this domain earned him the singular mission from Julius Caesar to create the public library of Rome. He began by having plans for it drawn up while he collected Greek books and—this was a new twist—Roman texts.

Several years later, this initial collection permitted the posthumous realization of Caesar's dream in the Atrium Libertatis, which faced the Curia. Among the busts of illustrious writers adorning the premises in accordance with a recently introduced style, the sole living author depicted was Varro. The booty of a bloody victory against an Illyrian people had permitted the consul Asinius Pollio, who was also an author at times, to finance the institution and, for doing so, to steal celebrity in the eyes of his contemporaries. Pliny said in his regard: *"Ingenia hominum rem publicam fecit"*—that is, "he has made genius a public property."

These words are less applicable to Augustus. Suetonius writes: "After becoming Pontifex Maximus . . . he collected whatever prophetic writings of Greek and Latin origin were in circulation either anonymously or under the names of authors of little repute and burned more than two thousand of them, retaining only the Sibylline books and making a choice even among these, which he kept in two gilded cases beneath the pedestal of the Palatine Apollo." The legend maintained that these nine books had been offered to the king Tarquin Priscus by the Sibyl of Cumae for the price of three hundred pieces of gold. When the king laughed, the Sibyl then burned three of the books and asked the same sum for the remaining six. "This old crone is mad," said the king. But on seeing her destroy three more books, he went completely pale and paid three hundred gold pieces for the last three prophetic books, for which act Rome still patted itself on the back.[16]

Censorship was part of the general mores even then, as denoted by the affair of Numa, the successor of Romulus, and his false library. In 181 B.C.E., this "library" was discovered in a buried chest that contained fourteen Greek works dealing with the philosophy of Pythagoras (who was born around two centuries *after* Numa), and the Senate subsequently ordered the praetor to destroy them. According to Clarence Forbes: "These books were bold forgeries, but it is clear someone wrote them and that they were burned. Thus the first attempt to introduce Greek philosophy into Rome, by means of subterfuge, was abortive." Suetonius adds that Augustus also had all the books about Julius Caesar's youth pulled from the shelves, because he felt they clashed with the official image that Augustus had created of Caesar. Albeit under the strictest supervision, Augustus did establish two libraries—the Palatine and the Octavian—and he was imitated in this way by many of his successors, such as Tiberius, Caligula, Vespasian, and Trajan, who each created at least one library.

These libraries frequently consisted of two buildings, one for Greek manuscripts and the other for Latin texts—for example, like the two that face each other in the sumptuous Ulpia of Trajan (named after Ulpius, whose column still stands quite straight between the two buildings, like the beam of a scales or a pontificating finger).

Libraries close to the gods, libraries close to the people: Emperors starting with Nero offered the Roman inhabitants the pleasure of increasingly beautiful public baths, which were both meeting places and centers of physical and mental culture. Available there to be borrowed and read, whether for distraction or instruction, were the classics of the ages as well as the latest works. Judging by a testimony from the year 350 C.E., the city included some twenty-nine public libraries. They were even proliferating throughout Italy and the provinces: Not only in Como and Tibur, but also in Dertona, Volsinium, Timgad, and Lyon, these baths were part of the design for Romanization.

How could Roman snobbism, born in the first century—that of the *Pax Romana*—fail to imitate the whim of emperors or the passion of celebrities? (For example, Cicero had a library in each of his villas along with an army of librarians to administer them.) It is Gaius Pollio's contemporary Vitruvius who set the architectural and decorative criteria for the self-respecting rich man's villa: "The rooms and libraries should be facing the sunrise, for their use demands morning light, and furthermore so that the books do not decay as much in these libraries as those that face the noon sun and sunset, which are subject to worms and humidity; for the same wind-borne humidity that gives birth to and nourishes worms also causes books to mold." Like regular and thermal baths, the library was an ornament of the house, its shelves "of cedar and ivory" ennobling and decorating dining rooms. The nouveau riche had three: one for Greek, one for Latin, and one for what language we shall never know.[17] Seneca and Lucian, however, inveighed against this inconsequential enthusiasm. What is the good of so many books that will never be read except for at most the incipit, which then serves as a title? We might add, what is the good of so many texts and so little philosophy while fate under various disguises was rumbling everywhere?

The fire is a gift of Rome: flames, agony, the odor of smoke permeating daily life, and more or less quickly quelled. But quite often a true apocalypse struck. The inventory of conflagrations[18] that tenaciously ravaged all or part of the Urbs is precise: no fewer than eighty-eight between the time of Romulus and the decline of the political capital. A Roman—if he survived—had the chance of seeing a good half-dozen fires over the course of a lifetime. Admissible or not, the causes of the disasters were numerous and repetitive: lightning, slave revolts, civil war, and every night, in each small street, the torches of anonymous citizens coming and going about their business, not to mention the fire that the Vestals were responsible for maintaining at all times. The wary Cicero reminds us that without the owner's consent, a cremation pyre should be located at least sixty feet from a private dwelling.

The points where the blazes began were almost always the same: Forum, Palatine, Capitol. And there was always a large library bordering the most heavily frequented areas. In 80 C.E., for example, the Field of Mars caught on fire, as did the Capital. Among the items on the impressive lists of losses compiled by Dio Cassius are Octavian's portico and its libraries. Domitian then sent people to dig through the collections in Alexandria for replacements for the lost scrolls "by dint of money," not without correcting the texts in passing.* In 188, lightning struck the temple of Jupiter Capitoline and, according to Orosius, known as the "mystic of catastrophe," destroyed *"bibliothecam illiam, maiorum cura studioque compositam"*—that is, his library, which he had organized with great zeal and care. Three years later, fire erupted in the warehouses of the Oriental shopkeepers and the resulting flames turned night to day around the Temple of Peace, the Forum, and Palatine. It is said that this was at the behest of Emperor Commodus. It is true that he mentioned it, but did he do it? In any case, a large number of libraries were destroyed, a fact deplored later by Dio Cassius, Herodian, and Galen.

When fate does not strike, man can take it upon himself to do so. For example, Sulla was the arsonist of July 6, 83 B.C.E.; the Sibylline books that had been so expensive were destroyed at this time and it was necessary to send emissaries to all the Mediterranean provinces in the hope of reconstructing the indispensable oracles.† Shortly thereafter, as denounced by Cicero, it was Clodius, Caesar's right-hand man, who "burned the Temple of the Nymphs in order to destroy . . . official tablets" that were deemed compromising. *Bis repetita:* A certain Q. Sosius set fire to the Tabularium, the building housing the archives, correspon-

---

*A French translator of Suetonius, Henri Ailloud, used the books from Pergamum, which were the only ones available at that time.

†Their ultimate destruction took place in 408 C.E., thanks to the general Flavius Stilicho, who favored Christianity.

dence, and laws, where three thousand tablets were turned to liquid, despite the fact that they were bronze. The obstinacy of memory is a new phenomenon, and power sometimes vacillated between pride and apprehension. Several arsonist slaves will clean house if necessary.

Quo Vadis? gave a starring role to the conflagration that erupted on July 19, 64, near the Palatine, in a quarter of shops and *insulae* (apartment buildings). Propelled by the sirocco, the fire spread for six days and nights, destroying the city before almost sputtering out at the foot of the Esquiline Hill, where Nero, touring the gardens of Maecenus, contemplated the inferno while reciting verses. The next day, the fire blazed into new life and on the ninth day, when it had finally been extinguished, only four out of fourteen "regions" of the city were still standing. Given that Nero had said that he "was shocked by the ugliness of the old buildings and by the narrow, winding streets," during these horrible nights one saw or wished to see some of his slaves carrying torches and helping the fire to spread. Sincerely sympathetic but checked by rumor, the emperor had no other recourse but to deal these losing cards to someone else. As Tacitus tells us, thus Nero "punished with the most frightful tortures those people whom the mob calls Christians and who are detested for their enormities," although it appears that the plotters of Piso were, unbeknownst, responsible. The fact remains that during this week the rare manuscripts of the important Palatine Apollo library, which housed thirty thousand *volumina,* disappeared along with those in all the other libraries located in the path of the flames, such as the library of the palace of Tiberius, which kept the 150 discourses of Cato, of which only several fragments remain.

As a consequence of the periodic conflagrations (whether intentional or not), the certain and definitive loss of all manner of works has been recorded: 109 pieces by Plautus; twenty-four by Ennius; forty by Accius; Cicero's philosophical treatise *Hortensius* as well as all his poetry, with the exception of a few verses; almost all of Varro; all the epics written during the time of Virgil; the greater part of the *Satyricon* (although its exact size is not known); 107 out of 142 volumes of the Roman history by Titus-Livy (including the one that holds the key to the mystery of Alexandria);

entire sections of Tacitus and Pliny the Elder (only thirty-seven books remain of the latter's *Natural History* out of the more than five hundred volumes he devoted to grammar, the art of war, and other subjects); and we will never benefit from Telephus of Pergamum's *Understanding Books*, *On the Selection and Acquisition of Books* by Herennius Philon, or the *Bibliophilia* by Damophilus of Bithynia.[19]

Lucretius explains volcanic eruptions not as the din caused by the anvils and forges of the Cyclops but by the existence of underground winds when they are overheated and enraged. Did Pliny have a moment to curse this infernal flatulence when an ocean of burning gases poured over and asphyxiated him in 79 C.E. near Vesuvius at Stabius? Following the advice of his people, he put a pillow over his head to protect himself from the incandescent pebbles that had begun to rain down heavily.

On August 24 and for four days altogether, the mountain spat cinders and rock and poured its 570-degree breath and then its vomit over the land, the people fleeing in vain, and the houses—the homes of both the poor and the merchants of Pompeii, as well as the summer residences of the Roman aristocrats in Herculaneum and even the most extraordinary structure of all, the villa of the Pisos. There Caesar's father-in-law had established a small palace of intelligence and culture: a series of inner courtyards, colonnades, pools, statues meticulously selected for their kinship to the philosophy of the premises, and a long arcade that led to a belvedere overlooking the sea, where a small group of sincere friends exchanged ideas while munching on sardines and onions. (The rich epicurean prided himself on his frugality.) The mentor of the house's mentor, the Greek philosopher Philodemus, installed in the villa his library as well as several copies each of his own works.

At the time of the tragedy, these elegant protagonists, Caesar and his father-in-law, had been dead for more than a century, although the luxurious dwelling was still a haven for reading. There were books in the tablinum beneath the peristyle, as well as in a *capsa*,* as if someone had

---

*This document carrier in the form of a hatbox is frequently depicted in marble attached to the right wrist of the great orators, where it consolidates support of the statue.

attempted to carry them off as he fled, and especially in that small room with its numbered niches and elegant shelving specially built for preserving volumes. Curiously, though some works were one to three centuries old at the time of the catastrophe, none of them was contemporary.

So here we have a library that was abruptly buried under seventy feet of magma and cement-hard oblivion. In 1752, a team of convicts commanded by a soldier built a vast network of tunnels at Heraculaneum, and these haphazard tubes strengthened interest in the find. But the coal-like sticks brought back to the surface from the tunnels were initially simply tossed into the trash. When it was realized that these were not rolled-up fishing nets but rather carbonized books, all that remained were 1,806. But how were they to be deciphered? The scientists peeled the volumina like hearts of palm to reach the parts that were less dark if not legible—one researcher spoke of "bark" and "marrow." In short, they made confetti out of them. One Father Antonio Piaggio even constructed a machine for unrolling the rigid papyri that offered a delicate touch and a slow, consistent pace beyond the ability of human hands. The results were modest: Four scrolls were unrolled in three years, and a few fragments were interpreted and placed in haphazard order.

Science fiction was next in line to make a stop in Herculaneum. Multispectral imaging, perfected by a NASA laboratory to determine the identities of precious minerals beneath the surface of remote planets, also made it possible to read black letters on a dark background—ink on anthracite—by the differentiating components according to their respective reflectivity. The documents analyzed, currently being translated in American and English universities, reveal that the major part of this library retrieved from the shadows is devoted to philosophy, particularly Stoic and Epicurean thought. Among the books uncovered is the work of Philodemus, a disciple of Epicurus, who would doubtless be much less important were it not for the eruption of the volcano; of Ennius; and a (complete) copy of *De rerum natura* (although never finished) by Lucretius, including, appropriately enough, his analysis of volcanic eruptions, which in principle is in Canto 6.

The vast majority of these treasures have not yet been read or even identified. Hundreds of scrolls remain stubbornly black, mute, and compact, some of them twenty-three centuries in age. There are hopes, however, that others are still held prisoner in this *villa dei papyri*. It was this hope that led the heir to a great computer fortune to offer $100 million over ten years for the restoration of the site and for a continued search for, in particular, other buried books.

Every age has its culture: In the eighteenth century, the king of Naples saw himself laying hands on Aristotle's manuscripts; the American media—CNN, for instance—boldly promise their viewers Horace and Virgil. Is there good reason to dream of finding a scroll by Pliny or one from a completely unknown poet, or to anticipate learning more about the occupant of the villa during the first century at the time of his death? All hopes are of course permitted, but Vesuvius seems to be entering a new phase of uneasy slumber.

Here is where the sword-and-sandals flick comes to an end and the film noir of true biblioclasty begins. With the first centuries of the common era, the characteristic and somewhat haphazard perniciousness of antique power started giving way to an organized absolutism aiming to nip in the bud any intellectual errantry. Like the Muslims after them, the early Christians (or Jews) are the people of a single book, a conviction that would often prompt the scorn if not the destruction of all other volumes.

Everything is in the Bible. An instruction for the apostles of the first half of the third century says simply, "If thou wouldst read historical narratives, thou hast the Book of Kings; but if wise men and philosophers, thou hast the Prophets . . . And if thou wish for songs, thou hast the Psalms of David."[20] This is what happened with Paul, whose personality, however, was forged by the reading of the pagans. (Like his Jewish mentor Gamaliel, who was already an original thinker, the majority of rabbis then believed the study of the Torah left no time for the Greek philosophers.) In Ephesus, Paul managed to convince many of those he converted "to bring books so they could be put together and set on fire in view of all; he evaluated them and found them worth fifty thousand silver denarii."* The commentators determined later that these were occult works, but we can consistently see that the word *magic* is such a target for blame that if the practice had not existed, it would have to have been invented. Diocletian invoked it in Alexandria against the Christians, and Jovian did in Antioch in 363 against the pagans, when, "in company of his joyful mistresses" (according to Suidas), he oversaw the destruction of the library that Julian had created in the temple built by Hadrian in memory of Trajan, who had adopted him as his successor.

The edict of February 23, 303, in which Diocletian snared three centuries of tolerance, is more frank: Demolish their churches and burn their books was his command. Augustine labeled this *persecutio codicum tradendorum,* the incrimination of the books that have been passed down to us. It is worth noting that this imperial order was by no means applied to Alexandria, Jerusalem, or Caesarea, a sign, no doubt, that the power of Rome had shrunk considerably. Conversely, in Cirta (today's Constantine, Algeria) the flamine Felix ordered the bishop to turn over to him all manuscripts. The bishop gave him a very large codex.

"Where is the rest?" barked the representative of the state.

Said the bishop, "The readers are holding on to them, but we are no traitors; order our deaths instead."

In total only thirty-three books were found and destroyed. The Christians used every subterfuge to resist. The armaria no longer contained anything but archives; books on medicine were turned over because the soldiers did not know how to read. Later historians would deem that Diocletian had done much to propagate Christianity.

Ammianus Marcellinus observed bitterly around 378 that certain Romans "detested science as if it were poison . . . the libraries are forever sealed as if they were tombs." The Nordic hordes then descended upon the capitals of antiquity, and the souls of the cities soared away, never to return. One by one, the cities fell; one by one, collections of books went up in smoke. Only the almost completely forgotten emperor

---

*Le Sueur bestowed upon the seventeenth century a particularly idiotic painting of this event (in the Louvre): At the feet of a pompously adorned crowd, a black slave on all fours is blowing on the reluctant flame licking at a handful of printed books.

Majorian, an original who tried to fight the corruption afflicting his administration, attacked the secularization of the monuments that were once the pride of the Roman Empire, for he knew that people needed to dream. It nevertheless happened that the majestic remnants of the empire now served as nothing more than a quarry for masons. "The temples which had escaped the zeal of the Christians were no longer inhabited, either by gods or men; the diminished crowds of Romans were lost in the immense space of their baths and porticoes; and the stately libraries and halls of justice became useless to an indolent generation whose repose was seldom disturbed either by study or business."[21] This discoverer of imperiled masterpieces was assassinated four years after his coronation, in 461.

In 546, Totila, king of the Ostrogoths, razed Rome. It is thought that the Palatine and the Ulpian, or what remained of them, now met their end, no doubt like the collection of Agapitus I, who was pope for one year. In his house we can see the walls of the library, still almost twenty feet high, with friezes and portraits overlooking the now vanished armaria and, on a marble lintel, the words BIBLIOTHECA AGAPETII A DXXXVI. Thus perish "all the libraries of Rome," observed Cassiodorus, who decided to leave and create a monastery and large library in Calabria, a calm region of which he owned a large part.

He made a very wise choice, for this famous Vivarium—which earned its name because it not only elevated his mind but also was used for raising fish—this place where he founded a new Alexandria in order to write in peace a reasonable description of all knowledge until he reached the age of ninety-five, would not long survive him. The Lombards descended, razing and burning. The residence of the popes in Lateran was the beneficiary of only some of Cassiodorus's works—the Christian books in his Vivarium, which had once rubbed shoulders with the most diverse selection of Greek and Roman classics. Radicalism was the winner: Gregory I, prefect of Rome, pope in 590, and future saint, ordered the remaining copies of Cicero, Titus-Livy, and many other authors of the great era burned for the sole reason that the young people of the sixth century clearly preferred reading them over the Christian scriptures. Starting with this pontiff, moreover, the mere proximity of a pagan book was enough to endanger a pious soul. He called himself "God's consul" and never hid his despising of books and culture in general. Isaac Disraeli swears that by ordering the burning of the Roman library, he also exonerated St. Augustine of the sin of plagiarism, because Augustine's *City of God* allegedly owed everything to Varro, whose last books disappeared at this time.

To tell the truth, the first works of the Christian writers did not seem to want to call attention to themselves. For example, Jerome wrote to the young and attractive Laeta in 403:

> May your treasures be, rather than silks or jewels, the manuscripts of the Holy Scriptures. But for these texts, think less on the gilding, Babylonian parchment, and arabesques, than on the conformity of the text and the precision of the punctuation. . . . Those who have ancient books with letters of gold and silver on purple hides and, to speak vulgarly, in initials—which are a weight on the page rather than an inscription—let them do as they please and leave, to me and mine our humble pages and transcriptions that are less remarkable for their beauty than for their relevance.

The literary style being targeted here is what we call *uncial,* script used from the third to the eighth century. Here the austere Jerome found a means of delaying the transmission of texts to future generations, for the truth is that its physical appearance also has weight in determining whether a book is saved, cared for, and handed down. For instance, a beautiful example of these same letters of St. Jerome was devoured in about 1500 in a priory of the Jura region by a bear whose appetite had been aroused by the aroma of fresh parchment.

CONSTANTINOPLE

Constantine the Great founded the imperial library of Byzantium in the very first years of the new Rome—in 330 C.E. Its wealth—and its misfortune—was unrivaled. Seven thousand books (not only Christian) were installed in the portico of the palace. Only "calligraphers of high degree, *antiquarii,* and recognized writers were employed there." One hundred years later its inventory had reached 120,000 volumes, no doubt an unsurpassable number in the world of 475. But then the incompetent Basiliscus usurped the throne for several troubled months, during which time direct political action was invented and after which a prodigious fire turned into a pile of ashes this collection that included, as some claim, a Homer in gold letters on a twelve-foot snakeskin.

A nobody named Tarasicodissa became emperor, known by the name Zeno. After he was driven away, he returned and made the library operational again. But things turned sour once more under the illiterate prince Leo the Isaurian. During his reign, iconoclasm came into existence and imagery was banned in the land of icons and mosaics between 721 and 841. The iconoclasts hated all illustrations and slew the iconodules who defended them. The academy was closed. Its library, created in 425, disappeared at this time, as did the library of theology, founded between 610 and 631 under the aegis of the patriarch. The library of theology was a victim of fire in 726, as was the public library.

On two or three occasions, emperors searched their palaces for works that could support their opinion in the quarrel over images, but such works could never be found. It was whispered that Leo the Isaurian was a secret admirer of Islam and had made a great bonfire of the thirty-five thousand books of the academy with its twelve professors at its center—but Byzantium was also the land of gossip.

Thanks to, among others, the empress Theodora, a former "courtesan of those the ancients called the infantry,"[22] iconoclasm went out of style; the Byzantine university was restored again to its immeasurable splendor under Basil I, emperor from 867 to 886.

A former ambassador, then tutor to Basil's children, the patriarch Photius (820–891) was the inventor of the *digest,* which would come to be called a *bibliotheca,* but not until the sixteenth century. Around 843, Photius began writing what he first called an "inventory and enumeration of the books we have read and of which our beloved brother Tarasius has requested a general analysis." In 379 chapters (and an equal number of codices) he summarized 386 major works from the time of Herodotus, rarities that sometimes came from afar, and entitled this vast work *Myriobiblon,* or *Ten Thousand Books.* This did not comprise only Christian or Hebrew books, but also pagan and profane works, which appeared to interest him more. Each notice opened with "It has been read . . ." followed by the title and commentary.[23] Jealous whispers insinuated that Photius had sold his Christian faith to a Jewish magician in exchange for success, wealth, and knowledge. It is true that a week before becoming patriarch he still had not entered the orders.[24] Once he fell into disgrace and was incarcerated, he complained to Basil that his sacks of manuscripts had been confiscated. Protesting was a mistake, however, for the eighth session of the eighth council made the decision to order the immediate burning of this library.[25]

A good many of the titles collected and analyzed by Photius are unknown to us: Two hundred eleven in the complete version described have disappeared and 110 have utterly vanished. But this labor of popularization, which was first intended for a single reader, contributed to the development of knowledge in the entire empire and allowed if not a challenge to unilateralist thinking, at least the transmission of the literature of antiquity—or at least what time has allowed to filter through.

How many thousands of books had the Byzantines amassed when the Crusaders arose? For the envoys of God, every city that did not surrender outright ("on mercy") was declared a prize of war, a declaration made all the easier because pillage provided the sole payment promised the soldiers. Even the Christian chronicler of the Crusades compared the pilgrim soldiers to "a cloud of locusts."

In 1204, Constantinople "exceeded measure in all things." The ravaging it suffered was equally excessive. The Franks made no secret of their scorn for this people of "scribes and scholars." They could be seen parading through the streets, displaying as trophies at the ends of their spears not banal bloody heads but inkpots, calami, and sheets of paper. The Greek historian and senator Nicetas wondered if anything else could have been expected of "ignorant folk who were so openly illiterate and barbaric." Villehardouin, of the other side, admitted: "Splendid palaces full of ancient art works and classic manuscripts were annihilated." The Alexandrian bibliophile Georgiades recalled that fire melted a colossal statue of a seated Hercules, a bronze by Lysippus that was so skillfully balanced on its axis that a man could make it revolve with one hand, and added, "[Y]ou can just imagine the manuscripts." Even the Crusaders' contemporaries were appalled because Saladin had behaved better in Jerusalem just seventeen years earlier.

> The palace was defiled with smoke and dirt and the gross intemperance of the Franks; whole streets had been consumed . . . and, as if they were conscious of their approaching exile, the industry of the Latins had been confined to the work of pillage and destruction . . . the literature of the Greeks had almost centered in the metropolis, and without computing the extent of our loss, we may drop a tear over the libraries that have perished in the terrible fire of Constantinople.[26]

This situation was not long to endure, however. In 1261 the stubborn imperial collection was restored in a wing of the Blachernae Palace by Michael VIII Paleologus when he recaptured Constantinople. The shelves were again replenished, albeit with a little less enthusiasm but enough to seduce the Spanish traveler Pero Tafur, although he did not love this city whose streets were filthy, whose residents were vicious and poorly clad, and whose palace was poorly maintained except for the cramped section where the emperor and his family closeted themselves. On the other hand, he saw "a marble gallery opening on arcades with tiled marble benches all around and with similarly crafted tables, placed end to end upon low columns; there are many books there, ancient texts and histories."[27] This is the final image of what disappeared some fifteen years later with the engulfing of the old world when the Turks took Constantinople on May 29, 1453. Because the city had resisted for eight weeks, the carnage lasted for three days and nights. There was an appalling number of dead—the corpses floated the length of the Bosporus, *"come fa i meloni per i canali,"** as a Venetian noted—and an even greater number of people were sold as slaves by the soldiers.

With Edward Gibbon, we "will more seriously deplore the loss of the Byzantine libraries, which were destroyed or scattered in the general confusion. One hundred twenty thousand manuscripts are said to have disappeared." But they were not lost to everyone, because the Turks were not Crusaders; several Italian booksellers were the beneficiaries of some of the volumes that were salvaged. "Baggage carts transported them by the thousands throughout Europe and Asia. For a bezant people sold ten volumes of Aristotle, Plato, or even theology or any other science. They ripped the precious metals that covered the richly decorated Gospels, then sometimes sold the now-mutilated copies, sometimes just cast them to the wind. They cast all the miniatures into the flames to keep their cook fires going."[28] A complete edition of the *Universal History* of Diodorus Siculus was destroyed on this day. After the sack it was said that the victor, Mehmed II al-Fatih, who then earned his nickname the Conqueror and lost his reputation as a poet, feebly attempted to reassemble some Greek and Latin manuscripts that had escaped the disaster, which (so he said) he would rather have avoided. At least, this is what his official chronicler Critobulus asserts.

---

*["Like melons in the canal." —*Trans.*]

THREE

ISLAM OF THE FIRST DAYS

———————— ◗ ————————

Heavens, what a pile! Whole ages perish there,
And one bright blaze turns learning into air.

ALEXANDER POPE, THE DUNCIAD

The man who *made* Islam was named Omar, or Umar, pronounced with a slight swallowing of the glottis to keep it closer to the tongue. Without his political genius, the Muslim religion would never have had more than a local audience and the Arab-against-Arab struggles would have suffocated at birth one of the world's most powerful civilizations. Its success emerged thanks to a luminous and unstoppable notion: All Muslims are joined in the *dar al-islam,* or "house of peace," and everything surrounding it constitutes the *dar al-harb,* or "territory of war." How could one not bring Islamic peace to this territory, by force if necessary?

Umar ibn al-Khattab was born around 586 C.E. (some claim 591) in Mecca, in the midst of the city's elite. Having little wealth but related through his mother to an influential clan, he initially violently opposed Muhammad's ambitions, then became his most ardent defender and followed him in the *hegira* in 622. He then became Muhammad's military adviser and, in 625, his father-in-law. On the death of the Prophet, he prevailed upon the Medinans to accept Abu Bakr (a fellow Meccan) as first caliph, then succeeded him in 634 and launched the great conquests before he was assassinated at the hands of a Persian slave on November 3, 644. Equally skilled at organizing the first *diwan* of the administration and sending troops (which, until that time, had been effective only at raiding caravans) to establish the empire in Syria, Mesopotamia, Khorassan, Iran, Egypt, and Libya, his hagiographer described him as austere, calculating, and pitiless. The times were not yet right for subtlety. According to the eminent Hellenist Hugh Lloyd-Jones, in the kind of understatement coined at Oxford, the majority of Arabs of year 641 "were no more evolved than the late Ayatollah Khomeini."

Thus the libraries of the first countries to be invaded experienced no mercy. It was in fact the will of Umar or the interpretation of his orders to which we owe the destruction, in 637, of Taysafun, or Ctesiphon. This ancient Sassanid capital is still famous for the gigantic vault of Taq Kisra, the palace where the powerful and learned Khosrau* reigned, from 531 to 579. Respecting, like Khosrau's predecessors, the Zoroastrian canon according to which all texts are sacred, the city welcomed with open arms the outlaws of Byzantium: Greek philosophers whose academy had just been dissolved and Syrian Christians and other Nestorians who were subsequently commissioned to translate books and enrich the royal collection, which already had a strong assembly of Indian scientific materials and Chinese religious treatises and medical books.

Founded by the same sovereign, Khosrau, and destroyed by the same Umar in 638, the city of Gondeshapur (Shahabad on today's map) is also regarded as having been an important scientific and cultural center. In that same place, the *Avesta* was codified and the rules of chess, invented in India, were refined; likewise, one could read there a *Khwatay-namak*, or *Book of Kings*, that would inspire the *Book of Kings* of Firdûsî. The universal library, with a wealth of works on medicine, philosophy, and astronomy, served as a model for Ma'mun two centuries later under the same name: house of wisdom. The splendor of the exceedingly brilliant and utterly forgotten Sassanid period left its mark on the Abbasids of Baghdad, who sought to surpass the Sassanids.

In 1375, Ibn Khaldun† deplored the devastating years of the Islamic

---

*[Also known as Anushirvan and Chosroes. —*Trans.*]

†[The eminent historian and philosopher, considered one of the fathers of modern historiography. —*Trans.*]

genesis: "What has become of the sciences of the Persians, whose writings were destroyed by Umar at the time of the conquest? Where are the sciences of the Chaldeans, the Assyrians, the inhabitants of Babylon?"

And what of the works of the Christians? As if he deemed their knowledge irrelevant, the great Tunisian historian said not a word about them. Yet he would not have been ignorant of the tragic example of Qaysariya, or Caesarea. The Caesarea of Palestine was described by the Jewish historian Flavius Josephus as "located between Jaffa and Dora," not far from Jerusalem, which was its sole intellectual rival. Its harbor was the preeminent deep-water port in the world, an easy and obligatory stop on the Egyptian maritime route. The town became an important city under Herod, then a bishopric at the time of Origen, who created a theology school there in 231, when Rabbi Oshays also opened a Judaic school in Caesarea. (It was here, perhaps, that the Talmud of Palestine was written.) The two institutions of this city were perfectly cosmopolitan and cooperated in a very civil manner.

Origen was a strange customer. He obeyed no authority, and in his youth he had himself castrated so that he might literally follow Jesus' words: "There are eunuchs who made themselves such because of the kingdom of heaven. Who can understand let him understand" (Matthew 19:12). Even in this era, he was not the sort of person anyone would want for a priest.

In his native Alexandria, Origen had obtained from a sponsor seven stenographers, an equal number of copyists, and several calligraphers who worked for him day and night publishing books in shifts. It is thought that this group completed six thousand books. Origen was banished from Egypt for his surreptitious ordination by the bishops of Jerusalem and Caesarea, and in 230 he settled in Caesarea, where he lived until his death in 254. During his time there, he again harvested texts from throughout Palestine and produced new ones. A student of his said: "No subject was prohibited . . . we were authorized to read all kinds of Greek and Eastern doctrines, spiritual or profane."

Origen's academy taught all the existing disciplines and was the starting point for a library whose fame grew rapidly. It was here, next to the beautiful beach, that Constantine began the vast undertaking to save on parchment the works of antiquity. Pamphilus, a rich Syrian, succeeded Origen and grew the library to thirty thousand volumes. He listed all its contents, the record of which has been lost, and this man of foresight also saw to it that a large number of copies of the Bible were created and stocked so that anyone who wanted one could have one. Next, Eusebius (circa 263–339) took over management of the collection and used its resources to the benefit of his *Historia Ecclesiastica* and the *Onomasticon,* the first geographical and historical studies of the Holy Land. He headed a team of calligraphers in 332 who were charged with the task of producing fifty copies of the Bible ordered by the emperor. The famous *Codex Sinaiticus* came from this lot.

In February 303, when Rome tried one last time to bring down Christianity by destroying its books and churches, those of Caesarea escaped destruction. Jerome was therefore able to make free use of these resources to write his *Vulgate,* the translation of the Bible into Latin. He mentions the presence of manuscripts that in his view were already quite old—such as the original of the Gospel of Matthew and the Hexaples of Origen, in which six versions of the Hebrew scriptures were aligned in six columns—and he noted that the transfer from deteriorating papyrus to parchment was proceeding nicely.

The conquest of Palestine by the Persians in 614 brought about the destruction of the library of Jerusalem without apparently affecting that of Caesarea, for Isidore of Seville still boasted of its wealth some fifteen years later. With the dual symbol of its harbor that opened directly onto the sea and its library that preserved, republished, and aided writing, this very mixed city situated at the center of the world was a small, unrecognized Alexandria in exclusive service to the Christian faith.

It was thus Umar's soldiers who earned the privilege of annihilating its thirty thousand manuscripts and almost as many human lives in October 640, after a siege of the city that lasted seven months. The Arabs were still not accustomed to facing resistance, and Caesarea was the last place to fall in this first wave of conquest. It was necessary to do Umar's bidding—so what could be more natural than that the second caliph be given the blame in the long-lived rumor about the false tragi-comic affair of the Alexandrian hammans?

Al-islam yahdimu ma qablahu: Islam destroys what is in front of it. The origin of this dubious *hadith* is not known, but it no doubt served as a religious slogan in the naïve beginnings of the hegira—and one that fire and blood have forever sinisterly colored. In Islam's first century, the actions of certain generals degenerated rapidly—for example, those of Qutayba ibn Muslim, who captured the land of Khwarezm in 712. All the inhabitants apostasized and then were slain if they knew how to write Khwaresmi or were scattered to the four corners of the world if they knew how to read it. This is why their knowledge and traditions are unknown today, says the Persian Pur Dawud. (Interestingly, a century later it was a Khwarezm native who left his name to history by inventing algebra in the *bayt al-hikma* [house of wisdom] of Baghdad under Ma'mun.) Abu Rayhan adds this terrible account: "Qutayba killed their scribes and *hirdads* [priests], and destroyed their writings and all their books, so as to make them an illiterate people. They were forced to rely on their memory for all the knowledge they needed. Over time, they forgot all the details that differentiated them and could only save in their memory the general concepts on which they all could agree."*

But there was first a time when the Muslims burned the Qur'an. Under the third caliph, Osman (a simplification of Uthman ibn 'Affan), who lived in Medina, the Arab conquests absorbed a number of territories such as Armenia, substantial portions of Persia, the Maghreb, and Nubia. Instead of Arabicizing the regions, Osman was satisfied with establishing a member of his family in them to supervise the takeover of the local finances, something that did not fail to provoke jealousy among some of the former combatants. The central power was fragile and the religion was still hesitant; Muhammad had been dead only a dozen years. Several versions of the Qur'an existed, for the message of the Prophet was

---

*These words are found in a text by the ayatollah Mutahari Murtadha, who was assassinated in 1979. They were translated into English by an Iranian propaganda organization. In reality, without exception, all the subsequent dynasties contributed to the eradication of the Khwarezm culture.

spread by word of mouth. In order to check the rising power of the *qurra* in the remote fiefs, who earned their living and undermined the local authorities by making themselves the keepers and readers of the Holy Book, the caliph decreed that only one authorized version of the Qur'an existed: that of the codex kept by Hafsa, daughter of Umar and fourth wife of Muhammad. The propaganda stated that she had been given this document by her father through Abu Bakr himself (who was also one of the Prophet's fathers-in-law and the first of the caliphs). To cut short the hair-splitting and backbiting, Uthman charged Muhammad's own secretary with the task of carefully supervising a copy of the Holy Book and then copies of the copy that would be imposed on all Muslim cities, such as Kufa, Basra, and Damascus, and all the existing books in such places would be seized and immediately consigned to the flames.

This was in fact done, albeit with great difficulty. In Kufa, in present-day Iraq, Abdullah ibn Mas'ud resisted, saying: "If I knew there was a place where a man knew the book of Allah better than I and if this place could be reached by camel, I would go immediately to meet him." The dispute grew more acrimonious between the partisans and adversaries of Caliph Uthman's official version of the Qur'an. He was assassinated in 656 and four years of civil wars followed. During this time, Marwan, governor of Medina, had gone to see Hafsa to obtain her copy, which she refused to give him. He told her, "I will wait for you to die," which is exactly what happened. Marwan then demanded the precious manuscript from Hafsa's brother, who had no choice but to comply. Marwan tore the document to pieces in view of all and proclaimed: "We have read what this contained and we do not wish that one day people might challenge the value of this original." It is clear that this engendered doubt and polemic, even to the extent that some contest the assumption that any written text existed before the copies of Medina. Nevertheless, it was the version of the Qur'an resulting from Uthman's manipulations that predominated in Islam for a long time, except in Kusa, where Mas'ud's version prevailed until the eleventh century. We know of as many as seven versions existing at the same time, and even today the Qur'an of Africa is not the one to which all Muslims refer.

In his fascinating and inexhaustible study of medieval Arab libraries, Yusef Eche amusedly reports that an Andalusian of the Golden Age saw in a student's home the fifty-sixth volume of a bibliography of everything that existed in the Arab language. He also added that this was not the last volume. The notices it contained were short: title, author name, date of death, and city of birth. If we estimate that there were twenty articles per page and know that each volume consisted, on average, of four hundred pages, we arrive at the impressive figure of 896,000 titles, equaling an annual production on 1,491 books for six hundred years of publishing starting from the second century of the hegira.

But even if this story brings to mind the one about "a man who saw a man . . . ," the assessment seems less exaggerated when we know that the libraries of Islam were also centers of production and creation, which contributed to an exponential development of their catalog. The first centuries of the hegira after the conquest were a period of openness that did not last, and during it we see the accumulation of mountains of translated texts from the outside world, especially Greek texts and, most specifically, scientific and technical works. The other source of this book growth was literature with a religious foundation, which was swelled by interpretations of the hadith, commentaries on commentaries, and records of the ambiguous and debatable jurisprudence that regulated every action and thought of the believer, allowing for endless disputes and constructions.

Nevertheless, whether or not profane or royally or privately owned, the vast collections of books of this era were all destined for tragedy. Tenth-century Córdoba experienced the most significant case of biblioclasty of the Middle Ages. We know all the ins and outs and the actors of this highly novel-like disaster in which one of the major libraries of history was calculatingly destroyed.

AL-ANDALUS

She was named Subh, Dawn, or rather Subh the Basque, because of her place of origin. She was the slave singer of the future caliph al-Hakam II, who loved her desperately over all the others in his harem (though it is said he did not like women—hence, his intimate name for her was Ja'far, a boy's name). She later gave him a son, Hisham, to ensure the survival of the dynasty, and she thereby acquired the title of *sultana valide*. Thus with regard to Subh, we are dealing with a *sayyida*, a lady. Al-Hakam had a Byzantine craftsman create two admirable ivory chests to offer "the most beloved of fertile women."[1] He was fifty years of age and had barely begun his rule.

From his father, Abd al-Rahman III, whose long reign as Andalusian Umayyade caliph was peaceful and munificent, al-Hakam had inherited and developed a taste for books and a passion for libraries. From childhood he had become accustomed to special envoys traveling throughout the known world in the service of his imagination, combing Cairo, Damascus, and Baghdad to use gold to entice respected scholars and authors to deliver the first copy of any new work to Córdoba, even before their own country could get wind of it. With the help of power and fortune, he continued acquiring works and even having books translated, categorized, and archived, thus exercising a state sponsorship of libraries. Immersed in the apparent success of a brand-new dynasty, as few other potentates did, al-Hakam used his library and culture to show that Córdoba was better than Baghdad.[2] His father had abrogated the caliphate at the expense of the Abbasids, whom he considered men of little worth. In order to assert himself, Abd al-Rahman had consumed one-third of the country's revenues in the thirty years it took to build an administrative and palatial city in the countryside, which to our eyes displays a sober and moving elegance but was seen by his contemporaries as an extravagant luxury.* The father sought to create a nation; his son, a center of culture.

His carefully collected books were organized in a logical manner: Appearing on the first page of each was the complete name of the author with his family ties, date of birth, and birthplace, as well as the titles of his other works. Its listing in the catalog included description and location. Along the walls of a long, vaulted hall and in adjacent storage

---

*Henceforth, the excavations of the "city of the flower," Medinet al-Zahra (Medina Azahara in Spanish), five miles south of Córdoba, were considered a visitor's attraction.

rooms were wooden frames the height of a man and nine feet wide, with shelves from top to bottom on which the books were arranged. There was an arrangement of this type for each branch of knowledge.[3]

When al-Hakam was disturbed by the recriminations of the clergy, who regularly demanded the banning of alcohol and other amusements, he responded that he would dearly love to discuss the matter but his chief treasurer had intimated to him that the tax on wine was paying for the new wing of his library, so his answer to the ban was no and he told the imams to cease diverting themselves from their prayers with futile requests.[4]

Within the perfumed shadow of this "motionless caliphate,"[5] Córdobans could therefore peruse and borrow thousands of incredible books: a history of Egypt or the Maghreb, the works of Shafi'f, a summary of the Talmud, Dioscorides' treatise in both Greek and Arabic, Orosius's *Against the Pagans* in Latin or a house translation, parts of the Hebrew and Christian scriptures, the tale of travels in Europe made by al-Tortushi, the *Kitab al-Aghani* that cost one thousand dinars—to cite only those titles that we know with certainty perished. The library of the Alcazar—for the bulk of the library was located not in Medinet al-Zahra but in the palace in the center of Córdoba, on the west side of the mosque—had become a veritable enterprise whose workshops permitted the learning of calligraphy, grammar, and the poetic arts as well as bookbinding. The researchers[6] have unearthed many details. Ibn Hazm swore that he had known Talid, the eunuch in charge of the sole index—a very efficient one, as the future would show. Lobna, the "unparalleled secretary," was involved in arranging with infinite precautions the *De material medica* in letters of gold to be offered to the emperor of Byzantium along with a trilingual monk to translate it orally. Lobna's colleague Fatima the Old manipulated the calamus with such elegance and confidence and was so honest that she died a virgin, or so it is claimed.

Today there exists a manuscript numbered MS 874 in the Qarawiyyin of Fez that was set down in calligraphy in June or July 970 for al-Hakam in his palace. This copy of the Mukhtasar is the sole authentic vestige*

---

*Discovered and recognized by E. Lévi Provençal around 1934.

of the legendary collection that was reputed to be immense. The content of its shelves has been estimated at four hundred thousand *mujalladat*. These were good-sized volumes, for the term *mujalladat* is used to designate leather-bound books. Even if the figure was lower than this, however, something that Pierre Guichard does not believe,[7] the total would still be fabulous, for the large contemporary European collections then each totaled around a thousand volumes. As proof of this opulence, we have the Córdoban inventory, which is a simple list of titles filling forty-four booklets of twenty pages each. Surprise: This document is written on paper, a fairly rough material to be sure compared to gazelle skin, but so very modern then. Although we lack formal proof, it is quite plausible that the first European paper was manufactured in Córdoba well before it was made in Jativa and centuries before it was made in Italy.

The beneficial halo of the institution was quite visible in the city, which teemed with booksellers, stationers, book dealers, and book enthusiasts. There were no fewer than 170 women who made their living from reproducing texts with their calami. Cadi ibn Futais kept six copyists at the same time he was accumulating masterpieces of calligraphy in a building whose interior was painted entirely green, a color that was said to facilitate reading. When his better friends coveted books to borrow, he ordered that copies be made for them so that they could keep them as their own. The mosque that inherited his properties in 1011 put his library on auction and realized no less than forty thousand gold dinars. The learned al-Ghafiki boasted of having the most complete library after that of the caliph, with a complete copy of the history of al-Tabari. This collection was also put on the block in 1041 and produced colossal sums: up to a quarter *mithkal* per page. Averroës, who it appears learned this from his grandfather, said: "When a scholar dies in Seville, his library is brought to Córdoba to be sold. When a singer or great musician dies in Córdoba, the instruments of his art are offered to the Sevillians."

Entering this tranquil scene was Ibn Abi Amir, called al-Mansur or Almanzor, for his fame extended to the far side of the Pyrenees. He received a fairly high level of education for a member of the minor

nobility. This devious social climber began his career in the judicial administration and soon became the steward for Subh's son. She needed him to
safeguard Hisham's destiny; Almanzor made use of Subh and Hisham a
hundredfold. Tongues began to wag, but almost overnight Almanzor was
selected by the caliph to be curator of properties by escheat, cadi of Seville,
and director of the mint. In these roles Almanzor drew copiously from
state funds to support his oversized lifestyle, and when he was caught with
his hand in the till, one of his political friends reimbursed the treasury.

The relationship binding this schemer to his master was more than
complex. The caliph displayed more than normal indulgence: Almanzor
was promoted to inspector of finance and was charged with the task of
overseeing the daily fortune al-Hakam poured into his armies, who were
in the Maghreb to contain the Berbers. Almanzor acquitted himself of
this ambiguous mission to the great satisfaction of not only his sovereign but also the soldiers in the field, who became his allies. At this very
moment, in 976, the caliph died. Almanzor strangled several viziers and
other claimants to keep Hisham II on the throne that devolved to the
caliph's son. Because Hisham was only eleven years old and "the soul of
an ass in human form," according to Ibn Sa'id, it was easy for his protec-
tor to seclude him in the depths of the palace "in order to allow him to
devote his time to exercises of piety." A large moat was even dug around
the palace, and the new caliph gradually delegated all of his powers to
Almanzor. Subh died in 999 from wounded vanity at not seeing her son
ruler. Almanzor accompanied her remains barefoot and gave the funeral
oration himself.

Now at the summit of power, he knew that the specious maneuvers
he had consistently used, his private life, and his liberal tastes—wasn't
he, too, an enthusiast of books who knew no bounds?—were the subject of increasingly bitter criticism on the part of the jurisconsults. In
Andalusia, these *fuqaha** were the *ulemas*† of Malakite obedience. During the entire history of Muslim Spain, these protectors of the most

---

*[Experts in Islamic jurisprudence. —*Ed.*]

†[Educated Muslim scholars. —*Ed.*]

narrow-minded orthodoxy could be found rooting through the souks of the cities—Seville in particular—in search of suspect books, the "books of the materialists and philosophers," in order to burn them on the spot, with the populace wholeheartedly applauding these festive disturbances. Governments hardly appreciated militias of this nature, but they bowed before the popular pressure they exerted with no moderation. As we shall see later, this phenomenon is not close to disappearing.

So, to assure himself of the support of the populist censors, Almanzor conceived the most radical action possible: Burn the library of the caliphs! Diabolically clever, he himself took part in the propitiation. Around him he gathered the very people who had advised him against proclaiming himself caliph: Ibn al-Makwi; the jurist al-Asili; the grammarian al-Zubaydi, who constructed the laborious refutations of the philosopher Ibn Masarra; and two or three others, including Muhammad ibn Yabqa ibn Zarb, who had devoted fifteen years of his life to the pursuit of the disciples of Ibn Masarra, "forcing them to retract their opinions and burning in their presence on the eastern side of the great mosque of Córdoba copies of the writings of the philosophy they held."[8]

Intoxicated with the power of transgression suddenly granted them, this clique of ulemas ripped the respectable books from the shelves and hurled them into the great patio of the palace, where they were to be burned to cinders until nothing was left.* Especially targeted were the works of ancient sciences, logic, astrology, and other non-Islamic notions. The "acceptable" materials were to be spared. Of these there were few: lexicography, grammar, and rules governing the division of property for succession. What was not burned was thrown into wells, followed by stones and mud. It was the apogee of Andalusia that was buried.

We might ask if, in this frenzy, the selection of titles was made with the precision intended (despite the eunuchs' classification of 400,000 volumes). With respect to Almanzor, however, he had no trouble recognizing and pointing out the most infamous works. He probably owned

---

*In 1823, Heinrich Heine drew inspiration from this episode for his poem *Almanzor,* a phrase that was prophetic, anticipating actions of 1933 (which we shall visit later).

the same books, for his library had been enriched in conjunction with that of al-Hakam, with whom he shared more than one passion.

One part of the caliphal collection that was spared was sold to pay al-Hakam's African soldiery, the six hundred Maghreb mercenaries whom he had used to stuff his army by "guaranteeing them benefits." It turned out that some books of the great Umayyad library remained, albeit those of lesser interest. The Berbers, however, were not overly demanding: They showed great pleasure in destroying them when they took Córdoba a short time later.

Appropriately enough for this time, the very time of Abd al-Rahman III, the word *faylasuf* first appeared in the Arabic language,[9] and its definition can be found in Greek medicine.* The first Andalusian philosopher was thus Ibn Masarra (883–931), an ascetic who lived hidden in the sierras near Córdoba and who escaped the Malakite inquisitors only through his obsessive need for secrecy. His doctrine, derived from Neoplatonism, was based on esoteric and symbolic teaching, and he took it as far as was possible for that era: Each individual's salvation could come from reflection as well as prophecy, and the Qur'an was not indispensable. This thought is still enough to get one's throat slit ten times in certain countries today. It is easy to see why the texts Ibn Masarra inspired and the people who defended them were the censors' most sought-after prey. The commentator and cadi of Toledo, Sa'id al-Andalusi, or Ibn Sa'id (1029–1070), testified on this subject: "These sciences were ill viewed by the old and criticized by the powerful; whoever studied them was suspect of heresy in their eyes and regarded as contaminated by heterodoxy. The majority of those who then had resolved to study philosophy lost their enthusiasm, lay low, and kept secret what they knew."[10]

Perhaps they expected a more enlightened age? To the contrary, however, the ages to follow were so dark that the period of the European Umayyads passes for a moment of dazzling purity.

---

*[*Faylasuf* means one in quest of the highest wisdom. —Ed.]

MEDIEVAL ISLAM IN THE EAST

Medieval Islam is an Olympus of libraries. Often inspired by a monarch's sincere inclination, they were first enriched by extensive diplomatic relations. In time, the prevalence of calligraphy, the sciences of bookbinding and papermaking, and, later still, the donation system, or *waaf,* helped libraries develop even more significantly, and their creation often concealed some well-rooted ulterior motives. Before long, the collections of princes or the powerful were divided into public libraries.

There are available precise descriptions of these sites for study, reading, and reflection. For example, before 990, al-Mugaddasi saw in Shiraz an immense vaulted hall, three sides of which opened onto a series of rooms, the *khaza'in.* All the walls were lined with wooden pigeon-holes sculpted three spans high (about twenty-eight inches) with doors that shut. In Cairo, al-Maqrizi saw that these shelves were divided with partitions to form compartments, each bearing a list of the works it contained, that could be locked with a key. On the *rufuf* (shelves), the books were piled flat in small pyramids, with titles abbreviated in calligraphy along the edges of the top or bottom of each volume. At the end of the tenth century, Ibn al-Nadim wrote the *Kitab al-Fihrist,* or index of everything written in Arabic, no matter what the subject or religion and origin of the author. We owe to this admirer of Aristotle, son of a bookseller in the Dar al-Rum, or Latin quarter of Baghdad, a precious testimony of a golden age of books known to us partially because of the two censuses that were taken of them.

The mathematical rigor of the Arabic language can be seen in the combining of the same root words to designate the public, semipublic, and private spaces that house books. First, there are the container: *bayt* (house), *dar* (building; in a dar there can be gathered several bayt around a courtyard), and finally *khizana,* literally meaning "warehouse" or "depot." Next are the contents: *hikma* (wisdom), *'ilm* (science), and *kutub* (books). The names arrived at from these words designate several kinds of places and activities, from the small archive to the collection in a large university. This is how we can say that the *bayt al-hikma* is a study center, the *dar al-'ilm* is a scientific academy, and the *khizanat al-kutub* designates a rather private library—one that often proves to be monumental.

The very first of these establishments was called bayt al-hikma, in imitation of the 555 Persian "house of wisdom." It was founded at the end of the seventh century in Baghdad in the first Umayyad caliph's palace of the Khadra and was especially developed by one of his descendants, Khalid ibn Yazid ibn Mu'awiya. This man had a strong penchant for alchemy and devoted much time (he was a pioneer in this respect) to the translation of Greek texts dealing with various speculations. These were subsequently blacklisted and despised, which he seems to have foreseen in this apologetic commentary he wrote toward the end of his life: "I am neither a scholar nor an ignoramus; I am only one who has collected books." These books formed a collection rich in medical science. It is said that during an epidemic that raged under Umar ibn Abd al-Aziz, they were generously distributed among the populace to help them heal.

In the heart of the circular city enclosed by the triple enceinte, the second Abbassid caliph, al-Mansur, gave new impetus to the growth of book collections based on scientific works inherited from antiquity—in other words, works in Greek. His successor, al-Mahdi, also encouraged the writing of new treatises in Arabic. Then, with Haroun al-Raschid (Baghdad caliph after al-Mahdi), the libraries of the conquered cities were carried to the translation studios and a second new house of wisdom, already a powerful institution that was bequeathed in 813 to Haroun's son, al-Ma'mun. "He devoted himself to the study of science wherever he could find it and to the exploration of hidden treasures," said Ibn Sa'id, somewhat grumpily. The emperors of Byzantium and other sovereigns were showered with gifts in return for the books of philosophy in their possession. In short order, fairly luxurious gifts compelled a flood of works by Plato, Aristotle, Hippocrates, Galen, Euclid, and Claudius Ptolemy.

Only the leaders of Cyprus were hesitant. An old counselor incited them to declare: "You should hasten to send these books, because the rational sciences will not be established in a country of religious institutions without corrupting it and sowing discord among the learned."

(There are at least three essentially parallel versions of this alleged, pretty scene.) The allegedly perverse effects of science did not prevent Baghdad from becoming a legendary center of translation, publishing, calligraphy, and binding endowed as well with an observatory where Muhammadan, Christian, Jewish, Zoroastrian, and Sabean scholars worked harmoniously on astronomical, mathematical, and cartographic research. The bayt al-hikma of the eleventh century was therefore "a popular library where freedom of expression ruled" and the "privileged place of a meeting between philosophy and religion."[11]

Al-Ma'mun, son of Haroun al-Rashid, died in 833. His other claim to fame is that he was the sole medieval Islamic leader to stand up openly to the fuqaha, however amiably, through the organization of controversies inside the bayt al-hikma, but also forcibly when he was away waging war and felt that the healthiest ideas for his people were not understood, especially in his absence. His enemies even said that he had created a kind of reverse Inquisition, in particular with the introduction of the idea that the Qur'an was a human work. This theory of Mutazilism born in the sixth century was never put forward as strongly as in the academy of Baghdad, where, moreover, nearly none of the many department heads was Arab and not all were Muhammadans.

There is no doubt that all this questioning was little appreciated by those for whom all necessary science is provided by the *sunna,* the pure, stark imitation of the alleged life of the Prophet. The Seljuks later arrived to avenge their frustration and bring the local culture back to a standstill. Yet they did destroy the library without it weighing too heavily on the conscience of the populace. The people had once again become traditionalists, and, as a consequence of the transfer of the capital (meaning only the elite) to Samarra in 836, this prestigious institution had been in an ongoing state of collapse, even to the point of losing its designation as bayt al-hikma and falling to the level of khizanat al-Ma'mun (the al-Ma'mun collection). The orthodox imprisonment that followed al-Ma'mun's rule was equal to the rationalist openness he had sought. Al-Mutawakkil even went so far as to pronounce an absolute ban on "reasoning" in matters of faith. Moreover, this tenth caliph was able to distinguish himself with the invention of the *ghiyar,* "the distinction," a piece of colored cloth that Christians and Jews were required to sew to the shoulder of their clothing.

It was during these years that the prolix historian and Sunni commentator al-Tabari felt obliged to spell out this precept: "No matter what the case, one should never destroy a book without knowing what's inside."[12] He agreed quite clearly, however, that books with unacceptable content should be destroyed, and this was exactly how matters proceeded. For example, in the following century, in 993, the minister Sabur, who had been a *katib* (writer), bought a building in al-Karkh, the liveliest and most educated quarter of Baghdad, and had it renovated— paved with marble and whitewashed—in order to display the handsomest books from his collection: 10,400 volumes, including nearly a hundred Qur'ans copied by several members of the famous Banu Muqla family of calligraphers.

The renown of this archive grew daily and attracted donations from great scholars and collectors. Eventually, complacency set in, and soon a library committee had to be formed to select or refuse the gifts. The collection had three directors: a librarian and his assistant, and a trustworthy servant, Tawfiq the Negress, who withdrew books from storage, entrusted them to copyists, then put them back in their place upon completion of copies. Unfortunately, the library's founder, his books, and the quarter were all on the side of the party of Ali, the Shiites. When the Seljuks came to power in 1059, the Sunnis finally had the opportunity to invest the Karka and descend upon the dar al-'ilm, which they burned from top to bottom. Once the fires were extinguished, the sultan dispersed the crowd that had begun to pillage and personally gathered the best of the books that still remained intact to send back home.

Also Shiite, the Fatimid power is known for giving several libraries to Cairo's turbulent history. For example, the chronicle graciously entitled *Audiences and Rides* reports that one day in 979, because his librarian was unable to find him the book he requested, founding caliph al-Mu'izz said, "So I went to the library myself, opened one of the cabinets, and remained standing at the place where I thought I might find the book;

this was at the beginning of the night. I examined the books and started leafing through whichever fell into my hands; thus I came upon passages that I wanted to study carefully. Then I reached for another book, and the same thing happened. And so I stood there and looked through one book after another. I no longer knew why I was there and even forgot to sit down. Not until I felt a violent pain in my legs as a result of standing for such a long time did I remember where I was."[13]

When this same al-Mu'izz decided to leave the delicious but far too narrow walls of what was not yet known as Tunisia in order to establish his court and government in Cairo, he ordered that first a "grand palace" be built with all the required "chancelleries and reserves," including that of books, the *khizanat al-kutub*. All was ready to receive him in 973. Ibn Killis, a Baghdad Jew who contributed greatly to the installation of the dynasty and was made a vizier, undoubtedly began this first caliphal collection. The name of the initial head librarian was Ali Shabusti, who died in the year 1000. Forty bookcases in the grand palace (the one on the east on the street of the two palaces) held at least eighteen thousand volumes covering ancient knowledge alone and one hundred thousand books total—a boundless wealth, with some pages bearing the script of the greatest masters of calligraphy: "I found there chests filled with the calumi carved by Ibn Muqla, Ibn Bawwab, and others."[14] The enthusiastic pride of the lord of these premises was later matched: When this or that title was mentioned in front of the next caliph, 'Aziz, he called for the display of his numerous copies, all of which were the creations of various famous hands and some of which were autographed. He had thirty copies of *The Eye,* a dictionary attributed to the grammarian Khalil, who died in 791; twenty copies of al-Tabari's chronicle of the world, including a version from the beginning of the century written in al-Tabari's own hand; and a hundred copies of the *Jamhara,* the anthology by the famous philologist Ibn Durayd, who died in 933.

A historian of Aleppo born just after the disappearance of the collection went so far as to swear that it had a wealth of some 1,600,000 volumes "of great value that have no peer in other lands for their authenticity, the beauty of their scripts and bindings, their singularity."

From this number we can drop a good zero (to make the figure one hundred sixty thousand volumes), this being the agreed-upon figure by all commentators, both hagiographers and foes. So that scholars could cross-check the often contradictory texts, an annex was installed at the side of the facing palace (the one on the west of Little Palace, which in principle was that of the prince and heir). The histories say it faced the Aqmar Mosque, which is still there. When he wanted to see the "newest additions," the caliph had only to cross the street, which he did in dignity on horseback. He left his mount on a special platform, which the librarians respectfully climbed to present him with the numerous acquisitions he had not seen yet. Within moments of this presentation, however, being unable to hold back, he would follow his servants and thread his way between the shelves to peruse to his heart's content.

Out of a substantial fraction of this grandiose patrimony of the caliphs was born the public institution on the same site, the current al-Khurunfush Street, two steps from the elegant sabil-kuttab that splits in two al-Mu'izz Street.

Caliph al-Hakim, who enjoyed a long reign, from 996 to his inexplicable death in 1021, was a charming and very simple man who was fond of young people, depite the fact that he happened to eviscerate them on occasion. During his rule he founded a house of science, borrowing the name that had been chosen by the Persian Sabur in Baghdad (house of knowledge or house of books, dar al-'ilm).* Inaugurated on Saturday, March 24, 1005, the collection was located in a building north of the Little Palace, where he still lived. (It should have been established in the facing building, but al-Hakim was an eccentric.) "People hastened to visit it, and there was no distinction of class, for it was intended for everyone." In the mind of its founder, "everyone" included all who wanted "to read books, copy them, and study them."

On the premises were held conferences on the religious sciences, phi-

---

*Despite this well-weighed choice, secretaries and historians designate the establishment under other names, such as al-hikma.

losophy, astrology, mathematics, grammar, and medicine. The building was "furnished and decorated . . . with curtains over each door and at the ends of every corridor." The noble stone walls were adorned with pleasingly sculpted wooden depictions of musicians and dancers. These were immediately turned to face the wall when the site was later transformed into a hospital, but it is still possible to see segments of them in the Islamic Museum of Cairo. The caliph made an extraordinary *waaf* of superb books in *khatt mansub,* or well-proportioned script (the word *calligraphy* does not exist in Arabic), and these were so beautiful that "their like had never been seen at any monarch's," said a courtesan singing their praises. The donation also included lands and dwellings in Fustat to cover its operating expenses. Its annual budget was 257 dinars: ten dinars for the straw mats and twelve for potable water; ninety dinars for paper to make the books; the librarian's salary of forty-eight dinars; the office boy's salary of fifteen dinars; purchases of ink and quills at twelve dinars; one dinar for the mending of the curtains; twelve dinars for the rebinding of books; and nine dinars for the felt carpet and winter coverings. We can note the considerable outlay for paper and that forty-eight dinars are missing from the total. About these, Maqrizi breathes not a word, but they may well have covered remuneration for the copyists. All the writing material was distributed free of charge, as was fresh drinking water. Such pains were taken for comfort and liberalism undoubtedly to alleviate the suspicions of the Sunnis: Not only was the dynasty Ismaili, but also the young and popular al-Hakim, an Ismaili, did not inspire them with confidence. This impelled him to name two of their scholars to the institution. The confrontation of their ideas perhaps took a wrong turn one day in 1009, for the dar al-'ilm was abruptly closed and the two Sunni scholars named to the dar al-'ilm by Hakim were decapitated. When it reopened a short while later, it officially advertised itself as an Ismaili center of study and propaganda.

During this time, the literary marvels of the grand palace remained considerable. In 1043–1044, a vizier gave the order to draw up an inventory, have it evaluated, and see to the repair of the bindings of the collection's books. We know that one expert, an astrolabe manufacturer, counted sixty-five hundred volumes among the pure sciences alone. The quality of this collection (soon to enjoy its hundredth year) was not reduced by the presence and works of the academy.

But then misfortune hammered the land: Between 1065 and 1072, the Nile did not once reach the necessary flood stage. Famine and anarchy managed to establish a strong foothold for seven long years, during which even the caliph's women were seen leaving the harem to beg in the streets while he remained in the depths of the palace, seated on a worthless rug in a bare room. He personally opened his cases and chests and, closing his eyes, invited his colleagues to take what they wished. In Fustat in 1068, for example, a caravan that transported the most beautiful books* for one hundred thousand dinars was seized by the vizier Abdu al-Faraj in compensation for a debt of only five thousand dinars owed him by the palace. Because the caliph's home was stripped of the usual security deposits that assume wealth, his books were stolen a month later, then were sold to a Moroccan buyer. Yet because no source mentions the arrival of this cargo on the Almoravid side, it is assumed that the booty disappeared somewhere between Alexandria and the brand-new city of Marrakech.

As the Turkish mercenaries had not been paid either, they followed the example set by the ministers, but this time stole books from the dar al-'ilm. They apparently sold this stock to the same buyers or else to Baghdadis, for when the buyers descended the Nile to Alexandria, they were raided by the Berber tribe the Luwata, who cut sandals out of the luxurious bindings and cooked their meals on fires fed with carefully scripted pages. According to legend, there were so many books burned that their ashes formed a tumulus that was quickly buried in the sand. For a long time it was known as the Hill of Books.

The house of science eventually reopened, but we do not know how. It resumed activities with such vigor that in 1119 it was abruptly shut down again on orders of the dictator al-Afdal, who, moreover, rigged the succession of Mustansir by having the official heir, Nizar, stabbed

---

*We owe the following precise calculation to R. W. Bulliet: one camel load equals approximately fifteen hundred books, thus some forty thousand books were involved in this withdrawal.

to death. (This is when the Nizarite opposition was hatched, and it gave birth to the sect known as the Assassins.) Four years later, however, with al-Afdal murdered by the caliph Amir, the reopening of the house of science was announced, but it appeared in a more restricted form south of the grand palace, thus on the outside, in order "to mitigate any scandal that might be prompted by the polemics that took place there, in complete freedom, on political and religious issues."[15] Located in the heart of what is now the Khan al-Khalili, in the ascending alley where notebooks are sold, it was in operation for another fifty years and escaped other snubs—until the rise of Saladin.

When the Kurd Salah al-Din won power in Egypt, he was quite happy at finding the Fatimid libraries, for they offered a means to pay his soldiers, and he dismembered the collections with few scruples, as he meant to cleanse the premises of Shiism. All that remained in the caliphal bookcases was 120,000 volumes, and the collection was still considered "one of the wonders of the world." It was the cadi al-Fadil who was charged with supervising the auctions, but given that he himself had founded an important university library in his madrasa on Darb al-Mloukhiya Street, his own self-interest led him to shamelessly falsify the dispersion of the books in order to turn them to his best advantage. He perhaps did not go so far as to tear off the bindings and immerse the codices in water in order to lessen their value, as it was rumored; he was too fond of books for that. One historian attests, though, that buyers convinced the governor of the palace, an illiterate Turk, that the books were riddled with worms and that he should throw them on the ground and shake them. Once they had been damaged by this treatment, they were able to buy them for ten pieces of silver and increase their investment tenfold.

Some ten years later, during the taking of Amid in Syria, Saladin personally offered al-Fadil his choice of books from the city's library. Seventy donkey loads were thus sent on the road to Fadiliyya. Depending on the commentator's tastes, the stock varied between thirty thousand and a million works, but al-Fadil's librarian declared 124,000. A sign of the library's wealth can be found in this story: The young son of al-Fadil asked to read the *Hamasa* of Abu Tammam, and al-Fadil requested that his thirty-five copies of this title be brought to him. As he pensively leafed through them, he commented: "This one was copied for me, this one is in the hand of a well-known calligrapher . . ." and so on, until he suddenly decided to send a servant to buy a one-dinar copy for the child.

In 1294 one book was all that remained of these large collections, which reached back to the beginnings of the previous dynasty and which the cadi had spent his life collecting: a Qur'an in Kufi script, said to be from the hand of the third caliph, Uthman, who was assassinated in 656, and for which al-Fadil had paid thirty thousand dinars. Indeed, it was so expensive that it had been locked in a special cupboard, which proved to be its salvation. During another period of intense famine, each of the students of the madrasa had exchanged a book a day for a small round bread, and at another time the fuqaha had carried away "armloads" of books to destroy them.[16]

During the Middle Ages, Cairo had four great private libraries. The first two belonged to Jews: the thirty thousand volumes of the physician Ephraim and an equal number at the home of the vizier Yakub ibn Killis. It was said that Ibn Killis had made his fortune by such dishonorable means that his generosity toward science was a gesture aimed at having his sins overlooked. The steward of his extraordinary palace disbursed at least a thousand gold dinars a month for books. In third place was the collection of al-Murrif, poet, doctor, and author of a commentary on Aristotle. The logician Sadid el-Din reported to Usaibi'a: "In [al-Murrif's] home I saw an immense chamber filled with books in cases. Most striking was not that he owned a thousand treatises on every discipline, but that he did not have one whose back was not covered with beautiful phrases describing their contents." We do not know the fate of these archives. The fourth, and most admirable, was that of the rich Fatimid prince Mahmud al-Dawla ibn Fatik:

"But the remnants of this collection are nothing but waterlogged scraps!" said Usaibi'a in surprise.

"Indeed," responded Sheik Sadid. "Let me tell you why. The prince liked nothing so much as reading and writing. He devoted himself to his passion every evening, almost immediately after alighting from his horse. He was an accomplished poet. When he suddenly died, his wife—she too was a princess of the ruling family—ordered his slaves to gather together all of Mahmud's books in the inner courtyard of his palace. There she sang the funeral oration while slowly casting into the large pool, one after another, all the books that had stolen his love from her."

The chronicle of Arab libraries cannot be complete unless it also takes into account the imaginal realm that surrounds them, both during and after their existence. In 999 Avicenna was eighteen years old and his prestige was already great enough to prompt an invitation to court from the sultan of Bukhara. "I found there," he said, "several rooms filled with books, which were arranged in cases, row upon row. One room was devoted to works on Arabic philology and poetry, another to jurisprudence and so forth . . . I inspected the catalog of ancient [Greek] authors and looked for the books I wanted; I saw in this collection books which few people have ever heard of and which I myself have never seen elsewhere, neither before or since." He made such good use of this library for his own development that when this collection burned to the ground, immediately there was born the legend that Avicenna had personally set the fire in order to prevent anyone else from becoming as learned as he was.

The other libraries of the Muslim world were generally the direct and intentional victims of countless conflicts of all kinds. Damascus, Aleppo, Ispahan, and Alamut numbered a body count in parchment as high as the one in flesh and blood. An example is tenth-century Basra. The dar al-'ilm was also a dar al-kutub, or house of books, founded by Ibn Siwar. "Subsidies were granted to all those who came there and diligently applied themselves to reading or transcribing the works." Al-Hariri comments: "When I returned home from abroad, I went to the dar al-kutub, which is the meeting place for men of letters and the place where natives and people from far-off lands gather." It seems that a certain astrologer who was accused of theft excited the greed of a chief of a Bedouin tribe camping not far from there and incited him to pillage the city, starting with the library and ending with the souk.

In the year 1080, Tripoli was a rich and shining port of Syria. As one of the first paper manufacturers outside of Asia, it produced a considerable quantity of books. It was said at the time that the library recently established there was already one of the richest in the world—some mention three million works, including fifty thousand Qur'ans and twenty thousand commentaries. One hundred eighty scribes were on permanent salary, which ensured that at least thirty were at work at any time day or night, says a Shiite in the service of the Banu 'Ammar, without batting an eye. This library was a dar al-'ilm, a university where both students and teachers reside on the premises.

Now it just so happened that the Crusaders had been besieging the city and blockading the port since 1099. On several occasions the inhabitants asked for help and reinforcements from the caliph. A message finally arrived in 1109, but it contained only the order to send to him a beautiful native of the city whom he'd heard about. This was the last straw; the people of Tripoli surrendered. The Firanj (Franks) were able to enter with fanfare, and because they had not been forced to fight, they proceeded to set fire to the library. "A priest—God curse him!—reacted in terror to the books he saw there. There was a shelf of Qur'ans. He opened a book, and it was the Qur'an, another was the Qur'an again. At the twentieth Qur'an he said 'This place contains nothing but Qur'ans. Let it be burned!'"[17] After the fire, there remained a few books, which were then stolen by the soldiers. The Crusades thereby created so much destruction that they established "a legacy of ill will"[18] between Muslims and Christians.

Rumor obviously describes the books of the sect known as the Assassins, which were destroyed by the Mongols in the Assassin fortress of Alamut in 1255, as dealing only with magic and murder. In truth it was much worse.

The first misfortune suffered by Islam was the Prophet's inability to guarantee his succession and the general desire to take possession of it. While the founders and partisans of the competing dynasties tore each other apart, many of the faithful believed that only Ali was worthy of the caliphate. Was he not kin to and cousin of Muhammad as the elder son of his adoptive father? We know that Ali was not tempted by this honor; when he finally accepted the responsibility of succession, he was killed, followed by his brother and his son. The frustration of the legitimists gave birth to Shiism and its main branch, Ismailism, from which issued the Fatimids, the Druzes, and the Nizarites. Nestled within these groups is the singular history of the Old Man of the Mountain as well as the much later appearance of the sagacious Aga Khan.

"As a child, at the age of seven I developed a passion for all forms of learning." These are the words of Hasan-i Sabbah, founder and first grand master of the Assassins' state, in a precocious autobiography whose title imparts a first lesson concerning the sect's creation: *The Adventures of Our Teacher.* He would never again be called anything but that: Sayyidna, our teacher. He was born in Qom (date unknown), and after training as a scribe and calligrapher, he devoted himself to more extensive studies. For this purpose he cut a path back and forth through Persia, Syria, and Egypt. He spent three years in Cairo (1078–1081), where, as we might imagine, he was given a royal welcome by the Fatimid authority. Crammed full of philosophical readings, the intellectual Hasan-i Sabbah became a missionary, or *da'i,* in 1071 and proceeded to spread the Ismaili doctrine. He was so successful at this that he was able to convince the occupant of the fortress of Alamut to allow him to take his place, adding that he would not allow the occupant to clear out without granting him three thousand dinars in compensation. We can see that this man had a plan, which allows insight into the reasons behind his years of calculated errantry and his attraction to the mountainous zones of Persia near the Caspian Sea: the Dailam.

As Ata Malik Juvaini describes it, "Alamut is a mountain which resembles a kneeling camel with its neck resting on the ground." Like his father, Juvaini was in the service of the Mongol invaders and took part in the progress of Hulugu, which, while he was governor of the "ghost town" called Baghdad, he recounted in detail with a certain verisimilitude that was nonetheless saturated with Sunni prejudice. Alamut means "eagle's nest" in the local tongue. The only way to reach this notch at the summit of a formidable rock was by a path overlooking a raging torrent. It was said that on top there were gardens, palaces, beautiful young girls whose virginity was restored every morning, and an immense library. Only the last of these advantages is true, for it was here that Sayyinda shut himself up and never left in the thirty-four years remaining in his life. He spent this time reading, meditating, writing—and giving orders. A constellation of similar fortresses were captured or built in the surrounding area as far as Syria, in the Jebel Bahra': Qadmus and Masyaf and several that housed collections of books on philosophy and a diverse array of knowledge. We might think we were seeing a Montaigne who had fallen in Wagner's cauldron.

The antagonism of Hasan-i Sabbah and the opponents of the Ismaili doctrine, in particular the Seljuks, exploded at the time of the succession of the Fatimid caliph in Cairo in 1094. As we saw earlier, Nizar, the heir, was removed from the picture by a Sunni plot. Sayyinda then launched a "new teaching" based on an esoteric mysticism of such effectiveness that it created and supported systematic political murder by suicide commandos, an action "as legitimate as rainwater." At least fifty caliphs, kings, and viziers fell beneath the daggers of the *fidayin** before the Mongols arrived to set all the erring ways of the locals to naught. In addition, the Mongols were not fooled; they began their destruction of the country with Alamut. Before this time, seven grand masters succeeded each other and other impregnable killers ruled over the Syrian branch, like the Old Man of the Mountain, who made such an impression on the Franks. This impressive Rashid al-Din Sinan held court at Masyaf, where he died in 1193.

Hulugu knew that the Assassins needed no hashish pellets in order to kill. (This rumor was started and spread by Marco Polo, who visited the region in 1273, and reached its apogee in Vladimir Bartol's 1938 novel, *Alamut*.) The fatal poison dwelt in the eloquence of the Ismaili intellectuals nurtured by their reading. Ghengis Khan's grandson Hulugu learned this from his grandfather, and in all the places he passed

---

*This word has often been translated as "devotee" or "sacrificed one," but in reality, it derives from "ransom," as in "May I serve as your ransom!" an ancient expression of the most exquisite courtesy.

through—Samarkand, Bukhara, Balkh, Herat, el Khwarizim—he never once forgot to burn every book he found. But at Alamut his hand was stayed by the devious Juvaini.

> Desirious of inspecting the library, the fame of which had spread throughout the world, I suggested to the King that the valuable books of Alamut ought not to be destroyed. He approved my words and gave the necessary orders; and I went to examine the library, from which I extracted whatever I found in the way of copies of the Koran and other choice books after the manner of *He brought forth the living from the dead . . .** I likewise picked out the astronomical instruments such as *kursis* [part of the astrolabe], armillary spheres, complete and partial astrolabes, and others . . . that were there. As for the remaining books, which related to their heresy and error and were neither founded on tradition nor supported by reason, I burnt them all.[19]

So, not satisfied with being a traitor to his country, Juvaini was also a hypocrite and a liar. He obtained the khan's promise not to destroy the library so that he could do the job himself at his own convenience, and, what's more, he said nothing of the fact that he took or copied a part of the Ismaili chronicles or writings of Hasan-i Sabbah, which he subsequently used for his own narrative. To bring the confusion to its peak, he recounted several pages earlier how one of the Alamut grand masters who wished to return to the Islamic fold invited, sometime between 1210 and 1221, the ulemas of Qazvin to climb up to the castle to visit the library of his father, grandfather, and the founder, and to remove and destroy any wicked works, all while swearing, "May God fill their tombs with fire!"

With the Ismailis of Alamut now reduced to dust, what could prevent the Mongols from reaching Baghdad?

---

*This is the beginning of verse 18 of *surah* (chapter 30 of the Qur'an), but the meaning of the phrase is not completely clear.

In the middle of the thirteenth century, the Abbassid capital contained thirty-six libraries. The most famous was that of the madrasa founded by the caliph al-Mustansi in 1233, to which sixty porters transported eighty thousand works. It was so admirable that the commentator al-Qalqashandi, although an Egyptian,[20] placed it at the top of his list of the great libraries, therefore ahead of that of the Fatimids in Cairo, which had a greater number of volumes. It was then that the hordes of Hulugu, charged by his elder brother to cleanse this part of the world that irritated his pride, swooped down on Baghdad and killed as many people as possible, starting with the caliph and his entire family—hundreds of thousands of residents, it is claimed. The famous calligrapher Yaqut al-Musta'simi, who had been at the court, owed his salvation only to his idea to hide at the top of a minaret.

Before the rivers of blood began flowing, Hulugu summoned the ulemas to ask them the following question: Which was better, a wicked Muslim sovereign or an infidel who would be just? It is important to know that Hulugu was actually a Buddhist, but did that really help him to select the right answer? Convinced they were going to lose their heads in any case, the sages did not breathe a word except for Ibn Tawus, who replied: the infidel. Not only did he say this in a firm voice, but also he made it a fatwa, which he signed and which earned him safe conduct from the carnage and a thousand-man escort for himself, his family, and all his books, after which he was named to an important post.*

Hulugu, now khan and wild about science and astronomy, also became a collector of scholarly works in his Maragha residence, not far from Tabriz, where he ordered the astronomer and philosopher Nasir al-Din al-Tusi to build an observatory. At this time this famous sage was sixty years old. Iranian and Ismaili, he had been the astronomer for Alamut. Under his leadership, Maragha, the brand-new Ilkhanid capital, attracted numerous experts from as far away as China to create

---

*Kohlberg provides a very precise study on the readings of this interesting thinker and character, but because his books were bequeathed to his descendants in the most bourgeois way possible, they cannot be cited here.

important planetary tables, which would later be rediscovered in Salamanca, where they allowed astronomer and rabbi Zacuto to establish his own *Almanach perpetuum*. Driven out of Spain, Zacuto made his skill available to the Portuguese court, and this was how, thanks to Alamut, Vasco da Gama was able to make his way around the Cape of Good Hope.

The Mongol Hulugu's taste for speculation and learning provides the full political meaning behind the sack of Baghdad. For a full week his troops doggedly burned the libraries or cast into the Tigris, as Ibn Khaldun said 120 years later, "books that exceeded all description . . . [I]t made a bridge over which crossed the foot soldiers and cavalry, and the water of the river turned black with the ink from the manuscripts." This windfall of an image was even transfused into the story of Aladdin: "During the night, the gates of Baghdad were sealed for fear that the heretics might take control and toss the books of science into the Tigris." A contemporary witness summed up the quasi-supernatural terror inspired by the Mongols: "They arrived ripping and burning, then making an about-face, they take all and vanish." But this favorable treatment applied only to small towns. In Baghdad, after slaughtering everyone, they systematically demolished observatories, hospitals, and universities, not to mention dikes and aqueducts, in such a way that the glorious city became impossible to restore.

And yet in 1401, Tamerlane's troops succeeded in doing even worse, both here and in Syria, where not a man nor a book nor a minaret remained standing. In front of a razed Baghdad in July, 120 towers were constructed, each consisting of 750 of the inhabitants' heads, after which even the warriors of Samarkand took flight because of the stench. No source, however, mentions any intentional and estimable destruction of Baghdad's books this particular year—perhaps there were no longer any to be had. But it has been noted that on at least two occasions, men possessing theoretical knowledge were spared from the massacre and sent to Samarkand, and that Ibn Khaldun—who had a great favor to ask of Timur (Tamerlane), which was granted—had several fairly long discussions with Timur and wanted to testify to the fact that the warlord prided himself on his history and displayed great courtesy toward scholars.

After a bouquet of fireworks like this, "the Arab world abandoned the scientific movement for centuries."* It was quickly forgotten that the libraries of Fez, Gaza, and Damascus had the fairly extraordinary privilege of offering their readers scrolls and codices and books on papyrus, parchment, and Hindu *ôles*.† The wealth of information and the opportunity to expand imagination were increased by the variety of languages and support materials.

Once these two savage and stammering centuries had passed, Islam presented the strange phenomenon of three regimes removed from one another but close in time that sought enlightenment through books: al-Ma'mun in Baghdad, the Umayyads in Córdoba, and the Fatimids in Cairo founded centers of discovery and reason. But once the year 1000 had passed, when the eyes of the West were not yet even blinking, the guillotine blade of orthodoxy fell upon the whole of Islam. From this moment the libraries bivouacked within the madrasas—it was much safer.

The schisms and blockades due to religion were a more frequent cause for the loss of Arab-Muslim libraries than pure stupidity, and the Europeans conflicts for the faith would make these their specialty. In fact, it has been shown that if the Abbassids and others before them had been less concerned with prayers, hairsplitting, and never-ending politico-religious plots (Sunni caliph, Shiite vizier, or vice versa), the Mongols would never have prevailed over them as easily as they did. The armies of the caliph al-Musta'sim in 1258 were in fact superior in number to the Mongol invaders.

---

*Thus Yusef Eche sighed during the '60s, without saying if he envisioned a return there one day.

†This word comes from the Tamil *ôlei*, the palm leaf cut into bound sheets that provided the pages of Indian books.

FOUR

PEOPLE OF THE BOOK

———— ◗ ————

God is a gaseous vertebrate.

ERNST HÄCKEL

Imagine two sons, says the twelfth-century *Sefer Hasidim:* "One of the two hates to lend his books, while the other does with good heart. In such a case the father should, without any hesitation, bequeath his entire library to the second, even if he is the younger."

As we saw in Cairo, and as was also true in Baghdad and Córdoba, the richness of the Jewish library in the medieval Arab world was remarkable. This is all the more true because such a collection rarely aimed at being universal. The reader with means collected only the books of Maimonides, Galen, Averroës, Claudius Ptolemy, Avicenna, Aristotle, and Hippocrates and arranged them around the Bible or the Talmud and even light and fictional works.[1] In northern Europe, on the other hand, the shelves were infinitely less laden, but they drew more attention, and, with it, hostility.

"Because of the blasphemous allusion to the Savior and the Virgin" that some claimed to see in the library of the Israelites, this collection, and in particular the Talmud, which often formed its unique basis, was the subject of a permanent and almost obsessive hunt. Although the Syrian king Antiochos had started the fad long before, it was a converted Jew named Nicolas Donin who, in 1239,[2] aroused the vigilance of Gregory XI regarding the hellish reading material of his former community.

In June the pope sent a secret circular to the monarchs and prelates of France, England, Spain, and Portugal in which the order was given that during the Sabbath of the next Lent, they were to take advantage of the time when all the Jews were in synagogue to collect all their books and send them to the mendicant brothers for analysis.

Because the procedure promised to be long and fastidious, only France agreed to it on March 3, 1240. Some rabbis dared present themselves before a *disputatio* presided over by the queen mother Blanche de Castille to contest vehemently the evil interpretation of their texts. It was a wasted effort. On May 15, 1248, after a period of time that would give the impression all had been read, the pope condemned Judaic literature and all its horrors. France, however, was not able to bear waiting until his verdict came in: The cremation of fourteen cartloads of books took place on a public square in Paris in 1241, followed by ten carts another day, perhaps in 1244. And in the decade of 1250 more were burned, because it was necessary to scrupulously execute the papal decision. In 1263, Clement IV enjoined the king of Aragon and his lords under pain of excommunication to compel the Jews to hand over all their books for examination. In 1299, it was Philip the Fair who ordered the judges to assist the inquisitors in the holy chore, and another three loads of books were burned in Paris as a result. The provinces were not left out: For example, Bernardo Gui had two cartloads of confiscated books paraded for several days through the streets of Toulouse, whose good people were always open to a little carnival fun, before the volumes were taken to be burned.

Thus a kind of papal routine was established: John XXII in 1320 and Alexander V in 1409 and in 1553 Julian III gave strict instructions for all the books from the Jewish shelf to be gone over with a fine-toothed comb, with an eye to getting rid of them. These books seem to form a virtual library displayed on the shelves of the centuries with an obstinacy that exacerbated an unvarying impulse to annihilate them. Another twelve thousand books to be burned were found in Cremona in 1569. It was so extreme, says one author, that it is admirable that the "Talamuz" (Talmud) was able to survive such fervor.

This is where the story of the Reuchlin report enters. Around 1508, a Jewish butcher recently baptized by the Dominicans and offered the benefits of a sinecure took pride in denouncing the horrors studding the texts of his former religion. Although he could read neither Hebrew nor Latin, the complaint of this man named Pfefferkorn made its way to Emperor Maximilian, who decided to officially pose this question: Should the books of the chosen people be legally confiscated in their entirety to be destroyed by fire? He ordered a report from two experts. One was the high inquisitor of Cologne, whose conclusions may as well have been written in advance, and the other was a law professor, Johannes Reuchlin.

A friend of Erasmus and a good Christian, this humanist had written a Hebrew grammar in 1506, and, like Marsilio Ficino and Pico dela Mirandola, whose company he also frequented, Reuchlin was a commentator on the kabbalah, in which, according to him, lay the base of the true Christian faith. He did not like Jews particularly, but he idolized books—and logic. His jurist response—a luminous and modern text, which recently has been translated by an American researcher and published by Paulist missionaries—can also be read as a metaphysical document. It is entitled *Recommendation Whether to Confiscate, Destroy and Burn All Jewish Books* and marks a red-letter date (1510) in the history of tolerance.

"Concives"—fellow citizens: Reuchlin launches his argument with the observation that the Jews are subjects of the emperor and benefit from the protection of the law. As a good rationalist, he erases the superstitious murk surrounding their literature by drawing up a complete panorama of it: scriptures, commentaries, treatises of philosophy and the various sciences, then poems, fairy tales, and satires. Perhaps in this final genre, he concedes, any who look for it can find anti-Christian sentiment, but this concerns only one book with "its own title, just as the author imagined it," and an entire people cannot be held responsible for individual expression.

For the rest, Reuchlin appeals to Aristotle and St. Jerome: How can we oppose what we do not understand? "If someone is taken by an urge to write against mathematicians and he knows nothing of mathematics or even arithmetic, wouldn't he make himself the laughingstock of all?" He then takes his readers into the realm of linguistics and the definition of truth and falseness, then on the dialectic of God, necessarily Hebrew. Let the Dominicans start by understanding; discussion can then follow. After this there is what may well be an argument of weight: If there were reasons to burn the Talmud, then our ancestors would have done so centuries ago, for they were much more zealous with regard to matters of Christian faith than we are.

This remarkable defense was one of the first texts to benefit from the stunning novelty of the printing press, and its publicity did not fail to bear fruit: More Israelite books were confiscated and burned and the writings of Reuchlin himself were burned by the Inquisition of Cologne, while he himself escaped death by fire as a heretic only through dying in 1522. Yet the first assault against general anti-Semitism had been waged. The publisher of today's edition notes, moreover, that the subtlest argument of this subtle *Recommendation* is in fact the first, in which the author suggests that German law differs from the Catholic law of Rome. One of Reuchlin's most attentive readers was named Martin Luther.

In sixteenth-century Venice distinction was made among the Jews of the Levant, who were settled there; those of the north, who were already regarded with ill favor; and the *ponentine,* who had earned that name by virtue of coming from the west, meaning Spain, which was expelling its Jewish population. Because the Jews were mostly without means, they lived in the ghetto. It was on them that misfortune fell first when it came to defending Christianity under attack by the Hebrew faith and the books that spread it.

The *esecutori contro la bestemmia* (executors against blasphemy) had the right to search houses and bookstores in order to empty them of the incriminated works and bring them to be burned without further ado, which was no one-time occurrence. In several months, hundreds of thousands of books were burned in areas as far away as Crete, which was then a Venetian domain. But in Venice itself, more were consumed than elsewhere, for this was where they were published. People such as

Daniel Bomberg, a Christian from Anvers, and the noble Giustiniani family paid a fortune in taxes for the right to publish these books. Eventually, in 1554, it was the powerful printers of His Serene Highness who obtained from the pope a softening of his anti-Judaic entreaties. Total and systematic destruction was replaced by strong censorship in advance of publication. Yet it was still possible to get around this, as was the case in 1568, when the esecutori again seized tens of thousands of books from warehouses,[3] burned them on the Piazza San Marco, and levied heavy fines on the publisher-printer. The trade in these works was so lucrative, however, that the presses were transported to the Greek island of Cephalonia and a large clandestine traffic was established.

Because the Hebrew letter is essentially considered divine, a fundamental aspect of the world of the Jewish book is the sacralization of writing of any kind. Hence the existence of that Ali Baba's cave for the seeker and the object of unexpected reflection for the philosopher that is known as the *geniza*. This is a reserve into which any book—even the *Sefer Torah*—or, by extension or indolence, any document, manuscript, or printed matter whatsoever that has fallen into disuse, should be put aside, piled up, forgotten, and "made secret." These should definitely not be thrown away, however, much less thrown into the fire. We can judge from this what a particularly traumatizing experience was dealt by the countless autos-da-fé of Hebrew literature throughout history. It was on December 6, 167 B.C.E., that the Syrian king Epiphanes initiated this process in his radical attempt to Hellenize the Jews. "Tossed into the fire after having been torn apart," the destruction of books in Jerusalem and Palestine was such a powerful event that it incited the Maccabean revolt. Each of the other examples we find over the course of the centuries verged ever more closely on sadism.

This is how the book of the *'am ha-sefer*, the People of the Book, flirted regularly with the flames. Sometimes this occurred for mediocre reasons, as with Herod the Great, who had all writings burned to conceal his Arab origin, the effect of which was to destroy the past of the other families going all the way back to the founding of the nation,[4] but more often it involved mystical reasons. Some of these even derived from pure myth: There exists a belief that the Book is not the good one. To satisfy this, everything that might be a challenge to this fraud would have been eliminated by fire, just as happened with the Qur'an and also, according to some, the gospels in Hebrew, which the Church would have destroyed in order to ensure that only the poor Greek translations survived. Thus, would book burnings have existed from the birth of monotheism, such as Ankhnaten[5] established? From there it is only one step to saying that monotheism without intolerance is unthinkable—a step that many have refrained from taking even hesitantly.

The history of Jewish thought not only is bathed in fire, but also offers the originality of its book burnings. The one that victimized Maimonides in Montpellier in 1233 is memorable because it was the Orthodox Jews who clearly knocked on the door of the Inquisition, which rubbed its hands, made a large fire out of the books regarded as heretical in Jewish eyes, then, after some reflection, extended it to all Jewish books, including the Talmud.

The stupidity of the messianic incidents engendered by Judaism leave nothing to envy with the stupidity of those of the Christians. Primarily Shabbethai Zebi, Baruchiah Russo, and Jacob Frank gave birth to enthusiasm and delirium that were perfectly comprehensible in a world culturally imprisoned in its taboos and things left unsaid. Its leitmotif and sufficient credo was "Blessed be you who allow what is forbidden." Harems of young virgins, incest, various profanations, and rape of all the dietary restrictions are commonplace rituals. Forming part of this was the doctrine of the destruction of the Book and of all books. For example, thousands of works were burned in 1757 on a public square in Podalia, and during the ceremonies, the good Frankists* wore sandals that had been cut out of the parchment of the Torah.

It should be no surprise to find numerous Web sites today that take seriously these opportunistic deviations, with which we should not confuse the more convoluted case of the Hasid Nachman of Breslau. We know nothing or almost nothing about him: Born in 1772 and dead of

---

*[Who also called themselves Zoharists. —*Trans.*]

tuberculosis in 1811, he spent his short life wandering, changing places, writing that he was the Messiah, and generally making himself detested. As is often the case with the "great initiates," succession did the rest. In this instance, his secretary, Nathan, divulged the singular teaching of this mystical rabbi whose essential message rested on an obsession with the necessary destruction of books. He embroidered on the concept of *sefer ha-nisraf*, the burned book, then he wrote a treatise bearing this title, which, with a perfect consistency, he consigned to the flames in 1808. He showed his students a piece of paper covered with notes in his handwriting and said, before burning it, "Numerous are the teachings on this page and numerous are the worlds that will feed on its smoke." Doing this quite obviously "brings light to the world."

Today, this maieutics by provocation will not shock anyone who has been around a bit, but it made a big noise at the time—so much that Nachman would go so far as to profess the obligation of casting all the sacred books into the fire because, just like the heretical books, they make it "impossible to approach the Blessed Name." This man is considered to be a saint today. Hundreds of thousands of faithful in the world, including the ultra-Orthodox of Judaism, practice most unusual devotions to him—without, however, going to the extreme of grabbing the box of matches, at least as far as we know. At the farthest point on the trajectory of his poetic thought—still according to his secretary, who may well have invented the whole thing—he had constructed the handsome theory of the *sefer ha-ganouz*: Above the burned book hides the absolute book. "No hand has touched it; not one eye has seen it."

FIVE

ASIA BEFORE THE TWENTIETH CENTURY

————— ❧ —————

This man will destroy my wall, as I have destroyed books,
and he will erase my memory, and he will be my shadow
and my mirror, and he will not know it.

JORGE LUIS BORGES

PAPER BURNS BETTER THAN BAMBOO

During the winter of 1899 the land of Anyang in China was gutted by terrible floods, and a rumor spread rapidly through the hamlets: "Dragon bones have been discovered, and there are lots of them." Young and old alike immediately converged on the two excavations where a landslide had disgorged strange whitish objects on which there could be seen carved pictograms. The peasants sold them to apothecaries, who ground them into powder of longevity and restored sexual energy. Everyone was happy.

The scholars were too, but their interest forced a rise in the price of bones. When the peasants learned that these were scientific discoveries requiring protection, they started scratching off the inscriptions to make it easier to sell their discoveries to the pharmacies without shame, until the philologist Luo Zhengyu managed to wrest from someone the name of the village of Xiaotun, which was next to the site of the discovery of the bones.[1] Proof was now available that a dynasty endowed with the art of writing existed in fourteenth-century B.C.E. China. Until this time, China had been saddled with the name Dunce in comparison to Sumer and Egypt, and finally it could be said that "it had earned its antiquity."

Members of the Shang dynasty, in fact, were practitioners of the *tabu* (high divination) using either the plastrons of tortoises or buffalo shoulder blades. In this approach, a red-hot iron or torch was brought next to the shell and a serrated line immediately cracked across it, which could then be interpreted. After this divination, the scapulomancer would impress his audience further by using a pointed object to write beneath the crack what he had decoded. "Divination *(bu)* on the yiyou day [the day with the cycle symbol *yiyou*], the twenty-second day of the sixty-day cycle: The Prince *(zi)* goes into the small hills . . . to catch wild boar with the net. He will catch some. . . . One, two. Divination on the yiyou day: He will probably not trap any." Otherwise they were used to record funeral bookkeeping records: "For the honorable elder brother of Ri Bing, a pig is brought as a sacrifice. For the deceased mother *(bi)* by the name of Ding, a pig is also slaughtered. Also for the deceased mother Mou, a pig. Also a pig for Father Yi."[2]

Not only the archaeologist finds such reading entertaining: The graphic system was already in place and functioning, even if the characters were casually drawn standing or lying, big or small, from left to right or right to left. Some five thousand of these have been counted. If a literature did exist then, it remains completely lost for the moment. (The wells heaped with divinatory bones cannot be regarded as archives and even less as libraries, as some American authors have successfully proposed. They should instead be compared to Jewish *guenizas* or computer trash bins.) Under the Zhou dynasty, on the other hand, actual texts were put together, and these still survive. The seer turned into an official scribe and the written language underwent its first codification, but it was not a resounding success: Only a thousand characters were authorized and they were gathered on bamboo.

The oldest monuments of Chinese literature date from this era (around 800 B.C.E.): the Book of Documents, the Book of Songs, and the Book of Changes. The meticulous Spring and Autumn Annals, as well as the Traditions, are classics of the next period. This implies that when the golden age of Chinese thought and philosophy got under way with Confucius, reading and collecting books was not a rarity among the wealthy: The surprising appearance of "one hundred schools" at the end of the Zhou period was accompanied by the blossoming of archaic but coherent libraries. Toward 500 B.C.E., Confucius crisscrossed the country and could feed his hunger for knowledge at these libraries. Lao-tzu (also known as Laozi) was the guardian of the Archives of Heaven, the royal library of Luoyang, and Mozi (Mo-tzu) would not travel without his personal wagons of books and maps. The wagonload of books, moreover, constitutes the measuring unit for knowledge. It was said of a highly cultivated man that he was a scholar of four or five wagons.

"[When the message] had more than one hundred words, it was written on a *ts'o* [a package of bamboo slips]; when it was fewer than one hundred words, it was written on a *fang* [a wooden board]."[3] Thin slices of bamboo and panels made of poplar or willow were undoubtedly the material used for texts from the Shang era until the third century B.C.E., silk *(si)* was added to these between the fifth and third centuries B.C.E. and was used for nearly a thousand years, though it remained expensive. As for paper *(zhi),* it made its discreet entrance into Chinese history around the second century C.E. It was by far the most combustible of the three materials. Its performance could only improve in this area as it became increasingly diaphanous, for the Chinese art of papermaking became more refined when the culture's primary material ceased to be first bamboo pulp, then hemp or white mulberry. Toward the seventh century it became the supple and silent substance composed of blue sandalwood fiber with a hint of straw and pure air that we now know.* So while a Western library does not easily catch on fire (contrary to what has often been written), books of Asiatic paper made with no glue and little bulk display a remarkable facility to ignite. In addition to causing fires that spread more rapidly and were more extensive, the technical

---

*This should never be called rice paper, which never actually existed.

improvement of paper in the Tang dynasty also enabled the transition from the scroll to the codex, with its sewn-in binding. Thus books could be piled flat, with their bottom edges pointed toward the outside of the shelves and the backs of the books facing right, with a strip bearing the title slipped between two volumes.

While awaiting this progress, however, the reader, even if he was master of the world, devoted himself to a culture of the most physical kind. Reading meant manipulating heavy and cumbersome bushels that had to be held at arms' length. The narrow strips of bamboo measured, on average, twenty inches long and carried about sixty characters in a single column, whereas the wooden tablets could each hold several lines. Strung like Venetian blinds, these strips could be rolled up into what was called a *juan* (scroll), which would remain the numbering unit of Chinese libraries even when books were made of silk or paper. A complete philosophical work such as the original version of the *Zhuangzi* (which was more than 100,000 characters, though the current text consists of only 65,200 characters) could represent around seventeen hundred strips of bamboo bound, for ease of handling, into a large number of *juan* that formed so many natural chapters. The word *juan* has often been translated as "book" (for example, Billeter refers to the thirty-three available books of the *Zhuangzi,* which we regard as a single book), and this has generated great confusion about library size, as occurred in the Library in Alexandria, with its papyrus chapter scrolls.

A tomb robber named Pichun* broke into a sepulchre from the time of Wei in 280 C.E. Using the light of torches that he fashioned from bushels of books, he found to his great disappointment that all the tomb

---

*Pronounced pit-chewn. Although it does not give the amateur the sound of the Chinese language from the get-go, the transliteration system known as Pinyin is precise and can be used in all languages, which was the reason it prevailed. For those who are interested, here are, quite roughly, the less obvious keys: *c* is pronounced like an aspirated *ts; j* sounds like *tj; q* sounds like *tch; x* sounds like the German *ch* in the word *Ich; z* is halfway between *ts* and *dz; zh* sounds like *dj; -ian* is pronounced *-ienn; I* is close to *eu* if preceded by the consonants *c, ch, s, sh, z, zh,* and *r*; and, finally, *u* sounds like *ou* [as in *you*] unless it has a diaeresis or if it follows the consonants *j, q, x,* and *y*. Examples: *juan* = tjuenn, *Zhuangzi* = djouangdzeu, *Li Si* = lisseu, *Qin* = tchin, *Shi* = sheu, *Sima Qian* = seumatchienn, and so on.

included, as the inventory ordered by Emperor Wu would show, were sixteen works of the past, each consisting of seventy-five *juan* of twenty-five hundred strips, equaling a total of one hundred thousand characters. One of these books was allegedly the *Zhushu Jinian,* Bamboo Annals, a mythic chronology that spanned a period from the time of legend to 299 B.C.E. This was truly an admirable discovery, but unfortunately no copies were made of the *Zhushu Jinian* and it was destroyed in the Yuan dynasty.[4]

It was out of these library collections in full bloom, clinking with their heavy columns of lapidary phrases, that the Qin dynasty was born, and the first actor in this drama was named Lü Buwei.

The richest man of his time, he was described thus: "He traveled, he bought cheap, and then sold dear." The first question he asked his father was "How much profit can I make if I sell pearls? What about jade?" Sima Qian adds that he attracted "landlords and adventurers," for he wished to use them in his efforts to subjugate the country. Among these supporters was Li Si, who became an important figure in his own right. Having little education, Lü bought a reputation as a literary figure with the work of the intellectuals he nurtured: the *Lüshi Chunqiu,* The Springs and Autumns of Mr. Lü.

He placed one of his own men on the throne of Qin, and as a bonus gave him one of his most beautiful concubines. She was pregnant to boot, the viper Sima Qian would later say. Hence the emphasis on the origin of Qin Shi Huangdi (Zheng): not only a bastard but also the son of a merchant.[5]

This was the situation when, in 259 B.C.E. the child Zheng was born. He became king at the age of thirteen, and Lü Buwei planned then to take back his concubine, whom he kept with an official lover so as not to personally incur the wrath of the young king. But Lü greatly underestimated the strong and monstrous personality of the young boy. Once Zheng came of age and could assume full rule, he drove away his mother's lover and thus exiled the one to whom he owed everything, including his very existence. As a result, Lü Buwei poisoned himself on the road to Szechuan.

With the use of espionage, misappropriation of public funds, and the bloodiest violence, the young despot Zheng required less than fifteen years to annihilate, one by one, the other six kingdoms of an immense China. In 221 he was the sole master of the land and assumed the title of emperor, which until that time had been used only in legend. For centuries to come, Zheng was no longer known by any name other than Qin Shi Huangdi, or "first august emperor of Qin." The sole mistake of his career was that he claimed to be founding a dynasty that would last for six thousand generations. It collapsed four years after his death, which was not long in coming.

Li Si was Qin Shi Huangdi's "left-hand adviser." It was with his help that the emperor succeeded in doing the unthinkable: putting China in order. This entailed standardization of writing, unification of money, establishment of weights and measures and wheel-axle size, and the construction of a wall connecting all the northern fortresses in a communication network, which included a veritable highway, the *shidao*, that went from the imperial summer residence near Xianyang to Inner Mongolia, a distance of five hundred miles. To better keep the country in hand, 120,000 aristocratic families were forced to settle in the capital and their weapons were melted down. Twenty centuries before the taking of the Bastille, then, feudalism was abolished—and the unanimously firm disapproval of four hundred eminent Confucians barely disturbed the emperor; he simply had them buried alive. Yet Li Si also wanted to bury the past, which was in fact beginning to collect more and increasingly physical and burdensome traces.

In 213, during the year's banquet, which had brought together seventy academics, words of misfortune undermined the toasts. One of the guests, perhaps emboldened by the yellow wine, said: "That one may refrain from taking antiquity as one's model in any given matter, and yet thrive, is a novel thing to my ears." A dead silence ensued, broken finally by the minister's glacial retort: "Men of letters do not model themselves on the present but study the past in order to denigrate the present age. Doing so, they sow alarm and doubt among the dark heads [ordinary people]." Then, turning to the emperor, he "proposed that all the official histories, with the exception of that of Qin, be burned and that all people of the empire . . . who dare possess classic literature and the writings of various philosophers bring their books to the military or administrative governors so that they could be burned indiscriminately."

This was not a sudden inspiration. The destruction of books as a tool of government had existed since the time of Shang Yang, two centuries earlier, ever since he had exhorted Duke Xiao "to burn the books so that the laws and ordinances can emerge."[6]

The monarch Qin's decree was most satisfying to his counselors from the legist school, for whom the state could govern only if the people were kept in a state of ignorance. "As for those who wish to study, let them take the bureaucrats as teachers," said Li Si, inspired by his former co-disciple and speedily eliminated competitor, Han Fei, who had declared, "In the state of the enlightened ruler, there are no literature or bamboo tablets; the law is the only doctrine. There are no words of ancient kings; the ministers are the only possible models." As these ministers alone had the right to teach, in imitation of the sovereign, the books they owned escaped the auto-da-fé—however briefly.

Thus banned were the "one hundred schools": the school of the laws, that of the Tao, that of Xunsi, who was the first skeptic philosopher. Xunsi was an original thinker who clearly expressed what he thought at a time in China when concepts were more often taught through means of parable and even anecdote, and he was also the teacher of Han Fei and Li Si.[7] Thus was ordered the burning of all the libraries and their contents, including the Book of Songs, the Book of Documents, the Book of Rites, and the Annals. Alone to be spared were the collection of divinations (the Book of Changes)—because the emperor was frightfully superstitious—and treatises concerning agriculture and medicine. Anyone who failed to comply within a month was tattooed on the face and sent as a convict to work on the construction of the Great Wall during the day and to perform guard duty there at night.

Did the Taoists take offense at these measures? Quite the contrary: For the strict and pure followers of the Tao, the abuse of reading concealed a source of mental indigestion. We can read in the *Zhuangzi*: "The mind that pursues study swells each day; the mind that practices the Tao shrinks each day. By shrinking, one attains *wu wei* (non-action); by not acting, there is nothing that cannot be done." Obviously, it is not forbidden to think that their particular and exclusive target was the Confucian gloss.

With the banning and burning decree, panic ensued everywhere. Numerous men of letters raced to conceal their books inside the walls of their houses, as Fu Shing did with the Book of Documents before he was disgraced and cast out into the street. When he managed to return to his home, however, he recovered twenty-nine sections of the historic classic. Kong Fu did the same in the house of Confucius. Sixty years later, when the family stumbled upon the hidden texts while enlarging the building, writing reforms had then (but not forever) made the texts unreadable. "The people of this time no longer knew that ancient characters once existed and they called [this] writing shaped like tadpoles."[8]

A pathetic and mysterious fate awaited Zheng, the most incredibly powerful of men. After cementing together his land, he embarked on secret provincial progresses on which his approach would be greeted by numerous *songdebai,* stelae singing the glory of his virtues, with text that was carved in *xiaozhuan.** It appears that Zheng the paranoid left this life on the road without having sensed death's imminent arrival. Nor did anyone else, it seemed, and for a certain number of days his escort unknowingly accompanied the emperor's corpse. As we know, his body ended up in a tomb about thirty square miles in size, which seven hundred thousand slaves gave their lives to build. All his sons and heirs subsequently died before their country's eyes, and Li Si was solemnly sawed in half widthwise.

As a consequence of the dynasty's precocious end, the year 208 B.C.E. was stamped with the onset of a philological and bibliophile frenzy in reverse proportion to what had been decreed eleven years earlier. Everyone of any account in the world of history, thought, and art was wearing

---

*This term is generally translated as "lesser seal script." Its writing is less ornate than the "greater seal script" *(dazhuan),* which had been in vogue until then. The new style was for each character to be written upright in the same rectangle. Reading it proved to be much easier and writing it a little less so, at least at the beginning.

himself out digging up, copying, analyzing, and hoarding any texts that had not vanished completely. The respect for writing that is a constant of the Chinese found itself forever strengthened from this. "The burning of the libraries and the construction of the Wall are perhaps operations that secretly cancel each other out," guessed Borges with amusement. This did not prevent the phrase "to burn the books and bury the scholars alive" from becoming a proverbial saying ready-made to describe a method of governing or even an action that was somewhat radical.

A crush of conflagrations: Chinese history consists of a long series of at least as many violent destructions of libraries as of their rebuilding. "We find repeatedly that no sooner was a national collection built up than it was partly destroyed or scattered, only to be recovered and restored in the succeeding dynasties, although in the process many works were lost beyond hope of recovery."[9] One Hundred Schools or One Hundred Flowers, the law of eternal return seems to be weaving together the resigned moments of a civilization in conformance with "its own doctrine of the dialectic of opposites."[10]

Whoever owns the books owns the world. Liu Bang, son of a peasant and founder of the Han dynasty, was utterly convinced of this and hastily sent a lieutenant to remove from the imperial library all the Qin documents he thought he might need. (Unfortunately, this disciplined soldier took only what had been specifically requested.) During the course of the final battles between Liu Bang, the future Han Gaozu, against his rival, Xiang Yu, Xiang burned down the capital in 207. The conflagration lasted for three months, during which time all of the very old books were lost: those belonging to the emperor, those belonging to the ministers, those that were hidden, and those that had been recently exhumed. The loss may well be greater than that caused by the 213 destruction decree and, in any case, can be added to that. It would require many long years and the lengthy reign of Emperor Wu, himself a bibliophile, for "the books to collect like mountains" (and enable Sima Qian to distill his *Shiji*).* Collectors were encouraged to bring their books to be copied,

---

Memoirs of a Historian or *Historical Memoirs,* depending on the translator.

as happened with many dynasties whose reigns were inaugurated with empty shelves. It was thus inevitable that there appeared many apocryphal texts, even fakes, when the compensation offered was so particularly attractive and librarians were so free with their funds. The ravages suffered by book collections were so frequent that the art of counterfeiting developed early on and reached such heights of skill under the Ming dynasty that Yuan-dynasty editions were commonly sold as being of the Sung dynasty. Books including prefaces and colophons were remorselessly mutilated in order to fabricate irreproachable fakes.

Just what a private library was in the second century B.C.E. is no longer a mystery thanks to the presumed son of the chancellor Li Cang, the marquis of Dai, who was buried in Mawangdui with the books he deemed essential—as well as with thirty-eight weapons, for the man was a warlord (a heritage that can be seen at the Hunan Museum in Changsha). His manuscripts were of silk, rolled inside lacquer chests with compartments and covered with around one hundred thousand characters in total. There were two copies of the *Tao te Ching* presented in an order different from the one we know, one of which was preceded by four mythical essays reputed to have perished in the great fire of 213: the *Four Classics of the Yellow Emperor,* which are manuals of Taoist conduct reserved for those who govern (a secret Lao-tzu, to some extent).[11] Also found were several works rich with teachings, including *Anecdotes and Discourses on the Spring and Autumn Periods* and *Letters on the Political Strategies of the Contending States.* There was also a copy of *Movement of the Five Planets,* which describes, for divinatory purposes, the orbits of Jupiter, Saturn, and Venus since the time of Qin Shi Huangdi (the seventy years that preceded the book's writing); the title *Study on Horses;* books on medicine, including marvelous plates using clothed and naked models; and three maps depicting the state of Chu, the garrisons, and the plan of the city with its walls and houses. Finally, there were *vade mecum* and books embodying the quintessence of the necessary knowledge for a gentleman of that day: history, strategy, astronomy, knowledge of horses and good physical condition, and a double dose of Lao-tzu for moral health.

With *tushu* referring to maps and texts, *tushuguan* has always been used to designate the Chinese public library (whereas the word *cangshu* is used to denote a private collection, for the primary meaning of this word is "to hide the works," a frequent necessity). It is not by chance that *tushu* is also the name of the diagram symbolizing the changes of the universe in archaic philosophy. For a long time, libraries made no distinction between territorial literature and archives.

The bibliography of China attempted by Han dynasty experts toward the very end of the first century B.C.E. came up with 670 titles. Yet these were survivors out of how many? This is precisely what we do not know. There were ten or one hundred times more titles, depending on the bias of the authors who have conjectured.* For instance, a declaration has been discovered among the Marxists of the 1970s, particularly in the review (very unusual today) entitled *Tel Quel:* The quite respectable scientist Joseph Needham maintained that Qin Shi Huangdi had not destroyed a single book. In fact, Needham comes perilously close to dismissing it as strictly gossip. But we should recall that the first emperor of Qin was the idol of Mao Tse-tung (Mao Zedong)—and of course the destruction prompted by the first of Qin's emperors was also overlooked as unthinkable by the rest of the world.

Out of the Han inventory, forty-one works have survived to the present, sixty-five have been more or less reconstructed using other sources, and the rest have vanished in smoke forever.

While the first catalogs are lost, classification in several summaries or surveys were adopted: general, classics, philosophy, poetry, military science, astronomy, mathematics, and the occult sciences. A philosopher might ask, however, for what purpose these were preserved. During the insurrection of then usurper Wang Mang in 23 B.C.E., the city of Chang'an was destroyed along with 13,269 juan. "This was the second literary catastrophe of our history," states Niu Hong.

The capital then became Luoyang under the eastern Han, and liter-

---

*Nothing is ever hopeless. In 2002, archaeologists unearthed around twenty thousand bamboo sheets in Liye, Hunan. The total found before that time had been only two thousand. Furthermore, these found volumes date from the time of Qin and note specific events that took place after unification.

ary men arrived there from every direction with so many sacks of manuscripts that "they could not be counted." An important imperial archive was born. Were you looking for the Sutra in forty-two entries? It is kept in the fourteenth aisle of the Hall of Stone on the Orchid Terrace. Other parts of the catalog were located in the Pavilion of the Unicorn or the Pavilion of Celestial Bliss—a poor name in this respect on that day in the year 190 C.E. when a general and his roughneck soldiers cleared out the court and trashed the premises: "All the literary works were hacked apart and scattered." Depending on their size, the books in silk served for curtains, tent roofs, and packing material; the smaller pages were turned into string. Nevertheless, seventy carts of books were recovered, half of which made it to Chang'an only in time to be burned there during the troubles of 208.

Niu Hong inventoried the complete destruction of the major libraries in a report he presented to Emperor Wen of the Sui in 583 C.E.: There were five such annihilations, "but he forgot one."* After the destruction by Qin Shi Huangdi followed by that of his capital Xianyang (which makes two) and that of Chang'an in 23, the other three disasters that he entered were that of the year 190 C.E., the sack of Luoyang by the Xiongnu in 311—where 10 percent of the books managed to be recovered (3,014 scrolls)—and the spontaneous book-burning by Emperor Yuan of the Liang. Incidentally, the report of 538 foreshadows both the formulation of censorship and copyright registration: It is not acceptable, Niu Hong said in substance, for a book not in the library of the emperor to be in a private library.

Rebirth was soon followed by disappearance. The imperial library became imperturbable and ever more sophisticated. Facing the Yang Palace, during the Sui dynasty (589–618 C.E.), was the Hall of Writings. There, "the windows, the bench cushions, the hangings on the cabinets, were all of exquisite beauty. All three aisles opened on to a room. Doors were covered with brocade tapestries, over which flew two immortals.

---

*This is according to Wu Guangqing, who found fourteen in all. For his part, Endymion Wilkinson suggests that the absolute catastrophe occurred "twelve times, at least."

Outside the doors a mechanism was hidden in the ground. When the emperor visited the Hall of Writings, palace servants held perfume burners, and when the ruler moved forward, he walked over the mechanism, causing the flying immortals to descend, take hold of the tapestry, and go back up to their original positions. The doors of the rooms and cabinets opened on their own. When the emperor left [the tapestries] would again drop down and [the doors] would shut."[12]

The imperial library became still more extensive: 2,655 titles on 48,169 scrolls were added under Xuanzong (712–756), who ordered the name of his palace to be changed to "the place where the sages gather" instead of "the place of the immortals."

In reality, it also became more mortal. Rebellions and the waves of invading Huigars, Tibetans, and Mongols occurred and caused great damage. The number of intentional and planned destructions is significant. On August 11, 1258, Kublai Khan ordered "the sending of emissaries everywhere who will seek out and take the texts named herein as well as the plates used to print them. Within a period of two months, [the texts] will be brought to Yanjing [Peking], where they will be piled up and where they will be destroyed by fire." He was acting on orders of his brother Mongke, but with impressive synchronicity his other brother Hulagu did even worse in Baghdad. Once emperor, Kublai forged ahead with the destruction of the entire Taoist canon, with the exception of the *Tao te Ching* (perhaps because this foundational text was inaccessible to the ordinary reader). From December 2, 1281, until the beginning of 1282, all copies (even those privately owned) and the wooden plates used to reprint the seven thousand volumes of the corpus were burned, including those in the newly conquered southern region of the country. Yet this action, as Zhuangzi had retorted long before, would be futile; the book does not exist in itself: "Books are only words, even if words are precious. What is precious in words are ideas."

At least two emperors intentionally destroyed their impressive collections. In 554, Yuan Di, his capital surrounded, consigned to the fire the 140,000 *juan* of which he was so proud. He threatened to throw himself on the same pyre but was held back only by his sleeve. He then broke on a column his sabers with their gold-covered and jewel-encrusted guards, saying: "Civil and military culture will disappear this night." Later it was said of him that what he liked about his books was their quantity, thus his love for them was not so deep. In truth he was so fond of literature that five readers would sit in relay at his bedside when he was ailing. Every time he dozed off, they would skip over a few pages. Also driven to destruction was Houzhu, the last of the Tang dynasty of the south. He ordered that his ten thousand books be burned rather than allow them to benefit his victorious opponent, who would become Taizu of the Sung dynasty. Why? Because knowledge is power. The day when a Chinese princess who had been married to a Tibetan king asked Emperor Xuanzong to send the classics to her, no doubt to fend off the deadly boredom of Lhasa, he found some bureaucratic drudge at the court to oppose the request because "knowledge of the classics would make our enemies too strong."

The gems of knowledge, however, did not fail to find their own way out of the treasury of the Son of Heaven and spread throughout his immense territory when China, almost casually, invented the printing press. Whereas the oldest vestige of a text printed on paper from wood blocks comes from the year 751, it was toward the end of the following century that books, not manuscripts, began to be produced and reproduced in an appreciable fashion. An official mentions an 883 C.E. quarter with bookstores in Chengdu where he could select from among books on geomancy, dream interpretation, and dictionaries printed by means of page-size plates that revealed several poorly printed and unreadable passages. What's more, large publishing projects of quality got under way in 950 with two complete and competing versions of the Confucian canon printed in Luoyang and Szechuan.[13] In an immense burst of enthusiasm, this time heralded the birth of personal libraries, an intensity that is obviously not foreign to the premillennial trauma of the auto-da-fé of the emperor who unified China. Their development incited imperial jealousy, if not pure and simple seizure. This is why, generally speaking, a Chinese collector of bygone days was always tight-fisted when it came to his books. If he loaned one, it would be only to a trusted friend, and this friend would bring him a jar of wine for the privilege of borrowing the smallest volume, and another jar when he returned it.[14]

We might get a good idea of classic Chinese bibliophilia: It was the garden of refinement and melancholy. We need only take a look at the seven collectors from Hangzhou, each of whom owned a large library and, without truly forming a group constituted as such, met on the shores of the western lake beneath their villas for evening parties that were generally well provided with alcoholic refreshment in order to exchange rare books, information, and, on a very few occasions, their own poems.

Among these dilettantes we are somewhat familiar with the name Wang Xian (1721–1770), who had the misfortune to win an imperial competition, for which reason he was compelled to accept a post at the Department of Fines with an office in Peking. He did not waste any time, however, before using the excuse of his parents' advanced age and his duties to them to be allowed to return once and for all to Hangzhou and his books. Trouble-free days slipped by in collating, punctuating, and analyzing with a steady brush the thousands of books held in his Zhenqitang, or Pavilion of Eminent Virtue. The same could also be said of his friends Wu Zhuo, Zhao Yu, and the others.

Zhao Yu was the oldest and most prestigious. He had descended on his mother's side from the Qi family, whose vast multidisciplinary library (itself a rarity at the end of the Ming dynasty) burned in 1597. This only propelled Qi Chengye to immediately create a new one that was even more admirable, which he left to his descendants along with a mania for books and a treatise on private bibliotheconomy, the first of its kind in China. Unfortunately, political vicissitudes brought about the ruin of the line at the same time as the dispersion of the books, and Zhao Yu recounted how, at the age of eighteen, he had made a pilgrimage to the ruins of the site where his ancestor had enjoyed his precious collection one hundred years earlier. Still there was the signboard above the entrance, which bore the two characters *kuang ting,* or Kiosk of the Solitary One, in the handwriting of the great calligrapher and painter Dong Qichang. Zhao Yu brought it back with him to Hangzhou and built a second library for no other reason but to crown its entrance with this panel. On his death, Quan Ziwang dedicated this distich to him: "To have children is not to die, to have culture is not to decay" *(You zi bu si, you wen bu xiu)*.

Except for that of Wang Xian, whose property spanned four generations, all these splendid collections quietly crumbled and disappeared upon the deaths of their owners. In the meantime, they had been able to contribute, or attempt to contribute (for it was still necessary for the gift to be accepted), to the bizarre erection of Emperor Qianlong's Siku Quanshu (complete library of the four branches of literature). Of the nine private donations that were accepted there, out of the hundreds throughout China that solicited this dangerous honor, five were from this circle of friends in Hangzhou.[15] They provided the imperial undertaking with some 1,905 ancient works, and in compensation each received an encyclopedia. But this was no shabby gift: Compiled in 1726 under Kangxi and printed in sixty-four copies under Yongzheng, the *Tushu Jicheng* offered 100 million characters for reading pleasure in 5,020 hand-sewn books.

A copy of this monumental publication, the *Siku Quanshu,* was offered for the same reason to Tianyige and was installed in 1561 in Ningbo. On reaching retirement, the mandarin Fan Qin (1506–1585) sought to house his collection of seventy thousand books, whose core was the Wanjuanlou collection of a family named Feng, which went back to 1086. This model library is a unique case. The building still exists in Ningbo, restocked by the state after all the misfortunes that befell it. The Tianyige had been the object of careful attention, though. Beneath the twenty-eight cedar cabinets in which the books of soft paper were piled, there were fixed blocks of *yingshi,* or anhydrite (gypsum), a stone that absorbs humidity. On the other hand, Fan Qin selected its name because *tianyi*—which can also mean "first under heaven"—is an invocation of water in the Book of Changes. Because Fan Qin had requested a building made of brick from which all heating and lighting was banned, the Tianyige managed to escape fire.

The secret of this collection's longevity is most odd: Fan Qin offered his heirs a choice between a mountain of silver—some ten thousand taels—and the library without a penny and an interdiction on selling it. His eldest son, Fan Dachong, spoke first and took the Tianyige without hesitation. His will was identical to his father's, and his son's will was identical to his, and so on for several generations. And all these successive heirs scrupulously applied this other commandment of its founder: "No stranger to the family shall enter nor will any book leave." Yet this should have been only a source of great amusement to the thieves who brazenly broke a hole in the wall some three centuries later, when Ningbo was invaded by the "long-haired soldiers" of Taiping, and in 1862 a considerable quantity of irreplaceable books were sold by weight to two workshops of Fenghua and Tang'ao, which converted them into ordinary paper for wrapping meat in the market.[16] Another thief had made a habit of entering the pavilion at night and carrying away armloads of books in a small boat. They could be found a day later in the bookstores of Shanghai, which ordered them by title for Western collectors. This went on until Zhang Yuanji, the director of the Commercial Press, was stirred into action and created a foundation to transfer the remains of the collection to the Hanfenlou, a reserve of rare books at the great library of Dongfang East, where everything was summarily destroyed by Japanese bombs in 1932.

> The sad fate of the modern book collection is not due solely to the destruction of wars and fires. People without means cannot collect books and those who can collect them are generally forced to disperse them because they lack the means for keeping them. What exists today may disappear tomorrow. South of the Great River [the Yangtze] there used to be innumerable book collections. But how many of them are still in existence? Only three or four.

This was the description of the situation by Huang Zongxi (Huang Tsung His), a famous man of letters at the beginning of the Qing (Ch'ing) dynasty.[17] He owned close to thirty thousand books, almost all of which he had read.

The China of the book is a vast body filled with black holes, an organism that has been quite largely and definitively mutilated. We can add to this monumental destruction the millions of great and small moments of self-censorship, discreet distortions of texts, and intentional omissions that have made the Chinese corpus forever rickety. Even the most peaceful dynasties were founded on the *wenziyu,* or condemnation, of subversive texts, using elimination and fraud for the purpose of propaganda. Ouyang Xiu did not like the works of Wudai and saw to it that they disappeared. The mandarin Gao Yuan destroyed history books, which he decreed as useless because they concerned past events. People got rid of anonymous texts they deemed untrustworthy. Each regime changed without hindrance what displeased it in the *yeshi* (chronology) of the times preceding it, and it was not only the printer who devoted himself to the practice of *chuimao quici,* "blowing through the hairs to find the defect."

One can never be too careful. There was a famous book enthusiast named Zhuangsu in Qinglongzhen during the time of the Yuan. Collected before his joyful eyes were at least eighty thousand juan of novels, poems, and history, all well organized in ten sections. In 1346, however, when the following emperor called for donations of books, Zhuangsu's heirs decided to burn his library for fear of incurring punishment for any objectionable content these books might hold. Under the Qing dynasty, many intellectuals of renown devoted their lives to risk-free studies such as archaeology and "the scientific study of the classics."

The Scienctific Study of the Classics was the name of an influential movement of 1736 to 1820 that swallowed up a large portion of intellectual energy which could have been dedicated to preparing the country's entrance into the modern world, and contributed in great part to its nineteenth-century slumber.[18] It was deemed preferable to avoid expressing personal opinions and even to refrain from writing anything so as not to risk writing a prohibited character. Truth in China is never naked, especially if it might upset the masters. There was a joke in China: *"Qing feng bu shi zi,"* "the fresh *(qing)* wind leafs the books in vain; it is unable to read the words that are written upon them." This means the people of Qing are cretins.*

The intellectuals who resisted this general drifting off course of Chinese society can be counted on one hand. Jean-François Billeter recalls the case of Li Zhi (1525–1602), iconoclast and anti-Pharisee, who, respecting nothing—not even literature—wrote these inadmissible words: "The people govern themselves, and will not accept being governed by any principles other than their own. . . . From birth, each man personally possesses a certain way of behaving, and no one needs Confucius to come give it to him. . . . The apostles of kindness use the virtues and the rites to rule over people's minds." So what remains for the skeptic? Books, of course: "All those who devote themselves to study seek to grasp within themselves the basis for life and death, the final word on their destiny. . . . A magpie could build a nest on their heads and they would not even notice." This singularly prudent man of letters had spiritually entitled his two principal books the *Book to Burn* and the *Book to Throw Away*. He committed suicide when the authorities, wearied by war, threw him in prison. The celebrity of Li Zhi "gives an idea of the degeneration reached by the mentality and the morals of the time," as determined by the following dynasty, during which the titles of his two books were quite decidedly taken literally.[19]

Emperor Quianlong (Ch'ien-lung) managed to display even more grandiose villainy than his predecessors, though he is seen in the eyes of his contemporaries and posterity as an ardent defender of Chinese literature. In 1772, the thirty-seventh year of his reign, he made the suggestion that both public and private libraries be searched, either by will of their collectors or by force, in order to find all the rare books of China (manuscripts or printed works) so that they could be collected in a gigantic corpus entitled *The Totality of Books, Quanshu,* in four sections *(Siku).* These four sections corresponded to the traditional catego-

---

*In Shanghai in 1936, the literary figure Chen Dengyuan wrote 524 pages on the building and destruction of Chinese libraries that are awaiting a translator. Among other benefits, they acquainted their readers with what would soon take place under Maoism.

ries and each had its own silk binding in an appropriate color: canonical books (green), historical books (red), philosophical (blue), and literary combinations and belles-lettres (gray). Under a single heading here is the absolute library, yet again as handsome as it is exhaustive: 79,337 juan were confiscated and entrusted to 3,286 calligraphers to copy for posterity. Printing would not have had nearly as good an effect.

On Chinese literature Quianlong said: "I have ordered [that these works] may flow down the river of time. But in case the [volumes sent] include books by Ming authors that opposed our house, they are to be set aside for destruction by fire." This effort degenerated fairly quickly into a titanic inquisitorial enterprise in which the agents of authority, using increasingly ambiguous criteria, went door-to-door throughout the empire in search of any books that might infuriate the emperor as well those that might please him. Thus starting with "any kind of literature produced from the end of the southern Sung [dynasty]" the directive evolved into the necessary seizure of *pianmiu* (erroneous) books; for example, a simple method of calligraphy such as the *shufa jingyan* by Wang Xihou (Wang Hsi-hou) could be judged unlawful.[20] On June 11, 1778, there was arranged an elephantine pyre of the numerous copies of seized books, which also included the wooden blocks used to print them, all of which had been held in storage at the Commission of Military Archives. A memoir writer noted tartly and boldly that given that wood for heating cost 2.7 taels for one thousand catties (or Chinese pounds), the palace had just realized a savings of 98.6 taels.[21]

This burning of books occurred on eighty separate occasions until 1782 and carried off all the editions of at least thirteen thousand ancient books, including some rarities, offered to the national undertaking by the most illustrious collectors in complete good faith—or else to earn the potentate's goodwill, perhaps even knowing the censorious motive behind the request.

"Nothing is lacking from what has existed over the course of the ages and the cosmos," wrote His Majesty in the preface of the *Siku*, in his own beautiful handwriting and not without that loftiness that is so distinctive of the emperors, which has also been referred to as shameless cheek or thoughtlessness. The fantasy of the prince and the paranoia of his devoted henchmen—unless it was the reverse—combined to create an immense void in the country's bibliography: In 1782 the *Jingshu Mulu* or *Index Expurgatorius* led this great editorial campaign to fabricating a lineup of 345 books to censor and 2,320 to utterly destroy. Only a fifth of these books earmarked for destruciton managed to find a hiding place—sometimes in France—that enabled them to survive to the present. All the rest were lost.

As for the *Siku Quanshu,* whose manufacture constituted the official purpose of the undertaking, it is miraculous that this rickety colossus did not vanish completely. Qianlong ordered four copies for himself, followed by three others intended as thank-you gifts to the provinces that had best collaborated with the endeavor. This was how one could still be found in Hangzhou, in its building of almost the same period on the shores of the western lake, the Wenlange. Publicly accessible, the *Siku Quanshu* could not avoid going up in flames during the upheavals caused by the Taiping, for whom this was somewhat of a vocation that was nourished, to some extent, by a degenerate Christianity. The first four versions (or rehashes), installed in pavilions built to measure in imitation of the Tianyige of Ningbo, were located inside the monarch's various residences, such as the summer palace, which was made famous by its destruction.

In 1860, France and England could not agree on anything except that the Chinese were at best acceptable as cannon fodder. Yet the country slumbering under a mountain of gold and silver, and, secondarily, millions of old unique books, required a pretext before a group could begin taking advantage of it.

On October 6, the French army succeeded in shaking off the English and entered the summer palace a night ahead of them—"a jeweler's fever dream," noted Hérisson. This secretary and interpreter for General Montauban gave an on-the-scene account—so descriptive that the war ministry subsequently tried to smother it[22]—of the destruction of these two hundred buildings in which five generations of emperors had amassed riches with an exuberance they did not permit themselves to display in the city. It was the bottles of fine Bordeaux that were first to disappear.

"One of the two victors had filled his pockets, which, when the other saw it, impelled him to fill his chests," Victor Hugo waxed all the more indignant as the incident bolstered his case against Napoleon III. The petty destruction of the Chinese "chimera" is clearly the work of a nation led by a "little man."* The English, in fact, had a method to their plundering: They organized an auction on the spot, taking only tobacco pouches, piasters, pearls, jade, and gold dining services. The French, however, acted like overgrown children: They used the princesses' wardrobes for costumes and fought each other for anything that was massive in size, particularly clocks and other automatons that had been manufactured in Europe. When the raiding reached monstrous proportions, the general Cousin de Montauban retreated to his tent. "Here and there in the park, groups were racing toward the palaces, the pagodas, the libraries, alas," said a perturbed Hérisson.

One of these libraries was precisely the building constructed to hold an entire copy of the *Siku Quanshu;* 3,461 titles, or 168,000 volumes, disappeared in smoke, a few on October 6 but most on October 18, when the *Times* correspondent being held hostage by the Chinese authorities was killed. Lord Elgin then decided to return to Yuanmingyuan to finish the destruction. This perverse vandalism is only somewhat surprising: It was his father who invented elginism† by dismembering the Parthenon. Furthermore, his interpreter was the renowned sinologist Thomas Francis Wade, who supposedly made out well by removing a substantial number of books from the summer palace. Montauban took no part in this punitive expedition and retreated again to his tent. He found it more politically profitable to burn down the Forbidden City.

Only one collection of the *Siku* remains complete: the "lead" copy housed in the Wenyuange behind the imperial palace. It was finally diverted to Taipei by the Kuomintang.[23] An incomplete copy was found in Chinese Turkestan after having passed through the hands of the

---

*[Victor Hugo denigrated Napoleon III publically as Napoleon le Petit, as opposed to his predecessor Napoleon the Great. —*Trans.*]

†[Cultural vandalism. —*Ed.*]

Russian army. The National Library in Peking was able to acquire the one from the palace of Chengde in 1917. Thus it did not suffer the fate of the *Yongle da dian,* another superhuman undertaking that would end even more wretchedly.

On his accession to the throne in 1403, Emperor Yongle asked Yao Guangxiao to set up a commission of 2,169 scholars to create the great encyclopedia of all Chinese knowledge. The creation of the Grand Canon of Yongle took four years and gave birth to 22,877 scrolls, seven to eight thousand essential works from the Spring and Autumn periods. An estimate of their content: 370 million characters on magnificent paper bordered with red silk, covered with perfect script in black lacquer with punctuation and notes in vermilion, all bound in imperial yellow damask silk. And as no more money remained to print it, there was only one copy—which was burned in its entirety in Nanking during the fall of the Ming dynasty. One copy was established in 1567, although far shorter than 2,422 juan and tangibly less luxurious. Qianlong's editors removed another 385 titles. The remainder were hastily purchased by the imperial academy, the Hanlin, or Forest of Brushes, for its already plentiful library, "quintessence of Chinese scholarship . . . the oldest and richest library in the world."[24] It so happens that the Hanlin Yuan had the misfortune of being located in the northwest corner of the Peking Legations Quarter, several yards away from the British Embassy, an entrenched camp during the siege of Peking in 1900.

The besieged were sanguine; the fearful respect of the Chinese populace for writings, especially those stamped with the red seal of the Son of Heaven, guaranteed this building would serve them as an inviolable rampart. So who then was responsible for burning down the Hanlin Yuan that Saturday, June 23? The Chinese claim it was the English. This is also what Wilkinson writes. It is incontestable that the building occupied a strategic position and its destruction would bring relief to the besieged. Or it may well have been the regular troops (though Muslim; the Boxer Rebellion was also a jihad) of General Dong Fuxiang, in the hope of, if not spreading the fire to the foreigners' buildings, then at least smoking them out. Furthermore, the besieging forces were in the windows of the neighboring buildings, shooting at anything that moved while "the old buildings burned like tinder with a roar that drowned out the steady rattle of the musketry." The quarter had eight wells, however, and a numerous albeit motley collection of arms for forming a bucket brigade.

Eventually, the north wind turned and the assault was finally repelled—but too late for the books. "In the East Court the small library was in ruins, the ornamental pond surrounding it was choked with debris; wooden printing blocks, manuscripts, and books were lying scattered about, trampled into the mire."[25] Everyone served himself: Children swiped the printing blocks to erect small barricades to play at being Boxers, too, and the soldiers gathered up the rest as travel souvenirs. All that was left of the legendary *Yongle da dian* was a miserable handful of scrolls. The British interpreter Lancelot Giles regretted that he was able to make off with only section number 13,345 of the encyclopedia—in other words, a single book of about twelve by twenty inches, which he felt was "hardly even a specimen." Giles was the son of Herbert Allen Giles, who had perfected a complicated system of romanizing Chinese that was added to the efforts already achieved in this regard by Wade in his work on the Yuanmingyuan.

Without pillaging, Sinology would never have existed. In conjunction with the transfer of all the gold and silver ingots of the country, the one hundred years beginning with the year 1900 saw a colossal transfer of texts to London and Paris from even the remotest regions of China, such as Dunhuang. Unimpeachable individuals felt quite seriously that they were working for the preservation and safekeeping of priceless documents at risk in a nation of scruffy wretches, an argument that could hold up in a pinch if it was one day combined with the intention of restitution, which is obviously not the case. (It has been gleefully noted that China has begun to draw up claims for the return of stolen cultural property. Once again the world's eighteen largest museums parried this with a common declaration released in December 2002, in which they retorted that they will never return anything.[26] But it is said that within two generations China will be the most powerful country in the world.) As an example, this is how the Tianyige became no more than a shadow of its former self by 1940. Foreign visitors traveled through the country followed by their moving vans and acquired books not by the title or by weight, but by the *wall*.[27] When they did pay, it was merely a few sapeques*—and they still imagined they were being charitable.

A marvelous salvation operation of archives and books reveals the extent of the state of abandon and scorn surrounding the empire on its deathbed, which its libraries also found themselves in as a result. This operation was also due to the same Luo Zhengyu who had intervened in the episode of the divinatory shoulder blades at the turn of the century and who won here the rarely shared title of benefactor of Chinese philology. In 1909, the Cabinet of Imperial Archives—made larger by a significant collection of books from the Wenyuange, the main imperial library—was on the point of collapsing under the weight of its decrepitude. The chancellor and reformer Chang Chihtung (Zhang Zhidong) decided that certain sections of it would form the base of the National Library of China but that all the useless items which had collected over three centuries would be burned, as tradition—and destiny—intended: Fifty to 60 percent of the archives were destroyed when the allies entered Peking in 1900. Luo Zhengyu managed to dissuade Chang Chihtung from this course and all the documents were sent to the Historical Museum of Wumen after the founding of the Republic.

Ten years later, the curator was strapped for cash and sold three-quarters of the collection for one thousand Mexican dollars to a paper merchant, who took away some 150,000 catties in jute sacks—a total of seventy-five tons. Some time later, while visiting Peking, Luo Zhengyu devoted himself to his favorite occupation, snooping around the booksellers', and he stumbled upon a letter of congratulations signed by the king of Korea and bearing the seal of the imperial cabinet. While waiting to transform his acquisition into paper to burn at funerals, the papermaker had begun selling off a part of it to the bookstores of Liulichang. Luo Zhengyu had to pay thirteen thousand dollars to carry it all away. He had a pavilion built to house it where it could be inventoried. This

---

*[The *sapeque*, or *sapek*, was a coin produced by France for use in Indochina. —*Trans.*]

deal ruined him financially, however, and he had to surrender the imperial collection to a Tianjin collector from whom the Institute of Philology and History acquired it in 1929 for eighteen thousand dollars. The affair caused a scandal, and Lu Xun wrote in a magazine: "Chinese, public property really is difficult to keep; if the authorities are incompetent, they ruin it, but if they are competent, they steal it."[28]

As the crowning blow to this period of dereliction, the Kuomintang stole the best of the rare books in Peking and Nanking in 1948 and 1949, as well as 7 percent of the Qing dynasty archives, which they then brought with them into exile on their island as evidence of the power of these literary possessions to which the Chinese still lend "magic and cosmological virtues"[29] and which are the mandatory guarantee and foundation of political power.

A new era began in China with the year 1900: The old beards of the middle of the world's Middle Kingdom had not realized to what an extent the hunger for lucre could overcome difficulties, erase thousands of miles, and unite the worst enemies, nor that new and particularly harsh technologies could appear without their knowledge, especially those based in revolting fashion on such a local and festive product as gunpowder. A new era had begun for China as China had begun: with the erasure of an irreplaceable portion of its memory.

INDIA AT THE SOURCES OF KNOWLEDGE

India covers 3 percent of the planet's surface and forms the cradle for several antagonistic religions, to which Islam has added its own brand of pepper. Myriad sects and the caste-system social framework form a highly inflammable material from which it is no anomaly that Buddhism eventually faded.*

Buddha had personally stopped one day in Nalanda. Na-alam-da, "insatiable in giving," is also one of his names. Today, under the name of

---

*It reappeared, however, within the most underprivileged social categories of the country, such as the untouchables.

Baragaon, which is west of Patna, the tall reddish orange ruins of Nalanda testify to the splendor of this university center created during the Gupta period (320–467 C.E.). This apparently was an ephemeral model of ecumenism: Brahminism and all the secular forms of knowledge were taught there. The audacious monk Xuanzang of *Journey to the West,* who had come here to harvest the essential Buddhist texts for China, described the glorious dynamism of this intellectual city during the seventh century. There he counted ten thousand people, including "the priests and foreign residents," which amounts to fifteen hundred priests for eighty-five hundred students. Teaching was free because the kings had granted this center the revenue of a hundred villages. The town held several buildings that were six to nine stories high, "licking the clouds," as an eighteenth-century stela described it; several conference halls; and numerous cells, including a niche to hold a lamp and another for books. The large library had the pretty name of Dharmaganja, meaning "at the market of faith." It consisted of three towers: Ratnasaggara, Raatnaranjaka, and Ratnodadhi, with Ratnodadhi dominating the complex, housing nine floors and the rarest and most venerated books, such as the tantric collection. While the number of the books collected at Nalanda is unknown, we do know that Xuanzang made two sojourns, one of fifteen months, in this paradise of texts to oversee the copying he had requested. In 672 his counterpart Yijing remained there for ten years and brought back four hundred books, including half a million *slokas,* the distiches of Sanskrit.

One day, two very poor beggars showed up during a sermon. They were *tirthikas,* heretics, which was the appellation bestowed on the adepts of Jainism, who obviously attributed the same label to the Buddhists. Some malicious novices who had been left unsupervised sprinkled them with water, which made them furious. It was said that after having prayed to the sun and asking its favor for twelve years at this site, thus purified they performed a *yajna* (a sacrificial fire ceremony), reciting the appropriate mantras in accordance with the Vedic scriptures before a sacred fire, then hurled its sacred living embers into the buildings. A great conflagration was started and the Ratnodadhi Tower was consumed in flames, along with the whole of the fabulous Nalanda library.

This story, which is still making the rounds, is attributed to a Tibetan pilgrim named Sharmasvamin, a troublemaker who allegedly visited the ruins of the tower in the middle of the thirteenth century, a short time after, in a more likely scenario, Nalanda and its books had been reduced to nothing in 1199 by Muslim invaders led by Bakhtiyar Khalji. This is because Odantapuri was located just east of Patna at this time (Ud dandapura, today Bihar), and it experienced a similar fate at the same time at the hands of these same Turko-Afghans. This Buddhist *vihara* was founded in the seventh century by King Gopala, who was no doubt inspired or stung by the example of Nalanda, and it was the model for Tibetan monasteries, the first of which was Bsam-Yas in 749. The incessant raids into India by the conquering Muslims were sometimes accompanied by the theft of libraries (such as that of the Iranian Nadir Shah in Delhi; the magnificent books of the Mogul emperors were then sold in Persia for almost nothing), which were often replaced by a center of Muslim education when they were not brutally culturally exterminated, as was the case in Vijayanagara in 1565.

Over the course of his initiatory journey, Xuanzang, who could be stopped by nothing but rumors of civil war (even then) in Sri Lanka, had pushed as far as Takshasila, or Taxila, the capital of Gandara. Nothing remained but piles of stones, but these were most curious, for the Buddhist temples there had Corinthian capitals. This exceptional crossroads of civilizations had in fact trembled successively under the feet of Darius, Alexander, Seleucus Nicator, Apollonius of Tyana, St. Thomas, and Mahmud of Ghazni. In the third century B.C.E., its governor was Asoka, who went on to become one of the famous kings of India, and was permeated by the spirit of Buddhism. Furthermore, Taxila was one of the first vihara and was at its apogee around the year 400, when Faxian, precursor of the Chinese pilgrim monks, visited it in search of manuscripts to copy. The library there was at the disposal of the five hundred teachers and equal number of students at the monastery, each of whom had to pay one thousand coins in advance for his long education, and the verb meaning "to learn," *sippam vacheti*, involved reading—yes, reading—the sciences. As bad luck would have it, the White

Huns, or Hephtalites, felt a kind of hatred toward Buddhism and strove to destroy all its physical as well as mental manifestations during the fifth century. This was how Taxila brutally vanished.

While in India, Buddhism turned the other, gentle cheek of nonviolence to its attackers and accepted its extinction. Its conflict with Hinduism was transported as it was, still smoking, into Sri Lanka, where it only made matters worse. The former Ceylon is ruled today by a Sinhalese authority colored by a somewhat chewed-over Buddhism that relies on a violent activism. On a daily basis it is confronted by a no-less-exacerbated Tamil opposition seeking independence, which we shall revisit later. The Buddhist philosophy, however, became acclimated to the isle first—and smoothly—around 220 B.C.E., influencing the language, thought, and literature. In the fourth century the presence of at least three monastic libraries with texts on ôles have been noted. As a follow-up to this tradition, King Parakramabahu I (1153–1186) decorated the country and his new capital, Polonnaruwa, with several libraries, the royal one of which was named Pol Gul-Vehera. But when King Magha of Kalinga in India landed soon afterward and ruled by terror from 1214 to 1255, these jumbles of books were among his favorite victims. Although Magha was not a Tamil, it would be the Tamils who incurred the blame for his misconduct. They had swarmed into the northern part of the country, and, during the thirteenth century, there was a library devoted to their works, the Sarasvati Mahalayam, which has incidentally been noted as having disappeared in a raging fire.

The spirit of the ancient Buddha also extended over the countries east of India. In Myanmar (Burma), the first books were made from strips of bamboo or palm leaves, then local folded paper, the *parabaik,* and carefully preserved in *sa-dike.* When the English took Yangon in 1855 and launched their bloody campaign of annexation, numerous scholarly and private libraries were burned. No doubt in order to preserve the essential works, King Mindon had built at the same time Kuthodaw, the indestructible library where the Theraveda is carved in Pali on 729 alabaster stelae, each close to five feet high. Thus the Buddhist canon "of the elders" covers six hectares near Mandalay. The surviving books on paper were later collected by Sir Charles Edward Bernard and, with his own collection of *mon* manuscripts, enabled the opening of the first public library in Burma, the Bernard Free Library. The roughly five thousand books that could be recovered following its destruction during World War II are the core of the present National Library, which boasts 618,000 printed volumes and 15,800 manuscripts and which perhaps will open its doors one day.

THE SWORD AND THE BRUSH

Prince Umayado no Oji ruled Japan from 593 to his death in 622. Also known by his posthumous name, Shotoku, it is to him we owe the massive importation of Chinese practices and knowledge and the decisive protection of Buddhism. For this purpose, not far from Nara he erected the Horyu-ji, which perhaps contains the oldest wooden structures in the world and where he placed his large library, the Yumedono, or Hall of Dreams.

Fragile wood and paper architecture is characteristic of Japan, thus fire is an ever-present component of life. Visitors today can frequently admire temples and palaces that have been rebuilt three or four times and are often almost contemporary. It goes without saying that the books made of *washi,* the paper created one page at a time with a technique consisting of aerating the pulp by imparting certain movements to the mold, were consumed by flames in a sigh. Nothing remains of the books making up the collections of the Heian nobles, the Confucian books preferred by Isonokami no Yakatsuga, whose Pavilion of Perfumed Herbs was open to all (meaning all the young aristocrats of his acquaintance, of course). Nor have any of the books survived from the palace of the emperor, poet, and calligrapher Saga, nor those of the Reizen-in, which went up in flames in 875 with all the contents of the *Nihonkoku genzai shomokuroku,* "list of the books currently found in Japan." When the sword replaced the calligraphy brush after the twelfth century, libraries became even more rare. Only the temples had book collections, but some of these were quite rich, such as that owned by the Tendai sect.

Corrupt and irrational—this was Oda Nobunaga's label for the Buddhists, whom he fought all his life. For generations they had formed a state within a state, rebellious even when power held them in favor. In the sixteenth century their power was at its peak and the Tendai sect, despite what the *daimyo* said about it, distinguished itself with the pragmatic rationalism it displayed by authorizing a vast blending of Zen with Shintoism. Things came to a head in 1571, when Nobunaga sent his armies to attack Mount Hiei, location of the Enryaku-ji monasteries, with the mission of reducing to ashes three thousand buildings, temples, schools, and libraries, and cutting the throats of sixteen hundred monks. Nobunaga's biography describes the event as follows: "The roar of the huge burning monastery, magnified by the cries of countless numbers of the old and the young, sounded and resounded to the ends of heaven and earth."[30] But this was no war of religion—far from it. Oda despised all the gods. Furthermore, to achieve his political ends and eradicate Buddhist teaching, he encouraged the arrival and establishment of the Kirishitan (from *Chrishtam,* the Portuguese word of that time for Christian) to such an extent that at his death, Japan had 150,000 baptized citizens. They seemed less dangerous to him, but the succeeding regents would have all the trouble in the world getting rid of them.

Few testimonies reveal an immoderate taste for the conservation of books in Japan. This makes all the more notable that of the learned regent Kaneyoshi (1402–1477), who was well versed in Chinese studies and a poet who led a very pleasant life, "enjoying his twenty-six children and a luxurious library, a vast storehouse of history and literature of the past. To his own eyes he appeared invulnerable and protected from the vacillations of destiny." The "senseless" war that erupted in 1467 caused him abruptly to lose all he held dear. In his journal he wrote:

In a very short time, a column of smoke was rising and the premises were soon destroyed. My library escaped the flames no doubt because the roof was tile and the walls were earth, but brigands of the neighboring area rushed in, assuming they would find money and objects of value there, and they soon staved in the door and scattered thousands of volumes. Not one of the Japanese or Chinese books, handed down through ten generation, was spared.[31]

The situation of Japanese public libraries changed in Edo starting in the seventeenth century, when each clan created its own collection, and especially during the following century, when the common people began educating themselves. Few large collections were formed and were perpetuated, however, even after the Meiji restoration. Except for the imperial library founded in 1872, all those created by will of the state were impoverished, poorly kept, and scorned by the people. They quickly become useless—and were bombed.

The sentiment of the impermanence of things as well as the attraction to all that is perfect, fresh, new, and in its first stages[32] permeates Japanese philosophy. Such notions are undoubtedly not foreign to the lack of haste shown in collecting and venerating those stale items that are books that have already been read. All of these, as Bashô says, soon become like dead combatants lying in the tall grass: *yume no ato,* "traces of dreams."

SIX

THE CHRISTIAN WEST

———— ❦ ————

So it is not surprising that we have so few ancient
writings; it is surprising that we have them.

GERTRUDE BURFORD RAWLINGS,
THE STORY OF BOOKS

INQUISITION

The popes invented the Inquisition to quell the Waldensian or Cathar radicals whose popular success offended them. This enterprise degenerated at once because of the zeal shown by the laymen charged with applying it, such as Robert le Bougre, Ferrier, "the hammer of the heretics," or Conrad de Marburg, who was so wicked he had to be killed.

With more finesse, the monks were next given the task to organize the network of suspicion. As we know, they were all powerful, their actions were covered by the most absolute secrecy, and they owed no explanations to anyone except the king when he knew there was reason to demand them. Rarely has a more effective system of domination been seen—one that did not have to waste money on tanks and gulags and which its own victims financed. Everyone from top to bottom in the hierarchies of the houses of the Inquisition personally enriched himself except, perhaps, two or three of the high inquisitors who were most steeped in asceticism. It is said that when all Jews, rich and poor, donated funds to offer Ferdinand of Spain six hundred thousand ducats in exchange for halting the

Inquisition, Cisneros, the grand master of the Holy Office, paid this sum to the king out of his own pocket. This makes it easy to understand the ease with which such a frightening number of subjects could be admonished and "released," the exact word that sent them to the stake.

In the Inquisition's tender years, it roasted—as Voltaire said in *Candide*—more bodies of men and women than it did libraries, and if there was a desire to put some book "to the test of fire," the first place to turn for guidance was the Holy See. This was the case until the Lateran Council in 1515 issued the bull *Inter sollicitudines* to put an end to this hesitation. Yes, of course it was necessary to eliminate the books "translated from Greek, from Hebrew, from Arabic, and from Chaldean, both into Latin or into profane tongues, books containing errors of faith and pernicious dogmas . . . as well as defamatory libels against figures of high rank." But despite the final stipulation, which is always a wise course to take, the writ appeared so harsh and sudden that even one of those in attendance—Alexis, bishop of Amalfi—declared that he supported the measure where new books were concerned, but not for ancient books. We are well aware that almost everywhere in northern Europe this kind of ordinance would never be applied, and Pope Leo X personally acted against it, as we shall see.

On the fairly clement territory of the non–Spanish Inquisition, we have seen that the capital of hate from which many libraries were more or less spared did not fail, however, to be spilled ruthlessly over the Jewish book, the preeminent "pestilential" book.

CATHOLIC SPAIN

Spain made the Inquisition such a beneficial tool of government that it had much difficulty giving it up and abolished it officially only in 1834. (I have learned, by the way, with a slight shudder, that the Vatican has preserved it into the present, but under another name.) With the sacred bonds of matrimony having joined Castile and Aragon and the reconquest of territory now finished, Isabelle and Ferdinand launched a vast operation of ethnic cleansing. The Castilian nobility in power, it should be noted, could find only one purpose in life: the elimination of Jews as property owners and rivals, which the common people applauded wholeheartedly without clearly knowing why. The order of expulsion was issued in March 1492. The only Jews who could remain were those who accepted baptism, those called the *conversos*.

Because the financial return for conversion of the Moors was actually quite meager, the evangelization of the Moors began gently until Cardinal Francisco Jiménez de Cisneros deemed the results too slow and, with the backing of the royal couple, brutally opted for coercion. Thus on December 18, 1499, three thousand Muslims were baptized by force. These Moors had been told to bring all their books with them so they could watch them burn on the Plaza de Vivarrambla in Grenada. The medical treatises were set aside and recovered by the University of Alcalá. This was a grandiose affair and far more exciting than the auto-da-fé of books Torquemada had organized almost on the sly and guiltily in his cloister of St. Etienne in Salamanca in 1490. Then there were burned barely six hundred volumes that were accused of referring to sorcery and Judaism. In contrast, the witnesses of Grenada, such as one Padre Alcalea, observed disappearing in smoke "truckloads" of magnificently scripted and illuminated manuscripts, many adorned with corners and clasps of silver or gold. Destruction is the most beautiful distraction. This spectacle left such an impression that the estimated number of books involved borders on sheer delirium: one to two million.[1]

Because this affair inspired a revolt, the response was even firmer: All Moors in Spain were baptized, including those in Aragon. To those who objected that this was an invalid sacrament because it was not performed with consent, the priests retorted that the Moors' frank and definitive option for baptism in preference to the stake was purely and simply the result of free choice. In 1511, the Infanta doña Juana decreed that the Moriscos—as the Moors were designated once they had been converted to Christianity—had to turn in all the books they owned. The search was now on for books of philosophy (they were few in number, for, with texts touching on theology and scholasticism, they had already been ordered to be cast into the flames under the rule of the Almoravids) and especially *los du su dañada ley y secta,* those of their wicked law and doctrine, which designated the Qur'ans and related works, and of these there were plenty. After this, the Arab language, names, and clothing were banned along with the custom of taking baths.

Finally, between 1609 and 1614, all Moriscos were expelled from Spain. This caused an economic collapse, particularly in the Valencia region, where there were three hundred thousand serving as quasi-slaves. "Now who is going to make our shoes?" moaned an archbishop. Shortly after the expulsion, Marcos de Guadalajara reports that numerous books were found in all the houses of Grenada, notwithstanding all the measures taken, and these were principally Qur'ans of great beauty, with strange characters and decorations that caused them to be mistaken for books of magic and sorcery.

During this same period, the Jews knew no relief, for the authorities suspected them of being absolutely insincere in the faith that had been violently imposed upon them. These leaders obtained permission from the pope to expand the domain of the Inquisition, without which the *marranos* (the name given the conversos "who practiced Judaism in secret") could not be confounded. Because the Castilian nobility were not particularly well instructed in business matters, the state's anti-Semitism ensured that from one day to the next, all the banks in the country became Genovese, which was not truly in Spain's best interest. Under the iron rule of Cisneros, the machinery of constraint was pushed to its fullest output: Humanism became an avatar of heresy and the name Erasmus was obligatorily replaced by *quidam* in quotes, as Christian mysticism itself appeared worrying and was thus a target for harassment.

Libertinage, meanwhile, was regarded as a springboard for religious doubt. "What are [these books] then, when placed in the hands of those of tender years, but a knife made available to a madman?"[2] This made for many titles to proscribe, so an index was published of books that could result in a death sentence if read, owned, sold, or printed. The publication of this list was "organized like an entertainment," with a parade, drums, and music.[3] The number of prohibited books did not cease to grow and was accelerated with the king's help. In short, all he needed to do was disinter the corpse of a wealthy man, convict him of heresy because of his reading material, and burn him in order for his entire legacy, minus one-fourth for the informer, to go to the Crown.

Analysis of the proscribed titles reveals that the review of the progress of dangerous ideas was rather erratic or, to the contrary, was prompted by pure opportunism. In the first half of the sixteenth century, the index showed evidence of a panicked fear of the "errors of Mahomet" and of "bibles in the common tongue," quickly joined by the Lutheran texts, the whole written in such amphigory that the courts did not know how to interpret them, hence the copious exchange of delayed letters.* Conversely, an index was produced by the Jesuits targeting only the books hostile to their order, which led to the pure defense of the monarchy in the 1790 list, which banned Voltaire, Locke, and Necker.†

When in doubt, the library destroyers of the sixteenth century were not satisfied applying the torch to the clearly designated titles, but would sometimes hazard a guess as to which ones needed to be burned. Their goodwill ensured, for example, the disappearance of an incalculable number of scientific books with positive or evil implications that they were incapable of clearly determining.[4]

The autos-da-fé of 1559 and 1560 were extremely brutal in nature: This time it was the Lutheran ideas that had to be driven back across the Pyrenees. The laws were subsequently made even tighter: a ban on studying abroad, with exceptions for Rome and two or three universities. Students and professors already on the other side of the border were summoned to return home and pass an examination from the Holy Office on their arrival. It was forbidden to import books or to read in any language other than Spanish. The king himself commonly spoke and read only Castilian, whereas his subjects spoke Dutch, Catalan, Arabic, French,

---

*For more details on this, see the work of Bartolomé Bennassar, who studied the phenomenon of the Inquisition throughout his career—perhaps even a bit too attentively, we might determine, for he seems lately to have discovered the subtlety, circumspection, and even the humanity of Spanish torture methods.

†Until I am informed otherwise, the last *Index Librorum Prohibitorum* dates only from 1966 and still sets the law. Montaigne's *Essays* still appears in it.

Italian, Portuguese, and English. Similar to the situation in Alexandria under Ptolemy Philadelphus, but for a diametrically opposed purpose, the holds of boats landing at Spanish ports were inspected and a representative of the Inquisition boarded them even before the customs agents.

Spanish libraries, private as well as public, were therefore under constant supervision, their contents subject to confiscation and destruction at the discretion of the authorities. "On October 25, 1566, Seville woke to find itself literally occupied by the *familiers,** who surrounded all the book shops. The commissioners placed seals upon these shops. This was followed by an examination of their collections, book by book."[5] On another occasion, twenty professors were ordered to clean the shelves of Salamanca of the *auctores damnati.* One expert asked for a raise from the Inquisition: Expurgating one Madrid library of books totaling a value of eighteen thousand ducats had taken more time than anticipated—eight hours a day over a period of four months. Conversely, the powerful bibliophile obviously made a habit of cheating. When, on his death, the sale was arranged of the collections of the above-suspicion don José Antonio de Salas, knight of the Calatrava order, 250 out of 2,424 books were found whose possession was punishable by death. In the same way, many "damned" works took the road not to the auto-da-fé but rather to the Escorial, which in 1639 owned at least 932 condemned books.[6]

This palace of deathly extravagance is easily the most disturbing pile of Christianity, made in the image of its master builder, King Philip II, who slept in tortured slumber in his small bedroom-sacristy. In 1566 this *rey papelero,* who never knew what he wanted but whom a Protestant pamphlet prettily accuses of distilling "Spanish Catholicon," forbade all his subjects to take baths as well as to use the Arab language: They were given three years to master the official tongue. He is less well known for his frenzied passion for books. The man who was then the most powerful in the world dreamed only of surpassing Rome, Florence, and

---

*[This was the name given the auxiliaries, public volunteers who, of course, acted on their own behalf. —*Trans.*]

Venice, home to the most prestigious known libraries, to construct an Alexandria for his own personal use. The sumptuous collection recounts that its attendant, José de Sigüenza, kept separate the Latin manuscripts, "unmixed with any other language," including a *De Baptismo parvulorum* from the very hand of St. Augustine, with "letters like our capitals and in the Lombard form or that of the Vandals who once lived in Africa, where there were many distinguished people." The "Hebrew, Arab, Italian, Castilian, and Persian [texts], as well as those from China and the Turks," were in another room, along with a codex "in the Malabar tongue." The Arab manuscripts are by far the most magnificent, with their gold Kufic letters on an azure background, the vowels in red and the diacritics in a deep blue made from actual pulverized lapis lazuli. But so many of these masterpieces had been made to disappear over the preceding years that it was now necessary to search in the Maghreb, after which the Morisco Alonso de Castillo was ordered to Grenada and Córdoba to purchase all that remained, which were no doubt few in number.

The Escorial, however, owned the greatest part of the royal Moroccan Library: four thousand manuscripts stolen in 1612 from Moulay Zidan. When Zidan fled with all his possessions, he had them shipped from Agadir on the *Notre Dame de la Garde,* a French galley whose captain took flight on the pretext that the sultan refused to pay in advance. The Spanish fleet inspected the vessel, and once Zidan's sons were restored to power, they spent the rest of their days futilely demanding their library be returned from the king of Spain and calling for damages from the king of France.[7]

But all this effort went for naught, for once the books were installed on the subtly aromatic shelves of the Regia Laurentina, a firecracker exploding in the college next door caused a huge conflagration in this stone monstrosity that raged for fifteen days and generated such intense heat that its thirty steeples melted. "In the library of printed books," says Padre Julian Zarco, "the flames managed to enter through the door, but tenfold heroic efforts at every moment during the first three days in an incredible, titanic, and desperate battle, prevented the advance of the fire, and that part of the building remained intact, although it had caught fire at the very beginning of the conflagration."[8] Yet some two thousand to four thousand Arab manuscripts that had been piled in a corner of the upper main cloister became the prey of voracious flames when the Turkish standard caught fire, for this trophy of the Battle of Lepanto was made of dried silk and had been stretched out over the books. According to the testimony of Padre Francisco de los Santos, however:

> [T]he Qur'an, with numerous other books from this inventory, escaped because they had been scattered about in different places, as well as ancient objects of value that were housed here. Much remained of the other books, Greek, Latin, and other languages, originals and copies, because they had been carried out; the rest burned along with the shelves and paintings decorating the room. Because it was so high, these could not be saved. Two chandeliers of gilded metal from the boastful Turk collapsed as well as other mathematical instruments, medals, and pagan idols, and because the walls were lined with painted walnut shelves and the rooms also contained desks and other wooden objects, the intensity of the fire only increased, so violently that one would have thought oneself in hell.[9]

More than three thousand works disappeared in this hall, including 650 Greek works, which, when added to the two thousand of the main cloister, makes the total four thousand to five thousand lost manuscripts, including the *Lucensus,* a famous manuscript of Visigoth counsel; the works of Dioscorides; and the nineteen volumes of *The Natural History of the Indies,* by the Toledo native Francisco Hernández, which described the flora, fauna, and customs of Mexico with colored illustrations he himself had drawn.

The monks saved a certain number of books (such as the very respectable *Beato de Liébana,* with its 119 eleventh-century miniatures) by tossing them through the windows to the esplanade and by hastily walling up the doors to prevent the fire from spreading. Little remained, however, of the eight thousand Arab manuscripts; an inventory taken one hundred years later counted only 1,824, "remote survivors, perhaps, of the great libraries of ancient Córdoba."[10]

When Spain had fallen so low that Joseph Bonaparte was sent to govern it, the palatial library was obviously shamelessly left to deteriorate. The French government then entrusted the mission of transferring the Escorial collections to Paris, to an *afrancesado* (the name bestowed on those who did not believe the country could emerge from its stagnation without outside help; in the eyes of many, they were simply collaborators). José Antonio Conde, an expert in Arabic matters, experienced a burst of patriotism and hid the precious works in the convent of the Trinity in Madrid, holding the chests beneath a mountain of worthless printed matter. For a period of five years they were overlooked. When the little-respected king Fernando VII expressed a desire to see them back on their gilded shelves, the literary world of Madrid opposed it: The collection would be better protected and appreciated at the Real. It was during this confused period that a number of manuscripts of the highest value found themselves all alone on the road to the sales room: The French government was able to acquire the *Cancionero de Baena;* the Chamber of Deputies carried away a rare Aztec codex (the Bourbon Codex, for thirteen hundred francs); a splendidly illuminated Greek collection of the gospels was taken at a bargain price by the British Museum; and another one was removed by the Pierpoint Morgan in New York. An inventory made in 1839 revealed that in this way the Regia Laurentina had lost a good twentieth of its most magnificent manuscripts and 1,608 rare printed works.

Irony of ironies: If in his time the envoy of Philip II was unable to find many handsome Arab manuscripts to purchase in Andalusia, it was because they had found haven in Fez and Tunis during the persecutions of the Muslims of Grenada and elsewhere during the previous century. It was his own father, Charles V, who was partially responsible for their definitive destruction when he went to take back Tunis from the Turk Chairadin Barbarossa, or Khayr ad-Din, in July 1535. This was an important affair—it was necessary to mount a vigorous reaction to the irresistible whittling away of Europe by Suleiman the Magnificent, which would soon threaten Spain itself. Inordinately large forces were thus thrown against La Goulette and the soldiers were given three days to spread horror throughout the capital. This is how it was recounted in his "complete discourse and true" by the squire Guillaume de Montoche:

> Immediately after the entry of His Majesty into the city of Thunes, he was followed by the Spanish infantry and other soldiers, who began to unrestrainedly break down doors and windows, entering the houses and killing the Moors that remained within, then pillaged and sacked all that was in vaults, wells and cisterns, and shops of merchants, where they found great booty, as also in the mesquites [mosques] and temples of said Moors, there where, after having broken and destroyed, several beautiful books, including some that had been very handsomely bound, gilded with gold and scripted in Arabic letters, some of these same soldiers took *pyliers* [mortars] of gray jasper and other rich stones . . .[11]

In this obscure chapter where Spain shined so noticeably, one cannot fail to take note of the refreshing and unique figure of don Enrique d'Aragon, marquis of Villena, who was born in 1384 of both royal Castilian and Aragonese blood. Dedicated by his father to the profession of weapons, he was inculcated into the military arts at a very tender age, which immediately spurred him to become a poet. Intoxicated by history, he spoke several languages; to the great astonishment of his fellow swashbucklers don Enrique quickly gained renown if not popularity for his science of divination and his art of interpreting sneezes. It is easy to see why he had "the lukewarm esteem of kings and was little respected by the ferocious knights of Spain";[12] they found him small and fat, too given to good cheer, and even more given to the sins of the flesh. Furthermore, he left his wife and wrote numerous books, all of which have disappeared, including the *Art of Cutting* (meats, fish, and fruits), and he even proposed a large school that would enable the young of the nobility to acquire the elements of a science propitious for the good management of life. He gave up his earldom of Tinea to become grand master of the Order of Calatrava, a title the king rapidly took away from him, in consequence of which, it seems, he had nothing left to live for and died in 1434.

The wildest rumors were spread about him, notably that he had his body cut into small pieces and placed in a jar in order to attain eternity, and that Andromeda's herb conferred invisibility upon him. Without delay, King John II ordered Fra Lope de Barrientos to seize the marquis's considerable library and tell him what he thought of it. The majority of its books were burned in great pomp on the square in front of the Dominican monastery of Madrid, where the marquis was buried. The rest were kept by Brother Lope himself—on the king's orders, he claimed—to help him write sometime in the future a large book condemning the occult sciences. In fact, he found sufficient interesting material to write at least two such books. While the library atoned for the cursed books it contained, these remained safe and propagated the crime.

THE NEW WORLD

"Our world has lately discovered another, no less large, populous, and manifold than itself, but so new and so infantile that it is still being taught its A, B, C . . . I very much fear that we shall have greatly hastened the decline and ruin of this other hemisphere by our contagion that we shall have made it pay quite dearly for our opinions and our arts."[13] Who but Montaigne could see so far in 1588 to understand so quickly and speak so clearly?

Hardly had the Spanish set foot in the New World when they introduced the Inquisition there. The queen had decreed that the only people eligible to emigrate and settle on these virgin lands would be the bearers of a certificate of *limpienza de sangre,* said purity being guaranteed by an ancestry of four generations of *catolicos viejos.* Yet this did not take into account that these candidates for the journey would set sail with many unverified servants, that many shipowners as well as many of the sailors on ships bound for this destination were Jewish, not to mention the easily committed fraud of choosing a name from an old tombstone forgotten in a cemetery. Thus Cisneros introduced the Inquisition in the Indies in July 1517, to keep watch over the communities of conversos that managed to establish themselves there in the blink of an eye, and which was not directed against the natives, who were then considered *casi monos,* almost monkeys.* Don't worry: Their turn for torment would come. It was simply delayed by a legal technicality: Because the Inquisition concerned only Christians, the natives would first have to be baptized before it could examine them.

There is little likelihood that the immigrants brought large collections of books with them. The inhabitants of the New World would almost have been able to lend them theirs. On the second meeting with Cortez, he was given numerous gifts made of gold and two books "such that the Indians possess."

The Incan emperor Pachahutec, or "he who transforms the earth," called together the historians and chiefs of the conquered tribes in 1450. He "questioned them at length and had the principal events that marked the reign of their ancestors depicted on large plaques adorned with gold, which he placed in the Temple of the Sun, which only he and the scholars he designated could enter."[14] They served there *como librerias,* like libraries, said Sarmiento de Gamboa. When the Spaniards took Peru, this archive, or rather this myth of an archive, had vanished. We do not know if it was annihilated to remove it from the cultural memory or if was simply carried off as booty. In any event, the Spaniards would have destroyed it because "to get the cinnamon, you need to cut down the tree; to get wool, you need to kill the vicuna."

On the other hand, they remained speechless before the "whole rooms" of *quipus,* knotted colored cords that were used as memory aids not only for bookkeeping connected to llamas and the details of a rigid bureaucratic and social organization but also to keep track of historical

---

*This belief endured: Much later, the Benedictine Peñalosa wrote this phrase in 1629 (cited by Alfred Tozzer).

events and astronomy. A conqueror has no imagination; otherwise he would have stayed home. None of Pizarro's companions had the curiosity to seek an explanation for these cords for the fifty years these documents remained in place. They were finally ordered burned by the Council of Lima of 1583 because of the magic spells that such mysterious objects most certainly contained. Thus there is no one today who can give anything but a perfunctory explanation for their use or the limits of their lost meaning.

Juan de Zumárraga, bishop of Mexico, then high inquisitor of Spain outside the walls between 1536 and 1543, proudly burned all the Aztec codices that the conflagrations of Cortez had missed—all the *tonal-amatl*, the sacred books that he sent his agents to collect or that were found gathered together in the *amoxcalli*, the halls of archives. This was undoubtedly a considerable quantity: Fortunately, we have the Mendoza Codex to testify that by way of tribute "twenty-four thousand *resmas* of paper* were to be provided annually to the warehouses of the master of Tenochtitlan," Montezuma II, and a distinction was even made between "the yellow sheets of Amacozitlan and the white rolls of Tepoztlan."[15] Thus in 1529, Zumárraga had the library of "the most cultivated capital in Anahuac, and the great depository of the national archives"[16] brought to the market square of Tlaltelolco until they formed "a mountain heap," which the monks approached, brandishing their torches and singing. Thousands of polychrome pages went up in smoke. The conquistador was there to kill and capture, the cleric to erase; the bishop fulfilled his mission while satisfying his conscious desire to destroy the pride and memory of the native peoples. "The missionaries believed in good faith that the Mexican Church could be erected only on the ruins of the indigenous religions," Robert Ricard tried to justify as late as 1933, but added in annoyance: "A missionary is no antiquarian!"

The pre-Columbian American book was such a sophisticated and original construction that it could easily have inspired the revulsion of the nouveau riche of the printed page. Using sheets made from the

---

*More exactly, *pilli* of twenty sheets, the paper, of course, *amatl*.

hammered fiber of ficus sapwood bark (Mayan *huun* or Aztec *amatl*), folded like an accordion or sewn, covered with a layer of lime that was better to hold the pigment, the codex could record a chronology; serve as a book of divination; consist of mythological and astronomical information; and describe martial exploits, although epic myths and poems were transmitted orally and rarely written. What the indigenous peoples used instead of letters was a vocabulary of recognizable and abstract objects, animals, grimacing faces, or highly stylized death's heads that could not help but ruffle the feathers of the Franciscans. Before Peter Martyr d'Anghiera, an Italian humanist who had visited Alexandria, pointed out that they were pictograms and therefore texts, they were regarded at best as collections of models for jewelers and embroiderers. These characters sometimes even brought to mind *horresco referens*, Arabic, *"Tiran a arabescos,"* shuddered a novice, Lopez Medel.

The Teo-Amoxtli, a collection of the Toltec's sacred books compiled by the astrologer Huematzion in Tula around 660, states that there were quite ancient writings in Guatemala. They were alluded to by Las Casas, the same one who, as many believe, was an ardent defender of the Indians and burned with joyous stubbornness everything he could find in the way of manuscripts or "works of the demon." Copan in Hondouras may well have been "the Mecca or Jerusalem of an unknown people," says the explorer John Lloyd Stephens. The natives of this district had revolted against the Spanish occupiers in 1530, to the natives' great misfortune. Garcia de Palacio, who visited and admired the city in 1576, observed: "They no longer have any books on their antiquities; I even believe there is only one book, and it is mine." According to the Spanish, the Aborigines of Nicaragua also possessed manuscripts painted in black and red on deer hide, which were about one hand in width and some twenty-eight to thirty-two feet in length, folded like an accordion. Fernández de Oviedo said, mincing no words: "Although not a letter was depicted upon them, these pages were not without meaning."[17]

While there remain some fourteen books from Aztec temples (including one in Vienna on sixty-five deer hides), we know of only three or four meager survivors in rather poor shape from those of the Mayan caciques:

One, appropriately, is in Mexico; another, which is quite beautiful but evanescent, is in Paris and is nicknamed the Peresianus because it was found in an envelope marked "Perez"—it is only Parisian (Parisinus) by chance; yet another—forty-five pages from the year 1000—is in Dresden; and Madrid is home to the most diverse and complete one, which has been studied so thoroughly that the specialists have even pointed out the spelling errors, if they can be described as such, which they label as dyslexic. This codex was purchased from the descendants of Cortez.

The Franciscan Diego de Landa Calderón, born in 1524, was one of the first preachers to enter the Yucatán. He offers an example—even more than Zumárraga, if that is possible—of the right-thinking nuisance. Because he had studied the mores of the Maya and decoded their glyphs, their infamies seemed even more cruel and cynical to him. We can read in his *Account of Matters in the Yucatán:*

> These people also used certain characters or letters, which they wrote in their books about the antiquities and their sciences; with these, and with figures, and certain signs in the figures, they understood their matters, made them known, and taught them. We found a large number of books written with these letters, but as they contained nothing but superstition and lies of the devil, we burned them all, which impressed them greatly and caused them much pain, *lo qual a maravilla sentian, y les deva pena.*[18]

Landa, then bishop of thirty-seven years, added just for good measure two hundred strokes of the whip to each of the nobles he forced to attend this spectacle.

The Maya of the third century carved their calendars on stone, but this practice had come to an end in 889, the date that may well mark the first appearance of their books.[19] When the Spaniards appeared, the Yucatán civilization was in decline, which was how, in 1561, the invaders managed to pull off the feat of destroying almost the entire body of the country's writings in a single blow. These were faithfully stored in a secret reserve in Mani, which had been the seat of the Tutul Xiu dynasty.[20] Hadn't that ancient masterpiece of oral tradition drawn in the Teo-Amoxtli, the Popul Vuh, announced the coming of such a fate: "This is First Book, written in days of old, but whose face is hidden [today] from he who sees and thinks."[21]

Barely thirty years later, José de Acosta mentions those "books of leaves, bound or folded, in which the learned Indians kept the distribution of their times and the knowledge of plants, animals, and other things of nature and the ancient customs, in a way of great neatness and carefulness. . . . The Indians were not alone in regretting this loss, also sincerely regretted by many Spaniards who desired to learn more of the country's secrets."[22] It should be mentioned, however, that Acosta was a Jesuit.

The vision of the world that guided the Jesuits—their strategy, if you prefer—diverges from that of their fellow Catholics: Scientific research and education form part of their essential admissible concerns. Athanasius Kircher was one of the most curious (in both meanings of the word) men of Christianity. It was his peers who would give their names to the lakes and mountains of the moon. There was another somewhere in 1595 who wrote a Tupinamba grammar, the *lingau geral,* or common tongue of the Amazonians. And who else but a band of Jesuits could have buckled down to the task of putting together a seven-thousand-page Chinese dictionary known as the *Grand Ricci?** Wherever they found themselves, they needed libraries. For example, in California, where only a few isolated brothers became the first permanent residents in 1697, the colonial presence in a pueblo could sometimes be summed up as one soldier and one missionary. When the king of Spain had the Jesuits expelled a century later, they had thirteen libraries in California totaling 1,855 books, including twenty-two titles and forty authors who were on the index. Manuel de Nobrega arrived in Bahia, Brazil, in 1549 with five colleagues. Between the gifts of the king and the pope, to which

---

*This is more an encyclopedic data bank of 13,500 characters, which required fifty years to complete, starting in 1952; the Chinese words are transliterated in Wade-Giles, a system with which only ghosts are now familiar.

were added the acquisitions of a wealthy congregation, the library of the local college had fifteen thousand books as well as a catalog and an annual operating budget before it was scattered. Its value was estimated at 5,976.69 reis. In the meantime, the institution served to train the local elite from Rio, São Paulo, and Maranaho, each of whom collected more than five thousand books at dozens of other sites: "[N]o establishment, whatever its remoteness inland or upriver, did not lack the embellishment of at least a room of books."[23]

Because the Jesuits were hindering, or so he claimed, his rational and modern ideas for running the state and also a little because of a rumor that was circulating about their gold mines in Brazil,* the marquis of Pombal obtained King João's consent to expel the order from Portuguese territory in 1759. Charles III did the same in 1767 in the Spanish colonies because he coveted their holdings in Paraguay. Within the space of one day, the arrogant brothers found themselves out on the street. The Spanish king, for example, wrote a secret decree that was suddenly read to those targeted in their beds at midnight: They had the right to take with them only their breviaries, snuff, and chocolates.

This was how books from California to Chile ended up confiscated or forgotten and left to rot, burned or stolen, sent back to Europe, or sold as wrapping paper to pastry makers. In Rio de Janeiro, 4,701 books were left to molder for sixteen years before those that were on the index or concerned the Company of Jesus were sent back to Portugal, with the books on theology handed over to the bishop of Rio and others "given to individuals able to take care of them." Seven hundred thirty-four titles that seemed of no interest to the viceroy, such as the works of Plato, were burned. The Jesuit collections of Córdoba (Argentina) and Merida (Venezuela) were requisitioned by the Dominicans. In Santiago, in Chile, they formed the embryo of the national library, whose expansion continued shamelessly with the invasion of Peru in 1881. The Chilean army selected the library of Lima as the ideal barracks for three years and a

---

*But the real reason was the opposition of the Jesuits to the enslavement of the Indians, which ensured that they encountered unanimous rejection. It should be added that such a noble attitude was greatly facilitated by their importation of slaves from Africa.

good third of the 150,000 books there were used in the latrines on a daily basis, after which 8,790 copies were taken away to end up on the bookshelves of Santiago—where they still may be.

Not only did the most beautiful libraries of South America suffer from the consequences of the expulsion of the Jesuits, but Pompal's scheme against Brazil backfired as well. The eviction of the Jesuits encouraged the emergence of Creole power and the march to Brazilian independence in 1822.[24] Above all, it incited the collapse of an educational system and a voluntarism that—who knows?—could have offered the continent a chance of producing a few more poets and a few less dictators or drug traffickers.

FROM THE MIDDLE AGES
TO THE AGE OF REVOLUTIONS

Almighty Author and Lover of Peace, scatter the nations that delight in war, which is above all a plague injurious for books, . . . so many shrines of eternal truth.

RICHARD DE BURY

"The library is the true treasure of a monastery; to be without one would be like a kitchen without pots."[25] It required many generations and many wild ups and downs, though, to arrive at this observation made in 1632, one that did not fail to hasten wide-scale plundering.

During the centuries before the year 1000, the great libraries of the West can be summed up as a handful of codices at the bottom of a padlocked chest, and thus do not give much work to a contemporary researcher.[26] When the word *library** appeared on an inventory, it could sometimes be defined as only a Bible. But hardly had the monastic collection become a bit richer, in conjunction with other, more visible

---

*In addition to the building and collection, *library* also designated, at certain times, the catalog of books as well as their descriptions (as with Photius). Better yet, Roger Chartier points out, the *Bibliotheca bibliothecarum curis secundis auctior,* by Philippe Labbé (Paris, 1664), compiles a list of the authors of these libraries.

possessions on the outside, than misfortune arrived at a gallop in the form of the Huns, Saracens, or Vikings. The Abbey of Tours was sacked no fewer than six times in fifty years. This often led to the little that was left being shut away, often to be lost due to an excess of precaution, as was the case for the tenth-century papal library that was so carefully sheltered within a *Turris carteleria* [Cartulary Tower] made expressly for this purpose, so that no one ever consulted the books it contained. They eventually fell apart.

The son of Charlemagne lived in Toulouse until the death of his father, who had made him king of Aquitaine at the age of three. Becoming Louis I in 814, he began by burning the library of the imperial and paternal court of Aix-la-Chapelle, which quite obviously consisted of Unica, or sole copies of works existing, and thus deprived posterity of an entire range of French and Germanic literature. In addition to the numerous manuscripts produced by the poets and scholars whose company Charlemagne had sought, Louis cleansed the premises of the prostitutes who had been given their ease there and forced his bawdy sisters to take the veil in the most secluded reaches of convents. No one could have been any more devout or puritanical; he was consequently nicknamed the Pious. Without him, the Dark Ages, also known as the Middle Ages, would inevitably have ended sooner.

The meager monastic libraries—when they existed, for certain congregations felt that faith had no need of any reading material, however holy—developed extremely slowly by means of the manual reproduction methods of the scriptoria, originally a Benedictine specialty. In this headquarters for text treatment (we are quite far from Arab calligraphy and light-years from the Chinese art of writing), the copyist aligned with mechanical meticulousness the millions of lines by reed or quill that formed the book after the illuminator cooked up his ornaments with the ingredients of an alchemist. Despite the exceptional conviction of Alcuin, who was educated in England and came to France to repeat to the monks of St. Martin of Tours, "better to copy books than to cultivate the vine," the brothers showed evidence of an intentional poor understanding. (The abbey library became one of the most renowned of its time, however, before being reduced to ashes in 905.) Calligraphers, therefore, are not intellectuals, bibliophiles, or even aesthetes. One of their phrases would be, as at the Vivarium of Cassiodorus, "Satan receives a number of wounds equal to the divine words copied by the monk." (At the same time, but at the other end of the earth, the Buddhist was also copying his sutras, but for immediate spiritual benefit.) So there is nothing surprising in the fact that the monastery libraries were poorly used, if at all, or that they were neither maintained nor defended against predators of all kinds. For example, Monte Cassini, "the Sinai of the Middle Ages,"[27] managed an active scriptorium in the eleventh century that published Greek and Roman authors as well as the scriptures, but when Boccaccio wanted to visit the premises with an easy-to-imagine book enthusiast's palpitation, he was told, "Just go there; it's open." It was so open, in fact, that grass was growing between the lecterns and rain had fallen on the dust of books whose covers had long since been torn off.

Fortunately, knowledge was not long in finding new nests. Gradually, collections of books appeared that had been put together for educational purposes inside the cathedrals, which were forerunners of the universities: Notre Dame of Paris under the leadership of Peter Abelard, Hildesheim, Barcelona, and Durham, which had a wealth of 570 volumes in 1200. (The Sorbonne's collection numbered 1,720 in 1332.) First lined up in armaria, the growing quantities of books soon required the creation of a separate room where individuals could work during the day, for candles were forbidden. The collections generally consisted of anthologies or summaries of all kinds, bibles, patristic texts, lives of martyrs, and sometimes a little history. Private collections soon emerged, then came the printing press. Catalogs grew in variety.

The great Western collections were born in the fifteenth and sixteenth centuries in the residences of the kings and princes, sometimes in the homes of their counselors, often prefiguring the crucible of future national libraries. But before that, they suffered the full brunt of repercussions of years of vicissitudes in which amateurism, emotionally maladjusted decisions, and ideological free-for-alls prevailed over more generous and more defensible realizations.

The most advanced country for bibliophilia, England, was the champion of chaos and crudeness when it came to books. By all evidence this authorized the following: Spottiswood,[28] in his *History of the Church and State of Scotland,* says that when the English king Edward I defeated William Wallace in 1298, he did all in his power "to extirpate the Scots" who lived in Scotland and therefore "abolished the ancient Laws, made the Ecclesiastic Rites adopt the form of those of England, destroyed the ancient monuments raised by the Romans or their descendants, burned all the Registers as well as the famous Restennoth Library where, among many other books, were housed the books that King Fergus II brought back with him from Rome," the city he had sacked in 400. This archive had been stored in a monastery on the Isle of Iona, whose only village was named Sodor from the time it had still been teeming with druids, priestesses, and refugees from Atlantis.

Richard Aungerville de Bury, bishop of Durham, decided to establish a new college in Oxford to which he donated his exceptional personal library, with five Benedictines as administrators. A collector for as long as could be remembered, his diplomatic missions for Edward III had allowed him to travel through the Europe of libraries, copyists, and archives in order to satisfy his passion for books of all appearance and on any subject at all. He describes this with equal measure of pedantry and inspiration in his *Philobiblon,* Love of Books. Exaggeration claimed Bury owned more books than all the rest in England put together. William de Chambre testifies that the bishop had piles of books in all his castles and that piles were always strewn across his bedroom floor to such an extent that no one could take a step without tripping over them. On the day following his death in 1345, the sale of his fifteen thousand books (some wet blankets maintain it was no more than five thousand volumes) was not enough to cover the huge debts he had contracted acquiring them, and his college began operations with its bookshelves empty.

Henry VIII is apparently the one who contributed most to the poor reputation of his truculent country. Forbidden to divorce as he saw fit and for several other reasons, we know that he made England a religiously eccentric country whose sovereign also serves as its own pope. The dissolution of the religious orders and the closing of eight hundred monasteries, along with the confiscation of all their possessions that this decision brought about, was not a bad affair, but its regrettable corollary was the destruction of some rich libraries. It is estimated that some three thousand volumes were then lost. Of course, the most admired manuscripts of the time found a path to the royal collection and several intermediary experts were no doubt also able to satisfy their interests, but the rest were ostensibly used to light lamps, shine shoes, and clean out chamber pots. After the antiquarian John Leland had raked through everything for his king and "retained many good authors," the rest were left to the tender mercies of the mercenaries, who shed them as quickly as they could and for the first price offered, as illustrated by the case of one merchant who was able to purchase two noble and complete libraries for forty shillings and, rather than try to resell them, found their contents more useful as a reserve of "waste paper," or toilet paper, for ten years. He did say he was far from having finished all his books.[29]

Edward VI showed himself a worthy successor of his famous father by ordering his minions to destroy all reading material smacking of "old learning." The degree of the ancient culture's wickedness was apparently based on the frequency of illuminated capital letters. It is as much to say that almost all the books of all the wealthy libraries were incriminated. There is the case of Westminster, for example, which was compelled to decontaminate itself of its superstitions, legends, and other missals by order of a writ in the royal hand, to which another hand had added as a postscript that they must "tear all the gold clasps from their bindings and turn them over to Sir Anthony Aucher," who, we assume, was charged with the execution of the writ. Hence this contemptuous line by a chronicler: "Here avarice had a very thin disguise and the courtiers discovered of what spirit they were to a remarkable degree."[30] Whole cartloads of books were taken indiscriminately and so zealously from the library of Oxford that mathematical treatises disappeared as surely as if they had been concocted in the monasteries. No great respect was shown even to the collection of Humphrey, the duke of Gloucester and brother of King Henry V, deemed the most beautiful of its time. (Depending on who counted, it held 281 to six hundred books, but all of the greatest luxury.) Even the shelves were sold, according to some because there was nothing left to put on them and according to others in order to erase the very memory of books capable of contradicting what was called, in distinguished English, the "nouveau sçavoir" (new learning).

Matthew Parker, archbishop of Canterbury; William Cecil, counselor to Queen Elizabeth; and other noted scholars such as Cotton and Bodley, having by their own initiative collected from the merchants the remnants of these collections that had escaped burning, the little (no more than 2 percent)[31] they managed to gather formed famous collections a century later, the core of the three greatest contemporary archives: that of Corpus Christi in Cambridge, the Bodleian of Oxford, and the British Library.

The systematic incineration of all the books possessed by a man or a community was a less rare discipline in Great Britain than elsewhere; it was not an everyday occurrence. Yet the burning of books in great pomp by the hand of the hangman was, in certain periods, routine at Westminster, and can be counted in the hundreds in any case, whether motivated by political, religious, or moral reasons.[32] In general, the symbolic destruction of a single copy of the condemned work was deemed satisfactory. The authorities sent all manner of documents into the flames. The measure became so banal that, decades later, Samuel Pepys noted impartially in his diary: "Saw the hangman burn, by vote of Parliament, two old acts, the one for constituting us a commonwealth, and the others I have forgot." The practice eventually faded away in London just at the time the Parisians were discovering it: Rousseau's *Émile* and the major part of Voltaire's works were the most famous victims.

The Renaissance's Dances of Death

With a new day, new ideas were given free rein, from the most outrageous gnostic divagations to speculations full of the spirit of the Reformation. Their combined effects on libraries could make the ferocities of the Inquisition pass for pointillist acts.

The richest man in the world, Cosimo de Medici (1389–1464), conducted his quest for books like the emperors of antiquity. Not content with acquiring excellent collections, such as the eight hundred works owned by Niccolò Niccoli, for which he paid twice because this connoisseur was also his debtor and died in debt, the top European banker commissioned his agents to buy him books from the four corners of Christendom and even—he had negotiated the right from Sultan Mehmed II—the Orient, although the librarian Vespasiano da Bisticci was working on location. At one time, forty-five copyists toiled twenty-two months to produce two hundred richly bound and perfectly scripted works.[33]

Gian Francesco Poggio Bracciolini also bore his share to the Marciana of the prince, which received its name because it was located within the enceinte of St. Mark's Monastery. Poggio is a Renaissance figure, a famous calligrapher to whom we owe the "humanist" form of letters, which literally humanized the withered Caroline minuscule. This modern man was no less a formidable hunter of ancient manuscripts and succeeded in bringing back to his place in Italy from France, Germany, and elsewhere in Italy, often by copying them in his own elegant hand, which was easier for his doddering constituents to read than Gothic script, a considerable number of the texts of Cicero, Lucretius, Lactantius, and Quintilian, which he unearthed from monasteries ignorant of their presence, or so he claimed. His voracious appetite was equaled only by his cunning and self-assurance. On the occasion of councils, he would present himself in isolated monasteries as an envoy of His Holiness, inspect the library, and have the fine abbot hand over manuscripts of staggering value, such as the *De Architectura,* by Vitruvius, in ten volumes, which was, perhaps, on the slippery slope to oblivion in St. Gall. Poggio was not afraid to state that Germany was a "prison where the Roman classics were held captive by Teutonic barbarians" nor to display a similar negligence of the books he grabbed. He and other antiquarians of his stripe lost, once copied, almost as many manuscripts as they had recovered: Pages of Cicero, Catullus, Pliny, and Tacitus vanished, and even the famous *Cena*

Trimalchionis, which Poggio unearthed in Cologne in 1423, just missed evaporating completely when Niccolò Niccoli borrowed and lost the only copy. If it had not resurfaced in 1650, in Trau, Dalmatia, we would have a completely muddled notion of the *Satyricon.*

During the Middle Ages, the palimpsest was a terrible laminator of classic texts that seemed to have gone out of style at a time when parchment was expensive: Many authors got the "downside" and may remain thus hidden today beneath a long-winded discourse by a Church Father deemed to be an utter bore but definitively respected for its antiquity. In the sixteenth century we have to reckon on the casualness of the humanists: "Manuscripts were often treated with scant respect by the printers to whom they had been entrusted."[34] The trade was new; why would anyone imagine that what we call "the copy" should be returned to its owner? Here is a research topic for the young student in archival sciences: Verify if any part of the corresponding manuscript survives for any book printed before 1501.

Cosimo de Medici was not only a bibliophile and reader. Aware of the philosophical implications of the fall of the ancient—and Christian—world in Constantinople, with the help of Marsilio Ficino he reconstructed Plato's Academy and introduced to the University of Florence the teaching of classic Greek, forgotten for seven hundred years. Florence thus knew or heard speak of the Bibliotheca privata Cosimi, located in the palace, and of the Bibliotheca publica gentis Mediceae, which was commonly known as the Publica or Marciana. Poggio bequeathed him a good many of his discoveries and Pico della Mirandola was planning to do the same with the good thousand books he owned, but an adverse fate diverted them to Venice, where a fire destroyed them during the seventeenth century.

Cosimo's grandson Lorenzo the Magnificent showed himself equal to such a legacy: Highly literate and himself a poet (though not in Latin, but rather in Tuscan, which was new), he continued to enhance the collections. He could have become besotted with the great novelty that would one day be called the incunabulum, but this was not the case. "Those who own the rare and costly manuscripts of the past, with

their admirable calligraphy, regard unkindly their raw and ugly reproductions [when] obtained by mechanical means."[35] No one, unless he
is the owner, would dare contest the fact that the Gutenberg Bible is
one of the most mediocre books of the century. Florence, moreover,
would not have its first printer until 1477, much later than Mainz or
even Naples. Lorenzo therefore spent thousands of ducats every year
acquiring books. He sent "the renowned Jean Lascaris two times to
the East for the sole purpose of unearthing ancient manuscripts. On
his second journey, Lascaris brought back two hundred Greek works,
eighty of which were completely unknown."[36] On his deathbed, the
Magnificent had only this to say to Pico and Politian: "I would wish
death had spared me a bit longer and allowed me to finish your libraries." Lorenzo was forty-three years old. He had no idea that he had
introduced the devil into the place.

He had carried on the Platonic circle of his grandfather. Pico della
Mirandola was a member, and it was he who gave the unwelcome
advice to name Savonarola as prior of St. Mark. Hardly had Savonarola
assumed his post when the uncontrollable Dominican hurled himself into
a radical denunciation of the Church, debauchery, and the Medicis combined as well the whole "horde of the Roman Sodom." While Lorenzo
was dying, Savonarola became the guru of the Florentines, thanks to a
French king who was passing that way in pursuit of his own chimeras:
Charles VIII in 1494. Following this, the last Medicis were driven away
and all their holdings were pillaged, including their munificent libraries.
Raiding palaces was then commonplace and tolerated by the authorities,
or prompted to a certain extent in this case. It should be noted that at
the twelfth and final Lateran Council, it was decided to put an end to
the custom of authorizing the people to take what they pleased from the
home of an individual just elected pope because he would not be returning. Unscrupulous types had made a habit of sowing false rumors of
election in order to arrange juicy pillaging opportunities.

In this instance, the Seignory put its hands on the books the populace
had overlooked or did not have time to carry off and had the audacity to
sell them back to the monastery of St. Mark for three thousand ducats.

This put the monastery in debt, for it had a total of only two thousand ducats in its account.

Savonarola dipped into these shelves and offered to the prelates supporting him luxurious editions of Ovid, Tibullus, Catullus, and Martial, thereby ridding the monastery of "the evil books infecting it." Did he not preach constantly that Plato, among others, should be sent "to burn in the devil's house"? In fact soon, as his favor began to fall, this was what he did. He founded militias of child magistrates who were charged with going first to their parents, then to all houses, to take all "dishonest things": art objects, adornments, perfumes and mirrors, "infamous books such as the Morgante and others . . ." He named this cultural revolution that was uncorked on the *Bruciamento delle vanità* the burning of the vanities, Anathema.

During Carnival in 1497, on the square of the Seignory there was erected a "scaffold in the form of a pyramid; at its base were placed masks, false beards, mountebank costumes, and other diabolical novelties; above were the books of Latin and Italian poets, the *Morgante,* the works of Boccaccio, Petrarch, and similar writers," then paintings depicting famous Florentine beauties. An aghast Venetian merchant offered twenty thousand ecus for all of it. By way of response, his portrait was rapidly drawn and added to the pile. The hollow interior was filled with flammable materials. After Mass, communion, and procession, the children set fire to it and accompanied the crackling of the flames with their joyous and holy canticles to the sound of the trumpets of the Seignory and the bells of the Palazzo Vecchio. A year later, the whole thing was started over again.

But Savonarola could not carry it off to heaven. On May 23, 1498, he himself was excommunicated, hanged, and burned, his writings cast to the winds, all to the sound of the same bells and trumpets in front of the same gawkers.

Twenty-two chests, the small portion of the Medici libraries still housed at the St. Mark Monastery, were redeemed and given a haven in Rome by Lorenzo's son Giovanni, who, five years later, would become Pope Leo X. He agreed to pay only 2,652 ducats and the monastery lost money. (The attentive reader will note that the family was paying for Niccoli's books a third time, if any were still part of the collection.) The least tormented of all the popes (Giovanni confessed: "As God has granted us the papacy, let's enjoy it then!"), he was also an unscrupulous book hunter. He felt that all the members of the clergy had the mission of procuring books for him and delegated agents who were sometimes outright traffickers, "from the shores of the ocean to the confines of Asia." The first five books of Titus-Livy are in Florence today thanks to him. When they were spirited away from the Corbie Monastery in France, there was a dreadful outcry equal in intensity to the emotion generated by their discovery. Until that time, the texts had been regarded as lost forever. The booty passed discreetly from hand to hand until it reached that of the pope, who paid the unheard-of sum of five hundred ducats to his supplier. Then, instead of returning the manuscripts, he had a copy of his edition printed "in a beautiful binding" and sent to the prior of Corbie, accompanied by a plenary indulgence for his church and a letter "so that he would recognize that this theft brought him more profit than harm."

At the same time His Holiness was utilizing all the facilities offered by the pontificate for fattening his personal library, the Vatican library grew only from 3,650 to 4,700 volumes. It should be further noted that during the sack of Rome in 1527, the collection "suffered tangible damage and the efforts to develop it were partially undone."[37] It is therefore the name of this bibliophile pope who is associated with one of the most historically hostile measures against reading. On May 4, 1515, the Lateran Council decreed that in order to eradicate the "too numerous errors in the past and even more dreadful in the future," everything of a nature to shake the faith would be burned. Satisfied with this impossible visionary formulation, it designated no authors or titles. These were provided, however, with the bull *Exurge Domina* of 1520, which put Luther on the index. The Council of Ten in Venice refused to promulgate it and authorized its reading only in churches when the last of the faithful had departed.

In 1523, Pope Clement VII, who was a nephew of Lorenzo the Magnificent, sent back to Florence all the books owned by the Medicis and charged Michelangelo with the task of building (but he only drew it) the Laurentian Library to welcome and offer to the public, in 1571, the remnants of the acquisitions of Cosimo and his grandson. All the same, this was 10,500 volumes, seven hundred from before the year 1000, including a Virgil from the fourth or fifth century; the oldest copy of the Bible; the original of Justinian's *Pandects* (533); the Codex Amiatinus; the oldest copy of the Vulgate; and other, similar titles that let our imaginations run wild about the obscure riches that were lost in November 1494.

Yet the very first of the great humanist libraries was founded not in Italy but in Hungary, and its luxuriousness was such that it could not have failed to inspire the Medicis. When he was elected king of Hungary at the age of fifteen, Matthias Corvinus already owned a fine collection of handsome books. His tutor had been the chancellor Johannes Vitez, about whom the greatest bookseller of the era, Vespasiano da Bisticci, said: "There are very few books in Latin that he does not own." A letter from 1471 informs us that Matthias had a permanent agent named Blandius, *"minator noster,"* our illuminator, charged with the task of supplying him with wonders plundered or commissioned from Italy. In the eastern wing of the palace at Buda, which overlooked the Danube, he had painted on its vaulted ceiling the astral theme of the precise moment he was crowned king of Bohemia in 1469.

His riches were juxtaposed beneath these providential heavens. The base collection was that of his predecessor, Sigismund of Luxembourg, who was the German Holy Roman Emperor and already frequented the company of Italian humanists such as Poggio Bracciolini, who definitely shows up everywhere. Added to these were books confiscated from disgraced chancellors and the library of Matthias's second wife, Beatrice of Aragon, the princess of Naples. All of this was in very good taste; the king merely wished that the principal productions of the human mind could be found here. The librarian Marzio Galeotto notes that a third of the books were from before 1470, their pages decorated "à la Florentine," with simple white foliation, the rest being of the greatest magnificence, as shown by the two hundred remnants. The king appreciated genius, like that of the famous illustrator Attavente degli Attavanti, and because he corresponded regularly with Marsilio Ficino, the books were in Greek as well as in Latin and Hebrew. There is nothing staggering about their quantity—today it is thought they numbered around three thousand—but with "the treasures equal to the number of books," visitors thought themselves "not in a library but, as they say, in the lap of Jupiter."[38]

Hungary was well managed; after the brutal death of the king in 1490, an ordinance prevented his son Janos from disposing of any books except those intended for his personal use. He had been stealing and selling them for his own benefit. While the Corvinian Library was no longer the center of humanist exchanges, as it had been during the lifetime of its founder, at least there was a desire to preserve its integrity. It then officially became the national library, the first of its kind in Europe. It would perhaps be there still if Turkish troops had not arrived and destroyed it. It seems that the father of Matthias had led several expeditions crowned by success against the Ottomans; they had to scrub clean their humiliation.

"Shadow of God upon the Earth" was how Suleiman the Magnificent liked to describe himself. It was he who extended the grip of Constantinople as far as it would ever reach. He conquered Belgrade, Iraq, and the island of Rhodes; terrified Vienna; and made Hungary into an Ottoman country. Upon the sultan's arrival into Buda and Pest in 1526, he ordered the city burned with the exception of the palace. "Because he was living there, he did not feel it convenient to have it burned," the official journalists who followed him declared fairly realistically. Everything else was subject to sword and pillage by the army—including the library wing and everything else that had "belonged to the miserable king." For public opinion and the intellectuals of the sixteenth and seventeenth centuries, the Turks then acquired the evil reputation that they would long seek to undo because Suleiman's troops "tore them [the books] to pieces, for some, or scattered them for other uses after tearing off the silver work for the rest." As for the Corvinian Library, "Asiatic barbarism had destroyed it."[39] By way of ex libris, King Matthias had all the bindings emblazoned. It is estimated that a tenth escaped disaster and reappeared, easily recognizable, a short while later in the markets of Constantinople. Today 216 "corvinas" have been identified scattered in forty-eight libraries in forty-four cities of fourteen countries.

This exotic villainy wrote "paid" on the unbalanced accounts of the Crusades. Starting now, the Europeans' making mincemeat of each other would be confined to home. This was the birth of a Europe of social, political, and religious conflagrations. Thus, instead of taking their measure against the Turks, in May 1527 the half-Spanish, half-German troops of Charles V promptly took the fork in the road that led toward Rome. Dispatches of the time describe strewn through the streets the manuscripts and documents from the archives, which were eventually spread out to serve as bedding for horses. The lead seals on the papal bulls were melted down to make bullets and the Protestant hero Sebastian Schertlin von Burtenbach proudly recounted: "We devastated Rome and burned the greater part of the city . . . destroyed all the work of the copyists, the registers, letters, and documents of state."[40]

The Bauernkrieg, or Peasants War, was expedited in two years: 1524 and 1525. This uprising of German serfs and the bourgeoisie was a veritable revolution before the fact. As always, the down-and-out who believed in it were massacred and the rich profited from it: The princes used this opportunity to recover ecclesiastical holdings and further increase their power. (In France, the peasants of the Beauvaisis and the Soissonnais preceded the Germans by more than a century: The Jacquerie behaved "like rabid dogs" and only the Black Plague prevailed.) Despite its tragic defeat, this catharsis sparked an immense cleansing of the land parallel to the Reformation: No fewer than a thousand fortified castles were burned and at least as many monasteries (sixty-two in Thuringia alone), of which hundreds of libraries were systematically destroyed if the assailants were left to their own devices, and were exchanged for a few coins if the fighters were somewhat organized.

All the illiterate peasants knew was that somewhere in these bizarre objects known as books their intolerable debts were consigned, unless they viewed them as symbols of an enigmatic world that would never share its privileges or benefits. Thus at the residence of the Augustinians of Anhausen they tore to pieces twelve hundred volumes valued at three hundred florins; in St. Blasien near Freiburg they "threw, tore, and burned" the library's contents; in the one at Ebrach the damage was assessed at five hundred florins. In Kempton, the abbot swore a complaint against those who "took apart and carried off the registers, letters, books, and documents." In Maihingen they made three piles from the three thousand books there: They set fire to the first one, the second was thrown into the water, and the rest served as "bumfodder," as they say, and so on to Reinhardsbrunn, where the library was totally destroyed, and to Bamberg, and to Wettenhausen . . .

At first somewhat favorable to the cause of the rebels, Luther eventually drew the line: "If the arquebus is not used, they will become one hundred times more wicked." Their misconduct in the monastic libraries, however, should have delighted the man who had also written that nothing was more "insane, useless, and dangerous" than the books of monks; in a word, real "donkey shit." Meanwhile, Luther's former disciple, Thoman Muntzer, went even further. Radicalized to the point of calling his former teacher "Miss Martin" because of how soft his overall doctrine appeared to him, he became so active in the very leadership of the rebels that he ended his days tortured and beheaded. Friedrich Engels wrote his great work with a totally partisan but impassioned narrative of this savage history, in which Goethe also found his provender, albeit much more bland, with *Götz von Berlichingen*.

The idea was in the air of Europe: A library was power; it was the corruption of conscience. The populists did not have, do not have, and generally speaking will never have any great difficulty in getting narrow-minded people (which was how Engels himself labeled the peasants) to accept the notion that owning no books was preferable to having any, and especially to having many. The anti-intellectual had all the right cards for pounding out the leitmotif of all religions: The ignorant are chosen to redeem the world—and for usurping the label of "freethinker" as the Beghards, Adamites, Taborites, shepherd crusaders, and flagellants more or less did. "No one should own, take in hand, or read any other books but the Old or New Testament; they are sufficient unto themselves for the salvation of the soul."[41]

Speaking thus was the illiterate Jean Matthys, a baker from Haarlem and self-proclaimed envoy of God who became the prophet and first grand master of the Anabaptists entrenched in the city of Münster, where they were baptized a second time, which was punished by death elsewhere. After two years, the city was taken by treason and all there were slain. In 1534, however, the beginning of their rebellion, as at Montségur and in other places at other times, it can be seen that the audacity and madness of their decision blinded them. Euphoria was at its peak, and any kind of aberration could be ordered. "When they sacked the cathedral, they took particular delight in defiling, tearing up, and burning the books and manuscripts of its old library."[42] The city archives and account books were destroyed on another day: Yesterday was no more and heaven was not far away. Finally, on Sunday, March 15, the baker-prophet, just like the friendly coordinator of our vacation villages, decreed that it was necessary to immediately go in search of all the city's books, whatever their contents, even and especially those in private collections; bring them before the cathedral; and reduce them to ashes. This made a mountain of fire around which people danced themselves into a stupor. The market value of this loss was estimated at twenty thousand gold florins. The Landesknechts, who had been besieging the city for fifteen months with the hope of making their fortunes by pillaging "the pearl of Westphalia," received eighteen florins in all, after having exterminated its inhabitants, who had been reduced to devouring each other.

The Palatina Library of the University of Heidelberg had escaped all the disasters of these times. Its destiny is exemplary, although quite uncommon. Expanded over the course of the sixteenth century with the books bequeathed to it by its professors, it consisted of six hundred books in 1396. It was categorized and indexed in 1466, when its contents had grown to sixteen hundred titles in 841 volumes, but the bequests of private collections brought the titles to sixty-four hundred in 1556: forty-eight hundred printed volumes, five hundred manuscripts on parchment, and six hundred manuscripts on paper. It was at this time that the Lutheran elector Ottheinrich decreed that his successors acquire fifty florins' worth of books at the Frankfurt Fair each year, the consequence of which was to make the collection a modern one in which contemporary literature was greater in number than

the medieval and scholastic texts. The fabulous books left in 1584 by
Ulrich Fugger caused it to double in size and made it the most important archive in Europe, rivaling that of the Vatican. (The first Fuggers
were the precursors of fifteenth-century capitalism; their descendants
were born millionaires in florins and became erudite humanists in the
sixteenth century. Ulrich Fugger was Protestant.) This rivaling could
not be tolerated.

In some ways it could be said that once again in the history of libraries, Rome imposed its order. During the very confusing Thirty Years'
War, the head of the Holy League appropriated the Palatina and offered
it to the pope by means of a strategic deal he had succeeded in complet-
ing. But no doubt in order to avoid the fingers of His Holiness coming
into contact with covers that Huguenot hands had touched, he had the
bindings removed from the thirteen thousand printed books and thirty-
five hundred manuscripts, then had glued to the flaps of their new skins
this dubious ex libris: *"Sum de bibliotheca Heidelberga capta spolim
fecit et Gregoria XV trophaeum misit Maximiliaus dux Bavariae"*—that
is, "I am from the library that Maximilian, duke of Bavaria, took as
booty in Heidelberg and sent as a trophy to Gregory XV." This was
in 1623. The University of Heidelberg then enthusiastically rebuilt its
book collection, but it was completely destroyed during the Palatinate
war of succession in 1693, when the city was razed. A new one was
started in 1710. The Vatican even consented to return 847 books in
1826, and Paris (at the cost of laborious exchanges) only one volume—
but one of primary importance: the Codex Manesse, a compilation of
poetry from the year 1300 illustrated with 137 miniatures, which later
escaped the thefts, bombings, and confiscations—a loss of only forty
thousand copies—of the Hitler era.

As we now know, it was the abuses committed by the Holy See that
had opened the door to Calvinism in France some dozens of years earlier, and which contributed to the repeated atrocities, reprisals, rapes,
and murders that characterized the Wars of Religion.

Books suffered all the more as the still omnipresent illuminators of
the time brought them to the attention of the Huguenot troopers just like

the relics of the saints and statues of the Crucifixion as apparatus for evangelizing among the illiterate. How could the *brisimages** not hurl themselves with irrepressible enthusiasm on an abbey such as Coloumbs, which boasted of possessing one of Christ's foreskins, or, in Soissons, the finger of St. Thomas (a possession illegally acquired in Constantinople in 1204)?[43] So have at the goods of the Church, went the hue and cry against the libraries: St.-Médard; St.-Jean-des-Vignes; Hautvillers near Reims; Poitiers; Cluny, where the manuscripts were violently torn apart as "being all books of Mass." The Calvinist Theodore de Bèze acknowledged he felt some contrition. As Catherine Brisac says: "Numerous libraries of religious establishments, secular as well as regular, were put to the sack by the Huguenots in this part of France. The case of Lyon (1562) has remained famous but it is far from being alone. Many institutions witnessed the disappearance of their manuscripts." This was the case again at the abbey of Jumièges in 1562, which was sacked by Montmorency's ill-disciplined soldiers. At St.-Euverte they "broke into splinters the rostrums and everything that was made of wood and set a fire into which they tossed all the books of the abbey." Similarly, this occurred in St.-Gilles in 1563, and at St.-Benoit-sur-Loire in 1568, where the Benedictine library founded by Macarius in 1146 was three-quarters destroyed by Coligny's German mercenaries. Coligny, however, was wise enough to remove a quantity of books in extremis, which quickly found a safe haven on more refined and scholarly shelves, such as those of Sweden's Queen Christina.

Ronsard vainly tried to gently remind de Bèze that France "is not a Gothic land, nor is it a Tartar or Scythian region; it is the one where you were born." Only fire cures fire, but as there were nowhere—and for good reason—any magnificent Protestant libraries or idols to burn in return, Catholics had to resort to St. Bartholomew.[†] Then, having become like one of the many statues he had urged his minions to mutilate, Admiral Coligny was finally "hanged by his feet for lack of a head."

---

*[Image breakers. —*Trans.*]

†[A Catholic massacre of Huguenots promised amnesty by Marie de Medici that occurred on St. Bartholomew's Day. —*Trans.*]

Revolutions and Evaluations

A monk is seen from the back leafing through an album of pictures of naked women with a large carafe of wine at his left, while a rat is attempting to scale the decorative woodwork of the cabinets of books from which sausages are hanging. Certain shelves are barricaded with chains, and others reveal that many books are already missing. Those that remain are leaning toward the left or right, positions that contribute to breaking their bindings. This frightful engraving from the album *Images des abus dans les monastères* (1784)[44] illustrates fairly well the anticlerical mentality born under Voltaire and the general crisis of confidence that led to the great upheaval in eighteenth-century Europe, when knowledge, like power, changed hands in an immense turmoil of libraries. This sometimes took place gently, but generally occurred in fairly deplorable fashion—especially in France.

Four episodes of this transfer of confessional and aristocratic possessions to our embryonic collective entities attract the most attention and illustrate the toppling of a world: the relinquishment of the Jesuits, because it was as monumental as it was urbane; the revolution without revolutionaries in Austria, which could have set the example to follow; the great French adventure as model of catastrophic incompetence; and the picturesque career of the Bavarian Aretino, which was inspired partially by the French adventure.

L'Onguent pour la brûlure, ou le secret pour empêcher les Jésuites de brûler les livres (Ointment for Burns, or The Secret for Preventing the Jesuits from Burning Books), by Jean Barbier d'Aucour, appeared in 1670, went through six editions in the seventeenth century, and was republished in 1826. This successful Jansenist pamphlet raised a hue and cry against the unpopular "Pères fagots,"* whom Rome had begun to view poorly for their praising of the depth and charm of Confucian rites, whereas the Christian strategy up to this time sought the immediate and radical extinction of all beliefs wherever it set foot. Portugal and Spain were thus not alone in ridding themselves of the burdensome Society of

---

*[Father Firewood. —*Trans.*]

Jesus.[45] Since 1761, the French parliament had ordered burned the works of twenty-three brother-authors, which had been declared contrary to Christian morality, and subsequently closed their schools. A year later, the congregation was prohibited and all its movable goods and properties were confiscated. There were close to three thousand brothers who lost everything, including their daily bread. The order's general Lorenzo Rizzi then relieved them of their vows, and several diehards set off for more-welcoming horizons in Poland. In order to prevent any return and claims, however, the "family pact" of the Bourbons sought to obtain from Rome the official abolition of the order. "I would rather have my two hands cut off," the pope responded. Close to the next day, he died from cardiac arrest and was replaced by a more pliable Clement XIV. The annihilation of the Company of Jesus was therefore proclaimed on August 16, 1773, by the brief *Dominus ac Redemptor* (obviously *Dominus ac Predator* would have been more honest). General Ricci was sent to die a slow death in the prison of the Holy Angel Castle, and his twenty-three thousand companions melted away into the countryside from San Diego to Shanghai without a murmur. In order to become ordained, they had to swear to obey the decisions of His Holiness no matter how they perceived them. The sole protest came from Catherine the Great, who declared that because the national education in Poland was her main concern, she considered the pope's order null and void. No one dared question her on it.

This was because Ignatius Loyola knew that education took precedence in all things and that only books permit it. Even while he condemned Terence, Erasmus, or Luther to the flames, he proclaimed in his *Regulae Societatis Iesu* (1540–1556) that at the rector's pleasure, each college must have a library with a key for everyone who needed it and that furthermore, the teachers were encouraged to build their own "professional" collection, despite their vow of poverty. This would be added to the common collection upon their death. This could pose a problem only sometimes, given the number of titles that should not have been included.

This is why, between 1762 and 1773, a thousand of the world's libraries found themselves, in the space of a day's time, without any teachers or servants, sometimes even with their doors left gaping. Not only did the heads of the provinces have to abandon their own book collections in haste, but in accordance with Ignatius's wishes, there was at least one library of good size for each of the seven hundred Jesuit monasteries and schools. Many of these were destroyed or left abandoned after a careful pillaging by the very instigators of the writ of Rome, and a number of book-lovers' treasures suddenly made their appearance in the great collections of Europe. It was also observed that the bookshelves of the Franciscans and Dominicans had also become considerably enriched. Despite the discreet raids that accompanied each inventory, numerous universities also created at that time several municipal collections that benefited from this manna. Booksellers became rich. In Rouen, for example, the adjudication of a sale by one of them took 208 hours. In Lyon, the catalog of the bookseller François de Los Rios began in 1777 with these words: "One could perhaps be surprised to see . . . that such a large number of rare and singular books have come into my possession, and in such a short while. . . ."[46]

When Pius VII repealed the measure of interdiction forty-one years later, demands for the reopening of the Jesuit schools proliferated throughout the world (eighty-six in France alone). But the rehabilitated brothers, despite the memory of the "black impostures" evoked by Blaise Pascal,* could only turn down these proposals for a time; they were either too old or too young and no longer had any books with with which to teach.

As carts collapse under their load of books as they toil along a muddy path in the Alps, from time to time the cart driver throws an encyclopedia or an atlas beneath the shoes of the horses that are stuck in the mud. Before the dumbstruck peasants, these were the libraries of the Austrian monasteries heading to the storehouses of the state. This image is most likely imaginary, but its great popularity speaks volumes about

---

*This memory perhaps explains the relative discretion of their return to grace and that in particular no systematic study has ever been made of the exact fate of their property. "You then find yourself before the void," is the response of the management of the Jesuit archives to the venturesome.

the collective trauma that Joseph II inflicted on his country by trying to revolutionize it before its time. "My empire will no longer be the theater for an abominable intolerance," he wrote to his head librarian, van Swieten. With that, freedom of worship and freedom of the press were instituted and the death penalty and censorship were abolished along with serfdom and feudalism. The nobility now had to pay property taxes on their unproductive lands. This man was much more than the enlightened despot customarily depicted; he was a madman of reason and a veritable hothead of good government. He gave the theaters of Vienna to actors to manage, and one hundred years before everyone else did so, he increased the number of schools and made education both mandatory and secular. With complete simplicity he declared he was following the path "traced centuries ago by Zoroaster and Confucius, which, fortunately for the human race, has now become that of the sovereigns." Who of our current leaders would ever be capable of uttering such a phrase?

"At a time when the apostates were still imprisoned inside four walls, the greatest minds were still chained in the libraries of the cloisters. Joseph freed all these prisoners." This anonymous text that claimed itself "translated from the German" appeared in 1787, barely five years after the emperor eliminated all the orders that produced neither science nor charity, on seeing that the Church owned three-eighths of Austria and that the bishops were millionaires. Seven hundred eighty-three congregations were thus dissolved and thirty-six thousand monks returned home with a nest egg. The buildings were transformed into schools or lodgings, and the money formed a religious fund that provided serious financing for the creation of hospitals, orphanages, and maternity wards.

Meanwhile, the libraries were condemned to be broken up and their contents scattered, after they had been passed through a sieve to pull out any treasures. Manuscripts and codices swelled the collection of the imperial library (the future National Library), which still shows today the registers of what was transferred. (I should note here that Gottfried van Swieten, its prefect from 1777 to 1803, launched a sizable innovation: card catalogs. Before that time, record books were always incomplete and muddled.) The withdrawals made by this archive were of the most modest kind but followed strict criteria: five hundred incunabula, for example, and fifteen medieval manuscripts, all in all from the Carthusian Abbey of Gaming,[47] from which twelve thousand other titles were transported to the university of Vienna, which still left several thousand to be sold at auction and several hundred to be stolen by the local peasants. Despite the numerous cases of destruction through ignorance or pulping, the universities of Linz, Innsbruck, Prague, and Graz, among others, were beneficiaries of this great *renovatio ecclesiae.* Contrary to what took place in France, at no time was any monk seen to be mistreated or any book damaged, especially because of its edifying content. Furthermore, as stipulated by the emperor, a monastic library could avoid seizure by the state. Thus the Premonstratensians of Strahov in Prague decided to open their collection to researchers. The consequence of this is that the five thousand manuscripts are still visible in their august place beneath the spectacular Baroque ceilings dating from 1727.

In order to be acceptable, the avant-garde in principle have to arise from the social depths. Having succeeded in making himself detested by the entire continent for attempting to impose novelty from on high, Joseph II seems to have started backtracking shortly before the end of his too short reign, influenced by the events in Paris,[48] although, as luck would have it, he did not have to learn of his sister's decapitation. All his reforms were brutally repealed starting in 1792 by his successor, a champion of reaction—save one, which remained established in the land: the redistribution of books. Ever since this singular reign, historians have been contemplating the hypothesis of Joseph II influencing his brother-in-law Louis XVI with his modernist ideas. Hadn't Joseph lent Louis his support when Louis was entering into one of the most intimate domains at the beginning of his marriage?

Whatever it may be, the French Revolution would not have been a bad thing at heart if it, too, had abolished the death penalty and inculcated the inviolability of the book. Yet these virtues were still too new to be widely desired. Only Sade advocated the first (yet another effort and this honest man would have expressed his desires for the second).[49]

It was said that the miscreants of that time who mounted the scaffold in tight rows still retained a little belief in the hereafter. Furthermore, the prevailing mood was so hot that Voltaire and Rousseau also would have been guillotined if they had been in the hands of the people. In such an overheated climate, the violent nationalization of the country could only bring in its own lot of false good ideas, fraud, and crass stupidity. Grenoble rebaptized as Grelibre or the reine-claude as the citoyenne-claude,* is part of the eloquent epiphenomena of this gigantic drain, which "has no need of scholars" or which sees the Sorbonne as "a shrewd and vain body, enemy of philosophy and humanity."

The unleashing of the hecatomb of books goes back to November 2, 1789, when all the ecclesiastic and religious possessions were transferred "into the hands of the nation," which had a real need to bail itself out without the structural means of organizing the plundering. For lands, buildings, and ciborium encrusted with rubies, the matter was simple and the capital quantifiable. But libraries? These were entire halls of dusty books where, here or there, perhaps, someone in the know could unearth something of sure value, putting aside the incunabulum or richly illuminated manuscript that has nothing in common with the price fetched by the gold threads of a chasuble.

So just what are libraries, then? For the nation they are an indecipherable dead weight, for the bureaucrats an empoisoned directive; but above all, they are the symbol of tyranny in the eyes of the restless. The hunt for Crown and fleur-de-lis was fashionable and a healthy occupation for the ordinary folk, but hammering out the coats of arms on the stone imposts was less convenient than ripping off the covers of books and lacerating their illustrations. When the mobs entered the shops of the booksellers to purify their stock, the sellers could only applaud. The national library had been the "royal library" just yesterday: All the books therein bore the marks of infamy. One La Harpe demanded their systematic elimination and a new binding, which the mathematician

---

*[The despised noble in Grenoble would be replaced with the word *free (libre)*, and the *queen (reine)* of 'Reine-Claude' (greengage) is replaced by *citizen (citoyenne)* —*Trans.*]

reckoned would cost three million "just for the exterior letters" and that "there would not be enough leathers prepared for the job."[50] They had to be satisfied with stamping "RF" all over them, in red, if possible. On the other hand, because several individuals had seriously entertained the idea of burning the national library in its entirety, there was no shortage of autos-da-fé. In Marseilles, in Toulouse, and in Paris, for example, on June 19, 1792, a German witness noted in his diary that an "immense quantity of volumes was burned on the Place Vendôme in front of the statue of Louis XVI. I went there and could still see the glowing ashes. There were many people gathered around it, warming their hands and feet as a very cold north wind was blowing, and I warmed myself on it like the others." This temporary improvement of his comfort was granted by, among other bound combustibles, 163 portfolios containing titles of knighthood and nobility. On August 7, another 582 volumes and files were incinerated on the same spot. The Office of Orders was no more than a memory.[51]

The first decree of confiscation of libraries did not enjoy much success; the monks created obstructions and lied and the municipalities often sided with them. Furthermore, municipal officers were often disheartened in advance by these collections, which we can assume consisted in large part of breviaries, missals, and collections of canticles and the lives of saints. They knew they would be paid only for whatever good books they impounded. The provinces began selling them "by the pound," despite the law forbidding it. A new decree was issued in March 1790: The officers had eight days to visit the premises and inventory the book collections. Transfers began. In January 1791, the injunctions were more pressing and "on pain of being held responsible for their negligence," the municipalities began to more efficiently extract books from the monasteries.

This laid the ground for the first major question: What to do with these four million books? (In fact, there were three times as many.) Should they be destroyed? The French street quickly grew weary of conscripted labor. Should they be given away? In his "Plan for What May Be Done with the National Books,"[52] the former abbot Tuet noted that selling them in bulk would net little return, whereas the education of the people was of urgent necessity. But there remained a question about all these religious trinkets, which were worth less than nothing according to the new canons and whose quantity remained a mystery. This was why [Jean] d'Ormesson, still the king's librarian and soon to be executed, launched a phenomenal project: the Universal Library of France, an idea that passed for scientific and beneficial, but whose underlying intent was obviously to plunder the departments* of the bibliographical treasures and leave them with the task of disposing of the blessed religious rubbish. One of the keys to this matter was that Paris had thrown itself into a total war against the whole world starting with the French provinces, considered as henchmen of feudalism and, even worse, sources of the geographical individualism then called federalism, the worst of crimes. The heart of the tragedy can be found there, in this new Oedipal relationship occupying intellectual sensitivities of the time and made concrete by rising and falling flutters of correspondence, and bursts of cold, even comtemptuous, instructions that generated those laborious and sometimes irritated justifications that the human race sprouts like garlic.

This enabled this technocracy before the fact to inundate the territory with a standardized filing system targeting each book in every library. The backs of playing cards were used to record all the essential bibliographical information concerning each book, and these were sent every four months to the United Committees "in boxes well wrapped in waxed canvas inside and out." But this enterprise would not have the success hoped for, because many excuses of the following nature were offered for their lack of compliance: "We have the honor of observing that our very numerous duties . . ." or else, "We keenly regret, Sirs, having deferred the sending of this portrait, but it seems such a trivial task . . ." Meanwhile, those catalogs that were received remained scant. The only "regular" thing about this one "was the writing," whereas this other one from Sarregeumines allegedly inventorying the library of the

---

*[French administrative districts. —*Trans.*]

Benedictines of St. Avold would be perfect if it were not missing "the date it was printed, the name of the bookseller, and the city, the format, and the name of the publisher or the translator."

This grandiose plan for cataloging the existing books in France was abandoned after five years, but it had already revealed a reality with terrifying future implications: An entire heritage of libraries that would rapidly be increased with those of the émigrés, those of the people condemned to death, and those of suspects of all kinds was at the mercy of uneducated if not completely ignorant and at the very least entirely unmotivated individuals. The abbot Gregory[53] denounced "the negligence of the administrators, who undoubtedly did not neglect to collect their salaries . . . the majority being inept copyists who have adulterated the titles of the works, altered their dates, confused editions, and sent on useless catalogs" at whose ends can be read, for example, "in addition, three or four hundred volumes in English, German, Greek, Hebrew, or an indecipherable script, old and bound in parchmant, which we did not believe was necessary to list and which would have taken too long to describe, etc." Then, despite the sobriety of their covers, it was these that were "perhaps the most valuable books of these hoards: . . . the *sans-culottes* of the libraries." For Gregory, these books undoubtedly escaped the censor "beneath the modest envelope of parchment," whereas those "in which despotism consigned its extravagances and its rages almost always had the honor of morocco leather."

The disasters of the inventorying went hand in glove with—or, rather, masked—the consequences of the autos-da-fé and the general pillaging, whether due to the books sold by the weight or to theft by the bureaucrats themselves.

Gregory lodged an accusation: "They squandered things away. They claimed that ten thousand volumes had disappeared from the only library of Méjanes in Aix; and it was known that the rogues had not failed to make their selections." And several months later, he raged:

The pillaging starts with the libraries. . . . The booksellers, whose self-interest they found difficult to set aside, are profiting from the circumstances. . . . The majority of the administrators who are not selling their charges are leaving these bibliographical riches prey to insects, dust, and rain. We have recently learned that in Arnay the books have been stored in barrels . . . books in barrels! . . . The rush to destroy and consign to the flames: You realize that this step is more expeditious than that of inventorying. This is what was done in Narbonne, where many books were sent to the arsenal, and in Fontaine lès Dijon, where the Feuillants library was sent to the scrap heap and thrown in the room of old paper.[54]

Yes, "the artillery services displayed no less a keen desire for the old books than the paper manufacturers" such as Didot in Essonnes. "Sending the books to the arsenal" does not mean that the soldiers were aspiring to educate themselves, but that they were ripping out the pages to use in making cartridge bags, the little packets of gunpowder they stuffed down their gun barrels. In this way, perhaps, the lead ball that the enemy might receive in the brain might have been well seasoned with the thoughts of the best philosophers. As for the room of old paper, this was the antechamber of the pulper, otherwise known as "the reviser," which was the name given to a strange innovation that the scarcity of rags had brought onto the scene: recycling.[55]

In 1791, the Constituent Assembly ended its session without having made any decision on this point: Should this huge mass of books be used for public education or should it be discarded? The Revolution hesitated between vengeance and "regeneration." In response to a certain Boissy d'Anglas, who said in *Quelques idées sur les art* with regard to the French "it is therefore not a question of teaching them to do without, but to enjoy," a certain Urbain Domergue, a purist from Aubagne who suddenly found himself head of the Bibliography, said: "Let's bring the scalpel into our vast collections of books and cut off all the gangrenous limbs of the bibliographical body." This ardent visionary did not suggest burning the books but rather sending them where they could be bought by the country's enemies and give them "vertigo and delirium." From the beginning, Romme had wisely felt that it would be better to save everything, "leaving to time and philosophy the task of purifying our libraries." Boissy again, at the Committee for Public Education: "You possess an immense library . . . which still lacks many books; let them be placed therein as soon as possible, and may France, at least, not take any away that one is not sure to find there." Concerning the "purifying examination . . . such a doctrine is nothing other than barbarism and darkness . . . it is not by burning books that you will replace them with better ones. . . . But if among them there was one single idea that could be useful to humanity's happiness, that could accelerate its mental development or extend the circle of its education, ah, without a doubt, by setting it afire you will have commited a crime that the centuries will not wash clean."

These arguments will ultimately win the case and bring about the acceptance of the perspective of "numerous and sufficiently diverse" libraries, thanks mainly "to the guilty desertion of the cowardly enemies of our freedom." But the distinguishing feature of perspectives is that we do not see the end as imminent. It was first necessary to face many tragedies that were as predictable as they were inevitable, such as the affair of the "warehouses."

On November 29, 1793, Achard, librarian of Marseilles, stood up against the individuals "ceaselessly requesting that all books be burned as useless or harmful" and suggested that everything be stored in a warehouse until the matter had been ruled upon. Domergue was thus driven off. The convention passed the Committee of Public Education as a matter of top urgency and two months later decreed that there would be a library in each of the 545 districts. Those among them who had rid themselves of their books began to eye those of their neighbors. Others, in contrast, concluded they were now free to sell off their clutter at reduced rates. The Gaillac District announced proudly that it had unearthed "two intelligent citizens" to choose the best books to keep. The executive commission thundered back: "Any kind of triage is absolutely forbidden; they should inventory every book no matter what it is." This was an underestimation of the stubbornness of the Tarnais natives. Because he had been ordered to list the books by starting on the left side of the warehouse and continuing to the right, the librarian Blaney Laisné stumbled upon the first book whose title displeased him and threw it in the trash because he did not wish to make himself look ridiculous by putting it on the list. Furthermore, he said, because the administration had not furnished him anything to make the files, then it "clearly permits me to take the margin of an old Gothic antiphonary that has no beginning or end to make up for the lack of playing cards. If this is having the mind of a vandal, then I confess to you that I have one without knowing it. . . . Consequently, I have continued my work, which will soon have reached perfection."

The Constituent Assembly had already issued strict instructions for protecting the books, describing how to guard against humidity, rats, and fire. "As much order as possible will be employed when moving them so that the divisions already established in the libraries may be kept." This was a sweet dream: When they transferred the library of the Château de Piré in Rennes to its assigned warehouse, the soldiers, proud as peacocks, distributed the books among the crowds gathered to watch the processions; moreover, the national guardsmen responsible for protecting them from thieves "had . . . ripped up the books to light their pipes or feed the fire in their guard rooms." What to do "against the spendthrifts, who were principally the police or other soldiers, and even porters?" Chances were great that the responsibilities of the future librarian would be greatly reduced, either "because there were few good ones, or they had been removed, lost, or damaged during the trips they had been forced to take [he checked them in and signed for them] incomplete works, rotting volumes, and others that fell to pieces."

In the majority of cases, the warehouses were synonymous with chaos. In Périgueux it was discovered that "the libraries of all the warehouses had been mixed together" and in Calais, "all the books were piled pell-mell in an attic," while in the Nièvre "the unraveling I was forced to do cost me a great deal of time . . . one of my fellow citizens had become a victim of his zeal by rooting through this unhealthy storehouse." A danger was corroborated by the guard of the Belfort warehouse:[56] "Picture a shapeless heap of more than ten thousand volumes of all sizes in the middle of a bare room. . . . Because the majority of these books had not been opened for more than a century, they spread a poison that was constantly forcing me to leave, and which caused grave afflictions from which I long suffered."

When on 5 Germinal Year 9 the minister of the interior decided to add the books from the Versailles warehouse to the Paris collection, some 127,100 volumes, the inspector of the triage, d'Aigrefeuille, brought back only thirty thousand books. The rest—but how many truly remained—had been delivered by him to the pulper and sold by their weight at that same site. At the end of 1789, the librarian of Paris, Ameilhon, could count on 169 religious or ecclesiastical houses, and, if the monks were not lying, in all there were 808,120 volumes to find room for, and, after adding the books of the émigrés, there were enough for nine warehouses in Paris, which was reduced to two in Year 5, then just one by Year 10, and this last operation took two years. (The monks, however, often lied: For example, the Carthusians divvied up the monastery's library among all the cells and each monk swore that these one hundred or so volumes were his personal property, but the deceit was finally exposed.)

Each month for a good decade cartloads of printed books and manuscripts rattled through the streets of Paris in opposite directions, perhaps sometimes crossing the paths of their legitimate owners on their way to the morning slaughter. How many books were lost due to these illogical movements? The curators did not care, for they, like all those who exercised the slightest responsibility during the Directory were completely devoid of scruples. A certain Dambreville who was in charge of the warehouse of Louis-la-Culture selected 9,595 books to keep for his personal library at home. This collection was selected with such intelligence that when it was reincorporated as a whole into the Cordeliers* warehouse, the First Consul granted it to himself as his personal library.[57]

---

*[Franciscan friars. —*Trans.*]

To speak in the style of the times, the hatred of books contended with corruption and negligence; no one knew which caused the greater harm, villainy or stupidity. In 1794, the idea of the greater good was foremost: The churches were deemed propitious for the installation of laboratories for manufacturing saltpeter, and the former Abbey of St. Germain welcomed the salpêtrière Germain: "A vast reservoir was installed in the very middle of the nave, a forge in the cloister, and a coal storage in the abbatial palace" (Louis Réau has forgotten the mound of fodder). The conflagration was almost inevitable if not programmed. During the month of August, the major portion of 49,387 printed books and 7,072 manuscripts of the library went up in smoke.[58] A few large handfuls in shabby condition were recovered for a few coins by Pierre Dubrowski, a secretary of the Russian embassy who had received earlier practice during the pillaging of the books of the Bastille: Incunabula and illuminated vellums whose price today is incalculable (such as the *Great Chronicles of St. Denis* that belonged to the duke of Burgundy, Philip the Good, or the *Epistles of St. Jerome* in French verse that were illustrated for Louis XII in 1509) immediately found themselves in the residence of Catherine II of Russia, near the libraries of Diderot and Voltaire or many others that were no less extraordinary, such as that of Lamoignon at the castle of Baville. The czarina knew her duty and had taste, so the Jacobins called her the "trollop of the north."

No, the Republic of these few years had no need of scholars. On the other hand, they did need books, more and more of them. The war against Europe was eating up industrial-sized quantities of cartridge bags and there was a chronic scarcity of paper. During the Years 6 and 7 then, the fifteen thousand folios at the Cordeliers warehouse were pulled because the large formats were preferred by the manufacturers. The Château de Sceaux, constructed for Colbert by Perrault, was razed by the Directory so that its roofing could supply lead for bullets, and the pages from the admirable library of the duke of Penthièvre could wrap the charges. During this time up to the Restoration, the cleansing of the book would continue. In total, between 1789 and 1803, ten to twelve million books were moved, re-sorted, and damaged so that whatever was not destroyed was in large part lost. Thanks to ideas that were without doubt generous but impossible to master, the French Revolution prompted the annihilation of "the network of private libraries, sometimes open to the public, that had been slowly formed over the course of the centuries."[59] The extent of this disaster would bring about, as reverse reaction,[60] the cultural intervention of the state whose effects would be noted until the end of the twentieth century. But today, this danger has passed. Aren't we instead witnessing the replacement of this absolutism by the sponsorship of anything goes?

The Freiherr (baron) Johann Christoph von Aretin (1772–1824) was certainly "one of the more detested men of the Munich intelligentsia."[61] Historian and member of the academies of Munich and Göttingen, throughout his short life he was an avid collector of scandals, women, and books, and even incurred some difficulties after he seemingly stabbed one of his adversaries.

A fanatic admirer of the Enlightenment and the French Revolution, he spent three dreamlike months at the National Library in Paris in 1801, in the midst of a great hysteria of armfuls of books everywhere. He specifically took away with him the notion of what should not be done and tried to keep it in mind when he was given the responsibility of skimming the best out of the armaria of the seventy-three abbeys of a secularized Bavaria. At the head of forty moving men, we see him, without any second thoughts, "extracting the brain from the corpses of the monasteries" with an eye to enriching the Hofbibliothek of the duchy, soon to be the kingdom of Wittelsbach: Polling, Schäftlarn, Tegernsee (Merovingian manuscripts were hidden beneath the monks' beds), and so forth. In the monastery of Benediktbeuern, a pretty building had been built separately to protect the books from a potential fire. Retin appreciated the comfort and chose from it 7,231 manuscripts, incunabula, and other rare documents. Here was the site of the discovery of a collection of 318 somewhat awkward songs in kitchen Latin entitled *Carmina burana*. The tens of thousands of works that did not find grace in the baron's eyes were left to be auctioned, as elsewhere. It is estimated that the impounded Bavarian libraries held a million and a half books, from which two hundred thousand works enriched the shelves of the future Bayerische Staatsbibliothek.* Yet whereas a large number of printed works were also sent on to the university of Landshut, a quantity certainly greater than half the total ended up as paper pulp, as was the case for the entire library of Rottenbuch.

While, all things considered, Aretin was able to prevent the creation of the infamous book warehouses *à la française* by the backbreaking task of personally selecting the works on-site, he could not avoid the flooding of the city of Munich, which rapidly crumbled under the jumbles of books that came in without being inventoried. The baron's scholarly enemies took advantage of this to denigrate him. He ended up as a minor judge in a remote location. In the meantime, an ex-Benedictine was chosen to put things in order. This Martin Schrettinger, who had worked with Aretin and contributed to his fall, took his charge quite seriously. He showed in 1809 that "the memory of the librarian should be separable from the organization of the books; otherwise, every time the librarian changes, the book collection loses its functionality and, because of that, ceases to be a library." For the first time we are dealing with Bibliothek-Wissenkraft, thus "science." The fairly urticating word *bibliotheconomy* is not far off. For once the world has truly taken a turn.

One of the most horrific cases of book destruction took place in Paris in 1871, while the entire nation was momentarily staggering on its foundations. In one night, three large libraries were reduced to piles of damp ashes. Even if their losses had been minor, the event would have been of major importance: French society, literary society in particular, found its mirror in the event.

In May of this year, the working-class people of Paris who had refused the shame of 1870 and formed an embryonic state within a state were bloodily put down. During their few days of grace, the Commune had tried to legislate, in hobbled fashion, a revolutionary direction

---

*The German speaker will enjoy going through the cozy exhibition catalog devoted to this entire history, its actors, and its *Cimelien,* from November 2003 to January 2004: *Lebendiges Büchererbe.*

while caught in a pincer between the Prussian army in Vincennes and the French army at Versailles. They thought they might vanquish both of them, except the two forces were in cahoots. Enthusiastic gestures multiplied in this completely unrealistic ambience, the most important of which took place on April 6: the 137th battalion of the National Guard brought out the guillotine and burned it on Voltaire Square (which is now named after Leon Blum). On May 16 it was the turn of the Vendôme Column, which was pulled down, as Heinrich Heine had prophesied thirty years earlier. These symbolic actions contributed to an irrevocable sense acquired by all the other actions, even those due to panic. No one realized that if the "gangstercratic and good for nothing"[62] Commune had been truly driven to destroy the libraries, it would have gone after them sooner and not after secondary institutions.

The end of the dream was not long in coming: The regular troops invaded the city. The first conflagration was on May 22: "The Ministry of Finance burned down. It had been shelled all day with some of the missiles intended for the terrace of the Tuileries, and the papers stored in its attic caught fire." On the night of May 23 and the morning of May 24, all the large civic buildings in the center of the capital were on fire: the Council of State, the Palace of Justice, the Tuileries, and, finally, the Hôtel de Ville. While the fires were primarily sparked by the incessant pounding by Thiers's cannons, the last two were apparently the work of the federates abandoning their positions, or even the work of *petroleuses.** The flames "told the conqueror of Paris that he would not recover his former place and that these monarchical monuments would no longer be home to monarchy."[63]

Nothing remained of the collections of the Council of State, the Hôtel de Ville, or, most important, the twenty-four thousand richly bound and odd works, the typographical masterpieces that had been collected at the Louvre by a succession of its former occupants, both kings and princesses.

---

*[Female arsonists who were active during the Commune period. —*Trans.*]

What wonders! The most magnificent editions, the most hand-some copies were kept there and they were not entrusted to the hands of just anyone, even for a moment's examination. More than one famous bibliophile had to cool his heels waiting for the curator, who never relinquished the keys that kept these rare treasures locked away. There were books of hours with illuminations and drawings that must have exhausted the talent and patience of artists who devoted an entire lifetime to make a single book ordered by a sovereign.[64]

But the beauty of this library was nothing next to its infinite uniqueness: It was also one of many secrets, often state secrets, for it contained works that had been banned or eliminated. This was the case, to mention but one example, of the complete collection of the *Mercure de France*. The Épernon family had ordered it bought up and destroyed everywhere in order to suppress the story of a public humiliation suffered in the seventeenth century by the duke of that time, the governor of Guyana, who had certainly deserved it and who accepted it nobly—but his heirs took umbrage. The entire collection of the catalogs of the Crown took up sixty volumes, all lost. A decision had been recently taken to move the collection of the Museum's books here, but procrastination had delayed this transfer, thus sparing them.

Nothing thus remains of the three Parisian collections outside of the detailed inventories that were established rapidly—quite rapidly—by Henri Baudrillart, Inspector General of Libraries; Louis Paris, director of the Historical Office, and Patrice Salin, bureau chief of the Council of State. The immensity of the loss was staggering; yet the indignation of its reporters and public opinion were blown out of proportion. The thirty thousand men, women, and children killed in the streets or lined up to be machine-gunned at the Place du Châtelet would not get off so well.

As Salin said: "Distressing display of actions by the populace . . . its coarse appetites . . . its stupid rages . . . its idiotic turf . . . burning the Library of the Louvre, guardian of rarities now lost forever! The Hôtel de Ville, the cradle of our municipal franchises whose archives and library contained historic treasures, unique originals, so useful for the city's history." For Michel Cornudet, these "stupid brutes . . . were only tools; the true authors are elsewhere; they are in journalism, at the bar, in literature, in the Institute perhaps . . . it is they who, with their writing or speeches, perverted the soul of this people, who excited them against God and his ministers, who taught them materialism whose consequence is pleasure at any price . . . it is they whom we must defy and [from whom] protect the children of the people and our own if we wish to avoid the same causes leading to similar effects."[65]

Abbé Lacroix threaded his way from Versailles in search of his bishop, a hostage who had already been shot. While trying to avoid jostling the buckets of the dangerous potassium picrate intended to blow up the city, he searched meanwhile for some soul to save. Just then a firing squad at the Palais Royale was about to execute one of those presumed responsible for the burning of the Council of State. Young and quite pale, the victim yelled: "Finish me off!" Did the abbé really propose to give him his blessing? "I don't want that!" the young man responded before receiving a bullet in the forehead. At the Tuileries, "It was the residence of the kings of France, destroyed by fire . . . the enemy within have kept their sacred oath!" Of the Hôtel de Ville, "We have nothing but an immense blaze . . . what riches, what precious documents annihilated in the space of a few hours and by what hands!" Indeed, said the municipal counselor Gilles, going him one better, "Wretches, driven by the instinct of destruction, destroyed in several hours the rarest and perhaps most irreproachable treasure, the most tangible in the heart of true Parisians," 120,000 missals, including the missal of Juvenal des Ursins, recently bought by the city for a sum of thirty-six thousand francs, and three albums of manuscript plans by Ledoux. Yet the librarian Jules Cousin, named to that post in September 1870, also said that he found "more manure than pearls [there], a jumble of modern books, pure bookstore merchandise, a servitude rather than a service . . . everything remains to be done in this Augean library" that received such little respect, where he led "Homeric battles to have books returned, which the bigwigs requisition as if they were at the market, with never a thought about returning them." This devotee, if ever there was one, "dismissed by the Communards and on vacation for the Nationalists," in July offered the city his own six thousand volumes as compensation, a gift that he would have much trouble having accepted and which would eventually form the embryo of the Historical Library of the city of Paris.[66]

A tourist, Sir William Erskine, came running: "I just saw ruins of the Hôtel de Ville of Paris lovingly caressed by a splendid sunset . . . it was superb. The people of the Commune are frightful rogues, I won't disagree with you on that point, but what artists! And they are not aware of their work; they don't know what they did! It is even more admirable."[67] With the exception of this perfidious testimony intended only to reignite the flame of Franco-British relations, the response was mainly a general outcry.

The avalanche of hatred poured upon the federates still appears astounding. There is nothing disconcerting about what comes from some old beards well established in the cogs of power: The era was the apogee of the bourgeoisie, whose "chief ambition was to move from mahogany to rosewood"[68] and dreaded above all the slightest shudder of the established order.

Yet except for some rare rascals (Rimbaud, Verlaine, Villiers) and Catulle Mendès, who saw everything, no writer allowed himself to be even remotely touched by the poignant and desperate fate of the people of Paris as by Elie Reclus: "Everything is burning! The Versailliards started it, the federates continued it. . . . Burn all that will burn. Precipitated to the bottom of the abyss, plunged into the gulf of disasters, when so many living chests are pierced through, when so many brains that think are crushed, when we are drowning in a sea of blood, what do monuments, statues, books and paintings, papers and tapestry do for us?" To the contrary, we see the entire writing class (for example, Comptesse de Ségur and Elémir Bourges) following the lead of the most puerile reaction or preceding it with disproportionate fury.* Ernest Renan

---

*In his preface to *La Semaine sanglante* [The Bloody Week], Geneva, 1964, the president of the Académie Goncourt, Lucien Descaves, still criticized Maxime Vuillaume for having adopted the obscene language of the people in *Pere Duchêne*. He later pointed out that Vuillaume "founded" a journal *(La Misère),* which eventually folded, to no one's surprise.

sets the tone and explains in erudite fashion: "The immense majority of human minds are impervious to the truths, no matter how lowly they may be." Zola praised family and commerce; to Flaubert, the perturbed small proprietor did not hide his narrow-mindedness and dreamed of a France ruled by "an iron hand"; while George Sand measured her words. The great damage suffered by French letters, the burning of the library—there it is. We thought we had great writers, but they were only pretty phrasemongers in slippers. Devoid of the slightest sensitivity are the Gautiers, Goncourts, and Frances from whom compassion was not hoped but at least an intimation that it was another future knocking on the door of their suburban bungalow. Worse than having no vision, they were totally lacking in chic.

Therefore, Victor Hugo (it is always Victor Hugo) again displayed his uniqueness by staking his reputation and winning. He was in Brussels, where, in *L'Année terrible* [The Terrible Year], he took a position totally opposed to that of the literary genus, which earned him additional troubles and endless insults from his colleagues. ("Until now we thought he was French," said Barbey d'Aubrevilly; "an old lunatic" was Sarcey's judgment.) This anthology contained the famous poem "Whose Fault?" written in a rush and redeemed only by its outcome: "I don't know how to read," retorts the arsonist the poet scolds for destroying the library. Yet only books can lift him from his social rut, hence the title. It so happens that all the writers of this era, with the exception of George Sand, rejected the idea of a mandatory, secular, free public education, which was the great idea of the Paris Commune, daughter of the Convention, without which *Madame Bovary* would have remained a work known only to preppies.

Yet the futility of agonizing over whether there are too many or too few books was already amusing Louis-Sébastien Mercier when he wrote in 1781: "The tireless hands of the grocers, the druggists, the butter merchants, and so forth have destroyed on a daily basis as many books and pamphlets as are being printed. [Without] all these happily destructive hands . . . the mass of printed paper would swell to a most uncomfortable point and in the end drive all the owners and renters from their homes." This striking *Tableau de Paris* subsequently inspired this observation: "My *Book of Songs* will serve the grocer to make paper bags in which he will pour coffee and tobacco for the old ladies of the future." In 1885, in *Lutèce,* this was what Heinrich Heine prognosticated the "victorious proletariat" would bring us. Mercier then concluded with his natural Taoism: "One notes the same proportion between the manufacture of books and their destruction as exists between life and death, a consolation I address to all those whom the multitude of books irks or annoys."

SEVEN

THE NEW BIBLIOCLASTS

———— ❧ ————

You are made of paper and to paper you will return.

WALTER MEHRING, *THE LOST LIBRARY*

The United States maintains that never before 9/11 had it been attacked on its own territory. Yet this is not true: The British attacked the United States in 1812. On August 24, 1814, the invading British army set fire to the U.S. Capitol and to the three thousand books of its young Library of Congress, whose first acquisition of books had taken place not long before in London (740 titles) and had been established in Washington, D.C., in 1800.

At close to the same time, the great Moscow fire of September 15, 1812, was lit, it is said, by ex-convicts at the instigation of the city's governor, who was none other than Rostopchin, father of the future Comptesse de Ségur. Prepared long in advance, this action intended to drive out the Grognards* and left nothing of the large and admirable wooden city. Numerous libraries escaped Napoleon in this rather radical manner, the most valuable being that of Count Dimitri Buturline (1763–1829), often confused for his relative of the same name, who was the czar's aide-de-camp. Count Buturline, much less discouraged than he might have been given that his fortune was intact, then established a second brilliant collection in Florence, from which numerous Italian editions of great value were

---

*[Soldiers of Napoleon's Old Guard. —*Trans.*]

acquired between 1839 and 1841 by the Bodleian Library at Oxford.

The scientific progress made at the end of the nineteenth century was highly beneficial to artillery and aviation. Bombing from a distance or from the air finally allowed for setting fire to enemy cities without the undue risks incurred by setting them alight by hand. The rules of the game had changed and the world's imagination had suddenly grown larger.

BOOKS IN WARS

For many cities that had the (admittedly) fairly common misfortune to find themselves at the same location at several-year intervals, the Franco-Prussian war was a two-strike disaster. This, in any case, was what the people of Strasbourg, Louvain, Arras, and a number of other communities thought.

The France of Napoleon III could rest assured that Strasbourg was ready to confront the Prussian assault of 1870. With its strong and handsome ramparts, the city would "defend itself as long as one soldier, one cracker, one cartridge remain," proclaimed the prefect, Baron Plon, on August 10 as he watched the last train for Paris leave prior to the complete quarantine of the zone. Unfortunately, no one had foreseen the long range of the enemy's artillery, which began serenely demolishing the city from Hausbergen. The bombardment lasted an entire month, and after having been hit by 193,722 shells, the city was forced to surrender. On the night of August 24, St. Bartholomew's day, the pillaging was unchecked. On this night the library, along with its four hundred thousand books, went up in flames. In the smoking rubble was the collection from the Molsheim Charterhouse, which had been seized in 1792 and which consisted of 4,133 volumes and 486 manuscripts, including a large folio with 344 paintings (the Abbess Herrade de Landsberg's *Hortus deliciarum* from the twelfth century). The ashes of hundreds of manuscripts were mixed with those of thousands of incunabula as well as the proceedings of the trial of Gutenberg versus the Heirs of His Former Associate Dritzhen—a piece that sheds a little light upon the convoluted schemes of the father of European printing.

A Franco-German library had been toppled into the past—and it so happened that Strasbourg found itself under bombardment again in 1943–1944. In 1870, it had taken a month of shelling day and night to cause the deaths of 362 inhabitants, but in 1943, aviation made it possible to surpass this result, with 1,239 killed in just three flyovers. The people of Strasbourg would prefer to forget the splendor of this progress: The bombs carried the colors of the Allies.

Once the Germans were gone, the region hastened to burn the German books that had replaced thousands of works in French. The illustrator Tomi Ungerer, then a high school student in Colmar, was one of the rare people to speak of the burning: "Like a déjà vu, everything that was German had to go into a great bonfire; the great library, which had been expanded at the time of the kaiser, was reduced to ashes. Goethe, Schiller, even the plaster busts of the Greek and Roman philosophers went into it."[1]

Its geographical position made Louvain (capital of the Flemish Brabant), located sixteen miles east of Brussels, both a European university center since the fifteenth century and a target for large conflicts. Founded in 1426, the university had welcomed Erasmus, Justus Lipsius, and Mercator. Vesalius learned Arab science there and created modern medicine there by writing his book on anatomy. Like Erasmus, Jansenius taught there for twenty-eight years, and his *Augustinius,* which caused a big commotion, was printed there.

It was not until 1636, however, that the true development of the library got under way. The archbishop of Malines, Jacques Boonen, gave it an annual endowment and named the first librarian. In 1793, it was installed in new premises adjacent to the cloth market. In addition to prestigious gifts it received, its collections were enriched by the benefit of the legal deposit that was extended to it in 1759. The Directory closed the university in 1795, and with no great haste the National Library of Paris appropriated five thousand of its best volumes. It suffered from thefts in 1798 and public sales in 1807, which, however, did not prevent the establishment from reopening in 1826, with reorganized and expanded library collections. This enabled the library of what was now the Catholic University to grow quickly from sixty thousand items to 250,000 in 1835. Yet three hundred thousand volumes from this establishment were destroyed in several hours on August 14, 1914.

Louvain had already surrendered and the German army, commanded by General von Boehn, was traversing it at night, on its way to "better" things farther ahead. A rifle shot came from a window. Perhaps it was a German reservist who had discharged his gun by accident and not a sniper (this is still a subject of contention), but the laws of war were firm: Any house from which a gun has been fired after surrender will be razed and its inhabitants put to the sword. Irritation, then general panic, ensued: Fifteen hundred homes were burned down, two hundred men were executed, and the rest of the populace was carried off in captivity. Nothing was left of the city but a pile of ashes. To set an example, the soldiers began their destruction with the Halle, which contained a thousand incunabula and hundreds of manuscripts. Vesalius's original copy of the *Fabrica,* on the structure of the human body, met its end in this pile of wall sections mixed in, according to a witness, with "an enormous mound of burned paper . . . including the foundational charter from 1426 . . . [A]ll we pulled from the still-warm ashes were the copper clasps of old folios." Such an action "expressed the rage of the German before the reistance of a pure idea," dared Henri Bergson. Meanwhile, Wilhelm II, described in a postcard as a "modern Nero," sent this laconic telegram to Woodrow Wilson: "Louvain has been justly chastised."

This did not prove to be a permanent setback, however. The library emerged from nothing in 1928 thanks to an innovation called international aid. England contributed to the serious German effort (which, in accordance with the terms of the Treaty of Versailles, provided 350,000 to 400,000 volumes) and to the efforts of Japan, whose emperor, Hirohito, offered a valuable Japanese collection, including an eleventh-century manuscript and incunabula that dated much earlier than Gutenberg's. Special thanks are owed for the assistance of the United States, which provided a substantial number of books and the reconstruction of the building itself. *"Furore teutonico diruta, dono americano restituta"* was what Yankee architect Whitney Warren had carved on the balustrade of the facade: "What German madness destroyed, an American gift restored."

Did the old cardinal Mercier feebly accept this outrageous motto? This provoked a fine scandal, and high and low sentiments were mixed, though it is, in fact, hard to envision any future and essential university collaboration with Germany for an institution that posted such a cutting epigraph on its facade. Yet who raised the loudest clamor against this perfectly acceptable sentiment that precluded any future collaboration with similar German institutions? Unfortunately, it was Léon Degrelle, already a monarchist and a future eager collaborator with the Nazis. The apologist for Catholic Action was also hopeless in Latin: He castigated a solecism in the inscription (according to him, the ablative *teutonica* was necessary, but *furor* is masculine) and from this argued that the epigraph had not been submitted to the cardinal; otherwise, the religious leader would have corrected it. During this time the balustrade, which had not yet been installed, was broken by some nighttime foes, then was remade and put in place without the Latin expression, which was far too inane.

Thus completed and installed, the great library of Louvain was the symbol of Western fraternity and finally held about a million books— which were totally destroyed by German artillery during the night of May 16, 1940. It seems the tower of the Halle, which rises above the library and bears a strong resemblance to the steeple of the Giralda in Seville, allowed the gunners to adjust their sights. By 5:30 A.M., no books remained intact. This time, the Wehrmacht declined any responsibility with an alarming display of bad faith and found, after an investigation, that the British were guilty, just as they no doubt were in 1914. Belgium was in fact neutral during World War II, but was placed in the worst spot in the world for neutrality. Indeed, its other book collections suffered terrible disasters, even if what had recently taken place in Poland clearly heralded the misfortune to come and permitted some precautionary measures to be taken. Only the Royal Library remained almost completely intact—but not those of St. Trond, Gand, and Tournai (71,456 hundred-year-old volumes were lost out of a total of seventy-five thousand).

Arras: The Benedictines of St. Vaast had here arranged their book collection, which was combined with those of the other abbeys in the surrounding area, such as those of the Augustines of Mount St. Eloi, along with that of the academy of Arras. Nevertheless, in July 1915, bombs destroyed the fifty thousand printed books still in the area, though the majority of manuscripts had been moved elsewhere over time. Hardly had the archive been rebuilt and its collection put back together, however, when it was again damaged, in 1940.

The list of the libraries destroyed by bombing between 1940 and 1944 is impressive, but it is also dreadfully repetitious: the municipal library of Tours (two hundred thousand books destroyed), the library in Beauvais (forty-two thousand), the library in Douai (110,000 volumes), that of Chartres (twenty-three thousand), and so forth. In Chartres alone there was housed a treasure of two thousand manuscripts, including the *Heptateuchon,* or book of teaching the seven liberal arts (in which Thierry de Chartres, 1100–1150, was the first to introduce the little science available from the Arab world to the Roman world). This library was supposedly in safe storage, but the occupying forces, seeking to make a good impression, ordered the manuscripts' return to their home in the city hall. It was there that an errant bomb, perhaps an English explosive, destroyed the archive on May 26, 1944. Because some pages were only carbonized by the heat, however, the same methods that have proved so beneficial at Herculaneum are now being applied to these works to allow the never published texts to reappear.[2]

In France alone, nineteen municipal libraries and two university libraries lost two million volumes.[3] In the deserted library of Laon of the "collapsed doorway," Captain Ernst Jünger made a casual and peaceful erudite promenade on June 12, 1940, in the midst of abandoned manuscripts and autographs:

> I rifled through this tranquil spot like a bee in dry clover until night began to fall. . . . [S]uch treasures are priceless; they are abandoned only when one is utterly defeated. I will add this: While I was hold-

ing these sheets in my hands, I hardly thought about how they were worth millions, and that without a doubt I perhaps represented the only soul in this city who understood their true value. In fairly ambiguous fashion, the poet of steel confesses he envisoned finding a safe place for "the documents and Elzevirs,"* then revised himself: "So I left them under neither lock nor key, where they were."

Italy had the rare privilege of being on the receiving end of both German and Allied bombs, which combined their efforts to achieve identical results: More than two million printed books and thirty-nine thousand manuscripts were decimated. For example, in 1944, the Colombaria in Florence, the library of the Academy of Letters and Sciences, was utterly destroyed.

This mountain of ashes is small, however, when compared to that of Great Britain, which suffered twenty million books burned during the Blitz or destroyed by firefighters' water. More than one fourth of these were destroyed in December 1940 in the booksellers quarter of Paternoster Row, whose shops even the famous London fire of 1666 failed to evict. In Coventry there was recorded a loss of 150,000 volumes, works whose quality was so impressive to the public imagination that the name of this beautiful city near Stratford-on-Avon gave birth to a terrible, albeit ephemeral, neologism: coventrated. The library there had indeed been coventrated. Adolf Hitler was convinced that this carpet-bombing would pound the British into submission, but showed how little he knew the English. For example, even when the Blitz was at its heaviest, the libraries never interrupted their loaning practices. As recounted by a London librarian, an old woman came by who was distraught because she could not find the book she had recently borrowed. "I must have swept it out with the wreckage of my ceiling," she said.

It was not long, however, before Hitler's somewhat muddled idea was borrowed to his own great disdvantage. Seeing no other solution

---

*[The Elzevirs were a family of important Dutch printers who worked from 1583 to 1712. —*Trans.*]

but to advocate heavy and "extremely devastating, exterminating" bombardment, Churchill saw his wishes fulfilled by the February 1942 decision to destroy "the morale of the enemy civilian population and, in particular, that of industrial workers." The glow cast by burning Dresden could be seen more than forty miles away; the effect of ten thousand tons of incendiary bombs dropped on Hamburg at 1:00 A.M. on July 27, 1943, caused the temperature at sixty-five hundred feet to rise so high that the Royal Air Force had to abort its bombing campaign after twenty minutes. Even then, the British were the beneficiaries of the assistance of American aviation, whose notable contribution was that this was the first raid to have been baptized with a code name: Operation Gomorrah.[4] In the streets the temperature exceeded 1,832 degrees Fahrenheit.

Ten million books from German public collections were burned simply from the bombings; thus, taking into account the likely private losses, one fourth to one third of all the country's books were lost. Among the 131 cities bombed, thirty were targeted particularly heavily and were hit several times, to the extent that all or part of the various libraries was lost in twenty-seven cities, such as Dresden, Leipzig, Darmstadt, Berlin, Frankfurt, Hamburg, Munich, Münster, Stuttgart, and Cassel. UNESCO's list of twenty-four cities is incomplete: Breslau, Göttingen, and Jena, cited by Johnson, should be added to it, as should Baden, where the Badische Landesbibliothek lost its 350,000 books on September 3, 1944, because the bureaucracy had not authorized their transfer to a safe location, as is reported by Hilda Stubbings in an essay dedicated to the library under bombardment. But is this work even talking about the same country? Baden is the sole German destruction noted in this study (with the exception of the 1933 auto-da-fé in Berlin), and the essay's main emphasis falls on the largely effective pains taken by the personnel of German libraries to protect their collections.

Even the deepest cellars could do nothing for books when incendiary bombs struck. In Dresden, the Anglo-American bombings of February 13–15, 1945, destroyed the entire downtown area, 70 percent of its industrial potential, and caused the death of thirty-five thousand people. How could its three important libraries have been saved—the Sächsische Landesbibliothek of the province of Saxony, the municipal Stadtbibliothek, and that of the Verein für Erdkunde, the Geographical Society? In the smoke of the burning pages glided the ghosts of thousands of incunabula, including one of the first illustrated books, printed in Paris by Jehan Bonhomme, Jacques Millet's *The Destruction of Troy* from 1448. Also a victim was the sole surviving example of the 1533 edition of *Pantagruel,* from the publisher François Juste.

In addition to the amputations suffered by its municipal and university libraries, in an air raid in December 1943, the city of Leipzig lost the sixty thousand works collected at the Museum of the Book. There is no doubt that the genesis of each of these murdered institutions deserves at least a paragraph, but the automatic nature of their accumulation in such a short span of years winds up causing doubt as to the value of the task. What is the use of reading or educating ourselves when the world looks as though it is ending, which was the case for a moment during the course of World War II? This is how Claude Simon expressed it in *The Flanders Road:*

> I answered in return that if the contents of the thousands of books in that irreplaceable library had been powerless to prevent things like the bombing that destroyed them from happening, I couldn't really see what loss to humanity was represented by the loss under a hail of bombs of those thousands of books and papers, obviously devoid of the slightest use. This was followed by a detailed list of things of definite value, the objects of prime importance that we have a much greater need of here than the entire contents of that famous library of Leipzig, namely shoes, underwear, wool clothing, soap, cigarettes, sausage, sugar, canned goods . . .

Dällenbach replied in the postface of the book that "if books are revealed to be so ridiculous when confronted by the chaotic force of elemental reality, then what is the use of narrating and writing . . . *The*

Flanders Road?" Despondency is also the tone taken by Walter Mehring during the Anschluss, "surrounded by howling demons frothing at the mouth in every street," when he fled Vienna, leaving behind his library. "I ran away so I would not be transformed into a pillar of salt, leaving behind that protective wall my father had built for me from thousands of books. Each of these books held an anathema cast by that white magic that allowed my father, the enlightened man and atheist who believed in progress, to feel he was defended from a return to the rule of demons and darkness."[5] But for his part, Ernst Jünger remains unshakable: "Kirchhorst, April 9, 1944. Contemplating the enormous mass of books destroyed by the bombardments. Ancient books will become even rarer . . . this even offers its advantages—like that of bringing the mind back to what is essential. . . . In a general manner, the collective speed of life will bring about a vast development of public libraries."[6]

This spilling of a million and a half tons of fire and iron over German cities by the Allied forces has become a taboo topic for the two generations that followed the time of World War II. That this would be the case in France or among British intellectuals is easy to understand, but it was also the case in Germany, as, shortly before his accidental death, Winifred Georg Sebald recently underscored with an essay that caused a stir in Germany: *Luftkrieg und Literatur.* This return to a problematical amnesia has apparently triggered the opening of a floodgate, for better or for worse—as can be seen in Jörg Friedrich's *Der Brand.*

Meanwhile, during this same time in Japan, the war in the Pacific (the official name the Pacific War takes on all its irony in English) reduced to dust an incalculable number of libraries and books that burned like oakum if they were from before 1800. In Tokyo, the planes of the free world made four thousand raids in a year and a half: Eight libraries were razed, buildings and all; three quarters of the libraries suffered damage; and the largest library of all, the Hibiya Public Library, located between the palace and the Imperial Hotel, suffered the greatest hurt.

Created under the Meiji dynasty, this institution had initially benefited from the movement of its collection—first by trucks, then by carts, and finally by knapsacks—but these efforts were not enough; the last two hundred thousand titles disappeared in the space of a few hours. Also lost were forty thousand volumes at Waseda University; sixty-nine thousand at the Ministry of Foreign Affairs; 15,528 at the Patent Office; 46,695 at the Cabinet Library; and all the books at the Ministry of Agriculture and the Sea. When the American army landed in Japan in 1945, only five thousand books remained in the entire country.[7] Interestingly, when they collaborated on the rebuilding of the libraries and educational system, the occupying forces were alarmed by the complication of Japanese writing and advocated its transliteration, though this idea was eventually sent packing.

NAZISM AND HOLOCAUST

Whereas the catastrophes mentioned above can be considered as collateral damage of "an elemental nature"—an ungovernable deluge of bombs and shells falling from anonymous skies like presents from Santa Claus—the devastation organized by the Nazis obviously offers a completely different scope of unsparing significance.

It seems that the quantity of the Nazi destruction was on a par with that of the opposing camp, if we accept the figure of one hundred thousand volumes lost in the Soviet Union, as put forth by a 1958 study,[8] but we shall have to revisit this point. As for the quality of the devastation, it had its direct source in the 1925 wild imaginings of Hitler and in the decisions of 1933, the year that witnessed the formulation of a war against "intellectual nihilism" through the burning of books on which a new humanity was allegedly able to build itself. This did have a precedent:[9] In 1817 in Iena, pan-Germanic students organized a large book-burning event at Wartburg Castle. The significant difference, however, is that the books at Wartburg were fake, cobbled together with notebooks of old paper on which were written by hand the titles of works the students found contemptible.

Hitler was named chancellor on January 30, 1933. As of February 2, all publications containing "inaccurate information" were banned.

Nothing could be simpler, except to cross out the "inaccuracies" as well. Librarians immediately began making preparations for the bonfire of May 10 while the League of Combat for German Culture sent instructions to student associations for the purpose of ridding the land of "Judeo-Asiatic poison." In the confidences he made to Hermann Rauschning, the Führer stated: "We are barbarians and that is what we want to be. It is an honorable word." But this was a red herring: Numerous libraries throughout Europe were carefully relocated (352,000 books discriminately chosen from the Jewish and Slavic communities of Paris alone), in complete contradiction to the imbecilic propaganda fulminated by the Third Reich's theatrical autos-da-fé.

So, on May 10, 1933, at 10:00 P.M., on Berlin's Opera Square, "a delegation of students paraded by, preceded by music played by a Storm Trooper band . . . students wearing their official guild dress, all carrying torches. The firemen watered the pyre with gasoline and set it alight. Trucks arrived carrying the books, and the students formed human chains to cast them into the flames."[10] As reported in the *Illustration*: "With each new packet of books cast into the flames, a voice declared the name of the implicated author and pronounced the sentence of execution:

First thesis: Against materialism and class struggle, for a unified people and an ideal concept of life, I commit to the flames the works of Marx and Kautsky.

Second thesis: Against moral decay and for morality and discipline and family and state spirit, I commit to the flames the works of Heinrich Mann, Ernst Glaser, and Erich Kästner.

Third thesis: Against petty sentiment and the political betrayal of the people and the state, I commit to the flames the works of Friedrich Wilhelm Förster.

Fourth thesis: Against spiritual corruption and the exaggeration and unhealthy complication of sexuality and for the nobility of the human soul, I commit to the flames the works of Sigmund Freud.

Fifth thesis: Against the falsification of our history and the denigration of its great historical figures and for respect for our past, I commit to the flames the works of Emil Ludwig and Werner Hegemann.

Sixth thesis: Against foreign journalists and their Judeo-democratic tendencies and for working consciously and responsibly on the task of national reconstruction, I commit to the flames the works of Theodor Wolff and Georg Bernhard.

Seventh thesis: Against the literary betrayal of the soldiers of the Great War and for the education of the people by healthy principles, I commit to the flames the works of Erich Maria Remarque.

Eighth thesis: Against the mutilation of the German language and for the cultivation of this most precious legacy of our people, I commit to the flames the works of Alfred Kerr.

Ninth thesis: Against arrogance and presumptuousness and for respect and veneration of the immortality of the German spirit, I commit to the flames the works of Tucholsky and Ossietzky."

Among the twenty to twenty-five thousand copies of books burned that evening, cast into the flames were the books of several other authors, such as those of Stefan Zweig. According to the *Illustration,* this display of pathos entitled Feuersprüche, Adages of the Fire, was the personal work of Goebbels, who arrived at midnight and, to the roar of hurrahs, announced that "the time had passed when the filth and impurities of the Jewish Asphaltlitteratur [sidewalk literature] would fill the libraries and where science, cut off behind doctrines, was isolated from life!"

It is interesting that though the *Illustration* devoted an entire page with photos to the May 10 event, pointing out that similar activities took place simultaneously in several large cities and that "henceforth, the freedom to think no longer exists in Germany," it also printed in its July 1 issue a second page, entitled "What Books Were Burned in Berlin?" Despite a few minor errors, in this much more in-depth article, the author compares the burning to the burnings of the Spanish Inquisition and Savonarola; analyzes with an insight that is rare for a simple reporter the books that were involved; and ends by citing, for the first time, the phrase taken from a "subsidized" theatrical play by Hans Johst that was destined to become famous, albeit distorted: "When I hear the word *culture,* I pull out my Browning."

A small mystery hovers over this: In this rather magnificently produced magazine, which is neither particularly leftist nor basically intellectual, this semblance of a warning cry is signed by Irene Chevreuse, whose name—or rather pseudonym—never again appears. Look at the journal *L'Intansigeant,* for example, which was feebly satisfied with a caricature of Hitler in a toga with a lyre and the caption "Nero . . . in paper." With the notable exception of Romain Rolland and Barbusse, few French intellectuals were flustered by the Nazi movement, which loudly announced its true spirit and, worse, threatened their rights as authors. Already, fascination was exerting its well-known power. Even an obscure baron, Robert Fabre-Luce, immediately applauded this display of freshness: "Book burnings, which have been depicted in rather ridiculous fashion as a sin against the mind, are to the contrary, in my opinion, the symbol of a spiritual renaissance for all those who are healthy, noble, and honest."[11] Meanwhile, Sigmund Freud snorted and said: "Only our books? Once they would have burned us with them."

Joseph Roth exhibited a more bitter tone: "We who are German writers of Jewish blood, in these days when the smoke from our burning books is rising toward heaven, should recognize above all that we are defeated. . . . We were in the front rows of those defending Europe, and we were bludgeoned first." This was a terrible line of thought, as if suspended in the void: In six years, Joseph Roth was dead and would never experience the most horrific development of what he had intuited.

Thirty similar "acts of faith" followed in succession between May 10 and June 21, prompting the strange appearance of three Libraries of Burned Books, specializing in the works of Voltaire, Einstein, Freud, Marx, Engels, Remarque, and so on, as well as the first studies of Hitlerism and the German opposition papers. These libraries first grew in London in March 1934, under the aegis of Countess Oxford and Asquith; next, they grew in Paris, in the delightful hamlet of artist studios called the City of Flowers on 65 boulevard Arago.

The inauguration of the Deutsche Freiheitsbibliothek (German Free-dom Library) took place on the anniversary of the auto-da-fé, under the leadership of Heinrich Mann, André Gide, Romain Rolland, H. G. Wells, and Lion Feuchtwanger. The brilliant Red propagandist Willi Münzenberg and the writer Alfred Kantorowicz were among its driv-ing forces; the first ended up a millionaire in Moscow and the other dashed off to fight in Spain. The absurdity of history contrived matters such that once France declared war, the "decree of November 18, 1939, concerning measures with regard to individuals posing a danger to the national defense" immediately brought about the library's closing by the French police and the seizure of its collection of twenty thousand works, of which fourteen hundred discreetly found their way to the National Library less than two months later (the rest are still being looked for). This "donation by the prefecture of police" bears the order number 335052 in the catalog of printed-work acquisitions. Other unidentified collections seem to have been combined with it, and the overall selection was grouped under the Bolshevik label "communards, revolutionaries, Marxists, and French communists."

The third Freiheitsbibliothek was located in New York, at the Brook-lyn Jewish Center. Five hundred people were in attendance to hear Ein-stein's speech the day it opened in December 1934, although the major-ity of the American press was operating in "postive thinking" mode: They thought that once in power, the Nazis would start behaving like adults. Furthermore, ten years later, a commission[12] charged with study-ing the situation of destroyed European libraries and how the United States might play a role in the reconstruction of the educational system ("A New Problem for the Civilized World") deemed that the Germans had acted in a spirit of "reprisals and punishment." It is as if the world was deemed a large day-care center.

Actually, only once were books targeted in a pure act of reprisal: Toward the end of the war, in Naples, a German soldier was shot by an Italian resistant in the street running adjacent to the Library of the Royal Society. The following Sunday, September 19, 1943, several truckloads of Brandkommando arrived carrying cans of gasoline. They entered the library, calmly sprinkled the reading rooms and all the shelves from floor to ceiling, and tossed grenades into each room as they retreated from the building. They then prevented the firemen from approaching the burning structure. Three days later, two hundred thousand treasures of the country's ancient history had been transformed into smoke and ash.

Hardly had the fires of 1933 been extinguished when, with great hubbub, Goebbels inaugurated "the Book, weapon of the German mind!" The stranglehold on the Third Reich's public libraries was all the greater because a large number of their noteworthy directors wanted to remain at their posts in order to extend their work or avoid interruption of their scholarly research.[13] The most inane kind of propaganda literature was thus established on solid and consenting ground, where it attempted to fill the void left by the systematic purging of all the authors designated for the fire. In 1983, Leo Löwenthal ironically noted the idea of seeing "the Nazi phoenix rising out of Jewish and communist ashes."[14]

What was exacted in the libraries of the occupied territories was immediate and even more brutal, without any festive character. In January 1934, Alfred Rosenberg was put in charge of the supervision of publications, propaganda, and (soon) pillaging—one naturally leading to the other. Despite the rivalry of Goebbels and Goering, who sought only to enrich his personal collections, Rosenberg displayed a flawless efficiency. The Einsatzstab Rosenberg,[15] created in 1939, was given the authority to inspect all libraries and other cultural establishments and to confiscate anything that hindered the furtherance of the Nazi Party's goals. In contrast to Goering, Rosenberg felt that works of art were secondary, and he ordered that "all archives and all scientific property belonging to our ideological opponents be placed at my disposal."[16] But these fine words concealed some very sordid operations and disorganized gestures. It is not always easy to distinguish censorship from lucre and brutality.

There was also a fourth motive for the destruction of books (along with ideological advancement, personal enrichment, and punishment): a genocide of the genius of a people that corresponds to genocide of the flesh. The Hitlerians applied the first and not the second where they required manual labor without name or memory, but with the

Jews they resorted to the second, which gives food for thought.

After a decree in Czechoslovakia in 1939, all students were ordered to find a definite manual occupation within forty-eight hours. A decree in autumn 1942 enjoined the university libraries to turn over to the German army any ancient works and original editions in their possession. The Nazis specifically sought the works of Czech writers, contemporary or otherwise, such as those of fifteenth-century reformer Jan Hus, Aloïs Erassek, and the poet Victor Dieck. Not only were the works of Czech and Jewish authors pulled from the shelves, but also pulled were the translations of all English, French, and Russian authors, which left quite empty the 411 affected collections. The minister of state and Reichskommissar of the protectorate, K. H. Frank, declared at the onset: "The Czechs"—like the Poles—"are good only to serve as workers or farmhands."

In Poland, on December 13, 1939, the Gauleiter of the Warthgau published the order with which all public and private libraries had to comply. As soon as the decree was in force, all collections were seized and submitted to the Buchsammelstelle, where experts skimmed the best from a stock of two million books, with an eye to sending them to either Berlin or Posen (the German name for Poznan), where it had been recently decided to establish a non-Polish "state library." The remainder became used paper to be recycled—and this was what happened in 102 libraries from Krakow to Warsaw, as well as to the thirty-eight thousand handsome volumes from the Polish parliament. Meanwhile, the archives from the diocese of Pelilin, which had a wealth of twelfth-century manuscripts, saw their precious works used to heat the furnaces of a sugar refinery.

The case of Poland is comparatively the most serious of all the plundered countries:[17] More than sixteen million volumes, 70 to 80 percent of the country's total, vanished from the public libraries, and the rest were gathered into a single archive, where they lost their identity. Half of the country's printers shut their doors. For five years not a single publication was authorized (but twelve hundred titles nevertheless appeared clandestinely), which, as explained with awkward candor by the *Verordnungsblatt* of November 5, 1940, was to "satisfy the primitive needs of distraction and amusement, for the purpose of diverting the attention of intellectual circles as much as possible from conspiracy and political debates, which could encourage the development of anti-German sentiment."

The end of this aberrant situation was even worse: The Warsaw Uprising bought about the action of the Brandkommando, fire-bearing soldiers whose special mission consisted of burning down libraries. In October 1944, the Krasinski, with its fifteenth- to eighteenth-century books collected in its five cellar levels after they were extracted from their original institutions, disappeared at the hands of the Brandkommando, as did the Rapperswil Collection, a considerable assortment on the country's history that émigrés laboriously accumulated in Switzerland until the blessed day of Poland's independence in 1918, which permitted its installation in Poland. In January 1945, the incendiary squads similarly destroyed the Bibliotheka Publiczna and its three hundred thousand volumes. Meanwhile, the librarians of the Narodova, the National Library, had laboriously moved 170,000 books to a safe site on the orders of and under the guidance of German officers, who set fire to the building when they left.

In Slovenia, all the libraries were purged, and use of the Slovene language was considered an act of sabotage. In Belgrade, the National Library was razed and its hundreds of thousands of printed books and Serbian manuscripts were reduced to ashes. In Greece, Athens lost the greater part of the books of its university, while the volumes of three American colleges were used to heat these institutions.

The damage was the lightest in the Netherlands: There the occupier was satisfied to pick out the undesirable reading material and lock it away in a "hall of poison," an unintended homage to Chateaubriand.

This orchestrated Germanization bears a striking resemblance to the crudest forms of vandalism, as can be seen, for example, in Yasnaja Polyana, the museum property in Russia where Leo Tolstoy was born and lived. The soldiers who occupied it for six weeks apparently had nothing to do but to destroy all the books and manuscripts there—and even the remains of the author of *Anna Karenina,* which they had dug out of the ground. The same desacralization was inflicted on the houses of Pushkin and Chekhov, not to mention those of Russian musicians. When an employee of the Tolstoy Museum suggested finding logs for the fireplace in order to spare some books, an officer named Schwartz answered: "We don't need a wood fire; we are going to burn anything connected with the name of your Tolstoy." Nevertheless, it seems that the Germans had too much respect for Russian books to get rid of them immediately; they frequently sent them to their leaders if they seemed to have obvious commercial value, as Obersturmführer Dr. Forster testified:

> At Zarskoje Selo [in] Emperor Alexander's palace . . . a large library containing six thousand to seven thousand volumes in French and more than five thousand books and manuscripts in Russian were removed. . . . We reaped a rich harvest in the library of the Ukrainian Academy of Science, treasuring rare manuscripts of Persian, Abyssinian, and Chinese literature; Russian and Ukrainian chronicles; the first-edition books printed by the first Russian printer, Ivan Fjodorov. . . . In Kharkov, several thousand valuable books in deluxe editions were seized from the Korolenko Library and sent to Berlin. The remaining books were destroyed.[18]

Soldiers paved the muddy main street with several layers of encyclopedias to facilitate the passing of military vehicles. This is a classic stereotype that can be likened to the actions of the Mongols in Baghdad in 1258 and the Austrian carts of 1785.

The 646,000 volumes burned in Smolensk or in the other Russian republics seem small when compared to the four million books burned in Kiev. Faced with the German advance, Stalin decided to practice a scorched-earth policy in the Ukraine: Anything that could not be taken out was to be destroyed. The rapid pace of the Wehrmacht prevented this considerable task from being completed. Two years later, Hitler gave the exact same order: For example, the German army took Rembrandt's self-portrait but not the 19,200 libraries of the country. This time the order was executed with impeccable efficiency. (They destroyed everything they could not take with them.) Nevertheless, on April 28, 1995, Germany returned some seven hundred valuable volumes. If this seems too few, we can remember that by the end of the 1940s there may not have been many more than this left. Among the damage caused by Allied bombs we should not forget to count the destruction of the plundered books that had been brought to Berlin. To a certain extent, nothing is ever lost.

The Nazi plan for books was a machine from which nothing could escape. Considerable Parisian libraries were spirited away in no time at all. In 1875, the Russians of Paris had formed a fairly consequential library. In fact, Turgenev had given it so much assistance that upon his death it adopted his name. Having accumulated a wealth of some one hundred thousand volumes, the city of Paris provided it with a home in a private mansion in 1938, on 11 rue de la Bûcherie. Two years later, the German Occupation army came up with an offer to purchase these books—which, of course, was turned down. Consequently, they stole all of them. At the end of the war, the greatest portion was found in Poland, where the Red Army took possession of them.

As for the rich library that the Polish had established in Paris in 1838, it found a pretty home fifteen years later in a seventeenth-century mansion on the quai d'Orleans. Almost immediately on taking Paris, the Gestapo invested the premises and, in June 1940, sent to Poznan cases of books, archives, and maps that had been collected over the years. Partial restitution (nearly forty-five thousand volumes) was agreed to during the 1950s, and at the same time a quantity of books that made the round-trip from Warsaw to Moscow were left in Poland with the consent of the library on the quai d'Orleans in order to restock the devastated shelves of Poland.

Finally, the Ukrainian collection excited the lust of the Third Reich. Hitler already had his plans for Russia. Symon Petliura, former president of the Directory of the Ukrainian government in exile, had been assassinated in Paris in 1926 by a Jewish anarchist, no doubt to avenge the deaths caused by Ukrainian pogroms, but perhaps also as a result of a dark Franco-Soviet plot. The Ukrainian immigrants then founded a library around the archives of the vanished state, which rapidly grew to twenty thousand books. This world center of the Ukraine outside its borders was visited in December 1941 by the Gestapo and was put *mis deutschem Schutz* (under German protection). Its contents were then carried back over the Rhine during the following month.

Nevertheless, the people of the Einsatzstab Reischsleiter Rosenberg für die besetzten Gebiete (ERR) found it of no practical interest, and, scattered and forgotten, it was seemingly abandoned to its fate and partially stored in Ratibor. From time to time, however, a researcher came across one of its books in the large archives of Kiev, Minsk, or Moscow, and today the Ukrainian Symon Petliura Library still operates on the rue de Palestine and boasts fifty-seven volumes.[19]

Parallel to these three important collections were hundreds of private Russian libraries that were taken away (Souvarine, Bukanov, Ossorgin, and so forth), and their fate is unknown—as is that of the seventy-one cases of books from the Czech library in Paris and the 144 cases from the International Institute of Social History on the rue Michelet in Paris.

Because the National Library of France sent the major part of its most valuable collections to Bordelais castles, Paris could sleep tranquilly. The German service for the protection of libraries, the Bibliotheksschutz, found very bourgeois accommodations in the Louvois mansion, which faced the National Library, and from there it exercised its mission of censorship and misappropriation—not only on the rue de Richelieu,* but also in all public and private collections. The lists of prohibited books (first, the Bernhard List of 143 titles and seven hundred thousand copies confiscated; then the Otto Lists 1, 2, and 3, which were established with the undoubtedly forced help of the Hachette and Filipacchi publishing houses and which designated about three thousand titles), were promulgated and imposed on everyone, even the used-book sellers on the quais. Interestingly, we can note in passing that any translation of *Mein Kampf* was on the banned-book lists, no doubt for encouraging readers to learn German. With the exception of the famous writers who

---

*[Site of the Bibliothèque Nationale of France, although part of the collection is now housed at its new building on the rue de Tolbiac. —*Trans.*]

lost their reputations, the France of books emerged from the war fairly unscathed. This is a fate that we can compare to the much more momentous one assigned to Jewish libraries, as we shall see.

If he had been born one hundred years later, Heinrich Heine might instead have written the opposite, just to keep his words from becoming cliche: "There where they burn men, they will eventually burn books." Given the fact that he was also a Jew, a debauched individual, and a pal of the young Karl Marx, he would not have been allowed to express himself for very long: Nazi-era anthologies that were obliged to publish his very popular lieder supplied them with the attribution "author unknown."

At this point, the parallel between holocaust and auto-da-fé diverged in a very odd fashion. In the beginning, one perverse effect of a creeping racism is that the people feeling threatened burn their libraries ahead of time. The Jews discovered, however, what a slow and difficult process this is—even in a stove. Some then threw their books over bridges, lost them in the woods, or mailed them in packages to invented addresses.[20] Even before the pogroms, the Jews, even more than the communists, cosmopolitans, and freethinkers, knew that their reading material betrayed them. A book in Hebrew is relatively easy to recognize, even for a policeman. (When in doubt, however, the police sometimes also seized copies of Homer.) The book-loving frenzy of the Third Reich inspired sarcasm among the erudite: As Chaïm Aron Kaplan wrote in his journal in 1939, "The Nazis have stolen not only our material possessions, but also our reputation as the People of the Book!"[21]

Before 1939, Poland was home to 251 Jewish libraries, which gathered some 1,650,000 volumes—in other words, more than half of the Judaica and Hebraica in Europe. Next to specific large institutions such as the grand synagogue of Warsaw and the two archives of Vilnius, the Strashun (from the name of its founder) and the Yiddisher, significant numbers of manuscripts and books printed in Hebrew were collected at the Publiczna or at the National, in particular in the Rapperswil Collection. Fire apparently made no distinction when it carried off these libraries, as we have seen. The Brandkommando knew full well what they were doing when they burned down the synagogues and books of Bedzin and Poznan, as they did in Lublin:

> For us it was a matter of particular pride destroying the Talmudic library . . . we had thrown the gigantic library out of the building and had it transported to the market square to set it on fire, which lasted twenty hours. The Jews of Lublin were gathered all around and weeping bitterly, to the point of almost deafening us with their cries. We had the military band come over, and with their shouts of joy the soldiers drowned out the sobs of the Jews.[22]

Elsewhere, soldiers waited for a rabbi to attempt to defend his imperishable Torah so that they could push him on top of it into the fire. In the Strashun, in Vilnius, the curator and grandson of the founder opted to commit suicide rather than collaborate on the inventory of the collection before it was seized. Two scholars had to be released temporarily from prison to do the work in his stead. The parameters of inventory were fairly simple, but nonetheless required a semblance of expertise: All the books in Hebrew published after 1800 could be sent to the pulp mill, except those dealing with the history and nature of Judaism.

Too much efficiency, however, brought about saturation. There were too many Torahs in Frankfurt; scrolls of them were piled nine feet thick in the cellar of the institute there. It was suggested that their parchment be used for binding, but these instructions did not inspire bibliophilia: One day, five cases of rare books were destroyed to make room on a train for pigs bought on the black market.

While the Italian fascists instituted a noteworthy auto-da-fé in 1938 in Turin's Piazza Carlina, anti-Semitism was not really their strong suit. It was after their fall, which occurred on October 16, 1943, that 1,041 individuals from the ghetto of Rome were gathered to be *liquidiert* in Auschwitz (this is the only time this instruction appeared in writing), while the pope closed his eyes, perhaps to pray.

Two days earlier, the ERR had finished its business with the libraries of the synagogue in Rome,[23] including that of the rabbinical college and especially that of the community, whose reputations inspired the wildest fantasies because these institutions were not cataloged. In fact, their successive guardians had barely established lists of acquisitions. But thanks to an examination made in 1934 by Isaia Sonne, it is certain that the collection went back to the first years of Christianity and the Caesars; had been considerably expanded during the Middle Ages and after the expulsions of the Jews from Spain and Sicily; and amply represented the golden age of Roman and Venetian printing of the sixteenth century, including an eighteen-volume Talmud of Daniel Bomberg. It was, in short, a dream library. The men of the ERR spent a month there, in a fever, it seems. In fact, a lieutenant

[w]ith hands as cautious and sensitive as the finest needlewoman, skims, touches, caresses papyri and incunabula, leafs through manuscripts and rare editions, peruses parchments and palimpsests. The varying degrees of caution in his touch, the heedfulness of his gestures, are quickly adapted to the importance of each work. For the most part, those texts were written in exotic languages, but when the officer opens to a page, as happens to certain particularly gifted readers who can instantly find desired and meaningful passages, his gaze is riveted, his eyes become bright. In those aristocratic hands, the books, as though subjected to the cruel and bloodless torture of an exquisite sadism, reveal everything. Later, it became known that the SS officer was a distinguished scholar of paleology and Semitic philology.[24]

On October 11, this man openly telephoned the transport firm Otto and Rosoni, then hung up and told the secretary of the archive that it was seized property; if a single book was moved, she would pay with her life. Immediately, the president of the Jewish community, Ugo Foa, paid court to the ministers in an attempt to stave off the disaster—but his attempts were in vain. Two German railroad cars arrived on October

14 and took everything they could possibly fit, more than ten thousand works that were carefully stacked and separated by kraft paper. Whereas the Germans took infinite pains to line up the books in the cars, however, the *facchini* of the Italian company, who were hired to bring them down from the building, threw a certain number out the windows of the back wall to men gathered below. "We will come back to get the rest," the officers of the ERR warned as the convoy departed. But they did not return. Forty-eight hours later, the Judenrazzia took place, as if the result of careful and discreet coordination, as noted by the historians.

These books were given the greatest care when bombs began to rain over Frankfurt: A good half came back to Rome (but only fifteen individuals returned out of those who had been rounded up). Not only was Hebraica no longer destroyed, but it also became the object of a covetuous search by the Nazis. Around four hundred thousand examples were gathered in the new library of Poznan, where a chair on the "Jewish question" had been created. The library—known as the headquarters of the security of the Third Reich, or RSHA in Berlin—stole, collected, and lost close to three million books on Judaism and other Hitlerian concerns such as Freemasonry. This was notably the case for the kabbalistic treasures that Adolf Eichmann ordered seized in 1938 in Vienna, where, in the 1920s, the Israelitische Kultusgemeinde had amassed one third of all known incunabula in Hebrew, including 625 manuscripts that dazzled researchers and bibliophiles. In March 1939, these texts took the road to Berlin; six were found and returned to the Viennese Jewish community around 1950 and a seventh was seized quite recently (a *sepher yetzirah,* or "book of instruction," from the fourteenth century)[25] by U.S. customs after an auction. In 1939, some two hundred to three hundred thousand volumes of the library that had not been sent to Germany were pulped.

For his part, Rosenberg had received a direct order from the Führer on January 29, 1940, to found a Nazi university (Die Hohe Schule) after the war near Chiem See, in Bavaria. After careful thought, it was determined that the departments in this institution of higher learning would be Judaism, Freemasonry, communism, racial biology, and so on. On March 26, 1941, in Frankfurt, he at least had time to create one essential element of the university: the Institute for Jewish Research (Erforschung der Judenfrage), which was to permit "the critical study of the spiritual foundations and tactics of our ideological adversary." Thanks to Rosenberg's ERR, by 1943 the pillaged libraries permitted the accumulation there of 550,000 books (and this was only half of what had already been seized but had not yet arrived), something they had "never before been capable of putting together." Seven hundred chests of books came from the Universal Israelite Alliance on the rue Bruyère in Paris—but only a fraction of these were returned after the war. Five libraries of the Parisian Rothschilds* sat next to the stock of the Lipschütz Library,† rabbinical schools, and various other collections from Amsterdam (the Rosenthaliana and the Sefarada amounted to forty-five thousand titles), Thessalonica, Kiev, Vilnius, and Riga.[26]

When Vichy France attempted to take part in the mad scramble, Berlin raised the objection that because Germany had liberated Europe from Jewish domination, it had first right to the "small indemnity that this pillaging brought in; furthermore the Jewish holdings had themselves been acquired illegally in the beginning . . . For example, the German origin of Jewish wealth is irrefutably established in history with respect to the Rothschild family." The Germans made this quite clear: "The seizure of Jewish cultural goods constitutes only a measure of relatively insignificant reprisal against the Jew, our adversary for dozens of years."[27]

The ERR worked quickly. Fifteen days were all they required to

---

*The Édouard Rothschild collection included six thousand volumes, that of Guy included three thousand volumes, that of Maurice included six thousand volumes, and that of Rober counted ten thousand titles. Added to these were the three thousand works sniffed out at the family's hunting lodge in Armainvilliers. In addition there were the 760 cases of century-old archives from the bank.

†Around twenty thousand books. José Corti testifies: "The German army was not in Paris eight days before its moving teams descended on the place d'Odéon to pilfer all of its books, as if the pillaging of this old library was one of the most pressing objectives of Hitler's war. It is true that Lipschütz was Jewish and owned treasures of Hebraica."

empty the bookshelves of Paris, both public and private. Léon Blum "loved beautiful books, rare thought, and the company of cultivated individuals; he lived a refined life in a very handsome apartment,"[28] but suddenly nothing remained in his "splendid library." The same occurred in the home of Jean Zay on January 10, 1941, and that of Georges Mandel the following week, and that of Jules Moch, Jules Romains, Marc Bloch, Tristan Bernard, Julien Benda, and Henri Maspero, among others. Nonetheless, the ERR did its work well and respected categorization as much as it could. For example, at the Israelite Alliance, before they were moved, tens of thousands of books were first photographed on their shelves, foot by foot.

Johannes Pohl was the man of the hour. An expert who had studied for this purpose in Jerusalem, he crisscrossed Europe in order to select the best the Jewish libraries could offer the Erforschung. He deplored the fact that when his back was turned, the officers made their choices based on the prettiness of the binding. In Vilnius only twenty thousand books out of one hundred thousand were good enough for him; the rest were made into pulped paper. In Thessalonica, he could be found in a nest of libraries and bookstores that had survived since the time don Gedalya founded his publishing house of Hebrew and Ladino books around 1513. For more than five centuries, the city had been a kind of hidden Jerusalem that had lived on with the consent of the Ottoman sultans. Despite seven major fires that carried off some fabulous collections, the houses overflowed with ancient Pentateuchs, Haggadot, and Mahzorim, illuminated manuscripts and scrolls, Judeo-Spanish novels, and other complas collections from the early days of printing. Herr Doktor Pohl left his instructions and trust with a crew that consisted of a poet, a policeman, and an Armenian translator. The booty: ten thousand first-rate selections. Destination: Frankfurt.

Pohl coined a slogan, *Judenforschung ohne Juden* (Jewish studies without Jews), straight out of Rosenberg's dreams. Thanks to the efforts of Pohl and Rosenberg, the most formidable collection of documents in Hebrew or on the Jewish world ever gathered together was divided up among Poznan, Berlin, and Frankfurt. Based on the extortion and extermination of its owners, poorly cataloged and never really installed properly, this superhuman library served no purpose and was soon partially destroyed by bombings and then pillaged again. What philosophical secret did these meticulous initiators think they would find there? No one seems to have studied this ambiguous aspect of the bibliophiliac impulse of national socialism, perhaps based on a fantasy, however misunderstood, which allowed the filtering through of Rosenberg's expression "our ideological enemy." On the other hand, what should have been considered was that such a systematic plunge into the rich Jewish culture would eventually inspire the opposite of its purpose—that is, a chink in the a priori hostility of some "student."

When the Office of the Military Government of the United States (OMGUS)—that is, Eisenhower and his men—occupied Frankfurt, three million books stolen by the Nazis were gathered in Offenbach in the factory of IG Farben (I. G. Farbenfabriken), the famous cartel that not only invented Zyklon B, but also gave wings to the fledgling chancellor Hitler. Captain Seymour J. Pomrenze and his team competently conducted the restitution, and by the end of 1946, they had found the owners of two thirds of the books.

As for the rest, however, because they were from libraries from which Rosenberg's ERR collected, multiple American delegations warily watched each other circling around them. They knew full well that nobody was going to reclaim them. A Professor James Michael wrote the State Department with no beating around the bush: "Europe is no longer a center of Jewish culture and spirituality and there is little likelihood it will become one again someday." The JCRF, the American foundation for restoring Jewish culture, made a moderate show of resistance: "Every time we stumble across an owner of at least six books," wrote its general secretary, Hannah Arendt, "we will do everything possible to find him or his heirs."[29] Thus 150,000 orphaned books made the journey to American libraries, mainly the Library of Congress, which had sent someone on a mission to Frankfurt in the beginning of 1946.

But enough on this quest for Israelite libraries for the purpose of some unknown illumination. Seen from Paris, the reality was much more sordid. Jean Cassou wrote: "Jew is the name given to the object of aggression and depredation. Being Jewish means destined to be plundered, dismembered, cooked. The average folk here call the place where we live a basement or a cellar. But the average folk here would never conceive of building an immense system of thought and extending it over the entire national destiny." It is a fact that parallel to the munificent plunderings of the ERR, which eventually became the vacuum cleaner of artworks for Goering, a subdivision for pillaging even the poor was put into place in Janaury 1942. This was known as the M-Aktion, or Furniture Action, the main purpose of which was to take possession of all the household effects of "the Jews who have fled or are still leaving" Holland, Belgium, Luxembourg, and France. Its leader was Baron Kurt von Behr, who became the black sheep of his family in short order; who had once been an antique dealer on the avenue de Tokyo; and who now wore fantasy uniforms and had reserved a table at Maxim's every night for two years. A detainee in charge of the sorting of Marcel Lob's books described him as a real "wartime bandit." It was said that there remained not even a single piece of paper or an open bottle of milk in the 69,619 apartments (thirty-eight thousand in Paris alone) that he boasted he emptied.

The contents of the Paris apartments were brought to "Camp Austerlitz," a big barn of a place with four stories located at 43 quai de la Gare, where four hundred prisoners taken from the Drancy had to sort through pianos, jewels, tableware, toys, and so forth. There were "stalls of all sorts; one would think one was at a department store."[30] From time to time, "these gentlemen" came to pick out objects for their girlfriends, and these had to be wrapped like a gift or they would leave an address so they could be delivered. As testified by a witness at the Eichmann trial, it happened frequently that the prisoners had to unload their own possessions from delivery trucks. The collections of the German politician Norbert Marx, Mark Bloch, and the son of Emile Durkheim must have been sent there, perhaps even in the company of the "469 kilograms" of Walter Benjamin's collection, seized from the rue Dombasle while the writer was fleeing to his death.[31]

The actor Robert Manuel, who was also a "librarian" at Austerlitz, witnessed the arrival and disappearance of his large collection of nineteenth-century theater bills as well as the library of Gustave Cohen, that of Fernand Worms (the entire Lemerre catalog), and that of René Blum. In one week he once had to sort through 15,999 books, the most beautiful of which were gathered in a large garage located at 104 rue de Richelieu and which the publisher Verdier-Dufour weeded out before the rest of the books were sent away to be pulped.

The prisoners at Austerlitz also indulged in acts of systematic sabotage. While one woman said she struck the soundboards of pianos with a hammer so that they would never again sound right, Robert Manuel destroyed one volume out of each collection of complete works and tore a page out of every single book of any quality. For his part, Marcel Lob stole and hid those books that a bibliophile or scientist would find interesting, such as the luxury editions of the Kra Collection and the notes and cards of Professor Ascoli—but, he added, everything disappeared in the fire that put an end to "this original enterprise," although "before the fire, the premises had been pillaged . . . first by the Nazis then by the people of the neighborhood."[32]

The often useless wealth of the poor collected by M-Aktion was sent away in 26,984 wagons as part of 674 convoys to furnish the occupied regions east of Germany. Yet all things pertaining to cultural heritage were still reserved for the ERR by order of the Führer. We know that in Belgium, on February 12, 1943, twenty-five chests of books were sent from the sorting center in Anvers to a special warehouse on the rue Livourne in Brussels. From the Parisian Jewish libraries, 442 chests were sent to the Third Reich on August 8, 1944, according to von Behr's last report. Nonetheless, all the trains in the world would not have been enough: Hundreds of thousands of books remained on the platform.

With the war barely ended, the temporary government of France made it a priority to settle the fate of the stolen books. In November 1944 there was created a "subcommission of the book, of the Commision of Artistic Recovery" (SCL). The ordinance of April 11, 1945, set the terms of the devolutions: Restore to their rightful owners all identifiable plundered books and give the rest—especially books of a "professional" nature—to libraries that had suffered during the war or under the Occupation.

Commitment to reequipping the country as soon as possible seems to have arisen out of a fine administrative sentiment, but these measures appear hasty and rather cynical. It was common knowledge that the large majority of library owners did not have ex libris and, more important, would not be coming back. For example, Strasbourg's department of plundered goods, which recovered about a million books collected by the Germans "whose owners could never be found," asked in a French that was as flawed as it was thoughtful, "What are the practical rules for the attribution or sale of these books?" Chance is objective: In the same file of the National Archives was a stray testimony about a concierge of the rue des Écouffes in Paris, who, like hundreds of others, appropriated the bedroom furniture of renters whom the Gestapo had recently taken. She told a neighbor who found this a bit quick: "They're done for." (A bureaucrat wrote a note in blue pencil on the letter he received on this subject: "Find out if it was she who denounced them.")

According to a member of the commission in September 1945: "There are few complete collections. The Germans made an initial weeding at the quai de Gare and a second on the rue de Richelieu. In addition, there are bookstores that bought the books. We should have no illusions about the quality of the books. It is certain that valuable books were sent to Germany. What we are doing has primarily a moral value." In the meantime, the SCL was able to search for the stolen collections in Frankfurt, though they brought back only a derisory million books because of the complex network of warehouses storing them, the destruction caused by the bombing, and Soviet obstruction. Out of these one million books, seven hundred thousand no longer had any owners.[33] Added to these were the three hundred thousand copies found by Camille Bloch, a member of the institute and head of the recovery commission, in the garage on the rue de Richelieu. The sorting of these books proved almost impossible. Convinced that their possessions would remain grouped together and protected through all changes, "the victims of this plundering had put their names in the first volume and neglected to do so in those that followed." To make matters worse, there was not enough personnel to do the sorting.

In addition, it should be noted that the French administration was unable to refrain from applying moral constraints; its backers were always susceptible to intoxication based on absurdity: "Works of an immoral or pornographic nature will be turned over to the Estraide,* who will sell them on behalf of the plundered with the proviso that the books are to be pulped." By virtue of this, absolutely no title deviating from bourgeois norms appeared in the meticulous and countless records of library restitutions (handfuls of books) to their rightful owners. In the restitution was begun a ballet of ghosts that resembled a distribution of prizes, if not a lottery: Vladimir Jankelevitch went away with forty-five volumes of philosophy plus some Russian books and books on music; Jules Romains was certainly delighted to recover his personal archives, but there were far fewer books available to him—eighteen in all; the Turgenev Library recovered 2,682 volumes valued at 390,100 francs; and the Israelite Consistory got back only several hundred books. It was obviously easier to recognize what had come from institutions than what had been property of regular citizens: One Monsieur Lazare carried away under his arm a Bible in two volumes and six prayer books valued at two hundred francs, and a Monsieur Bloch of Lyon had a take that consisted of four novels by Kipling, Milton's *Paradise Lost,* and volumes 1, 2, and 4 of the 1908 Cassel *Complete Shakespeare,* with "severely damaged red bindings."

In a deserted Camp Austerlitz, moldering in the warehouse at the edge of the Seine, were anonymous piles of books that were sordidly stolen from people who had been sent to their deaths or who had fled with nothing but the clothes on their backs. A leaden air of mystery smothered the site. It is supposed that because of a bombardment on August 23, 1944, a fire broke out there, and soon nothing remained of the teddy bears, cozy corners, and novels by Delly;† nor did anything

---

*[A charity group that gave assistance to the poor of that time. —*Trans.*]

†[This is the pseudonym of Frédéric and Jeanne (his sister) Petitjean de la Rosière, whose sentimental novels were quite popular at that time. —*Trans.*]

remain of the building that had held them, which was soon rebuilt by its owner. Left was only the quai de Gare itself, which has been rebaptized Panhard-et-Levassor, for in Paris the automobile always triumphs over the railroad.* We can thus note that there is now not the slightest trace "of what was itself an operation of erasure."[34]

In addition, because the state has a duty to remember only when public opinion thinks to remind it of that duty, a confounding frivolity seems to have governed the selection of this very area to build the new National Library of France. The superstitious would say that this could only guarantee bad luck.†

It took thirteen months of pharaonic efforts to carry Adolf Hitler's treasures up the steep-sided paths (on which the trucks slipped so often that it was necessary to use oxen) to the snowy hiding place he had chosen for them: a former salt mine above Alt Aussee in Austria. This was not far from his birthplace in the city of Linz, where he planned to build a museum to himself with a large library as revenge against Vienna for slighting him. Because the personnel charged with blowing up all of it as the Americans approached had fled the scene, the Americans discovered in the galleries, in addition to the 6,755 paintings by the masters, 119 chests of the Führer's personal books. In other words, out of the sixteen thousand books the Führer thought he had, there were found only three thousand or four thousand volumes, of which twelve hundred now remain in the Rare Book Collection of the Library of Congress, which is always in the forefront of these endeavors.[35] Also found were the 237 chests of books that Rosenberg had collected.

Two observations deserve mention: First, these collections belonged mainly to the Rothschilds, which of course simplified their restitution. This perhaps betrays an odd fantasy: Just like the parvenu gangster who ceaselessly steps into the shoes of the bourgeois businessman,

---

*[René Panhard and Émile Levassor created the first French auto-manufacturing firm in 1890. —*Trans.*]

†This Parisian stutter disturbed Winifred G. Sebald deeply enough to encourage him to slip the land of the warehouse under that of the National Library itself at the end of his last novel, entitled, appropriately enough, *Austerlitz.*

the anti-Semite surrounds himself with Jewish goods. Second, all the reports, notes, and letters that Hitler had to read during the last year of his life were typed by a special machine that produced letters that were each 0.9 inch tall, because Hitler was on the verge of losing his eyesight. Therefore, all of these books that had crisscrossed Europe in every direction and had been stored away with the stubbornness of a blind beetle were a complete waste.

At the exact moment when Alfred Rosenberg was hanged in October 1946, three million surviving books had been collected in the suburbs of Frankfurt to be sorted and returned, for better or worse, to their rightful owners. Rosenberg was from Riga, Latvia, and a rumor circulating in the halls of the Third Reich added to his already dubious history the fact that his great-great-grandmother was Jewish. This may well have been what impelled Rosenberg, the theoretician of Nazism, to overdo the anti-Semitism he displayed both in his editorials and in the Führer's ears, which were undoubtedly already full. Several years later, librarians sighed at the thought that the fixed notions of this extremely methodical man eventually contributed to the non-destruction of an incalculable number of books that had come within a hair's breadth of apocalypse.

AN END-OF-THE-CENTURY WORLD TOUR

The Former Soviet Union

Before bombing made smoking carcasses of its buildings and a large portion of its books, the National Library of Prussia had succeeded in distributing two thirds of its collection to thirty-two warehouses. The part of the cake that the Red Army sliced from Berlin contained fourteen of these, housing (more poorly than well) eight hundred thousand books. An equal number were housed on the Polish side, and twice this number were kept in the American portion. For long months these remained at the mercy of the weather and other dangers. In fact, the most urgent priority of the "book brigades" that had been formed to scour German bookshelves was to seek out everything the Hitlerians deemed "ideologically dangerous," then everything directly or indirectly touching on Nazism. Numerous German institutions had fallen into Soviet hands, which was how the eighty thousand ancient books of the Martin Luther Library were judged "to be of no interest" whereas the Nietzsche Archive was frenetically emptied to be packed away in cold storage—with the exception of his works on ancient Greece, which were no doubt considered to be an inoffensive pet hobby of "the sworn enemy of the working class."

Mrs. Lieutenant General Margarita Rudomino, leader of these brigades, proved to be not such a bad sort at heart: She exulted when she placed her hands on an original edition of *The Pickwick Papers* accompanied by a letter from the author.[36] Her name was subsequently given to the Library of Foreign Language Works in Moscow, whose intended purpose was to impart culture to the masses, then perhaps pursue its task, at present, of restituting some of the eleven million or twelve million books relocated from Germany, the major portion of which originally came from France.

Unfortunately, only a meager third of these volumes were identified and relocated, and even this required the work of terribly obstinate and clever seekers such as Patricia Grimsted, "the spy of the archives," as she was nicknamed with annoyance by the numerous officials she put in the hot seat. For two or three generations, no information on restitution was obtained. Even now, no official request has been formulated. We harvest only freshly polished *fins de non-recevoir** from the Quai d'Orsay when the status of Franco-Russian negotiations on the restitution libraries is brought up, even if only regarding both side's figures and stocktaking attempts. It undoubtedly has been more urgent to recover the archives of the intelligence and police services or those of the Masonic lodges.

As with the Symon Petliura Library, Moscow distributed the Turgenev Collection, the entirety of which fell into its hands from Paris by

---

*[According to Bouvier's Law Dictionary, this is a term of French law regarding "an exception or plea founded on law, which, without entering into the merits of the action, shows that the plaintiff has no right to bring it, either because the time during which it should have been brought has elapsed, . . . or that there has been a compromise, accord, and satisfaction, or any other cause which has destroyed the right of action which once existed." —*Trans.*]

way of Poland, through several establishments as far away as Sakhalin Island. Recently (within the last twelve years) Russia has ceased refusing to mention the retrocession to the Turgenev Collection (now on the rue Valence) of some of what belongs to it. After much bargaining, 118 books have found their way home to the collection's shelves, which its enthusiastic organizers say is a small victory over both Nazism and Stalinism. Yet the bulk of the collection will never return: Its "degenerate" portion, some tens of millions of books, was ordered burned in 1955 by officers who recently supplied personal testimony to its nature, and the same fate certainly purified the Petliura Library. This is the season of confessions. The director of libraries at the ministry of culture admitted that millions of "literary trophies" were rotting under pigeon excrement in an abandoned church in Uzkoe, near Moscow. Patricia Grimsted adds that the collections of Léon Blum, Emmanuel Berl, and others are simply part of the presidential library in Minsk.

The size of Stalinian destructive accomplishments far outstrips the imagination, and witnesses are only beginning to appear. It is believed that the administration's recourse to gulags, purges, trials, firing squads, and mass deportation was accompanied by a systematic reduction of reading as a source of identity or potential focal point for deviation. The extent of this remains unknown.

The Tartars of the Golden Horde founded the khanate of Crimea in the thirteenth century. This state, annexed by Russia in 1783, became a theater of nonstop persecution until the 1945 deportation of its inhabitants, who were convicted of sympathizing with the enemy during World War II. Stalin ordered them sent to Uzbekistan and banned totally the use of their language. At the same time, all their monuments, libraries, and archives were systematically destroyed in their own country. They were not allowed to return to their memory-less homeland until well after 1990.

Although Estonia had been administered by foreign capitals since 1220, its inhabitants had succeeded in maintaining their language and culture. In fact, an Estonian literature appeared in the nineteenth century. The mass deportations from Estonia organized by the USSR led to the replacement of more than half the population by other forced emigrants. Outlawed in the 769 public libraries that existed in 1940 were books smacking of a literature that could incite social unrest or provocation, which could tend to justify man's exploitation of man, and those that could inspire hatred or chauvinism as well as religious struggle. Consequently, 2,600,000 books were burned and nothing remains on the shelves of ancient Estonian literature.

The National Library of Lithuania was founded in 1919 and held two hundred thousand volumes in 1941. The German army eliminated 19,175 of these, and the USSR, which reoccupied the country later, determined to "get rid of ideologically dangerous publications in our libraries," and subsequently performed all manner of devastation. In 1950, thirty tons of reading materials were sent to the pulp mill in Petrasiunai alone. Ordinarily, the books went directly to the central heating furnace of the library for the greater good of its users. As a result, each of these institutions had only a very slender catalog; what was not burned was locked away in so-called safe deposit boxes—tens of thousands of titles. It should be noted that Lithuania was also the Soviet republic that had the highest number of *samizdats* per inhabitants during all their years behind the Iron Curtain.

Stalin planned to deport to the remotest reaches of Siberia the entire Israelite population living in the European part of Russia, but his death prevented this. Since 1936, state anti-Semitism had been so strong that Russian Jews experienced relative tranquillity only during the war years, when they were used to obtain a certificate of planetary antifascism for their government. But starting in 1943, the persecution resumed with even greater force, along with the eradication of the very idea of Jewishness. In the USSR, there were too many Jews for Stalin's liking, but there could not be a "Jewish question" there. To remedy this, all books making even the slightest allusion to Jewish culture were eliminated, Lenin's speeches in favor of the Jews were expurgated, and even a geometry book that showed two superimposed triangles was banned as an obvious mark of Zionist propaganda. In addition, the use of Hebrew was banned in the 1920s, and after World War II it was the turn of Yiddish to be banned. All Israelite artists, journalists, and writers were arrested en masse, and all of their production vanished from bookstores and libraries, while the press was unleashed on these "people of no country" and on these "cosmopolitains," perhaps for the purpose of preparing their exile.

The tension suddenly dropped on March 5, 1953, however. When the boots were finally pulled off the Guide's cadaver, the majority of the regime's figures, such as Khrushchev and the KGB's Andropov, hastened to burn any compromising documents. Now, we can find practically nothing about the subject of "outdated [books] that are not going to be used again."[37]

"The greatest catastrophe of the century in the world of libraries" (though I don't know what jury determines the prizewinners) befell the Academy of Sciences of the USSR in 1988. It was 8:00 P.M. on Sunday, February 14, when the fire began on the third floor in the periodicals room. When it was finally extinguished the next day at twilight, four hundred thousand books had been reduced to ashes and 3,600,000 others were permanently damaged by water, smoke, and extreme temperatures. The librarians knew right away that the Baer Collection (a collection of foreign scientific books) was largely destroyed; the rest of the destruction consisted primarily of works that went back, in some cases, to the seventeenth century. The impact on the Russians and great-book enthusiasts was terrible, but the disaster was even more traumatic for those who still harbored any illusions about the perfection of the state.

The first article, a short piece that appeared three days later on page 4 of the *Sovietskaia Rossiia,* noted the abnormally high number of fires on Vassilevski Island, where many university buildings and governmental institutions were concentrated, all prey to the absolute slack of the bureaucrats. Vladimir Filov, director of the library, responded in a perfect Soviet manner the following day in an official article. He contended that only several handfuls of newspapers and perhaps some 1930s-era books had been burned. As time passed, however, the bureaucracy's wooden language began to display fissures. Several hours later it was simultaneously learned that Filov had been suddenly hospitalized for health reasons and that his departments had not thought it worth asking for help or advice from the nearby National Library, but instead had ordered a bulldozer to remove the waterlogged books along with the rubble. A mob raced to the site and scaled the fences to try to prevent the bulldozing, although the panicked officials swore there were no books left to be saved there. The bulldozer operator then pulled the key from the ignition and sided with the people, like Potemkin crushing Chernobyl.

A radio appeal enlisted the support of all the inhabitants of the future ex-Leningrad to help dry the books on the clotheslines at their houses. In this way, eight hundred thousand (only six hundred thousand, according to another story) were restored to the collections, while one of the vice presidents of the Academy of Sciences took the unheard-of initiative of requesting assistance from American librarians who had experienced a similar catastrophe in the Los Angeles Central Library fire in 1986, two years earlier. Nevertheless, the intervention of the famous magnate of Occidental Petroleum, Armand Hammer, who had become rich from Marxist Leninism, was required to obtain the services of three experts, who did not reach the scene until nine days later. In the meantime, 250,000 books were rushed to the freezers of a local fish-packing plant.

China

In the twentieth century, China once again held the record for convulsions and drama in this chapter of the history of the book.

The bombings, fires, pillaging, and confiscations from Japanese aggression had ravaged considerably the northeast regions of China, and three quarters of the large public university and smaller private libraries were concentrated in the battle zone. More than half of the books in that region were destroyed or carried off, such as the four hundred thousand volumes of the Dongfang Tushuguan installed by the Commercial Press in Shanghai, which were burned along with the Hanfenlou, the collection of rare books from the Sung and Yuan dynasties, including the survivors of Tianyige. During the sack of Nanking, the priceless manuscripts of the Sinological Library of Jiangsu disappeared; the soldiers spent several days taking them away before demolishing the building. From 1925 to 1936 the number of Chinese public libraries had grown from 502 to 4,041, but the three years of war that followed destroyed twenty-five hundred of them at one blow. Bombardments affected private collections with equal efficiency.

Yet shells and theft were not solely responsible for the destruction. Many personal libraries were burned by their owners, because even to own a book in English or to own "anti-Japanese literature," which amounted to the same thing, was a crime punishable by death. Weren't Shakespeare and the Bible both written in the language of the enemy? What's more, the Japanese police in the occupied territories were known to be horribly tenacious: They were "much given to looking for the black cat in a dark room which is not there."[38] This paralysis also compelled the owners of books to sell them to be transformed into *huanhun zhi*, "returned soul paper" or "reincarnate paper." In addition, bookstores already sold their books by the pound. This recycling struck a death blow to "cartloads of well-printed volumes, classics, imperial encyclopedias, poetical works, etc. [. . .] As a result of such 'reincarnation' books printed in the late Manchu dynasty and the early years of the Republic which ought to be very common here, have now become rarities. It would be an interesting inquiry to find out what topical literature has been printed on the paper in which an edition of, let us say, Confucian Analects has become reincarnate."[39]

Once routed, the Japanese began considering the transfer of the remaining large Chinese collections—but it was too late. They no longer had enough transport at their disposal. Still, they managed to take with them from the Forbidden City two thousand chests of manuscripts and from the National Library in Nanking seven hundred precious books.[40] It was precisely to avoid this fate that reference works and books in foreign languages from this institution traveled across China to follow the government to Chongqing, in Szechuan, and returned three years later. Jiang Fucong was the head director of the National Library before departing for Taiwan during the debacle of the Kuomintang—but not without bringing with him a large part of the collection. This man was a pure symbol of cultural universality, a rare bird in China who reminded people that "knowledge," in Chinese, is *shu xiang,* "book perfume." He compared this notion to what Richard Aungerville de Bury said in the fourteenth century when he treated himself to browsing in secondhand Parisian bookstores, which were "more aromatic than any spice shop." Jiang prided himself on peppering his speech with Latin and French quotes. It is easy to see why he took refuge in Taipei, where he directed the museum; he would not have lasted long in the new China.

Despite a considerable donation of books by the United States,[41] barely nine hundred university and public libraries remained in mainland China by the middle of the 1940s, and even fewer books were available in 1949, after the Nationalist withdrawal.[42] Thirty years after the conflicts ended, the situation had worsened to a lamentable degree: This period of time witnessed the unfolding of the Maoist saga, with all its devastation.

In classic fashion, China began carrying out the "liberation" of Tibet in 1949. The insurrection of Lhasa prompted a brutal repression in which eighty-seven thousand Tibetans were exterminated. An operation of genocide followed on the heels of this insurrection. Eliminated were about six thousand monasteries, most of which housed a library that was destroyed on the spot. As in its other colonies (Xinjiang [Chinese Turkestan] and Inner Mongolia), Peking (Beijing) has recently resorted to a less brutal recipe of subduing these regions: relocating Chinese nationals to live there, with ten Han for every one native. This is why the Gsung-'bum* are found instead in India.

"Great disorder across the land will lead to great order": This is what the convoluted Mao Tse-tung essentially said when he let loose the youth into the streets in August 1966—his indirect method of getting rid of Liu Shaoqi. In the beginning, the high school and college students merely baited their professors, then university authorities. The matter

---

*[The collected Buddhist writings of a Tibetan or Mongolian lama. —*Ed.*]

could have ended there, but on August 18, Mao personally slipped on a Red Guard armband, and on August 23, the first issue of the *Daily Journal of the People* congratulated the students for having thus swept away "the dust of the old ideas and cultural customs of the exploiters." This was a green light for anarchy: Two months later 4,922 of the 6,843 historical sites in Beijing had been damaged and 33,695 houses had been invaded and rifled through in search of anything that might denote a bourgeois attitude, whether books or old paintings.

After having made the rich peasants and counterrevolutionaries pay for their so-called black crimes, it was time to attack the "gray zones," the intellectuals. One hundred forty thousand people in Beijing were afflicted, and 7,682 of these died. Because the Red Guard traveled at the expense of the state, they could crisscross China to apply vigorously the "supreme directive" of Mao Tse-tung's philosophy. As a bonus, this allowed Mao to witness 13 million pass in review in front of his balcony on Tiananmen Square. He sought to remove only a political rival, but it would require the Red Army to end the new national cataclysm he unleashed. Another consequence of this: Because the political sabbath was extended for a number of years, Chinese culture was subjected to fire and blood for much longer than is commonly believed.

Mao was a librarian in Peking (later Beijing) in 1919, which, as the hagiographies proudly declare, was how he discovered Marx. This may also have been the source of his hatred for books and all things highly cultivated—no doubt because of a frustration or humiliation he suffered that remains unknown. In 1950 he instigated an auto-da-fé on books deemed reactionary as well as being enemies of the people. As the *New York Times* nobly protested, this was "a sign of weakness." All in all, however, this destruction was still timid or was little publicized.

Starting in 1963, Mao was powerfully assisted by his wife, Jiang Qing, to whom he conceded cultural affairs, given that she was once an actress. One scholarly periodical after another was suppressed along with other university publications. "Better to have uneducated workers than to have learned exploiters," was Mao's wife's leitmotif. Likewise, she dropped this comment at a meeting of librarians: "The cultural period between the Renaissance and the Cultural Revolution can be described as a complete void." At the Shanghai Library her disturbing acolyte Zhang Chunqiao proclaimed: "Of the millions of books here, only two shelves are worth preserving." Yao Wenyuan, another ineffable member of the Gang of Four, said: "Whoever acquires knowledge becomes bourgeois!"

It was due to this thinking that the owner of a collection of books was dragged down the street, arms outstretched like the wings of an airplane, wearing a dunce cap. He was then struck publicly until he confessed his crimes, after which he was conscripted to perform the vilest jobs among delighted farmworkers to whom he had to confess his guilt every morning if he wanted to eat. At this stage one can only deny oneself. Ba Jin wrote quite clearly about how he negated his own way of thinking after ten years of such Calvary—and for every Ba Jin, how many others went mad keeping their mouths clamped shut?* As they say, happy is the one who has no children to protect; he can at least kill himself.

"A regime this hostile to accumulated knowledge could not be expected to spare the libraries."[43] This meant that even favored intellectuals were reduced to the rank of boilermaker of words who worked for the masses, meaning the Party, and thus a library fell to the level of a machine tool. To sum up the philosophy of Zhang Chunqiao: Before 1949, all the Chinese books that were not Marxist were feudal. From 1949 to 1966, the majority were revisionist, and everything printed abroad was necessarily capitalist or else revisionist. As a result, millions of rare and not-so-rare books were extracted from institutions of public

---

*Ba Jin's testimony can be read in a collection of his chronicles, *Random Thoughts*. A thousand other grim details from this period that is now busily erasing itself can be found in books by Yan Jiaqi and by Barbara Barnouin. Ba Jin wanted a museum [of the Cultural Revolution] to be created. His wishes were finally answered, but in the most infamous fashion: In an enchanting old house on a tiny street in Beijing, fortunate foreigners can now drink a cocktail in the armchair where the unsavory Lin Biao (we are told) once placed his posterior or else enjoyed a meal (excellent) served by ravishing young women in Red Guard uniform. The heights of dubious humor are reached with the restaurant's name: Xin Hong Zi, the "new Red attitude." It goes without saying that this kind of establishment can open and stay open only with authorization from the highest levels of the administration.

or academic reading because they were deemed no longer to serve any purpose, and they were summarily sent to the pulp mill. During this time, no one seemed to wonder what the source was for all the paper for their Little Red Books, which were printed in quantities equal to every inhabitant, young and old, in a country that did not even have enough rice.

Far from the large cities the message was understood even more radically: Everything should be burned at once. This was the case of the Yunnan, the public libraries of the Fujian, a region where 224,023 out of 464,964 books were consigned to the flames; and in the Hubei, in the Jingzhou district, west of Wuhan, where four hundred thousand books and periodicals were destroyed.[44] The province of Liaoning lost two and a half-million books starting in May 1966, "according to statistics that remain incomplete."[45] In Jiangxi, the Red Guard chose the Lushan Library to serve as its dormitory. The library's employees were forced to find new jobs and the books were piled in dank storerooms, where they became food for various insects. When the odor of mold became intolerable, they were all burned.

It is also possible to read the testimonies of former Red Guards:

But most of all of idols and books. All the books that had been removed from the city libraries early in July and stored in the Workers' Palace of Culture were there—the yellow, the black, the poisonous books. Most of them were old hand-sewn volumes. *Golden Lotus, The Dream of the Red Chamber, Water Margin, The Romance of the Three Kingdoms, Tales Told in a Study*—all awaited burning. Shortly after six o'clock, fifty kilograms of kerosene were poured over the piles, which were then set afire. The flames leaped three stories high. . . . The flames of class struggle will never be extinguished.[46]

The very official photos taken by Li Zhensheng in the Heilongjiang remained secret a long time, as did many others, which eventually emerged and finally put a face on this "nation inhabited by accomplices and mute victims." They reveal the obtuse hate, the pleasure of humiliating and debasing during a time when "struggle meetings" [or educational meetings] alternated with the burning of Buddhist scriptures, which were considered "only dog farts," and the overturning of libraries. "Only the paperbacks are visible; the other books were used as projectiles."[47]

But while Mao's little soldiers were authorized to destroy any text that fell into their hands—archives, old and foreign books, calligraphy, and so forth—they did not find everything. At times, these bewildered groups let themselves be drawn into ideological discussions that ended by diverting them from their immediate objective, as happened one day in Beijing: The librarians agreed that they were right and began chanting slogans that essentially said, "Yes, let's pick out all the bad ones!" which allowed the time they needed to save the books. On another occasion, a librarian had the idea of using the energy of his riled detractors by offering to make them a Documentation of the Cultural Revolution room, where young people earnestly gathered 230 chests of tracts dated between September 1966 and August 1968. In the same way, the famous two-hundred-thousand-volume library of the Jesuits in Xuijahui (pronounced Zikawei in Shanghai dialect) was attacked in 1966 by a quarrelsome band who came looking for practice at pillaging by ransacking first a school, then a neighboring church, and burning all the books that they found there. The personnel at the church academy came to the doors and windows and defended the establishment, however (though they were persecuted and killed a short time later—but in the meantime, the collection was put in a safe location).*[48]

While snooping through shelves from the Xuijahui (Zikawei) era, researchers discovered a *Dictionnaire chinois, français et latin, publié d'après l'ordre de sa majesté l'empereur et roi Napoléon le grand* (Paris: Imperial Printing House, 1813) that was so large that an abridged

---

*With its storerooms restored and an ample reading room created in the former apartments of the superior, after July 2003 the former Jesuit library became a branch of the Shanghai Library. The library has removed the twenty thousand titles from its Chinese collection—whose 1930s-era catalog has largely vanished—but still has available its original collection of about eighty thousand works in foreign languages, a collection increased by the Royal Asiatic Society, its British counterpart and a branch of the Shanghai Library (whose listed building should be reopening as a home of significant Chinese manuscripts).

version of the French one was released in Hong Kong, but it was almost entirely destroyed by fire in 1863. Also discovered were the *Quartum Scriptum Oxoniense Doctoris subtilis Joanis Duns Scotis* (Venetiis: n.p., 1515) and Pierre Martial Cibot's *Lettre de Pékin sur le genie de la langue chinoise* (Brussels: n.p., 1773), which attempts nothing less than to establish the kinship between ideograms and hieroglyphs. Drowned among miles of sermons and other titles that were as edifying as they were useless were one of Benjamin Rabier's first albums; countless titles made famous for having been placed on the index; and an entire wall of Chinese yearbooks from the first half of the twentieth century, a priceless resource for historians. The paradox here is that communist China deserves praise for having protected and opened for researchers the only Jesuit library in the world *grosso modo*, intact within its own walls.

Finally, librarians were not alone when defending themselves and their collections and protection was afforded them from the higher spheres of power, which were forced to try to manage Mao's chaos. Tan Xianjin, who directed the Beijing Library, said of December 7, 1967: "[I]f Chou En-lai had not ordered the army to defend the library from attack by the Red Guard . . . I dread to think what might have happened to the National Library."[49] The garrison remained on the premises for an entire year before being replaced by *jungong xuandui*: "propaganda brigades made up of workers and soldiers,"[50] which were militias created to quell the young Red Guard members who refused to return to their studies.

A large part of the most valuble collections had been packed up by order of the minister of culture in May 1966, long before the troubles started, and was moved to the institutions of Gansu and Inner Mongolia, either because war with the USSR was expected or because those in high places knew that the Cultural Revolution was about to occur. Generally speaking, it is thought that the majority of libraries in the large cities remained padlocked for three to six years and, during that time, were inaccessible to both readers and rioting demonstrators. It is said, however, that there were those libraries that remained open as traps. The Department of Western Publications lay in wait for the unwary who came to obtain foreign books so it could denounce these patrons immediately—but in such instances it is not possible to be more precise: This period of Chinese history is still taboo and it remains impossible to hear from the last witnesses, who are growing more rare every day.

In this regard, it is highly regrettable that Gu Tinglong, who presided over the Shanghai Library and died in 1998, when he was almost one hundred years old, did not share his inside knowledge with anyone. During the 1950s, he and his aides had visited pulp and paper mills to recover in extremis the genealogical records of tens of thousands of Chinese families. (Today these forty-seven thousand volumes provide inestimable value for researchers.) He taught calligraphy during his lunch break and was undoubtedly the most uncomfortable witness of Zhang Chunqiao's purge of the institution when Zhang, made all powerful by the Cultural Revolution, eliminated fifty of the 360 librarians who might have been familiar with the anticommunist text he had written earlier under the pseudonym Di Ke.

In 1976, Mao Tse-tung and the members of the Gang of Four disappeared at the same time. While the authorities displayed images of Chinese weeping over the death of Mao, the entire country was riotously banqueting to celebrate the imprisonment of the Gang of Four. After eight days, not a drop of alcohol was to be had in Beijing. The official burial of the Cultural Revolution was followed, however, by a long, viscous trail of obscurantism. In 1979, China passed directly from "combating the Four Olds" to "fighting for the Four Modernizations," and the soon forgotten president Hua Guofeng even stated with a straight face that libraries would be built "to serve scientific research and the masses." Meanwhile, propaganda was making good headway with its unverifiable claims: "The administration of museums and cultural relics has restituted two million books to their former owners."[51]

Despite the excitement of the new times engendered by the new slogan of the hierarchy after the Tiananmen massacre in 1989—"Enrich yourselves" (whose unstated additional meaning is "and leave us alone")—China's misfortunes were now complete. For ten years the country had been stripped bare of public and private libraries, education, and reading material. The renewal of these activities required ten additional years to achieve any semblance of efficiency. Thus public and research libraries suffered particularly during this time for lack of any real publishing, lack of acquisitions from or communication with foreign countries, and lack of any formal training or cataloging skills. Second, if we might put it this way, was the national "debraining" that was supported by the humiliation of all the intellectuals, who no longer knew if they should just die or simply stoop to a lower level. Among the other consequences of this unprecedented period was the colossal decline of the cultural level of the young Chinese, who, for the first time in the history of the country, were severed from their past to such an extent that students read literary essays from the 1930s with great difficulty. They can be overheard muttering, "Our parents have nothing to teach us."

After twenty-two centuries, Qin Shi Huangdi's operation to wipe clean the slate has finally succeeded.

Cambodia

Though the implacable logic of the *hing xiao bing,* Mao's Little Red Soldiers, contributed a great deal to China's national ruin, the complexity of traditional Chinese society and the extent of the territory did not allow the ruin to reach the horrific heights attained by their Angkor counterparts.

Starting in 1975, in a Cambodia whose power had been liquidated by American machinations, and with its government's own incompetence, bands of Khmer Rouge suddenly exercised a bloody absolutism for three years, during which a third of the population died in a singular hallucinatory climate in which children were promoted as "instruments of the dictatorship of the Party." Only the teachers who managed to pass themselves off as imbeciles escaped; the other teachers all earned body bags. The strategy of Saloth Sar, known as Pol Pot, or of Khiru Thirith, Pol Pot's "minister of social action," was to raise an army of adolescents who hated all the reference points of the former society: ancestors, Buddhists, professors, and even their own parents. As a result of this principle, 5,857 schools; 1,987 pagodas; 108 mosques and churches; and 796 hospitals were destroyed.

War was declared on paper; money was eliminated, as were identity documents—indeed, owning a photo was punished by death. Of course, the book, whether an old-culture manuscript on latania leaves or a printed book from abroad, was designated a mortal and easily recognizable enemy. From the very first days of the stupefying and unique forced evacuation of Phnom Penh, young people in black garb raced to the libraries. First in line was the National Library.

> In the courtyard was a mountain of burned paper from which protruded partially consumed red, green, or white bindings. Torn-out pages were strewn on the stairs and across the floors of the different rooms. The precious documents that scholars from all over the world came to consult had been trampled, soaked by the rain that had fallen during the previous days, spattered with mud, and torn in pieces. They now lay scattered in the gardens and in the street running past the front of the building. . . . In the Buddhist Institute, one of the most important study centers of the country, seven hundred thousand documents in Khmer and Pali had been reduced to ashes and torn apart. The same was true for the Faculties of Letters, Sciences, and Pedagogy: Gigantic piles of books had been the fuel for an auto-da-fé near the Chakdomukh conference center.[52]

This story was still hot off the presses in 1976. By the time international opinion realized that the worst exaggerations were less than the reality, people had already begun forgetting Cambodia.

Sri Lanka

Colonialism always leaves behind some time bombs. For example, the British imported massive numbers of Tamil manual laborers in the nineteenth century to work on their tea and coffee plantations in Ceylon.

On May 31 and June 1, 1981, a band of police led by two ministers (according to some) or (according to the government) a mob of unidentified thugs attacked the Jaffna Library and burned down its two-story building, which was home to ninety-seven thousand books on paper and on ôles, including 150 manuscript treatises on secular herbalism and the sole copy of the *Yalpanam Vaipavma,* a history of Jaffna, which disappeared in the flames at the same time as the offices and contents of the separatist newspaper *Tamil Eelamadu.*

Twenty years later, the authorities launched a national campaign, "One book, one brick," that allowed the establishment to be rebuilt and restocked, but the Tamil Tigers remain opposed to its reopening if the 1981 assault is not given a permanent exhibit there. Hence the resignation of the Tamil Municipal Council (moderates).

In March 2003, the army still guarded this building, which remains closed, prudently and for an unknown period of time.

Kashmir

This wonderful mountainous valley, the name of which evokes luxury and elegance for Westerners, was often regarded as a striking example of Paradise on earth. Shared by Pakistan and India and under the watchful eye of China, which maintains a vigilant neutrality that consists primarily of force-feeding Islamabad with weapons, it has actually become the Paradise of bloody violence, murder in the streets, and the destruction of libraries, a phenomenon in Kashmir that offers the distinction of being almost permanent.

As it sits on the western slope of the Himalayas, Kashmir's ethnic distinctions were long respected by its Arab conquerors until its late Islamization at the coming of the mystic Ali Hamadhani in 1372. Terror was set loose in the fourteenth and fifteenth centuries with Sikandar, sultan from 1394 to 1416, and the forced conversion of Hindus for the purpose of eliminating the influence of the Kashmiri Pandits—the scholars and erudites of the old Sanskrit culture of Sharda Peeth (or "crucible of knowledge," the sacred name of Kashmir).

Therefore, Sikandar, as recorded by the poet Srivar "burned books, *saklan pustakan,* in the same way fire burns hay. . . . All the scintillating works faced destruction in the same manner the lotus flowers face with [*sic*] the onset of frosty winter."[53]

But here the friction of centuries has not played its customary role of softener. Fomented by the incessant pressure of Pakistani agents, Islamic attacks of libraries continue to occur. Their intellectual scope, however, has been expanded considerably: In the fires the writings of George Bernard Shaw, Milton, Shakespeare, and, most intolerable of all, Darwin have recently joined the national writers Jonraj, Somanand, Utpaldev, Kshemendra, and so on. Since 1998, the ravages of the Jamaat-I-Islami* have occurred in the middle of the day, generally at universities or even in libraries, such as the one that was vandalized in Batamloo. This collection specialized in the works of Marx and Engels and Jean-Paul Sartre.

The new official name of the country indicates that "Jammu and Kashmir" will never know peace. It should be renamed "crucible of insanity." In Srinagar there is even an Abdur Rahman Kondoo who recently founded an Islamic research center to which he donated his personal books as compensation for the destruction, which apparently he alone has reported, of the libraries of the Madinat al-'Ulm in Hazratbal and Islamiya College in Srinagar.

The collision of the Qur'an with *Das Kapital* may well seem a rearguard action. It is not.[54]

Cuba

During the summer of 2001, a merry little group of librarians in Cuba requested a book by George Orwell—any book by George Orwell. The sole three titles and copies on the island were located in the National Library, where, the librarians were told, they were unavailable for consultation. Apparently the National Library's director was planning to write an essay about Orwell and was keeping these titles in his office.

Cuba is at the forefront of progress: The sole Internet provider is the state.

---

*[The largest religious party in Pakistan. —*Trans.*]

It has been more than forty years since Fidel Castro said all he had to say to the intellectuals: "Inside the Revolution, there is everything. Outside the Revolution, nothing!" The result can be seen in the bookstores and the three million volumes in libraries: The known universe is reduced *grosso modo* to the life and works of Ernesto Guevara or his political kin. In 1999, a local journalist grumbled, hundreds of books offered by Spain were destroyed upon their arrival.

In its beginnings, the current government committed the very serious error of teaching all Cubans to read and write. As a result, the citizens keep asking to read. Consequently, today there exists a network of amateur booksellers who obtain (no one knows how) and discreetly provide armchair reading to the great displeasure of security personnel. Despite the petty annoyances, seizures, and arrests, there were about eighteen of these reckless individuals in 1998 and about sixty in 2003. Through them, European vacationers are thereby assured of finding a copy of *Animal Farm* to read at the edge of the pool.

France

The *zouaves* of Lamoricière had never heard any mention of the misconduct of the Crusaders in Tripoli in 1109. Nevertheless, they behaved in exactly the same fashion in Constantine in 1837: "The books from private libraries were tossed into the street, trampled upon, torn, and soiled by an unleashed soldiery who looked with hatred at the 'Alcorans,' which they saw in all Arab texts—for example, in the valuable translation of a work by Galen. . . . Several books were recovered by an educated officer who sent them under escort to Algiers, but they were burned en route by the soldiers to fight the cold of a harsh winter!" This is how former communist leader Sadek Hadjeres described the scene, adding that all of this conformed to the wise recommendation of Tocqueville: A conquered country should be ravaged.

Later, the Delta Commandos of the OAS* had their heads full of the

---

*[The Organization Armée Secrète, a French terrorist organization that opposed Algerian independence. —*Trans.*]

exploits of Lamoricière and other nobly named despots when they blew up the library of the University of Algiers and the municipal library of Oran on June 7, 1962, the day on which Jouhard had ordered an end to the attacks in Salan, as if the death of books represented a higher bid than the death of men or one last hurrah before leaving the country. Samir Hachani, assistant professor of bibliotheconomy at the University of Algiers, believes he can establish the figure lost in the fire at 252,258 volumes, or about half the collection. (The press gave a figure of only sixty thousand books lost.) The passive nature of the firefighting seemed no less criminal than the attack itself; at the time, the thinking in the street was, "We are not going away and leaving behind everything our fathers built," yet Hachani adds that based on his research, several thousand rare books, manuscripts from the end of the fifteenth century, and valuable documents had been discreetly transferred to the metropolis once the countdown to independence began. These items would have been directed toward the Center of the Archives d'outre-mer in Aix-en-Provence,[55] which claims that it has no knowledge of them and that they are none of its concern.

Some thirty years after this Algerian summer, the political party known as the National Front* began a progressive series of mayoral takeovers of cities in the south of France and began altering the catalog of the public libraries by eliminating "tropical literature" and "mono-maniacal" tendencies and canceling the subscription to *Libération*.† "It is time to give a good sweep of the broom to the libraries too," proclaimed the mayor of an Orange-turned-brown, where a pass of a magic wand suddenly caused the appearance on the shelves of books that had hitherto been avoided like the plague.[56] As condemned by Gilles Lacroix at the time, the democratic appearance of a "perverted pluralism" makes the case that (using the Front's rhetoric) "a racist book should balance out an anti-racist book."[57]

An inspection tour had to be expedited and the ministry of culture

---

*[The National Front is a right-wing party in France that uses anti-immigration as a theme to appeal to voters. —*Trans.*]

†[An independent leftist French newspaper. —*Trans.*]

coughed up two reports with purely theoretical fallout, which ecumenically invited the entire profession to reflect on the question "Does freedom of expression include the right to vileness?" The correct answer was yes for 18 percent of the total questioned, but this response was delivered in 2002, when, following the meltdown of the Left, one of every five French citizens proved to have been seduced by the extreme Right.

The spotlight was then trained back on the three cities sold to the devil. In the municipal libraries of Orange, Vitrolles, and Marignane it was then detected that "almost all qualified personnel had disappeared, the result of a drastic reduction in budgets and library use" (8 percent of the population of Orange, as opposed to 60 percent of Cavaillon, for example) and the application of a "moral standard": Houellebecq, yes, and Catherine Millet, no, noted an assistant in Vitrolles. And while the preferred theoreticians and publishers of the FN-MNR* now enjoyed greater shelf space, their dull literature attracted even fewer readers than one might think. The librarians of this allegiance knew, moreover, that their electorate was not made up of readers and put more energy into organizing "activities" around a carefully chosen subject, as observed by Gilles Eboli: "Atlantis, sophrology, megaliths, the golden number, the symbolism of the Grail," or even the language of the elves. Systematically resorting to these kinds of gewgaws presents a "danger hanging over the very mission of public libraries."[58]

The professional association consequently created a file called Resources Liberté [Freedom Resources] on its Web site (abf.asso.fr). Its purpose was and is to focus and give vitality to the mobilization that was set in motion after the librarial void had already been created in these three cities. So even today the situation is in a deep freeze: The servants of reading are constrained from the start while City Hall complains that it is unable to attract anyone but incompetents. An objective of totalitarianism has been obtained: bog down the enemy with an insurmountable contradiction.

---

*[Front National, Mouvement National Républicain, the alliance of the two main right-wing groups in France. —*Trans*]

Africa

It is high time to settle the fate of the ill-considered words once uttered by Amadou Ampâté Bah: every time an elder dies in Africa a library is burned.

The continent does in fact have its fair share of old ignoramuses, but these words imply definitively that things are going quite well over there and that the good Negro needs no libraries. It so happens, however, that he needs them more than those on the rest of the planet because the infrastructure in Africa is poor at best and nonexistent at worst. It is a region still ravaged by ethnic conflicts, sordid ambition, and permanent economic crisis. In the space of a generation Angola has lost between eighty and ninety of its libraries and their contents, and this negative report is the same for Rwanda, Congo, Sudan, and other African nations. Generally speaking, with the exception of Cape Town, South Africa, the only Africans who know what libraries are and who use them when they are available are schoolchildren.

We might like just one echo from a world to which the West customarily turns the deafest ear. "The building has deteriorated so badly that it is no exaggeration to say that it is a disaster," Tiburce Koffi, the new director of the National Library of the Ivory Coast, stated in 2000—although the Ivory Coast is one of the countries that are better off than their neighbors. Perhaps the sole possibility of remedying this situation could come from somewhere besides government. "But, Tiburce," retorted the minister of communication and culture, ship captain Henri-César Sama Damalan, "enough already with your story of a lack of books. So what if there are no books in the library? What difference would books make to the Ivory Coast?" The general outcry provoked by this response prompted Sama Damalan's press secretary to say he was only joking.[59]

In these countries that are so destitute that, for example, the word for *rainwater* is used for the national currency in one of them,* what good could be done by books owned communally? The answer is, quite obviously, that they could do a great deal of good, which is why libraries

---

* *Pula* in Botswana

are always among the first victims in coups d'état. Because there is no room here for a thorough explanation of reconstruction attempts,* I recommend reading Assia Issak's gripping report on the status of Maputo's disastrous but not desperate premises.

Not the least interesting example of a solution to libraries in lands of such destitution can be found in a recent report on Cajamarca, Peru, a region of great poverty where the public library exists solely by the will of the local inhabitants and manages to function without a building, hours, catalog, or salaries. This report, written in English and found in bookstores and online, also describes the steps taken by various foundations, associations, and nongovernment organizations (NGOs) to attempt to replace, often in realistic ways, the elders who burn.

Balkan Bosnia

In 1914, Archduke Francis Ferdinand had just left the picturesque neo-Moorish building of parliament when he was assassinated, thereby plunging the city of Sarajevo into notoriety.† It has been common knowledge since the tenth century that this region was one of the world's powder kegs, but the world tried to forget that it would always be so.

The building was erected in 1896 in the middle of the former Ottoman Quarter in a style that owes more to fin-de-siècle Viennese Orientalism than to Muslim architecture. After World War I, it became Sarajevo's city hall and its name, Vijecnica (pronounced: vi-yetch-nit-sa), was retained by the locals even after Tito installed the National Library there. It was as both the city hall and the national library that this building became an international and popular symbol of the city.

The building was immense, with four stories and about seven thousand square feet, 420 research chairs, 108 employees, and two million books and periodicals. Yet these figures say nothing of another

---

*These include the conservation efforts in Chinguetti and Ouadan, as described by Jean-Marie Arnoult. The public's interest, however, is more easily drawn to the lost and then rediscovered manuscripts dating from the first centuries of the hegira than to the problems of a lending library in a Zimbabwe village.

†[And plunging the world into World War I. —*Ed.*]

distinguishing feature: the blend of languages and cultures amassed in the place. Incunabula and manuscripts (the printing press did not reach Bosnia until 1866—copying by hand and calligraphy occurred there until the end of the nineteenth century) are written in Latin, English, Russian, Arabic, German, Italian, Spanish, Turkish, Hebrew, and Persian. Scripts used are Latin and Cyrillic; Arabic and Hebrew; and, of course, Glagolitic. Numerous books were also written in Alhamijado, or Adzamijski, which is the Arabic script used to transcribe the regional languages of Serbia, Croatia, and Bosnia. This cultural mosaic presented yet another aspect of the powder keg.

On August 25, 1992, the Serbs pounded the Vijecnica with their phosphorus bombs from four positions in the hills, from where they laid siege to the city. The following day they fired another forty bombs in the surrounding area to drive away the firefighters, though this was not actually necessary, for they had cut off the city's water supply.

The library burned for three days. Despite the danger, people came out of their homes to participate in the tragedy by trying to save whatever they could—even the smallest books—from the inferno. This was how the librarian named Aida was shot down by a sniper. "The sun was obscured by the smoke of the books and all over the city, sheets of burned paper, fragile pages of gray ash. Catch a page you could feel its heat and read a fragment of text in a strange kind of black and gray negative until, as the heat dissipated, the page melted to dust in your hands."[60]

Fallen into dust were the lexicographical works and personal papers of Ljubusak, the archives of the poet Kranjcevic and the literary critic Krsic, and the diplomatic materials from the end of the nineteenth century, when the colorful chancelleries jostled each other in Sarajevo. Also vanished in the blaze were all the contents of the Croatian and Serbian shelves. The aggressors apparently did not care about their own books, either. In fact, quite the contrary: The Serbian Nationalist Radovan Karadzic asserted, with disarming humor, that the Muslims burned the library themselves "because they did not like its architecture." The precision bombing by Karadzic's troops was no accident: They had already razed the Oriental Institute on May 17, with its 5,457 Islamic and Hebrew manuscripts; hundreds of thousands of documents illustrating the five centuries of the Ottoman presence; and ten thousand printed Turkish, Persian, Jewish, and Arab books. And why? Because in the institute's cabinets there was not only a trace of the non-Serbian occupiers and a symbol of coexistence, but also proof that for centuries countless Slavs had converted to Islam and lived peacefully in Bosnia.

This is why the Serbo-Federals strove, systematically and hatefully, to destroy the book collections in the land they intended to "cleanse." Hundreds of municipal, university, museum, commemorative, and monastery libraries were thus entirely or partially reduced to cinders. The list is too long to be included here,[61] yet the quantity is so large that it can be stated that the Serbs were the true winners of this war. Why the United Nations helped them by preventing their adversaries from defending themselves is a mystery that our children will have to mull.

In addition, reports abound of identical destruction in size, method, and motivation in Kosovo and Albania.[62] As an example, we can single out the town of Zadar in Dalmatia. When the Serbian army retreated from the territory in 1991, they were not sure what to do about the thousands of books that remained intact because there had been no bombing there. The officers therefore decided to create a large fire into which were tossed tens of thousands of printed books and Latinate manuscripts, selected according to how easily they could be understood. The smoke was visible for miles for twenty days; meanwhile, the soldiers used axes to demolish the library's sixty computers.

Hardly had the ashes of the Vijecnica been carried away by the wind than a mob of friends of the book descended on Sarajevo, denouncing in unison the hypocrisy of the international community and the reasons that this had been allowed to occur. Unfortunately, the misfortune of others sells, and for those who know how to draw media coverage to themselves, there is always a drama somewhere. Alas, once the cameras had left the scene, the disaster received minimal attention, even in response to official announcements. The Sarajevo Library was then truly condemned to a second death.

Once Austria had paid for the repairs to the roof in 1997, without which the walls themselves would not have survived, the curators and librarians who were still there had to face facts: All the aid that was promised would not be coming. In fact, perhaps none of it would come. There were numerous explanations for this: Other conflicts vacuumed away the funds; the money, it was thought, would be better spent for a more consensual project (the bridge in Mostar, for example); and perhaps it was suddenly realized that it was not a building, but a symbol, that needed to be rebuilt. The journalist Ellen Barry put her finger on the problem in the excellent architecture magazine *Metropolis*. In 1991, there were 501,000 inhabitants in Sarajevo. Half of these were Muslim, 28 percent were Serbian, 7 percent were Croatian, and 15 percent were classified as "other"—that is, Jews, who numbered in the tens of thousands. Today, 87 percent of the 360,000 people remaining in the city are of the Islamic faith, and there are no longer any Jews in Sarajevo. How could any monies restore at once the universality that the great library had amassed, with its centuries of routine, its colonizations, and its strata of immigrants?

So, ten years later, we can observe that while the cupola has been replaced, the walls remain waterlogged and fragile from four winters of snow and rain. This puts off to an improbable future the return of the library. In addition, its budget has been reduced by 60 percent, and the government no longer includes a ministry of culture.

The Israelites of Bosnia descended from the families driven out of Spain in 1492. One of these families crossed Europe with a 1314 haggadah, a book of 109 pages of striking and naïve calligraphy and illumination that left a record of its presence in Italy in 1510 and eventally came to rest in Sarajevo. In 1894, a young Cohen brought it to his schoolteacher and exchanged it for a few small coins to feed his family. Its value today is estimated at "close to a billion dollars." Given that a haggadah is a book of rites, biblical stories, and prayers connected to the feast of Passover, this copy bears the traces of its casual use during the course of successive feasts. In particular, it is stained with wine.

The book went to the National Museum in Sarajevo and became so famous that when the Wehrmacht entered the city in April 1941, its general requisitioned the valuable book in person. The curator at the time, Jozo Petricevic, a Croat, answered him: "We already gave it to one of your colonels yesterday. His name? We were not authorized to ask him for it." The general had the premises searched and had to be satisfied with the annals of the Sephardic Jews, which went back five centuries, as he had already done in Dubrovnik. The astute Jozo had surreptitiously entrusted the haggadah to a Muslim friend, an imam in the country who hid it beneath the stone of his mosque's threshold, where the book remained until the end of World War II.

Toward the end of 1991, Kemal Bakarsic—also a Muslim, but an atheist, as he explicitly described himself—who was then director of the library of the National Museum of Bosnia, took the initiative, along with his colleagues (who were similar to "silent shadows"), to move on foot the 250,000 books from the collection. This was how the Sarajevo haggadah ended up locked in the underground vaults of the Bank of Bosnia before the first bombardments of the Balkan war.

Finally, ten years later, the museum announced that it was preparing an exhibition of this astounding, wandering book, a perfect emblem of the mixed nature of the region, but also, perhaps, a detonator of brawls yet to come. Immediately citing the Dayton Accords, the Serbs of Bosnia declared that they were owners of one third of the valuable book. They did not go so far, however, as to demand its division into three equal pieces, but they did insist that the planned exhibition spend one of every three years in the ethnic capitals Banja Luka (Serbian) and Mostar (Croatian).

Consequently, the haggadah now remains buried inside a specially constructed strong room in Sarajevo and is shown only to those who have obtained an authorization from the three governmental authorities under the supervision of the three community leaders, each of whom has his own key.

Afghanistan

Because the region had never signed the world treaty honoring each nation's terms of copyright, all books could be published here without any constraint, which brought about a plethora of libraries in Afghanistan in the 1970s.

During the time of the Soviet occupation, every translator was a writer and vice versa. The weeding of "bourgeois" literature and the imposition of a prolecult did not last long enough to dull any minds. The Taliban* changed all of this, however. For it, any book that was not the Qur'an was worth less than music, which was already near the bottom of its scale. In Herat, the cultural capital of Afghanistan, a poet and former cultural minister of the country saw his large library sacked at the same time as that of the university. In 1996, it was the turn of the public library of Kabul.

Saïd Mansour Naderi, whose father was a mystic poet and who had written dozens of books, had created an Ismailian cultural center in Kabul called Hakim Nasser Khosrow Balkhi. Its activities were diverse: It published magazines and every year awarded prizes to artisans, researchers, and artists. It was especially renowned for its library, which was larger in both quality and quantity than any the country had ever before seen. On the arrival of the mujahideen, the Taymani Quarter, where Naderi had settled because of the neighborhood's Ismailian majority, found itself at the center of a civil war. Naderi quickly decided to move his institution to Pul-e-Khumri. This industrial city of three hundred thousand inhabitants was then called little Moscow and provided the state with 40 percent of its revenue. The girls and boys attending the university there dressed in European fashions, and it was where most of the intellectuals who did not leave the country came to live when the Taliban captured Kabul.

When the Taliban approached Mazar-e Sharif the following year, Naderi—who had launched the first international appeal against it and the Pakistanis—moved the library again, hiding it in the mountains. At this point, it contained fifty-five thousand books. Because the Taliban encountered stiff resistance at Mazar-e Sharif, only a small group of

---

*Contrary to what is often printed, this word is not plural, but rather singular—hence, not the plural of *taleb,* which means "any kind of student." Furthermore *mullah,* an approximate but suitable transcription of *mawla,* does not, in principle, have any reason to end in *h.*

fighters managed to make the climb to Pul-e-Khumri. They then disappeared. Thinking the assault was over, Naderi returned the books to their place in Pul-e-Khumri. In the meantime, he had officially donated them to his country, so that his heirs could not break up the collection.* The center then also consisted of a printer and a television studio and sculpture and carpet-making studios. It occupied a beautiful house that had once been home to the city hall, in a large park next to the river.

Launched by Mullah Omar, the black-turbaned Taliban invaded Pul-e-Khumri on August 12, 1998, at 10:30 A.M., following a nightlong battle against the Northern Alliance troops in Massoud. They went directly to the Hakim Center, machine-gunned its padlocked doors, and destroyed everything inside. Sculptures were hurled out the windows; books were cast into the water; fire broke out at the level of the printing press; and within three hours nothing was left. This was the story told by Latif Pedram, subdirector of the library. He had hidden in a nearby house and was able to see every stage of the disaster.

Once the city had been pacified, the newcomers set up their headquarters in the park, which they complacently trashed. No one knows why they also cut down the trees. On this day were destroyed complete collections of Afghan and Iranian periodicals and newspapers going back to the nineteenth century, as well as books that covered a variety of subjects: history, philosophy, literature, and religion. These included a large number of ancient manuscripts, both Qur'an-related and profane (such as the works of seventeenth-century poets and rare versions of *Shahnamé*, the Book of Kings) and all the decrees of the Aga Khan and the correspondence of Ismaili readers. It is therefore certain that a far-from-negligible part of the country's heritage is lost.

This should be seen as a real victory for those seeking to put an end to the predominance of Persian *(dari)* in Afghanistan culture. (Pashto is

---

*At the time, his son Jeff was known in California as a great enthusiast of AC/DC, beer, and Harley-Davidson motorcycles. After the fall of the Taliban, he returned home to start a new career as a warlord and resumed using his given name, Saïd Jaffar.

a poor language whose ancient literature is limited; it follows, says Latif Pedram, that a kind of inferiority complex would exist.)[63] It was also a success for the Sunni, who seek the end of Shiism in the region. Like other iconoclasts before it, the Taliban aimed to "pulverize the past"[64] in such a way that nothing could come back to challenge and compete with its indigent "rhetoric." It had not yet started changing the place-names; that could wait until later. For the Buddhas of Bamyian,* however, the treasures in the museum of Kabul,[65] and the library of Pul-e-Khumri, the evil was already done.

On hearing the news of the destroyed books, an old Iranian woman sighed: "This has already happened to us, my son," because the fragrance of the legend of Caliph Umar, who heated the hammans with undesirable books, also lingers in Persia. The sole remaining question is whether the little mullah of Kandahar, who is Caliph Umar's namesake, thought of this historical comparison.

Iraq

"A Country's Heritage Condemned by the United Nations" was the title of an article on Iraq in the January 2001 issue of *Archéologia*, in which we learned that, during the embargo, one hundred cuneiform tablets were leaving Iraq every day. The Gulf War of 1991 had already damaged a number of archaeological sites. With the subsequent starving of the population, sanctions brought about widespread, unauthorized excavations and theft. Hence there appeared what Western collectors dubbed a "golden age" of the country.

This is what Elisabeth Neffer wrote in the January 24, 2003, edition of the *Boston Globe*. She was a particularly well-informed journalist,† and wrote this story more than two months before the next invasion of the country. Her article examined the chaos and destruction immediately following the American action during the Gulf War (four thousand

---

*The fate of these has received much more attention than that of the Afghan libraries. Consequently, it has been noted that they were not very handsome, especially when compared to the Buddhas seen elsewhere—for example, in Fengxian, China.

†Elisabeth Neffer was killed in Iraq on May 9, 2003.

works were stolen, including two thousand treasures of which twelve have been recovered), which enabled her to describe what would happen again if nothing were done to prevent such looting. Numerous appeals were then launched by the world community of archaeologists, researchers, curators, and various bodies in the good graces of Blue Shield (the cultural equivalent of the Red Cross), but the sole result of this campaign was a violent polemic between the "patriotic" scholars grouped behind the White House and the opponents of the preannounced conflict.

The quiet listservs of the Internet, where scholarly information is customarily exchanged on incunabula or museum administration, suddenly exploded with invectives and revealed how intolerance could hide precisely where it was least expected. A good number of the American subscribers displayed open hostility to any mention of Iraq and slammed shut their portals. It was no less surprising to discover the lobbying by the American Council for Cultural Policy (ACCP), an association of billionaires and large art dealers who supported the White House in hopes of the abolition or relaxation of the Iraqi laws forbidding the exportation of antiquities. We know what happened: because the United States and Great Britain never ratified the 1954 Hague Convention decree on the protection of cultural items in the lands to which they, as nations, might bring misfortune, the leaders of these two countries had only their consciences for their guides. As for the soldiers . . .

The museums pillaged in Baghdad and Mosul in April 2003 under the ingratiating (to say the least) supervision of the Marines brought about the loss of thousands of clay books, including the Library of Sippar, only slightly less ancient than that of Ashurbanipal and discovered in 1986, such a short time ago that only two dozen of its eight hundred tablets had been analyzed, translated, and published (for example by Jeremy Black, in Oxford)* at the time of their loss. The toppling of the country's regime authorized every kind of misappropriation and

---

*Whether they disintegrated as a result of poor treatment due to incompetence and the embargo or were scattered and broken by thieves who followed the Assyriologists in the field—what is the difference?

destruction: The ten thousand archaeological sites in the country were transformed into self-service establishments. Nippur and the Temple of Enil and even Isin were devastated within a month. Thus was the sack of Iraq.

The National Library in Iraq was founded in 1961. The center of legal deposit during the 1980s, it held 417,000 volumes; 2,618 collections of newspapers and periodicals; and 4,412 rare books. Its possessions on the eve of the invasion were estimated at two million shelf marks, including "the greatest collection of Arab newspapers in the world." The National Archives, created eleven years later, was located in the same building, the Bab al-Mu'azzam. Housed there were the documents of the Hashemite government (1921–1958) and the Ottoman government (1534–1918), as well as those of the Jewish community, which was of great historical importance.

The winds of lunacy and mystery that blew over Baghdad between April 14 and April 21, 2003, stirred to life two fires that framed the pillage, although the neighborhood where the blazes occurred was shut down by the troops positioned just in front of the main entrance* and a curfew had been declared on the evening of the April 14. Insinuations were ventured that the disappearance of all the documents from the 1980s could have eased the minds of more than one person. The April 28, 2003, edition of the *Wall Street Journal* pointed out that white phosphorus was used. Nearly two hundred thousand books containing Hebrew texts were carried off by the librarians and stored at the Al-Haj Mosque a few days before the disaster.[66] Moving a library of two million volumes and twenty million archives appeared to be an operation greater in scope than the Iraqis were capable of handling, however. In addition, had these items been relocated, then the countless observers of 2002 would have inevitably noted it. Consequently, of the majority

---

*Based on the on-site observations of Édouard Métenier, of the French Near East Institute, in Nabil al-Tikriti's report of the Middle East Librarians Association at www-oi.uchicago.edu/OI/IRAQ/docs/mat.html, and based on an interview with Jean-Marie Arnoult (General Inspection of Libraries) on his return from missions to Baghdad. His report can be found at www.cfifla.asso.fr/conferences/berlin/irakarnoult.htm.

of books in the National Library, as Jean-Marie Arnoult says, "nothing remains, except a thick layer of ash in which you can bury your hand without encountering any resistance."

Fifteen hundred feet from the National Library the Awqaf Library, which, in addition to printed books, contained seventy-five hundred manuscripts collected from Baghdad mosques since 1920, was pillaged and burned at the same time as the National Library. Two-thirds of the most valuable works from its collection had been moved, however, and the remains were gathered in thirty-two metal trunks and were placed under an armed guard, whom the American soldiers hastened to kill. Following this, a rumor began circulating that the carefully padlocked trunks contained dollars, and that twenty-two of them were stolen by people who had TV marked on their chests and backs in red adhesive strips. The final ten trunks and their contents were turned into charcoal.

In the same quarter and destroyed the same evening was the Bayt al-Hikma, based on the glorious name from the time of the Abbassids. It had been founded in the 1980s to be used in the study of social sciences and economics. Once the building had been burned, many of the books that survived the blaze were shamelessly sold in the garden facing it. Though the central interuniversity library *(al-maktabat al-markaziya)* was spared, that of the Academy of Science was pillaged and sacked after a U.S. tank staved in the main doors so that a flag could be taken down, then disappeared, thus inviting the crowd of gaping onlookers to help themselves. No certain knowledge is available regarding the other archives, of which there were twenty. Yet the Saddam House of Manuscripts (Dar Saddam li-l-makhtutat), where the government had collected forty-seven thousand ancient works that were most often requisitioned or stolen (for example, from the Shiite holy places in Najaf and Karbala), was closed in January 2003, and its collections were moved to a fallout shelter by an energetic director. It is now named Dar al-makhtutat al-iraqiyya, House of the Manuscripts of Iraq.

Once all the Iraqi bookshelves are rebuilt, there is a good chance that a government that is much more fundamentalist than the ignominious Raïs Hussein will consider its prerogative to choose which books will stock them. Perhaps, then, the country will have moved from dictator to dictator and a half?

Thus after months of preparation, threats, and warnings from the press and from the specialists, both respected and timid, all it took was five days to confirm everyone's worst fears: Vanished from Mosul and Baghdad were the physical elements of the texts—both Assyrian tablets and Ottoman manuscripts—and the memories of a civilization. "For Iraq, it is year zero," said a British journalist who was in the thick of things.[67] A large brouhaha ensued in which it was difficult to distinguish emotion from disinformation. (Nothing was destroyed and almost nothing was stolen, spat a colonel who confused the manuscripts of the Dar Saddam li-l-makhtutat with the common items of the museum.) Likewise, UNESCO's wooden words of reconstruction prescriptions have jostled one another. The sole voice not heard is that of the local intellectuals, who, long before the fall of Hussein and even for centuries before (remember Layard), denounced the shameless colonialist immersion of Middle Eastern archaeology by Westerners and their concept of Mesopotamia as the cradle of humanity, in other words, the birthplace of European and American civilization.[68]

Yet during this time the media have made themselves the capable echo of the usual stream of mayflies attracted by the sunlamps. From Kabul, from Sarajevo they come and they go, hatching their three-hundred-line communiqués in which the only new information is "I was there." They are the jet set of the world's tragedies. It must be said that it was a fine party: It cost $100 billion.*

But next time, we must pay attention: During the first hours of any war the information that profoundly shocks the planet can be summed up in four words: The library is burning. Special envoys move on-site and by the next day the messages grow longer—about the number of books lost, the people responsible for the disaster, the scholars in tears, and so on. The following weeks see the arrival of experts with large expense accounts

---

*And for a fistful of billions more there could be lodging and dining facilities worthy of welcoming the tourists that are already champing at the bit. Baghdad, city of a thousand and one wars, is the travel destination now all the rage.

paid for by shadowy organizations and, with the increasing size of the detailed reports, it becomes more and more a matter of taking inventory, aiding, and rebuilding. The original offence is watered down, well-meaning promises flood in, and, in the months that follow, it becomes clear that the library had not burned *so much*. A year later, it is as if the burning never occurred. We can move on to the next tragedy.

This book may well be interminable. According to an April 23 *Business Journal* report of 2001, in March 2001, members of the Harvest Assembly of God Church burned all the books in a library near Pittsburgh that they saw as offensive to their god, including the works of Hemingway and Khalil Gibran. On March 28 of that year, it was the turn of the Jehovah's Witnesses in the former Soviet Georgia, and on May 15, 2001, nationalists and Muslims in Jakarta burned the bookshelves they deemed communist. Ad Libitum, the Web site of the American Library Association, ended up creating a daily column on the planetary pyre.

As of July 2003, however, Iraq still did not appear there.

This book's investigation began the day after the burning of the library of Sarajevo, and it is ending (because it is high time this book was sent to the printer) with the burning in Baghdad. Ten years have only confirmed the worsening fate of the ambitious and innocent search for knowledge in this beginning of the twenty-first century, where the hyperpowers are headed by leaders who grow more infantile as their power grows greater and who surround themselves with experts who will use no more than thirty nouns their entire lives and who cloak an inescapably geoeconomic appetite with the most simple quibbles.

"We are in a world war against terrorism, and those who do not agree are mostly terrorists." Here is something to authorize an Anchluss even among next-door neighbors—and to authorize other measures such as an order given librarians demanding they inform on users with suspect faces and reading material.[69]

All of this would be only somewhat disturbing if it did not jointly produce the cultural depigmentation with which we are all familiar. The depreciation of vocabulary and thought that this depigmentation kicked off fifty years ago, and which will undoubtedly not start retreating for ages, goes hand in glove with the simplification or coarseness adopted by the once respected media. The absence of humor and distance form part of the editorial code almost everywhere, just like that light intellectual touch given one by a well-stocked mental library, is also conspicuously absent. François Mauriac would have a devil of a time placing his *Bloc Notes* with a publisher, to give only one example in France—which is ecumenical to boot.

Will real life find a haven in the academic journals? There is something like a global organization of insignificance in the air, and everyone is delighted to collaborate with it each morning, with his small contribution striving to show himself the least profound, the least subtle, and the least learned as possible. We just saw Donald, now here's Dopey. This orchestration of life through the importance given moronic merchandise and the most rudimentary relations can obviously facilitate the entrance onto the stage of something always waiting in the wings and ready to fill the void of people's minds: religion. It, too, has had its external symbols transformed into gimmicks and has been rebaptized, through marketing, as *spirituality.*

We shall see (in chapter 10, no earlier) how the likely future of the great encyclopedic libraries can lend a hand to this infantile morning show.

EIGHT

PEACE DAMAGES

———— 🔥 ————

*You are pleasing to Rome as long as you are young; but
once you have been well-handled, crumpled, and stained,
you will be stuffed away and eaten by worms who
don't know how to read.*

HORACE, *EPISTLES* I, XX*

Cornelius Walford was born in London on April 2, 1827. He was an
insurer, a self-taught scholar, and an author of a book on the history of
life insurance. The thirty thousand books in his library were dispersed
at his death in 1885, which was a consequence of the malaria he contracted in America, where he had attended the International Convention
of Stenography.

He aroused the curiosity of the bibliophile Fernand Drujon with the
title of the conference he was invited to present at the second annual congress of the Library Association of the United Kingdom, held in Manchester in 1879: "On the Destruction of Libraries by Fire Considered
Practically and Historically." Drujon took with him to the grave his disappointment at never having read this text, which was aimed at selling
insurance policies as much as it was meant to amuse the bibliophile.

This is what it said, essentially: "A book is a very difficult object to
burn or otherwise destroy; it requires time and patience. Collectively,

---

*The work that doomed Condorcet when it was found in his pocket.

book collections will withstand consequential fires, as together they form a compact mass. The true danger for books comes from their environment: They are too often placed in buildings that are overall not truly adapted to their safekeeping." Only a new kind of construction, made from enameled iron, slate, and bricks, with shelves nestled into the walls, should house the new libraries, with great care taken in the placement of the fireplaces and their flues, "which always represent a danger." As for houses, even in the best designed and constructed in the country, "varied risks arise from the negligence of working people and domestics, because of smoking, drinking, reading in bed, and other events of daily life. . . . The presence of one or two *extincteurs* in every large house is happily becoming the rule and no longer the exception. . . . It is possible that chemistry may even render books incombustible." Incidentally, there was at that time the recipe of a certain Professor Folbarre for a more incombustible wood: "zinc sulfate, 55 pounds; American potash, 22 pounds; American alum, 44 pounds; manganese oxide, 22 pounds; sulfuric acid at 60 degrees, 22 pounds; and water, 55 pounds."

Cornelius Walford added to his printed conference text a laborious list of the libraries destroyed throughout Europe's history, which concludes with this cheerful advice: Write on clay. Because the Assyrian libraries were able to withstand the passing of time so well, why shouldn't we return to this material for our printed matter? It is so "wonderfully available!"

A beautiful library in olden days was lit with torches and warmed by open fireplaces and accumulated thousands of pages between its handsome drywood panels. Charles V, known as the Wise (1338–1380), who founded the Bastille and restored royal authority during the Hundred Years War, created a royal library at the Louvre in 1367. Because— despite his nickname—he lacked wisdom, he also ordered the university to provide thirty portable torches as well as a central chandelier made of silver so that the students would not cease their studies on the pretext that night was falling. The risks presented by such a practice cause librarians to shudder; the vast majority of public libraries throughout history strictly forbade the carrying of even the smallest light or heat source onto their premises. For a long time, libraries closed quite early.

Yet fires do not seem to have been reduced by the invention of concrete and iron shelves. During the last century in the United States alone, insurance companies investigated 359 significant library fire disasters that occurred between 1911 and 1961. Statistics cited negligence in the maintenance of buildings and electrical installations as the primary causes of misfortune and condemned as presenting record dangers the waste containers in the basements and the personal heaters used to make offices more comfortable. The frequency of American library fires remains distinctly staggering. The consequence of this is that the English language has a pretty word lacking in French: *arson*. Directly derived from the Latin verb *ardere*, "to burn," it is vaguely related to the French *ardeur* [ardor] and designates the intentional burning of someone else's property without his consent (the British dictionaries' definition) or implies burning "to get the insurance" (a definition added in many American dictionaries).

Water, however, damages books more surely than fire. Ever since the time of Noah, floods have carried off or dissolved knowledge. On a statistical level, the hoses of firefighters are responsible for the rest. This is easily overlooked because water seems weak, in some ways. The phrase "books on fire" obviously piques the imagination much more than does "drenched pages." Yet there is one occasion in which water gets its revenge and is emotionally quite striking: shipwreck. The library has not escaped this fate either, as we shall see.

The property of a public library belongs to the community; each user rightly considers him- or herself the legitimate owner. Problems arise because some believe their use is more important than that of their neighbor and either fail to return books or mutilate them. It should be noted that the prevention of theft has made much more noteworthy progress than the battle against fires. We still do not know how to fight fire with anything but water. (For a while, it was thought possible to use diffusers of carbon dioxide, a gas that extinguishes fires, but because it also stops the respiration of living creatures, we have opted for sprinklers.)

The elements, the sea, and theft display their hostility to the library in peacetime, but in the case of the private collection, the invincible foe of its integrity is the death of its owner. Here are a few well-chosen examples of libraries' natural calamities, organized chronologically.

THE ELEMENTS

The great fire of London in 1666 obviously made only a mouthful out of the libraries it crossed in its path. *"Flame, where are you going? Quo vadis?"* The bookshops of Paternoster Row had prudently stored their books in the crypt of St. Paul's Cathedral, but the fire found them all the same and consumed them entirely. Paternoster Row was located between Amen Corner and Ave Maria Lane, where the turners of rosary pearls had prospered for nearly an eternity. The guild of stationers, copyists, and booksellers had first gathered there in 1403. Despite repeated conflagrations, in 1813 it was still the biggest book market in the world.

Born on November 13, 1663, the Icelander Arne Magnusson knew Latin at the age of six and Greek at ten. No doubt he already had a fine library when he arrived at the University of Copenhagen in 1683. There, the king of Denmark entrusted him with the mission of returning to his country "for our own library some old and rare manuscripts"—for a similar earlier mission was lost at sea on its return voyage. It should be said that for the seventeenth-century bibliophile, Iceland was a gold mine of medieval manuscripts, except that they had deteriorated terribly from the time of the Reformation and the ascendancy of the printing press. Torn-out pages served as insoles, parts of clothing, and patterns for tailors, and the illuminated vellums were used as covers for modern printed books.

Thus, bit by bit, Arne Magnusson reconstructed all the books in the considerable collection he brought back to Copenhagen ten years later, and those that he kept for himself. When in 1729 a large fire broke out that destroyed half of the city, Magnusson's house also burned down, along with a good portion of this extraordinary library. He nevertheless was so convinced that the precautions taken by the municipality would protect him that he lent the city his sleigh. Thirty minutes was all that was needed to annihilate "the books impossible to find anywhere in the world." Magnusson fell ill and eventually died.

Ashburnham House, whose name foretells the curse that befell it, was where the books of the king of England were housed when, in 1731, a fire spread there from the flue of a paneled fireplace. It was 2 A.M. on a Saturday. Before fleeing themselves, the librarians threw out of the windows all they could gather from the smoke-filled rooms. In 1700, Sir Henry Cotton had donated the large library collected by his grandfather Robert. All his life, Robert was prohibited from entering the collection on orders of Charles I, who viewed it as a ferment of subversion. King William III accepted the collection fairly casually in the name of the nation, and no one ever enjoyed what it had to offer. This was a shame, for it contained a Genesis with a wealth of 250 miniatures that were reputed to have been created in Alexandria in the fifth and sixth centuries. After the fire, they were reduced to a handful of blackened fragments.

Yet the famous Lindisfarne Gospels managed to escape the blaze. The irreplaceable manuscripts from 958 had been divided among fourteen cabinets that were topped with the busts of the twelve Caesars as well as those of Cleopatra and Faustina, the hardy wife of Marcus Aurelius. *Beowolf*, the first great English poem, which had survived the purges of Henry VIII, was in the "Vitellius A-XV" section: It was the fifteenth book on the first shelf beneath the bust of Emperor Vitellius. Well sealed in its leather cover, this story of combat with monsters was pulled from the library with its carbonized layers and in 1753 joined the scant remnants of the collection at the British Museum, where nothing was done to prevent its continued deterioration until 1845. Two thousand letters from the text of *Beowulf* were, however, lost here.

The "no-popery" campaign subjected London to a week of fire and blood in June 1780, at which time the populace burned down the rich library of Lord Mansfield, who made a free man of any slave who reached the shores of England, unless, as Blades tells us, he had come from the shores of the colonies.

Thomas Jefferson (1743–1826), the third president of the United States (from 1800 to 1809), confessed to a "canine" appetite for books and constantly surrounded himself with them so that he would never waste an idle moment—for instance, when he waited for guests to come down to dine.

He had three libraries: Begun during his childhood, the first one burned in 1770 with Shadwell, his maternal house. In 1815, with no excessive elegance, the shrewd Jefferson sold the second to the government (6,487 volumes for $23,940). It formed the core of the new Library of Congress, the original having been burned down by the British in 1814. Though this price and collection made a good deal, the matter did not proceed entirely smoothly: Several members of Congress were frightened by the "radical" content of several texts—for example, those by Voltaire.

Jefferson's final library occupied his retirement years. He preferred the "delights" of "mathematical truths" to novels, that "mass of trash." The shelves crafted by the cabinetmaker of his little palace called Monticello were independent units that could be fitted on top of each other up to the ceiling and, if they needed to be moved, could be closed with a cover, like a coffin.

The Library of Congress, barely recovered from the wartime fire of 1814, disappeared again in less hostile flames in 1825. A third conflagration took place in 1851, eliminating two-thirds of the collection, which had grown to fifty-five thousand volumes. After this, the institution equipped itself with a stone floor and metal shelves.

Turku, the first capital of Finland, was later rebaptized Abo, when the country belonged for a time to Sweden. Nevertheless, the library of its academy, founded in 1640 within the enceinte of the castle, burned on September 4, 1827, with the rest of this pretty city that history made bilingual.

Likewise, in 1865, fire devastated the premises of Sotheby and Wilkinson the night before the sale of the Offor Library. Packed tightly on its shelves, after the fire the books were nothing more than oval-shaped pages surrounded by ash. A courageous bookseller acquired the lot, which he took away for a handful of guineas. According to Blades, one year later a thousand of these books were again offered to enthusiasts, trimmed and newly bound by the firm of Puttick and Simpson. The seventeen thousand volumes of the Humboldt Collection perished in the same fire; as Walford reports, the insurance policy protecting them had expired that very day at noon.

Andrew Wylie, president of the University of Indiana, founded that institution's library in 1823 and personally oversaw its acquisitions. We still have the catalog, which was printed in 1845 just before it was all consumed by flames on April 11. That was no lasting setback, however: The library was rebuilt and managed to collect thirteen thousand volumes, which burned again in 1883. Only two of these managed to be saved.

On the night of January 24, 1904, flames ravaged the Biblioteca Nazionale ed Universitaria in Turin, Italy. The cause was not explained, though "the electricity was blamed, again, for one of its customary short circuits"—but it appears that all the switches were off. The famous archive had already suffered a serious conflagration in 1659, but since that time, it had grown fabulously, though "the catalogs . . . were not updated." On the eve of the tragedy, the library contained thirty-eight rooms; 1,095 incunabula, including a *Romance of Lancelot of the Lake* in three folios on parchment by Vérard (Paris: n.p., 1491); 10,321 prints; 1,500 editions printed by the Aldes; 621 works of Hebraica; and 4,138 manuscripts, among them four of *Romance of the Rose* from the fourteenth century and one manuscript from the fifteenth century, *Le Chevalier errant* (The Wandering Knight) by the marquis de Saluzzo, a *Scriptores historiae augustae* that was decorated with miniatures and attributed to Pisanello, and, most important, the Book of Hours of Jean, duc de Berry, with seven illuminations undoubtedly by the brothers Van

Eyck, in a large chapel format intended to be read on a lectern. All were "reduced to three crusts blackened by smoke."

The hides of the books that were saved began to putrefy, which called for the use of gelatin, a delicate task. Treatment by steam and collodion was another option, but using this meant that the next fire would transform the manuscripts into "a veritable mass of flash paper." According to Georges Bourgin and Giovanni Gorrini, someone also mentioned the Vatican's use of "extremely sensitive electric recording devices that could alert the prefect himself, by means of an alarm, to any rise in temperature in the stacks." This use is worth noting and studying.

The earthquake of April 18, 1906, entirely destroyed the brand-new library of the University of Stanford, which had been erected without consulting the main librarian or even showing him the blueprints. This was followed by a widespread fire in San Francisco, which was nicknamed the "ham and eggs fire" because it caught people by surprise at breakfast before it consumed the two hundred thousand books in the city's public library.

Interestingly, three quarters of all seismic events merely knock the books from their shelves. For example, there were six hundred thousand books to be reshelved properly and some seventeen thousand to be rebound at the University of California, Northridge, after the San Fernando quake in 1971. Some earthquakes, however, are tenacious enough to cause the collapse of buildings that were in theory constructed to resist them.

At two minutes before noon on September 1, 1923, all the charcoal stoves in Tokyo must have been lit to prepare lunch when one of the strongest *jishin* in history struck. It was 7.9 on the Richter scale and caused 140,000 deaths in the Kanto. The fire that ensued lasted three days and razed 70 percent of the city, including numerous libraries. The National Library (DNL) has in its collection 248,000 doctoratal theses on earthquakes; as Theodore Welch points out, all of them are dated later than 1923, the year in which their predecessors burned.

Following the bibliophile's nightmare of Chilean occupation (1881–1883), Peru rebuilt its national library, but it perished in flames on May 10, 1943. Subsequently, according to Michel Lenoble, Chile became one of those admirable states in which customs seized works on Cubism on the pretext that they were Castroite propaganda.

Encyclopedic in spirit, the library of the French National Assembly and its thousands of books went up in flames on August 25, 1944, while Leclerc's division besieged the Palais Bourbon, occupied by the German bureaucracy. A complete list of the books lost is available at the BNF.* Saved by the wise decision to send them away to Libourne were eighty incunabula and, most important, hundreds of manuscripts that included Rousseau's *Confessions* and the Codex Borbonicus, the Aztec calendar bought for thirteen hundred francs in 1826, during the period of the Escurial's dereliction that followed the Napoleonization of Spain. Its core subject collections were focused exclusively on parliamentary history found in the complete *Gazette nationale* and the *Moniteur universal,* a newspaper founded on November 24, 1789, by the famous Lille librarian Charles Panckoucke. Today the library is some nineteen hundred manuscripts strong.

To avoid being drafted into the army, a student waited for the noon break to throw a match into a wastepaper basket on the seventh floor of the administrative building of Michigan State in Lansing on February 8, 1951. All the files were archived on this floor. The fire lasted fifteen hours, and the firefighters poured six thousand gallons of water per minute on it before it was brought under control. The Michigan State library was located on the second floor and its storage was in the basement. According to Goetz, the 22,400 books it lost were never threatened by fire at any time; they were lost through water damage.

The end of the 1960s witnessed an increase in the burning of university libraries in the United States, especially in New York and Washington,

---

*[The BNF is the national library of France. —*Trans.*]

as well as in Indiana. The Molotov cocktail was a frequent accessory in those days.

The blaze that reduced to ashes seventy thousand books in the Jewish Theological Seminary in New York in April 1966 is obscure in origin, but there are very interesting photos of tens of thousands of waterlogged books spread out to dry in the sunny courtyard during the following week.

On November 4, 1966, the Arno rose almost twenty feet and passed through Florence at fifty miles per hour, carrying away everything in its wake and leaving behind in the city's cellars and ground floors 500 million tons of mud mixed with fuel, animal corpses, automobiles, and sewage. Included in the devastation were the cellars and first floors of numerous libraries in this city of culture—such as the Colombaria, which had previously been destroyed in 1944. The Biblioteca Nazionale Centrale maintains that it housed 1,200,000 works in its basement, but that it fortunately kept the incunabula and manuscripts on the higher floors. For a solid month its director, Dottore Emmanuele Casamassima, never left the premises. Aided by thousands of volunteers fed on coffee, sandwiches, and good wine, he orchestrated the necessary cleaning and drying of the collection and the eight million cards of the catalog. (Altogether, this took a year, but the librarians took advantage of this opportunity to microfilm the catalog and collection.)

It seems that the librarians of the school of letters and philosophy did not share the same patience and selflessness. According to Arthur T. Hamlin, they quickly got rid of their thirty-five thousand muddy and malodorous books. Almost forty years after the flooding of the Arno, the team of twenty people who worked at the restoration center of the Nazionale had been reduced to fifteen, and thirty-five thousand volumes still remained to be treated—a good decade's worth of work.

We stubbornly give women's names to the hurricanes and tropical storms that regularly devastate a large part of American territory, which allows the newspapers afterward to write phrases such as "Celia was not at all gentle with the library." It has also been observed that the title *Gone With the Wind* often makes a comeback.

More recently, in 1986, the four hundred thousand books destroyed by consecutive fires that occurred two months apart and the seven hundred thousand volumes damaged by the firefighters' water at the Los Angeles Public Library show that preparation for catastrophes is still but a dream. These fires (April 23 and September 3) were criminal in origin, though hardly anything else is known about them.

On August 1, 1994, in Norwich, England, a gas leak and an employee turning on a light resulted in the county's one hundred thousand books and archives going up in smoke. Several eleventh-century manuscripts in the cellar suffered only from the inundation that followed the firefighters' intervention and were sent away to be freeze-dried (through a process known as lycophilization).

Water similarly caused problems in the United States. On July 28, 1997, in Fort Collins, Colorado, seven inches of rain fell in just a few hours. The Morgan Library, of the university there, had just been restored and expanded. During the rainstorm, a poorly constructed wall collapsed, allowing for the drowning of half a million books on the social sciences stacked in the cellars during the renovations. The loss was estimated at $22,500,000 or $36 million, depending on the source. This library had also been flooded in 1938 and again in 1951. It "paid the consequences" every time. A good deal of the current damage is being repaired by lycophilization, and one hundred thousand replacement works have been offered by other American institutions and an equal number have been digitized and are available only onscreen.

Water was also the cause of a more recent Boston Library disaster. On August 16, 1998, a $65-million renovation job had just been completed to enhance the city's public library and restore its frescoes by Puivis de Chavannes and Sargent—but no money was allocated to restore the plumbing in the basement. An age-old cast-iron pipe burst at one o'clock in the morning, drowning the storage areas and their contents under tons of questionable water.

The destruction continues in the twenty-first century. On May 21, 2001, a fire broke out in Seattle's Center for Urban Horticulture, a biogenetics research institute. It destroyed two million dollars' worth of scientific books. The eco-activists of the Earth Liberation Front (ELF) are the top suspects, yet one of the researchers at the center, an expert in GMOs, lamented, "All we are trying to do is improve the environment."

On May 29, 2002, the warehouse of publisher and distributor Les Belles Lettres went up in flames for no apparent reason. The victims: three million books, including the Universities of France Collection, better known under its nickname the Budé Collection, consisting of Greek and Roman classics as well as other rare, scholarly works on the Chinese, Indian, and Arab worlds, among others—truly belles lettres, we could say.

Although this destruction involves but one library, in a context of a general decline of knowledge, this disappearance of books, some of which were published and kept in inventory since 1960, is an absolute tragedy. Because their sales were microscopic, the logic of management will never support their reprinting. The books that Les Belles Lettres, a publisher that is a paragon of classical studies, felt morally obligated to keep in its catalog during the last century, despite lack of any financial benefit, can only end up in the oubliettes, sacked like those titles that the large libraries allow to drift toward a physical death because of how rarely they are consulted.

Even if getting rid of stock that doesn't move is a godsend for any publisher, such destruction is merely another hole in the countryside of French texts—or those in any other language. Would you like to discover the outrageous gossip of Procopius regarding Theodora or *Adolescent Eros*? No date is set for the reprint, you will be told. Out of the ashes of some sixteen hundred titles, twelve hundred will be reborn, though much more modest in appearance, of course. They are to be digitally printed and bound in a color reminiscent of the old candy-pink covers. And for the less saucy works—for example, the *correspondence* of Nicephorus Gregoras and even utterly ridiculous books such as *The Relationship of China with India,* written in 851 by Abu Zaid al-Hasan and based on travelers' tales—you will need to find a library that still owns these books.

Half of Europe was covered in a muddy soup in September 2002, and the tourists whose vacations were ruined mingled their lemon yellow raincoats with those of the consternated librarians. An incalculable number of books were left floating in an incomprehensible event whose consequences are still being evaluated almost everywhere.*

A fire destroyed the château of Luneville in Meurthe-et-Moselle on Thursday, January 2, 2003. It was the property of the defense ministry, and because television loves masterpieces that have been struck with misfortune, this "Lorraine Versailles" became a national cause in the space of a weekend—though its library remains without its eight thousand books of military interest.

Not only the West has suffered recently from the destruction by the elements. The six hundred stalls at the Calcutta Book Fair vanished in flames in forty minutes on February 3, 2003. Two-thirds of the exhibitors were very small publishers who had borrowed money and brought all their stock, as this was an opportunity for them to earn half their yearly sales figures, given the scant presence of bookstores in the country. Only the twenty-two British publishers present had taken out fire insurance. According to Ex Libris, they set up a fund to support their colleagues.

Finally, what can today rightfully be called the Lyon Affair deserves separate examination, because, if truth be told, Lyon is never completely at war or completely at peace. On Sunday, February 16, 1997, arson

---

*See, for example, www.unesco.org.

entirely destroyed the anarchist bookstore called La Plume Noire (The Black Feather) and all of its inventory. At about the same time—but this obviously has no connection—we can recall the ramming-vehicle and fire attacks on the synagogues of Minguettes in Vénissieux (October 14, 2000) and of La Duchère (March 23, 2002).

Similarly, in June 1999, in the particularly troubled ambience of the Plantin Affair, which revealed the repeated indulgence for revisionism from the universities Lyon II and Lyon III,[1] a fire suddenly broke out at the university library on the quai Claude Bernard. Founded in 1866, this important library originally housed several collections gathered after the separation of church and state, including that of the Oratorian Order of Tournon, a large seminary and archbishopric; seventeen thousand volumes from before 1800; manuscripts; and incunabula. Its buildings, constructed by Abraham Hirsch, became the law school and the school of the arts in 1930. Successive acquisitions and donations had pushed the total number of books in the collection to 469,000 when the fire broke out on Saturday, June 12 at 1:30 A.M. Lieutenant Colonel Serge Delaigue said it must have been smoldering for some hours in order to cause "the entire top floor to go up in flames" so suddenly. Against the black backdrop of the night sky, the city then saw the unforgettable flames fed by three hundred thousand books, which destroyed the roof.

A month later an investigation was opened to arson after traces of hydrocarbons and their spontaneous combustion were discovered at two spots in the blaze. The press noted in passing that tens of thousands of old theses submitted at Lyon II and Lyon III had been annihilated. "According to the experts, this scientific heritage would be very difficult to reconstruct."[2] After the surviving books had been sent for adequate treatment and after various committees began work on rebuilding the collection, and after the dome of the Hirsch was replaced, the investigation came to a standstill and time passed. On July 31, 2000, another fire broke out at the archives of the law courts. The firefighters were unable to enter the reserve, which was protected by an armor-plated door whose opening mechanism had been disabled by the heat. In the time it took to cut through it with a blowtorch, thousands of sealed documents were transformed into cinders,[3] including the tracts oddly blaming "the Jewish lobby for setting fire to the university library" and material that eventually would have allowed legal proceedings to be initiated against the academics whose theses had burned a year earlier.

A little more time passed. Finally, on Monday December 3, 2001, a nonsuit order was handed down: although the criminal origin of the fire was proved, the public minister decided against pursuing the matter, given the lack of results from the investigation. By December 2001, the matter had already been forgotten by any who may have taken an interest—except for some of the neighbors of the Hirsch. On this political crime "a fine offense of indifference has been grafted. . . . This nonsuit must not mean that there was no tragedy, no criminal act or even an event—that an attack against thought could be repeated by an attack against memory."[4]

It has been noted by the people of Lyon that at the time neither the minister of culture nor the minister of education ever showed himself or displayed any great loquacity concerning the deeper meaning of this tragedy. Suddenly, their names were also forgotten. The moral of the story is spelled out by an online encyclopedia, which asserts that the conflagration of the Lyon library was a pure accident.

It is an observation that heralds nothing good.

THE LIBRARY AT SEA

High pieces of furniture of violet-black ebony inlaid with brass, held upon their spacious shelves a large number of books, uniformly bound. They followed the contours of the room, terminating at the lower parts in large divans upholstered in chestnut brown leather and curved to offer the greatest comfort. . . .

"Captain Nemo," I said to my host, who had just spread out on one of the divans, "this is a library that would do honor to more than one palace on the continent, and I am absolutely amazed when I think that it can follow you into the depths of the sea."

Actually, the luxuriousness of the room with twelve thousand volumes, which Aronnax looks at here, is nothing next to the privilege of reading in the heart of the abyss. Here there is the fragile accumulation of paper, instrument of the platonic domination of the world, installed as if at home in the heart of darkness. In this reverse image of the fortress of Alamut, Jules Verne expresses the most powerful fantasy: domestication of the ocean. He triumphs over the anxiety inspired by the idea of sinking at the same time that he plays on the very final and brutal loss of books swallowed by the waves.

The effect of such a trauma is quite in keeping with its cause. The hair of the merchant Guarino Veronese immediately turned white when he witnessed the sinking in the Mediterranean of the boat carrying the unique manuscripts he had just acquired after the capture of Constantinople in 1453. The rich library of Gian Vincenzo Pinelli, claimed by his Neapolitan heirs after his death, was located in Padua, and was loaded, along with the rest of his effects, on three boats, two of which safely made it to port. The third was inspected by Turkish pirates. Furious at finding nothing on board but scholarly material, they threw the thirty-three chests into the sea. Says the humanist Peiresc: "This poor library was so unfortunate that it lost I know not how many chests to the Adriatic Sea while traveling from Venice to Ancona by order of the heirs." But all was not lost. According to Tiraboschi, Walford reports, the books washed up on to the beaches and were used to patch holes in boats. We know that numerous manuscripts from the two other vessels, as well as those that were plucked from the waves, were purchased for the Ambrosian in 1609.

The sea showed a crueler face to the Dutchman named Hudde who, Walford says, having made a fortune, threw himself into the study of China and its language and literature to such an extent that he even became a mandarin. Returning to his own land after thirty years, he saw his Chinese library sink beneath the waves. Shipwreck was a common occurrence. The history of the British East India Company shows it lost a third of its vessels with all that they had on board.

In 1819, the postal ship *Albion* was "the first merchant ship to be equipped with a library." Thus it was the first shipboard library to perish at sea (in April 1822, off the coast of Ireland). The library of La Pérouse, on board *La Boussole,* included 119 titles, among them Cook's voyages, Hawkesworth's voyages, and scientific works, which, according to Carlyle, suddenly "vanished trackless into blue Immensity." This shipwreck, which long remained a mystery, caused nineteenth-century imaginations to boil. Also notable is the case of the *Peacock,* a sloop that broke in two on July 18, 1841, and took down with it its crew and a collection of 150 scientific works "that found a sailor's grave."[5]

The first public libraries on ocean liners were formed from the books the officers shared with the first-class passengers. The Hamburg-America Company made a name for itself by having a "small library on board" each of its steamships. When these ships were transformed into floating palaces, the first step was to enlarge the rooms, including those for reading: In 1891, the library of the Cunard Line's *Campania* measured 210 square feet. It had a highly decorative, coffered ceiling with electric lights; the pillars holding it up were covered with blue velvet; and its mahogany paneled walls were enriched with Burmese rosewood. The books were housed in niches with glass doors to protect them from inclement weather.

The *City of New York* (Inman Line); the *Teutonic,* "well installed with good, standard books" near the promenade deck; and the Cunard Line's *Mauretania* ("one of the richest") were surpassed by the Hamburg-America Company's ships, says Calvin Winter. They held "the largest and most complete" libraries of the liners, one for each class, with books in four languages, totaling sixteen hundred to seventeen hundred per ship. This was also the case for the *Queen Mary* in 1936, with "two thousand volumes just for the cabin class, one fourth consisting of the best contemporary literature; sixteen hundred for tourist class; and one thousand in third class."[6]

A necessary distraction for these times without cinema and a confirmed social symbol, the assemblage of books sensibly lined on their costly shelves were an instrumental part of this floating world, which ventured across the seas with a renewed shudder every time the boat cast off and, from time to time, sank majestically beneath the ever-icy waves. The *Titanic,* for example, held two libraries. The first-class library was located on deck A and was decorated in Louis XV style, based on details borrowed from the château of Versailles. The books were loaded on in Southhampton, and we know that the selections of the book club the Times Library were part of it, including *The Old Dominion* by Mary Johnston, an 1899 work that related stories of escapes to London. A colonel who survived the disaster told how he had read and returned this work a few hours before the calamity. In second class, on deck C, there was a library that was thirty-eight feet by sixty feet, paneled in sycamore in the Colonial style and stocked with mahogany furnishings. Its books were housed in wardrobes with glass doors that lined one of the walls. As for the third-class passengers, whose doors were locked at night, the International Mercantile Marine Company had not deemed it worthwhile to supply them with a library.

> Then this vast outpouring of electrical wastes subsided, and soon the *Nautilus,* transformed into the coffin of Captain Nemo, lay resting at the bottom of the sea.

THEFT

The adventure of a library open to everyone cannot be separated from the history of crime, or at least of pilfering, which often opens the door to the worst crime: vandalism. Whether the book thief sees the book as a tool he cannot otherwise obtain (much like the student in the Middle Ages), something with which he can wrongly enrich his personal collection, or the means to earn his daily bread (through resale), the book of a public library constitutes the easiest prey in the world. In some Latin American countries today, it is enough to walk in and serve yourself. The ten centuries of existence of the library of Notre Dame of Paris are riddled with the purchases of new chains, appalling stocktakings, investigations, oaths, and sanctions against the unscrupulousness of the reader or the negligence of the sacristan who performs the duties of librarian.

But when it comes to pathological bibliophilia, the French remain rank amateurs. John Bagford (1650–1716), bootmaker, bibliophile, and founder of an antiquarian society, spent his life in libraries all across England, ripping out the title pages of 3,355 old books, with an eye to publishing *The Art of Typography,* a work that would never appear but for which he distributed a prospectus in 1707. Found in his collection are all the works of Cicero printed in 1606; the works of Ovid, Boccaccio, Swift, and Pepys; the intriguing *A Speedy Remedie against Spiritual Incontinencie,* from 1646; and *The Antipathy betweene the French and Spaniard* (1641) by Robert Gentilis. This concentration of a library of rare books was bound in one hundred folios that today, despite their provenance, are the pride of the British Library and an important subject of study. In fact, Howard did Bagford's portrait and had it engraved by Vertue.

Such a splendid love for books could not help but quickly create emulators. In 1749, Joseph Ames (1689–1759) published *Typographical Antiquities,* about which he was proud to say, "I chose not to make my book from catalogs, but used the books instead"—and in fact he tore out as many as 10,428 fragments that pleased him from books dating from 1474 to 1700.

If book theft is as old as bookstores and libraries, the latter more than the former are loath to speak about it, as if to do so would be to acknowledge their vulnerability and attract even more audacious abstractions. The National Library of France will give to anyone who asks a demonstration that theft does not exist. Scarcely noticeable there are a few "lack of space" and "absence noted after stocktaking" notices, which suggest that the work is really there but is in a new section or has been wrongly shelved and will eventually reappear in a generation or two; the researcher should plan to return then. The two copies of *Luftkrieg und Litteratur* by Sebald have been absent from the students' and researchers' shelves for almost a year—supposedly to be rebound. Bringing their absence to the attention of the upper echelons after having pointed it out to the middle echelons for six months was enough to see them back in their place—unbound, perhaps bought new.

There are, however, several studies of theft in public libraries accompanied by precise figures. These are English, by chance. Should we venture to mention it to Tolbiac,* we will be told in response that people of that nature prefer a job that is done to one that is well done; their statistics necessarily raise doubts and, to say the least, cannot be extrapolated. In short, only France knows, and France prefers things vague and out of focus. Millions have been spent at Tolbiac to counter shoplifting. This makes the rare shoplifters laugh, which annoys the numerous readers.

One of these colorful studies dates from 1935. Ralph Munn, director of the Carnegie Library of Pittsburgh, indignant about the petty theft of 134 books that had been noted for the year 1933, succeeded in reducing the number to forty-three by installing a monitor at the exit. Yet because the monitor intercepted 291 books that people were attempting to steal, it proved the phenomenon was greater than had been thought. Munn blamed this on the loss of a moral compass caused by the Depression. It had "popularized the idea that one could take anything not nailed to the ground or to the wall."

A specialized department of the British police conducted the other investigation, which is less amusing. At that time, the total number of all the books in the kingdom's libraries was estimated at two hundred million copies. The sole way to know if a book "missing from its place" was not merely the result of misshelving was to conduct a complete physical inventory; however, one third of the libraries did not have the means to perform this audit. The definitive absence of works from those who could meet the requirements of the investigation was 4.4 percent, meaning 8,800,000 books or 185 million in pounds sterling. It was noted, though, that the proportion fell to 1.9 percent for collections of fewer than ten thousand books, that it was generally higher for books acquired for less than a year, and that it involved mainly works of nonfiction.

The subjects of choice for thieves in the United Kingdom are, in decreasing order: sex, telepathy, foreign languages, black magic, music, and literature and the arts—with the emphasis on sex in the big cities and on black magic in the smaller communities. Agreement was made

---

*[Tolbiac is the name of the street on which the BNF is located. —*Trans.*]

on the effectiveness of the solution, which consisted of the tag or electronic marker, but only 36 percent of the libraries possessed the means to install these. All forbid backpacks and schoolbags, but none prevents the reader from keeping his coat on, as is called for in 8 percent of specialized libraries and 4 percent of academic libraries.

Well-organized professional thieves take advantage of the public collections of rare books to meet a growing demand that is less and less hindered by shame and better outfitted for communication. A Spanish priest and a Spanish professor stole 166 valuable books from the diocese of Zamora, and then sold them to institutions or collectors in San Francisco, Milan, Bogotá, and Paris between 1994 and 1996. In the teresiana of Mantua, five hundred works disappeared during the renovations of 2001. Out of the 260 known examples of *De revolutionibus orbium celestium* by Copernicus, a good percent (seven in 2002) are permanently being looked for by Interpol, and the FBI is searching for the forty-nine Chinese books—each of which is said to be more than one thousand years old—stolen from the Harvard University Library (though we know not how) by one or more connoisseurs. *De Humani Corporis Fabrica* by Vesalius (1552), stolen from Christ Church in 1995, recently reappeared in Niigata, Japan, in the library of the school of dental arts, to which it had been donated. Oxford loudly demanded it back, but because the work had traveled in the meantime among the hands of five or six English and American organizations and private citizens with sterling reputations for honesty, such as Sotheby's, this has become an actual case.[7] The thief was a specialist in Baroque music at the BBC who regularly gave conferences at Oxford University. He spent two years in prison, perhaps perfecting his Latin.

Whoever has the privilege of visiting the London Library on St. James's Square knows the unique experience of becoming, for several minutes or hours, his own librarian in a venerable building. The borrower buries himself in the narrow galleries on one of seven levels, in search of the desired book—or for something completely different, which would be even better. Founded in 1841 by Thomas Carlyle and several colleagues (George Eliot and Charles Dickens were early members), it is the largest private lending library in the world, with more than one million volumes. The annual dues are as high as 150 pounds. That the Queen Mother was its royal patron does not prevent a visitor from finding some forty shelf marks by or about Leon Trotsky, including two biographies in French. A borrower is thus among good company, and the integrity of the place always rested principally on the excellent education of its eighty-five hundred members—until 2002, when William Jacques was arrested.

He had been pillaging the library for four years, as he had done at the no less admirable library of Cambridge, where he was a student. Hundreds of well-chosen seventeenth-century editions thereby found themselves on the road to the sales room: the *Sidereus nuncios* and *Dialogo* by Galileo, a copy of *An Essay on the Principle of Population* by Malthus, as well as a first-edition Copernicus and one of Newton. It seems that the judges condemned the young man to an even heavier sentence because he had not read any of the books he pilfered.

This was fairly similar to the case of the thirty-two-year-old teacher with a degree in mechanical engineering attracted—we know not why—by ancient books. He was a self-taught Latin scholar and burglar who was mixed up in an affair straight out of a Gaston Leroux novel that took place at Mont-Sainte-Odile. The vaulted library of this monastery founded in the eighth century—where, incidentally, was created the *Hortus deliciarum,* which was burned in Strasbourg in 1870—was being emptied of its most admirable books on a regular basis, and the prayers and new locks could do nothing to halt it. As a discerning touch, the thief left a rose in passing. Confronted with such determination, disguised gendarmes blended in with the boarders and cameras were installed until a dark silhouette was finally spotted slipping out of a wardrobe, whose removable back allowed access to a secret door that opened onto a windowless room, where a rope hung. Apparently, this fan of medieval history had discovered the passage in an archaeology magazine.

After having gone through a dozen of the books, he returned the thousand volumes, including ten incunabula and manuscripts that he had stolen in valises. Once upon a time, the newspapers would have written: "To what depths can the frequenting of old books lead? The young man sighed in his cell." But the judge was sensitive to the thief's childlike joy in books and especially to the fact that he had returned everything. The teacher was spared a prison term. Magnanimity on one side of the Channel, severity on the other.

Despite his cleverness, the shadow of this amateur pales in comparison to obsessive personalities such as Stephen Blumberg, of the United States, who, in twenty years, had fine-tuned his interior decorating skills with a collection of 23,600 books at the expense of 268 public, private, and university archives in forty-five states and two Canadian provinces.[8] He made his acquisitions most often at night, like any ordinary burglar, which was the trade he also plied to earn a living, but he would also work during open hours by replacing the library stamps with his own. This is why he swallowed his rubber stamp the day he was arrested. The owners recovered their property when it could be identified, but because the thief had rubbed out or bleached the ex libris in the large majority of cases, his exceptional booty eventually ended up as part of a huge auction sponsored by the FBI at the beginning of the 1990s.

Because most libraries are unaware that their books have been stolen—a danger equal to that posed by frequent fires—American public institutions seem easy prey for professional thieves. A 1998 audit of the Library of Congress revealed that at least three hundred thousand of its titles were missing—a great enough quantity to set up a large library in an average-sized city. It is also estimated that twenty-seven thousand illustrations have vanished from its nineteenth-century books on travel and botany.

It was necessary for the Argentine National Library to catch red-handed Luis Alberto Videla with eight maps he had just cut from the *Theatrum orbis terrarum* in order to discover that at least 220 priceless documents from the seventeenth to nineteenth centuries had also vanished. Rather than blaming the incompetence of personnel, the Mafia was fingered. In truth, the collection is run much like a ghost library: For a total of 130,000 square feet there are fourteen guards present in eight-hour shifts, meaning there are only four people on duty at any one time. This affair of stealing allowed a horrified Buenos Aires to discover that the two million works in the National Library had never even been cataloged or insured, thus the full extent of its losses could never be known.[9]

For its part, Scotland Yard estimates that forty-five hundred maps and ancient blueprints are missing from European archives. In fact, a single page with good provenance can bring up to ten thousand pounds. The map rippers pass themselves off as somewhat comical scholars, with their overlarge raincoats, and have a deft hand with scissors to the detriment of cultural legacy. Among them are Peter Bellwood, of Leeds, and especially the ancient map seller Gilbert Bland, who made his cutting skills into an industry in the United States and Canada and most likely in European libraries as well. His shameful story is told by Miles Harvey.[10]

Crime turns petty when it strikes modest libraries: The complete atlas that is several decades old can be turned into a best seller once it is separated into single-lot maps that are then listed on sites such as eBay, which has definitely become the fence of the planet, offering cuneiform tablets from Mosul and small squares of ancient calligraphy on vellum mounted as jewels. Highly valued by apartment decorators, a page from a reasonably old atlas is worth at least fifty dollars. Generally speaking, it is probable that books of real paper (that is, handmade paper) bearing nice typography will one day suffer the same fate and end up cut up and sold in framed pages as if they were manuscripts. Perhaps next the pages of all physical books will exercise a frankly fetishistic attraction in a world of dematerialized knowledge.

DEATH

If God created man in his own image, it is legitimate for the philosopher to ask: Wouldn't heaven then be an immense library?

GASTON BACHELARD[11]

The obvious advantage of a belief like this is that building Paradise at home is within the reach of all of us. Who hasn't dreamed of this harem without eunuchs, a room whose walls are entirely paneled by books, where we can devour some subtle hodgepodge near the fireplace while the shadow of the flames lovingly—and silently—caresses the bindings?

Matthias Corvinus, Walter Benjamin, Enver Hoxha, and Nicolae Ceauşescu[12] each has the right not only to buy the books he wants but, more important, to keep them in his preferred order or disorder. Isn't my life only a rough draft of my library? Yes, without a doubt, for my library dies with me, unless not a single book ever changes place—ever. Walter Benjamin reminds us: "As Hegel said, it is only with darkness that the owl of Minerva begins its flight. It is only at the time of his death that the collector is understood." This was not the case with Montaigne: His books were offered to the parish priest of Auch, who made haste to pull out his wallet. Everything was lost at once: the books, the catalog, the very atmosphere of the tower where the author had lived "like a king."

People suspect that our choice of books is quite telling—but the way they are arranged is even more so. The collector can give books the most exquisite neutrality: "Monsieur Guermantes," says Proust, had all his books bound identically so that he no doubt saw "a greater kinship between *Eugénie Grandet* and *La Duchesse de Mers** than between *Eugénie Grandet* and a one-franc novel by Balzac."

The best example of the opposite situation is the Warburg Library, whose descriptions sometimes border on the fantastic. Aby Warburg was the eldest son of a major Hamburg banker. He said that his discovery on-site of Hopi culture in 1895 to 1896 enabled him to gain entrance into and to better analyze the Quattrocento, which he already knew quite well.[13] His obsession with books must have taken root practically at birth, because when he was eighteen, he offered to surrender his rights as eldest son to his brother Max in return for Max's promise to pay all his brother's bookstore bills. Fortunately for Max, this did not happen; he would have been the loser in that arrangement. In 1889, barely at the age of majority,

---

*A small, 287-page book by Countess Lionel de Chabrillan published in 1881 by Calmann-Lévy. We would know more about it if it were not held captive on microform at the National Library.

Aby Warburg obtained a sufficient allowance from his father to create a research library that he spent his life developing—and categorizing.

In 1911, this library had reached a size of fifteen thousand books, which Warburg exhausted himself "shifting about endlessly. Each progression shows his system of thought; every new idea on the inter-relationship of facts prompted him to change the position of the corresponding books."[14] For him, "the book one was looking for was not necessarily the book one needed." Until this time, categorization systems were in a line of descent from Bacon's order (1605), adopted by "that great gatherer" Gabriel de Naudé in his famous *Advis* and followed by Jean le Rond d'Alembert, then by Jacques-Charles Brunet in 1810. At the opposite extreme we have the decimal system of Melville Dewey, which appeared at the end of the nineteenth century (the prefix *100.* is assigned to philosophy, *200.* to religion, *300.* to the social sciences, and so forth), which is Bacon's system reversed and prevails in the world today because it tells us both what the book is and where it can be found.*

The devil take such logical reasoning! Aby Warburg made his life-work an art that consisted of making books more meaningful by their relation to their neighbors. According to his first director, Fritz Saxl, he located "books of philosophy next to books on astrology, magic, and folklore, and linked the sections on art with those on literature, religion, and philosophy. For Warburg, the study of philosophy was inseparable from that of so-called primitive mentality: Religion, literature, and art figure in the study of language; neither one nor the other can be isolated." The philosopher Ernst Cassirer went Saxl one better by saying:

---

*The Library Hotel, which opened recently in the shadow of the New York Public Library, categorizes its ten stories and sixty book-crammed rooms with this system. For example, room 800.002 is designated for the classics, and so on. Do not go in the wrong door, however: Room 800.001 contains the licentious shelf, no doubt for passing hellish nights. [In French libraries, *enfer*, "hell," is the section where forbidden books are housed. —*Trans.*] The idea is charming and the place is elegant. But in the land of copyright, the heirs are king: The Online Computer Library Center, which claims the right to Melville Dewey's estate and banks five hundred dollars a year per library using this system (in other words, a hundred million dollars for doing nothing more than adding a zero from time to time so the idea does not fall into the public domain), has filed a legal suit against the Library Hotel and demanded three years of its profits from the time it opened, thereby giving a new meaning to the word *bookworm*.

"From the sequence of the books emerged a series of images, themes, and original ideas in ever clearer fashion, and behind their complexity, I eventually saw standing out the clear and dominating figure of the man who had built this library, his personality as seeker plighted to a profound influence."

In the 1920s Warburg's large house had become a labyrinth of books nestled into every nook and cranny. He was thus forced to construct a new building designed especially to make obvious the new mental order, the itinerary represented in this library. In 1926 the institution was opened to researchers. It held more than one hundred thousand volumes divided into four branches: action, word, image, and orientation. Three years later, however, Aby Warburg was dead. In another three years the Berlin book-burning took place. The definite astuteness of its director and the family, who were Jewish, barely allowed this collection to escape an easily foreseeable fate. A selection of sixty thousand books in 531 cases quickly departed for London, where, from warehouses (during the war) to premises increasingly adapted for their display, they went through a series of moves and reinstallations. Today, the Warburg Institute on Woburn Square, with 350,000 titles, claims to reflect the "living thought" of its founder, no doubt because the titles are categorized according to his four original sections. The building on Heilwigstrasse, with its carefully thought-out details, where Aby Warburg housed not only his body but also his imagination, as it is put in *Great Freedom,* was bought and dolled up by the city of Hamburg so it could install its Art History Institute there.

The dispersal of collections breaks the cement of books and annuls their added value: When Saladin hawked the Fatimid Library in Cairo, a contemporary observed that the admirable order that made it so valuable was the first thing to disappear. Look, too, at the destroyed library of André Breton, which managed to juxtapose the irreconcilable: Gracq and Gorky and *Le Crapouillot* and Doctor Crocq, Junior. Although these examples involve only alphabetical comparisons, with the illustrious Breton, the archaic is ever combining with the sublime and vice versa.

Furthermore, we saw only the gilded tip of the iceberg during the famous sale of 2003,* because, on the rue Fontaine, an undetermined populace of insignificant works formed a vivid gangue from which the experts extracted all they thought was juicy. Even before their inspection of accounting dexterity, it is plausible that the writer's daughter—who, according to the newspapers, was a social worker—had demolished the collage and made gifts of entire cases of paperbacks, among which was a *Blue Guide to Brittany,* stripped of its bookplate. Who will read it, now that it has expired twice? René Char states he is, somewhat comically, "living where his stiff book is found." But is it his book or his *book* (see the Aristotle file)?

Perhaps the only one of its kind in the world, the Egyptian National Library offers the researcher a *maktabat almuhda,* a library of donations: Instead of adding to the magma of the general collection the books from the libraries bequeathed by the great writers, each of the thirty-three collections is displayed as it is, on U-shaped shelves that curve around the cells bearing the name of the deceased author. This arrangement makes it possible to visit a library of libraries. In succession, we can go through a group of highly polished and flattering bindings, rows of books in imitation leather that are not titled but are strictly numbered, or, conversely, collections of only stitched books, worn from intensive perusing and yellowed by tobacco. Each of them is a full-length portrait of its former owner. Often the same works can be found from one collection to the next, but they are never the same books—and they were no doubt understood differently.

In direct contrast to this is the collector whose atoms of tomorrow will be commingled with the other atoms of the cosmos, who arranges matters to ensure that the books he owns will be mixed in with those of the largest library on the planet without the slightest mark to distinguish them from their new neighbors, like the ashes of the deceased that are sprinkled over the soil of a vegetable garden. It is in this frame of mind

---

*[Breton's collection of books, art, and surrealist archives were sold at auction by the Drouot establishment to pay the large estate taxes due at the time of the death of his wife, Elisa. —*Trans.*]

that the narrator of *The Book of Sand* anonymously gets rid of a burdensome book, which he deposits on a shelf in the National Museum, by "trying not to look at its height or how far it is from the door." According to one of the many rumors surrounding the author, this is also the order given Borges's notary for the author's small and meager library, as in his novella *The Book of Sand.*

And at the extreme opposite, we have the example of Abu Hayyan al-Tawhidi.[15] Born in Baghdad, he died at almost the age of one hundred in 1023, perhaps in Shiraz, after a life spent wielding the calamus: His copied ten pages earned him ten dirhams, enough to live for one day. Viziers summoned him, spent time in his company, and then eventually drove him away. It should be said that his conversation could not have been any more profound, but after a certain number of exchanges and propositions, its highly unorthodox nature became evident. Al-Tawhidi had studied Ismaili and Sufi ideas as well as *falsafa* [pursuit of philosophy], and, in a word, he had become a *zindiq*, a freethinker, at a time when *zandaqa*, or freethinking, spelled death. The elegance of his highly valued discourse long delayed the coming of evening "where the sun of my age will go sleep." In the meantime, he wrote numerous books such as *Al-Imta' wa-l-mu'anasa* (Delight and Charm). He was much loved, and the preface to his *On Friendship* starts this way: "Above all, it is most helpful to be convinced that no friend exists, or anyone resembling a friend . . ."

Eventually, having become older than all his intimates, who had died, he set fire to his entire library and wrote: "It was painful to me to leave these books to people who would have mocked them and who would have stained my honor by studying them, rejoicing when they stumbled upon an omission or a mistake while leafing through them."

NINE

AN EMBARRASSMENT
OF MODERNITY

——————— ◗ ———————

In the ideal scenario,
the user would be unable to enter the library.

UMBERTO ECO, *THE NAME OF THE ROSE*

The bloody beak of the crow digs into the entrails of a palpitating pigeon. Prisoners behind the immense windows of the cloister—two livid Japanese; an old American with large, yellow glasses; two or three disconcerted students, one of whom is bearded—are watching this intense scene about which they can do nothing. They are all researchers at the National Library of France, distracted from their scholarly pursuits by the minor event of a bird that has just been stunned by flying into one of the bay windows* enclosing the trees of the central copse that are chained like bikes in a large suburban town. To prevent the feathered creatures from falling into the trap of transparency behind the trunks, silhouettes of blue gulls were finally glued onto the glass walls of the pit. Will the next pigeon sense the solid danger that stands directly behind the last pine? Wouldn't silhouettes of goldfish, instead of gulls, be more suitable?

———————

*Two hundred birds a year, according to the head administration. Thought has been given to establishing peregrine falcon nests at the tops of the towers. It seems these birds are the terror of crows, pigeons, and starlings—but then, what would terrorize the falcons?

Sometimes for better and sometimes for worse, the architect always strikes, whether in Alexandria or Montreal, Paris or San Francisco. Any historian of edifices built will tell you that the architectural gesture is made at the expense of the building's intended function. Yet the gesture can become downright criminal when it comes to libraries. Just as a book can cause the reader to forget his physical life in the pursuit of reading and reflection, the library environment should be drawn with more eraser than pencil. The sight of the mind kills the mind. It so happens that the new establishment on Tolbiac was conceived and realized through not only its users, librarians, and readers, but also the Ministry of Culture and even the most inconsequential intellectual, pushing away as much as possible.

Consequently, the project smacked of abberational provincialism from the very first sketch. Was it possible that not a single sycophant noted the sight of a book posed upright and open, a vision the four towers are allegedly meant to evoke, is torture to a bibliophile? We can then imagine a perverse dialogue, rife with misunderstanding, between the ill prince, in a dither from reading *Mont Analogue,* and the architect, who feels that this, now or never, is the occasion to surpass himself, though it is he who will soon be exceeded by the state-controlled weather vane. Everyone seems to find agreement on one point: Whoever aspires to knowledge is there to drool over it. Thus a prison—in addition, one dangerouse to enter—will be built for such individuals.* It is far away from everything: The closest metro station, brand new, with a name that comes within an inch of the crime of fraudulent advertising, is 772 steps away in good weather for a person with large strides and a pedometer in hand.

But this tragic story of ancient times has been widely told by, among others, Jean-Marc Mandosio, who often refrains from painting the

---

*Human appropriation of the hostile environment is a force against which even the best architect can do nothing. This natural mutation has already occurred at Tolbiac, sneakily beginning at the bottom: all the priceless, stainless-steel bathroom washbowls and basins that were intended to evoke a maximum security prison have recently been replaced by perfectly bourgeois white porcelain.

bleakest picture, despite a personal animosity that is a bit problematical at times, and François Stasse, who—almost—represents the other side.[1]

Tolbiac's evident future is a vast reading room with zenithlike lighting, as recommended by Jacques-François Blondel and his student Boullée,* which would take the place of the trees, long dead, at the level of what was named, in Grand Siècle fashion, *haut de jardin*.† The young students have returned to their university libraries instead of squatting on the site mythically created for people who never cracked open a single book.

An admirable ivory dome drawn by a disciple of Norman Foster rescues the parallelepipedal space wasted between the four towers and softens the silhouette. It is slightly evocative of Istanbul. Muffled and decorated in accordance with neo-Labroustian taste,‡ this pharaonic hall of three thousand alcoves welcomes the reader who clings to the reality of the book or seeks to flush out the rare idea. The tens of millions of volumes of the National Library are now gathered in a space of a few acres on two levels beneath the reading rooms, as they should be. The books can come and go in four minutes by means of a central well. The slide has been abandoned, and access to the premises from the street is through regular doors cut on each side of the pedestal, like the porch of honor, originally oriented toward the street intended for the library personnel's small autos. The towers, transparent again, now house offices and mainly the computer departments of the monumental BNF Online. Displays of geraniums are sometimes arranged over the handsome wooden terraces on the facade facing the Seine. Europe is flabbergasted.

Long before the building of the BNF, the prize for the most horrifying building scandal in the history of public libraries is, for the moment, held by San Francisco. Using a pastiche of the heavy, pretentious style called, in English, Beaux Arts, and having swallowed up $126 million

---

*[Blondel (1705–1774) and Étienne-Louis Boullée (1728–1799) were important French architects of the eighteenth century. —*Trans.*]

†[The Great Century (Grand Siècle) of France was 1598–1715, encompassing the reign of Louis XIV. *Haut de jardin* roughly translates as "upper garden." —*Trans.*]

‡[Referring to Henri Labrouste, 1801–1875, famous French architect. —*Trans.*]

in 1996, the new building in San Francisco kept its promise to be the avant-garde of the history of reading. Because it did not have enough room for its three million books, the management discreetly ordered that all those that had not been consulted in six years be sent to the dump, and the management was also ordered to rent a warehouse to store one third of the remaining stock until better arrangements could be made. Depending on the sources,[2] the quantity of books destroyed on the eve of the building's inauguration ranges somewhere between two hundred thousand and five hundred thousand volumes. Here, we can admire the dreadful conjugation of two young forces: architectural creativity and a love for dematerialized books. When the whole world, stupefied, learned that the British Library had done the same thing, we knew that the great extermination of libraries had begun.

A Hollywood-like desire to make a statement is partially to blame for the city of San Francisco's inability to resist the urge to bestow upon itself an affluent gadget under the aegis of science-fiction guru Kenneth E. Dowlin, author of *The Electronic Library* (already long obsolete), when a simple renovation of the "Old Main" would have cost ten times less. But this is not all that is involved here. There is also the profound presence of a purely American action that remains little known to (or carefully hidden from) the rest of the library world: *deaccession,* or how to get rid of books.

Whereas the English word *accession* defines the growth of a library by the addition of a book, *deaccession* expresses the annulment of this contribution and the elimination of the title from the catalog. In the catalogs of American booksellers it is common to read that such-and-such copy is a deaccession, and there are even merchants who specialize in books purchased from the community, whose stamp confers upon them a kind of pedigree. Given that the French word for *accession* is *acquisition,* its opposite is the term *désaccès* [deaccession] or *désacquis* [deacquisition]. Some librarians lean toward *dédomanialisé* [denationalized] or *désaffecté* [deconsecrated]. This dithering, however, is already an admission of guilt of sorts.

The libraries of the United States are foundations dedicated to a permanent quest for subsidies and financing. One of their major concerns is the enrichment of the collection, while another is the lack of space for a plethoric edition multiplied by the cost per square foot. Both of these factors combine to form one simple idea: Sell or discard. Capital execution takes place by shredding (the French term is *effilochage*, a papermaking term from the time of rag paper—at that time the French used the word *défilage*). Many institutions are reluctant to speak of this action, although it always appears in their account keeping: Figuring not far from the total number of books acquired during the year is the net quantity of books cataloged, the difference being what has disappeared.[3]

The very powerful American Library Association (ALA) acknowledges that no one knows when or where the phenomenon started and that no statistics on it are available. Yet a large number of deselection methods can be found in U.S. libraries, all intended for the apprentice. In the archives of the Glengarry Historical Society, for example, a certain David G. Anderson resorts to this expedient: "In order to purify the holdings of their secondary or superfluous elements and to reutilize the collections thereby obtained to develop or maintain the collection, every establishment (or collector) should have a deaccession policy. It is just good management." It is not necessary to surf the Internet very long to find announcements from the University of Illinois (the end of October), the University of Birmingham in Alabama, the Seattle Public Library (seventy-five to one hundred thousand books offered at each), and no doubt many other institutions regarding an annual sale of duplicate or outdated books.* Nevertheless, comments from the American taxpayer allow us to see a certain unease related to the practice. Who would want to leave their cherished libraries to such establishments?

Ba Jin left his library as well as his manuscripts to three institutions: the Museum of Modern Literature, the Shanghai Library, and the National Library in Beijing. About thirty thousand volumes were delivered in several trips in the crammed car of his daughter. All the copies

---

*The site www.librarybooksales.com has even chosen the slogan "Everyone wins!"

bore his signature: When he bought a book, he pulled a stick of ink and a brush from his pocket, wet the brush with his saliva, and wrote his name in it. Li Hui, a journalist of the *Renmin Ribao,* stumbled upon a copy of an old magazine in which he recognized Ba Jin's signature. A quick telephone call to the daughter of Ba Jin confirmed that all the copies of this magazine had been given to the National Library. Li Hui wrote a short piece on it for his newspaper. The next day, ten readers called him: They, too, had been able to buy books originally owned by Ba Jin.

As it turned out, the National Library had received 3,274 books (a unique collection of the complete works of Tolstoy, for example) from Ba Jin, including the fifth and last volume of his famous chronicles *Suixianglu* (Random Thoughts). His dismayed children requested the return of everything, most likely to give it to the Shanghai Library, and since December 2002, Li Hui has laid siege to the director of the National Library for an explanation. Yet the director is never in. It was at this time that the SARS epidemic began dominating news coverage to such an extent that we were deprived of the next episode of this saga, which gave a frightening lesson to the Chinese authorities, for whom secrecy is the ingredient *sine qua non* of good administration.[4]

Do French libraries throw away or sell their books? At least the National swears it does neither. Stuck between its patrimonial vocation and its role as legal depository, it can do nothing but keep its holdings and swell until it bursts or give its duplicates to its partners in the provinces. This activity is prettily described as *désherbage,* or "weeding," for those on the other side of the Channel and the Atlantic—as this term admits with uncustomary spontaneity that the books generously offered have a value equivalent to that of couch grass. It does seem, however, that the other institutions in the country have the right to pick up a little money out of the deal, after each title undergoes a thorough deaccession review by committee. Such is the principle, anyway, respected in Grenoble though not in in Poitiers, Brest, or Chambéry—but mum's the word; this is only a rumor.

Weeding was the subject of four concise pages in the annual report for the year 2000 of the activity of the General Inspection of Libraries, in which a writer who no doubt has developed a legitimate allergy to the book admitted to being "fairly frequently . . . surprised by the compact and fairly oppressive appearance of the shelves" of the establishments he visited. We can also read in the report that "the legal formalities connected with the necessary deaccession of the eliminated documents generally continue to be rather poorly carried out," and that among relegation to warehouse, pulp mill, gift, or sale, the sale "is probably the least popular."[5] This, however, is not certain.

The rare lending libraries that observe the procedure of weeding (the universities royally exempt themselves) and which, like that of the city of Grenoble, are not reluctant to discuss it offer lists of books that are worn from use or that are considered obsolete to a meeting of the municipal council before they become part of an annual sale or before they are sent to be pulped or are given as a reasonable gift (for example, to an association for the cultural development of any given penniless country).

Prices for sales to the public are fixed at 0.15 euro for a booklet to 7 euros for an encyclopedia, with the average classic set at .80 euro. The customers—especially those with a fetish for the *que sais-je**—start lining up early in the morning, and there is a limit of four graphic novels per person. Booksellers are discouraged from participating. This kind of sale causes a scandal when it takes place in the library building, but is much less controversial if held somewhere else. It is still necessary, however, to flood the city with leaflets before the sale, less to promote the windfall than to explain the meaning behind it. This is no doubt why the majority of France's libraries prefer sending books directly to be pulped. It represents one hundred times less work, but is nevertheless surrounded by a thick and discreet silence, as if it were shameful.

The scandal of Poitiers can be freely mentioned here—especially because it was seen on television. In the middle of August 1989, a Dumpster placed in the courtyard between the municipal library and the law

---

*[The "what do I know" series published by the University Presses of France, which provide introductory surveys of every topic imaginable. —*Trans.*]

school was suddenly filled with an undetermined number of eighteenth-and nineteenth-century books. Teachers served themselves delightedly from this bin, and the matter would have rested there if a bookseller who was hostile to the mayor at the time had not informed the newspapers that the city was throwing away books with an imminent plan for the removal of the archives. This caused a huge commotion. Dashing back from vacation, the poor director of the library, just several weeks from retirement, had to face the press and the audits ordered by the supervisory authorities while a general librarian was installed in Poitiers as an emergency measure to try to restore order to the house.

It took one year to find and compel the restitution of some of the "stray" books, which appeared in the homes of law professors who readily admitted to having books stamped Bibliothèque de Poitiers and Propriété de la Ville—an indication of stolen property. "If you find a book marked this way at a bookstore, which does not appear also to have the stamp marking its official removal from the catalog, then, in principle, you can just put it under your arm and leave without paying for it," said Jean-Marie Compt, the general librarian who had been rushed to the scene.

So, just what did happen in Poitiers? Did the director's assistant suffer the kind of sunstroke that often befalls public servants during the month of August? Was he trying to perform a good deed by getting a jump on what he imagined to be the superhuman task of the future transfer of the premises? He was not well liked. Without saying a word, his colleagues had simply allowed him to make matters worse. The report from the experts emphasized a number of dysfunctions at the library with respect to procedures and psychology. The Huchet report, in particular, clears the mayor of any evil intent. Nevertheless, all's well that ends well, as we all know: there is no longer a municipal library in Poitiers, but there is a François Mitterand Mediathèque, which is not at all the same thing—and its management never responded to any requests for information on the matter.

Thus libraries are now aware that they are mortal. Yet what do they fear above all else? Explosion. Here, I touch on a new plague that involves the exponential expansion of publishing: Throughout the world, hundreds of thousands of titles are added each year to those published the previous year throughout the world.* These titles clearly appear necessary to the publisher, a bit to the distributor, and sometimes only to the author. It is truly a parade, if we are to believe a 1982 study that estimates that each year 100 million paperbacks are destroyed by American publishers. "Few other enterprises routinely rely on the destruction of half their products to clear the market."[6]

The installation of new titles on bookstore shelves, in newspaper columns, and in library catalogs can be made only at the expense of other, older books, which sometimes provide a far better treatment of the same subject. This new library in relief is nourished by a kind of hollow, older library consisting of books that it would be a better idea to read than, say, this literary prizewinner of the day or that essay of the hour. The title *The Tempest* typed into the BNF server creates more than 120 listings for documents having to do with the air and weather before Shakespeare pops out of the compost. You can practically hear Caliban snickering.

Facing what should clearly be called a cataclysm, is the library going mad? We can find particularly alarming the affair of the British Library that raised such a fuss during the summer of 2000, when the press revealed that, at the least, eighty thousand books had been thrown out.[7] The 340-year-old institution had already had a good deal of trouble earning acceptance of its abandonment of the romantic rotunda of the British Museum for a new installation devoid of pride—a location that had already unleashed a flood of hostility and had even been dragged through the mud by one newspaper like a vulgar royal who had slept

---

*As we can read in Stasse, every year the BNF receives fifty thousand books sent just to fulfill copyright requirements, and then purchases an almost equal number of foreign books. Incidentally, these foreign titles are no doubt chosen with care, for they have to be paid for—so can we logically think that at some date in the far future the French collection will be, for the most part, synonymous with indigence when compared to the useful and intellectually more profound collection in other languages? As a small consolation, this question can be turned inside out, like a glove, to fit London or anywhere else, for that matter.

somewhere other than home one night. The simultaneous replacement of its director with a woman against a backdrop of privitization rumors did not fail to stir up the blaze.

All British subjects, even the illiterate, no doubt clung to the belief that the essential mission of this kind of establishment was to be "the library of last resort" from which no book that had ever existed in the United Kingdom could be missing. It appeared, nevertheless, that a researcher—a widely published author—stumbled upon five titles stamped "discarded," and, by way of explanation, was told that a new label was to be henceforth applied: "Selection for Survival," from the title of a 1989 report by a librarian from the University of Newcastle.

The general outcry provoked by this news increased tenfold when it was learned that the weeding had been entrusted to novice librarians, and it grew even louder when it encountered the ambiguous attitude of the new management, which had allowed circulation of a rumor that the practice in question had, in any event, been abandoned for lack of personnel. Under the circumstances, this was truly a far from sufficient explanation. The director of the collections, no doubt regretting being named Richard Bradbury, eventually abandoned the venerable library's customary reserve with a dryly stated declaration of three short sentences from which there emerged *a minima* that no rare books or copyright examples had been discarded. Over time, the indignation caused by old chimeras calmed down.

Then, in 2001, a new scandal broke, this time in the United States over the collections of foreign newspapers from the early part of the twentieth century, which the British Library had quietly rid itself of in 1997. The source of the disturbing revelation was Nicholson Baker, a writer known for his rages on the subject of unjust inventions (however microscopic in size) that are highly illustrative of modern decline—such as the plastic straw that is lighter than the old paper straw, which was nevertheless not heavy enough to sink to the bottom of a can of Coca-Cola—as well as for works that include a daring book which made him rich and famous. He discovered that London had spurned sixty thousand volumes, "thick as bricks," of bound weeklies and dailies, a stunning collection of newspapers from pre-Revolutionary Russia, 1920s Germany, and Occupied France, but also magnificent American sheets from 1900 with four-color Sunday supplements such as the *World* and Capone-era issues of the *Chicago Tribune*.

His investigation revealed that all of the U.S. archives had purged their stock of these cumbersome folios after having recorded them on black-and-white film. Baker acquired them himself to set up a foundation near his home in New Hampshire—the American Newspaper Repository. Seventy years of the *Chicago Tribune* cost $63,000, whereas the complete series on microfilm sells for $177,000. Baker writes: "We're at a bizarre moment in history when you can have the real thing for considerably less than it would cost to buy a set of crummy black-and-white snapshots of it, which you can't read without the help of a machine." For the rest, the British were quite clear: "Volumes for which there are no takers are destroyed." The translation of this terse statement is that such works would be sent to the mills to be pulped. It clearly seems that not a single library in the world wanted the offered albums, even for free.

Dostoyevsky saw the diversity and blended nature of a newspaper page as the best copy of the polyphonic image of life. Yet the exploration of the *New York Times* from 1945 on microfilm at the BNF actually brings to mind an autopsy in the dark.

Between 1850 and 1960, during the height of world literary production, billions of books were printed on abysmal paper—an acidic glue ate away the lignin of the wood, a process that no one knew how to eliminate. An internal reaction then also caused a change of color—an improvement on paper that was too blindingly white—a weakening of the fiber, and an increase in the stiffness of the pages, which made them brittle. This is why the prevailing belief among librarians is that because paper self-destructs, either it should be deacidified or its contents should be recorded on film, and sometimes both. Deacidification is a costly and laborious procedure whose long-term consequences are obviously not known yet.

Several large libraries have implemented large deacidification campaigns to halt the evolution of deteriorating paper. For example, in theory the new installation of the BNF allows the treatment of three hundred thousand volumes a year. Nevertheless, this determination is made ludicrous by the fact that not one government has decided to make permanent paper mandatory* in the publishing world, thus allowing the problem to grow unhindered. As for the transposition of an image of book contents onto microfilm, it seems that some archives are taking advantage of it to get rid of the burden of keeping the originals. That the process often requires the back of the book to be guillotined—a systematic procedure, at least for bound newspapers—makes the justification even easier: Newspapers must then be tossed.

But this "assault on paper," according to Baker, is based on an aberration: It is wrong to say that pages continue to deteriorate once the lignin has yellowed, and only those questionable bought-and-paid-for experts still dare state that the pages will crumble into dust. This is the amplified aftereffect of an old rumor started by microfilm manufacturers, who are well equipped for disinformation. In fact Bell and Howell, Xerox, Kodak, and other microcard companies could easily win this debate, for they were born in the world of espionage during the Cold War, and the librarians of the important American institutions maintained close ties with the CIA—many, in fact, were former members of the agency.

In 1973, the Library of Congress, among other institutions, invested in twenty-four cameras capable of producing two miles of microfilm a day. These needed to be fed. The librarians of the entire country thus threw themselves upon their books to give them the "double fold" test,

---

*The standards ISO 9706 and IS 111081 (1996) and the U.S. standard ANSI/NISO Z39 48 (1997) determine the quality of the paper made to last, which, it seems, should be made mandatory for every publication meant for a library or for every document to be archived. In addition, this would require the mandatory use of paper pulp entirely free of chlorine (totally chlorine-free, or TCF), which is far from being the case (elemental chlorine-free, or ECF, is allowed now). Sly wits have come up with the joke that the French book world respects primarily the standard they term ANLD (après nous le déluge). ["After us, the flood," a saying attributed to the Sun King, Louis XIV. —*Trans.*]

consisting of maliciously folding a page corner back and forth. If the paper broke, the book was a prime candidate for microfilming, which meant that readers would never again see it.

The current market for the reproduction of books decreed to be at risk in large libraries is estimated at $358 million in the United States alone. Librarians in Washington, London, and Paris refuse to acknowledge it but know full well that readers detest the microform (microfilm consists of reels, microfiche of flat sheets); to read it requires special machines that are noisy and always in use, and their screens are inevitably marred by various specks. In addition, to make it properly visible on the display terminal is a veritable chore: While a text on microfilm or microfiche can be consulted for a few moments for a verification or to find a quote, it is made distinctly illegible in its entirety through its tiring contrast of black and white or because it is frequently blurry when it is not actually scratched.

Each tome of the *Colección de documentos para la historia de Mexico* is represented by eight microfiches, but the index for its thirty-seven chapters is located at the end of the very last one. This means that the reader must engage in a game of constantly switching sheets (which quickly get out of order), but only if the image of this index is not completely blurred, which makes its twelve hundred pages useless. This book is effectively destroyed, just like Louis Baudin's *L'Empire Socialiste des Inka* and its "five acetate microfiches of sixty diazoid images 105 x 148 mm," a work whose lack of an index means it must be read it in its entirety, which requires a superhuman effort under these circumstances. The BNF Tolbiac has at its disposal seventy-six thousand microfilms and close to a million microfiches of so many works that a researcher will consult only under duress and whose paper originals he is forbidden by regulation to read. "The primary role of this house is conservation," a young employee scolds while looking askance at a patron. "You know, here most people work on recent books . . ."

Yet if by patient and indirect means we manage to see two or three original works—these still need to have been saved—we can note that the page color has perhaps turned a light orange or ocher, that in certain cases the edges tend to disintegrate slightly, but if the book is held and its pages turned cautiously (under the distrustful eye of the librarian, say, in a reserved section of the room for this purpose, which is called the hemicycle* in memory of the old days), there is no earthly reason why it will crumble into ruin. With regard to the danger posed by repeated use, this is also a fantasy: How many readers need to read Édouard Chavannes's *Les Livres chinois avant l'invention du papier*? Fewer than ten a century, no doubt, and a fairly limited number of football players among them. An extract of the *Journal asiatique ou recueil de mémoires, d'extraits et de notices relatif à l'histoire, à la philosophie, aux langues et à la literature des peuples orientaux*—a title of the kind a writer had time to make and read in former days, but one that is vaguely insolent today—was printed in 1905 on seventy-five pages in octavo on sturdy, excellent vellum paper with a satin finish, which is in perfect condition today and will be for centuries to come, except that one of the margins has become gray from the effect of the dust and raging pollution at the edge of the highway called the rue de Richelieu. The page offers the charm of a typographical composition, which beautifully integrates the famous Chinese characters, that was a specialty of the Imprimerie nationale (National Printer). Most likely printed in a fairly small number of copies at the author's expense, the thin pamphlet was bound temporarily by the National Library (copyright Seine no. 2022, 1905), and the collection did not deem it profitable to replace the binding with anything more solid, which would have to be broken in any case in order to photograph the text. This, then, is why the book is sick.

The most depressing information about this bogus, supposedly correct way to preserve collections is that, despite the assurances of the teeth pullers that accompany its advocacy, the plastic support materials of the microfiche and microfilm are perfectly perishable themselves and are already deteriorating. "Don't let that hold you back," replies the son

---

*[The hemicycle is the reading room of the BNF's original establishment on the rue de Richelieu. —*Trans.*]

of the microform seller. "Here is the CD-ROM—and then we will invent something even better," and on it goes.

At the current time, none of the solutions used or envisioned is truly reliable and guaranted over time. In addition, the transfer of data onto current disks will not prevent the frenzied evolution of materials, and nothing indicates that in the future there will be readers for a protection system deemed perfect today. Who remembers the somewhat dodgy and bizarre item called the floppy disk? It will thus be necessary with every new technological upheaval to start transfer of data at great expense and to perform regular verification procedures on the accurateness of the data—currently, this checking of data occurs every five years for the ordinary CD-ROM used for distributing the book online, and accuracy and usability are checked every twenty years for a century disk on glass sealed in titanium nitride or brass on which the original is allegedly kept. Given that public institutions are known for never getting the necessary funding for their building maintenance, we can only imagine that they will experience several major catastrophes before doing anything in the area of intangible information. This is the source of the grandiose paradox of spiraling, infinite expenditures that in no way relate to the cost of the original and that result from the decision to replace the paper book with its copy on another material—however insecure such replacement might be. Nevertheless, the transformation of life into bytes marches on and nothing can stop it.

Said that devil Louis-Sébastien Mercier so fittingly in 1771: "Our grandparents read novels in sixteen volumes, and these were not too long for their evenings. They were carried away by the mores, virtues, and combats of the old knighthood. Soon for us we will be reading only on screens."

TEN

FLAMEPROOF
KNOWLEDGE

———— ◗ ————

You can't consume much if you sit still and read books.

ALDOUS HUXLEY, *BRAVE NEW WORLD*

If American university libraries are getting rid of their books, it is for the purpose of buying fewer of them; their budgets show a greater preference for electronic equipment. Here is one consequence of this change: "At Colorado College Special Collections, we call the small books 'small.' They used to be called 'octavo,' for reasons still not clear to me." The ingénue wondering about this on the Internet in 2002 is a degree-holding librarian and archivist.[1] Would the height of relevance be a library with no past?

The collection of virtual books—meaning they are dematerialized and visible on computer terminals possibly before being printed—seems to confirm a hundredfold all the dizzying perspectives that books inspired when they were made of paper. Borges, for example, tells us: "I say that the library is endless." To better race toward this easy infinity where the book is no longer alone—maps, blueprints, images, and music all have no difficulty in finding a part in the farandole—the virtual book collection feeds primarily on everything that preexisted it by absorbing complete works in text mode or the increasingly numerous analogical facsimiles. These libraries include Gallica in France, with its collection approaching one hundred thousand books, and, in English, Project Gutenberg (6,267 books at the end of 2002), American Memory (Library of Congress), and what it is possible to discover through Bibliotheca universalis (the association of the national libraries of the richest nations) and Gabriel (the national libraries of all Europe).

It goes without saying that free, online reading is possible only for books in the public domain, although these boundary markers don't exist everywhere; the little mice can easily find the cheese. Many students now bless the widespread use of French or English around the world if only because they can download recent essays from university sites in the antipodes.

The second source (with the first being preexisting printed works) of the enrichment of the immense virtual library is the swarm of texts, along with the sounds and images that it generates every second, that flies into the hands of Internet users, seasoned specialists and amateurs alike, positioned elbow to elbow, who go online with the click of a keystroke. Bizzarely hatched in the nooks and crannies (if there are any nooks and crannies left) of the planetary brain, here they are commingled into a greater whole in a casualness that has no self-criticism or copyright. The intoxication of the electronic resource (the new name imposed on the library of the future) comes from the fact that everything is suggested, then offered to it; the copy/paste command replaces the pen, the click becomes the tic.

This cyber catalog will certainly replace the costly physical library for the majority of people, and much more quickly than anticipated,[2] but will it replace it completely? In the image of the expanding cosmos, the Internet is an unquantifiable future. In the eyes of the professional who surfs it every day, like a miner in the depths with battered fingers, almost all of it appears to consist of slag, plagiarism, and dead skins from sites that have molted—a vertiginous demonstration of stupidity and vulgarity. This observation is not important, in and of itself, to the extent that a lifetime would not be enough to profit from the information of a scientific level that the 5 percent remaining content allows us to obtain. Nevertheless, it shows that the new scriptuary galaxy does not superimpose itself over the old encyclopedic library in which everything, even the bad, can be used.

The problem posed by the storage of astronomical quantities of documents will be resolved—perhaps, though at a price as high as the preservation of these documents. As long as we work from paper, I do not see how the price of return will lower: Handling the pages of often fragile books involves skilled and precise manual labor. Yet the question of the faithfulness of the copy is already looming. Many electronic transfers of books are made from microfilm, an onerous process that provides somewhat fuzzy results but of which we can be sure that not a word is missing. This is not the case, however, if we want to work on the text obtained, say, for an extract of quotes—in which case, we would need to turn to character-recognition software such as optical character recognition (OCR) scanning. The experiment, easy and amusing, consists of scanning with a high-grade system, say, page 547 of Erik Orsenna's *L'Exposition coloniale*.[3] In OCR terms, *"l'amour de soeurs"* [sisterly love] is thus transformed into the love of *"saurs"* [smoked foods], which is much more aromatic. In *Pantagruel, "dist le compaignon"* [said the companion] is transformed into "disk the companion."

Of course, we can always pay a proofreader to compare the copies and follow the OCR scan page by page; administrative, bureaucratic waste has no price. When the National Library began digitizing its stock in 1992, it was declared that one hundred thousand volumes, or thirty million pages, would be transformed in three years. Yet by 1998 it had hardly achieved 80 percent of the results it hoped to reach. The page cost was close to 0.12 euro for the paper and 0.20 euro for the microform (ten or twenty times more in text mode, which is the only one useful for a researcher). With an average book length of 350 pages, copying a book works out to 42 to 70 euros minimum before it even goes online, not including the costs of transporting it, the selection, the implementation of the disk track function table/pagination—no one knows the real cost of its permanent presence in the ether of the Internet. If we can imagine that librarians—at least, those of today—would not raise a fuss if the backs of books were guillotined and the bindings broken, the BNF alone would require about a billion euros for all its stock to be consulted from a distance, and it goes without saying—although this is a taboo subject almost everywhere—that people would have to pay to use this service. At least, however, the problem of authors' rights would not come up.

What is about to take place has already happened before. The Athenian tyrant Pisistratus, who died in 527 B.C.E., proclaimed that he was buying the writings of Homer by the yard, at so much per line. It is easy to imagine that he suddenly discovered a great deal of Homer. This is what the grammarians Aristarchus and Zenodotus attempted to put right in Alexandria, by bringing to bear all their philological science or, in any case, their idea of what ancient texts were. "They studied the entire *Iliad* together, says Eustathius,[4] and corrected it as they pleased, and because it was too long to read and somewhat boring, they cut out several parts." Even earlier, Democritus felt the need to compile a Homeric glossary of rare and ancient words to facilitate reading. There was, then, no irony intended in Timon's answer to someone asking if a faithful version of Homer could be found no later than the third century B.C.E. Said Timon: "You can, if you stumble across one of the ancient copies, not one of the corrected ones today."

This transformation into air of a whole domain of knowledge is perhaps nothing more than a simple avatar of communication tools. The written work survives numerous traffic, not all of which it goes through without causing some harm. For example, this happened when the scroll* gave way to the form of the book we now know, the codex. This carving of the document into equal-sized rectangular pages that could be leafed through made it possible to skim through texts easily; the idea for it had been provided by the diptych of wax tablets.

This novelty was first synonymous with clandestinity. The Christians appreciated its platitude, if I dare say so. (Just try to hide a big scroll beneath your tunic!) When Christianity became a state religion under Constantine in 306, the codex had become the standard. The fourth

---

*From *rotulus,* meaning "read vertically," like the common computer, as opposed to *volumen,* "read laterally."

century busied itself with the transfer of texts onto pages made from hide, which were larger and more resistant than papyrus. This is when a fine purification that dares not speak its name goes to work: Obviously, what will be copied is only what is deemed worthy—as in Alexandria a few centuries earlier, as in Quianlong in eighteenth-century China, or even not far from there. "A pitiless manuscript tradition inspired by a narrow Confucionism constantly adulterated the poor works that had escaped by chance all manner of destruction." We owe this despondent assessment to Émile Gaspardone in 1935, when he compiled a large Annamite bibliography and was forced to note "no longer exists" at the end of one of every five listings.

In Peking as in Rome, the purifiers of Babel traveled through the pages, but this time, independent of any philological, confessional, or political concern, the rule was first shaped by the material: The theoretically infinite space—in at least one of its dimensions, leaves of papyrus glued to each other—must now be chopped to fit within a page closed on all four sides. This is not only why the major part of the images of antiquity were lost during this transition—a scribe is not an illustrator—but also why the volumen reduced the series of endless columns to two, most commonly, or a maximum of four. Texts were then amputated, and condensed versions began appearing. In complete good faith, we presume, a stratum of antiquity was reinterpreted to be more comprehensible to contemporary readers. "Only the works that, in the fourth and fifth centuries, seemed worthy of being read, because they still seemed relevant, were given the opportunity to make the transition from scroll to codex, and thus survive. . . . It is the breadth or narrowness of the era's tastes that determined our own cultural horizon."[5] We should also note in this regard that the weakness of the Western empires and the Islamic invasion aborted these salvage efforts, and that the world had to wait unitl the Renaissance to recover from antiquity whatever it was still possible to save.

The most formidable trump of the Internet, if not the only one with hypertext, is the power to update its information continuously. Newspapers have clearly grasped this and have dived in magisterially, to the point of competing with themselves and paving the way for their own disappearance by cashing in on the manna of advertising, especially services, promoting the sale of a complete hodgepodge from archived articles (which is frankly quite shabby, but, happily, not all do it) to theater tickets. We would expect as much vivacity from all the professional sites connected to culture and information. Let's pass over the numerous bodies and administrations whose electronic representations speak volumes on their pachyderm reality, but information sources such as general encyclopedias form the spearhead of this progress. It is understandable that their twenty-eight or thirty-two paper volumes—or even a CD-ROM—would be partially out of date when shipped from the printer, but a permanent information source for paid subscription should update itself the moment any given piece of data becomes official.

Yet any example chosen at random reveals that this is not the case: The Organization of the Islamic Congress (the United Nations of the Muslim world) comprises fifty-seven, not forty-five, nations. The online article in the *Encyclopaedia Britannica* has been out of date since 1948. As for its French subsidiary, Universalis, they were satisfied simply to put the raw mass of the paper edition online without verifying whether the screen highlighted any defects, including outdated data and personal opinions, empty phrases à la Roland Barthes, and openly tendentious information (for example, the burning of the Lyon library). A thorough, continuous updating should clear away all the dust, although it does open wider the window to the wind of disinformation.

If this kind of company is fallible, what can we expect from the creations of other corporations whose history is more noteworthy for their skill at rewarding (or duping) their shareholders than it is for producing and sharing learning? It is still acceptable, if somewhat despicable, for them to buy eminent publishing houses of dictionaries, encyclopedias, and reference books only to have them suddenly increase their profits tenfold by putting these publications online, but we may ask if all the scientific rigor that presided over their birth is to be followed in their digitalization and will carry over into the fine-tuning of the new contents. Based on how things have passed up to now, I would say the great electronic wave will more likely go toward intellectual simplification—meaning, mainly, the shortening of paragraphs, phrases, and words. It will end with summarizing, as Photius did, the books that people do not have the time to read or the means to understand. Louis-Sébastien Mercier earlier described this art of updating by placing its effects in the twenty-fifth century. Like Winston of *1984,* who adjusts Big Brother's past forecasts in accordance with the results obtained, it will be so easy then to change the meaning and the scope of certain historical events: when the analysis or summary replaces what has been named the document. Distortion on the sly will have an open field. The meaning of the word *digitilization* (which often slips into the French press in place of the French word *numérisation*) says it clearly: It is the installation of a venomous substance drawn from the digital.

In fact, computer language does only what is in its head, which is already fairly small and grows only by its own ignorance. Everything transpires as if conscienceless distortions and approximations facilitate domination of the conquered territory. The icon has severed its bonds with Russia; the adjective *virtual* replaces the immaterial—but only a short while ago it was merely a humble synonym for *potential.* Some of our most banal texts are thus in the process of taking on muffled ambiguities aimed at the readers of the day after tomorrow, who, in order to be penetrated, will have to be twice as clever as we are. This represents more lines for lexicographers to write—unless they decide to simply erase the original meanings given these words.

Three or four intangible infoconglomerates will soon share the copyright for all works essential to education and leisure, and our good old stone mastodons will become only long-distance content providers for research and advanced studies. Let's skip past the contradictory declarations of the institutions, the generally wooden language, and the exasperating slowness of the PDF format from certain providers, which sometimes allows the reader to drink his coffee between two pages of a digitalized 550-page book. All of these irritations will no doubt soon be forgotten with precocious rantings such as the invention of the e-book.

Skimming today through the enthusiasm of the year 2000 that was inspired by digitalized publishing and reading, we are struck by the strong odor the Internet imparts of decomposing bodies, broken links, and shops with closed curtains. Here is proof that everyone can be fooled, especially when everyone is urged to do so by the powers that be, with Microsoft and Adobe Systems leading the pack. We can see, however, a few bodies quivering among the cadavers: two or three publishers of technical documents for experts or accountants or dentist or surgeons, but primarily an armada of essays on flying saucers and the "true" Nostradamus, which provides confirmation of the natural tendency of the idea itself—one that, you could say, was interesting only on paper—to putrefy. Let's revisit the question of *litbouc** in twenty years, if you are really set on it.

London, at least, is convinced that the placement of the quasi-totality of collections online is the sole mission proposed for the future. Today, the British Library keenly desires to transform the lead of the past into future gold through a brand-new key position: the marketing director. Aided by a crew of one hundred, his mission is to create a modern brand image and advertising, and thereby accelerate the opening of the collection to the greatest number of the world's users. Facing the future with open arms means radical decisions: While truckloads of books and newspapers are being dematerialized, IBM is getting ready to pocket tens of millions of pounds sterling that could not be any less immaterial.

The architectural modesty of the new British Library already reads as the future, with its comfortable and pleasant work rooms that are well lit from the ceiling and with its armchairs—although unrecognized by home décor magazines—in which patrons can spend hours. Its efficient supervisory duties are performed by human beings, but the national library of each country will be open upon reservation only (on-site staff, as opposed to on-site computer technicians, will be scarce) for those who track the marginal science, the secret of a text deemed insufficiently worthy of world vaporization, and all those—often the same individuals—who, like the blind, demand contact with old books, the

---

*[This is an untranslatable pun on a homophone of *e-book* in French. *Litbouc,* which is a Rousselian neologism based on it sounding like *l'e-book,* means "read goat." —*Trans.*]

grain of the pages, that *sui generis* aroma, the reality of leafing through them, the *biblioteca de papel*, we might say ironically.

As can be seen in small-business trade the world over, only the specialized institutions will survive and thrive. The intermediary archive that currently satisfies (more than honorably) the needs and tastes of the public at large will vanish, for it, too, will soon be overequipped for electronic communication in the comfort of one's home. France certainly knows how to make good use of its language; it has rebaptized its municipal libraries [*bibliothèques*] médiathèques, because words beginning with *media* or *medio* reveal from the outset the vocation of what they designate.

It is easy to prophesize which of the these two readers—the pedestrian of books and the one who loads up his reading list and his credit card from his sofa—will still be able to generate a spark. But believe me, another literature will not fail to see the light of day—one that will seem new and will only be transcoded. The paper book will cease to be manufactured because the generalized desubstantialization of exchanges demands it: Liquid currency is vanishing from our pockets, and the newspaper has already become evanescent.

In the year 2100, students who express an interest in books will be told of the appalling process consisting of deforesting the Morvan or the Amazon (imagine them covered by trees) to operate the most complex factories ever built, which would never stop their release of dioxins in order to produce a sheet composed more of glue and chalk than paper pulp. This sheet would then be used to feed the print shops filled with Chaplinesque machines from which pallets of books that weigh a ton each are transported to warehouses, then wholesalers, who would send the new titles to a bookseller, who would give them to another transporter, after which a book would finally make its way out of the warehouse for a bookstore and eventually end up in someone's home, if not the pulp mill. And all of this rigmarole for ten to thirty units of the money of that time!

The incredulous young people will laugh, and they will take notes with a phonetic spell-checker that runs a constant stream of a flexible codex of two downloaded pages of all the works of the world mixed with music and films and sensations and aromas and heat. Sometimes one of their more marginal peers will pull out a text written as they were long ago, but he or she will rapidly abandon the deciphering of the swarm of ants called letters, whose relationship to ideas and facts now seems so little obvious that it causes a headache.

ELEVEN

EPILOGUE
Return to Alexandria

——————— ❦ ———————

> *The city of Alexandria will remain forever a symbol*
> *of letters and open-mindedness thanks to the writer*
> *Laurence Darel [sic] and his Alexandrian Quartet.*
>
> A RECENT ALEXANDRIAN TOURIST GUIDE

When receiving visitors, Professor El-Abbadi begins by inviting them out onto his balcony overlooking the site of the fire Caesar ordered set that destroyed the Great Library. It seems that the fire provides muted sound effects that ceaselessly permeate all conversation. In the span of a few moments the deed is done and visitors have caught Alexandrian fever.

An enthusiastic historian, the professor has devoted his life in one form or another to the mythical Great Library, and it was during the course of a conference in November 1972 that he floated the idea of rebuilding it. The president of the university, Lotfi Dewidar, took him at his word, and the project was officially launched in 1974, with the help of a third colleague, Fouad Helmy. Very familiar with the monstrous incompetence of the Egyptian administration, the trio decided to dispense with aid of any kind from Cairo. The matter seemed simple: the university owned the land on which the army was dozing, Helmy became governor, the scholarly world applauded.

Unfortunately, fate was not in their favor. A new university president reoriented the dossier toward a kind of cultural center; Helmy confronted Sadat over a nuclear center he was against, lost his post, and died; and a disappointed Dr. El-Abbadi left to teach in Beiruit. On his return in 1984, a new rector invited him to re-form a committee and, with the platonic but quite active aid of Moktar M'Bou, then president of a UNESCO that had a penchant for projects favoring the developing world (which was why it had so little money at its disposal), the first stone for the new library was laid in 1988, an architectural competition was initiated, and an appeal for funds was sent out to the international market. To reach this stage, the project for a university library, large and universal as it might be, had to be legally transformed into a state library and state project. This is where the generous and certainly not necessarily realistic original plan was undermined.

The first contributor, Prince Faisal of the United Arab Emirates, sent a check for $20 million. As soon as he learned of this, Saddam Hussein signed a check for twenty-one million dollars—and so on. As money poured in and an excellent, grandiose architectural scheme was chosen, this became too serious a matter for Hellenists, no matter how distinguished. One of the committee members, Mohsen Zahran, became the real boss and put a lid on the construction site, which had become a national if not international attraction. In 1993, the ground where the new library was being built was attacked by bulldozer, between one and five in the morning, and the remnants of the palace of the Ptolemys were thrown by the truckload into Lake Mareotis.[1]

The French archaeologist Jean-Yves Empereur as well as the architect and patron Muhammad Awad did all they could to alert world opinion, but the evil had been done. As the large reading hall of the new library descended fifty feet below sea level, it goes without saying that its foundations were beneath anything that could have been built in ancient times. A semblance of excavation work entrusted to Poland permitted in extremis the unearthing of two superb squares of mosaic, and finally a special museum was added to the basement of the new Alexandrian Library to display and attest to the royal nature of the terrain. Because Alexandria is an inexhaustible source of fantasies, it has been possible to read that the new library is feeding like a vampire on the corpse of the old one. The idea is charming, but the majority of historical speculations place the Mouseion farther west, generally not far from the crossroads formed by Nabi Daniel and Horeya Streets. Archaeology could pronounce an end to the mystery if it could step in as it usually does, but it is far from undertaking this role—it is known that any leader of an excavation is forced to spend more time in the administrative breach, trying to obtain an operating permit, than in the hole with his crews. So how, in this case, could the legendary Egyptian bureaucrats and housing developers have been allowed to prevent a mecca of science and history from being refused a permit? After all, wasn't the Rosetta stone discovered by Napoleon's sappers who interrupted the construction of a military site?

But this dustup would be just one additional example of universal servility before the yelping landowner* if it had not thrown the poor light of a bad omen upon the emerging archive.

Here is where the question of the books arises: This subject of perfectly natural concern for a library seems initially to have been treated in the most offhand manner at best, when all donations were solicited and welcome. For example, Saudi Arabia wholeheartedly offered eight hundred Qur'ans, and the incredible rummage sale of the university's ten thousand books took place during this same period. In the 1930s, the university had decided to install its library in a former Italian school, the Littoria, whose space, all at once, appeared desirable to the rector of the 1990s as a place to house the university's ever-growing number of office employees.

The rumor quickly circulated throughout Alexandria that tons of books were being offered in a hangar, each for the price of three Egyptian pounds (equal to a dollar at that time), no matter the size, age, or freshness of the volume. The Library for the Center of Alexandrian Studies was able to enrich itself with a small cabinet of travelers' tales from the eighteenth and nineteenth centuries stamped with the name of King

---

*France no longer has any lesson to teach anyone in this regard, because of the astonishing reduction in the budget allocated for archaeological conservation in 2002.

Fuad I, founder of the library. Still, they were among the last informed of this windfall and others were able to make off with works that were even more rare and worth much more. If this case of absolute weeding was not listed in chapter 9, it is because the university offered the collection to the new Bibliotheca Alexandrina, which turned it down.*

Now let's move past these events that are already forgotten and whose troubling implications are thus easily avoided by the former vice president of the World Bank, Ismael Sarageldin, 2003 director of the new Bibliotheca Alexandrina. Surrounded by the right people and, by all evidence, well advised, he has mastered the art of getting opposites to coexist and to take precautions against any and all eventualities. It was brought to his attention that the catalog of Bibliotheca Alexandrina included neither *The Satanic Verses* by Salmon Rushdie, *Mahomet* by Maxime Rodinson, *Awlad haratina* (the original version of *Sons of the Medina,* which earned Naguib Mahfouz a sharp knife in the back, though the French and English translations are in the collection), nor Haydar Haydar's the *Walima li A ʿshab al-Bahr (A Banquet for Seaweed),* a seven-hundred-page book that was first published in 1983 but whose 1992 reprinting prompted violent street protests in 2000 by the students of al-Azhar after an obscure imam who had not read it stated it was anathema. The problem this posed for the new Bibliotheca Alexandrina was that it showed proof of what, as seen from Europe, resembled appalling cowardice on the parts of the minister of culture and the president of the republic.† This kind of downward spiral is reminiscent of the Córdoban ulemas of a thousand years ago, whose exactions we run the risk of seeing repeated in Europe someday soon. All one of these individuals has to do is declare Mahfouz apostate in order to invest every believer (in principle) with the duty of putting to death this author. An

---

*In an interview, J.-Y. Empereur says the letter of refusal was signed only by Dr. Zahran, who contests it.

†Another stinging example of this can be found in the banning of a dozen books by the minister of culture and the condemnation of at least one of their authors to prison on the opening day of the International Book Fair of Cairo, January 24, 2001. See Tariq Hassan-Gordon, "Rights Group Upset over Banned Books," *Middle East Times* 14, no. 7, February 17–23, 2001.

enthralling and finely crafted study of the Centre d'Étude et de documentation economique (CEDEJ) by Mustapha al-Ahnaf[2] explains how to survive all this, at least in Cairo society.*

Books such as these, while they are not all extraordinarily good, now form part of the history of Islam. Dr. Sarageldin admits that a universal library cannot, in fact, refuse any book; he asks how it is possible to refute the theories of certain titles if it is impossible to read them. This is also one of the purposes served by libraries.[3] Consequently, such books are definitely there but, he says, in order to avoid any harmful action by some deranged individual, they are handed out only in the reserved section and on special request accompanied by personal identification.

With the exception of the manuscripts and rare books (which number sixty-five hundred, most of which were withdrawn from the municipal library), all the books at the new Bibliotheca Alexandrina are freely accessible. The immensity of the reading room and the small size of the collection (250,000 volumes, though up to this point the international press has highlighted the eight million volumes that could eventually be housed there) allow this kind of ease. Ismael Sarageldin is a delightful individual, and no one would be rude enough to ask him to find the four books to verify their presence. Coinciding with his enlistment was the promulgation of a special law referred to as Number 1 of the year 2001, followed by decree Number 76, which makes the new Alexandrian Library a private reserve for the head of state, protected from all his ministers and administrators, so that it might peacefully go about its business as a "center of intellectual, cultural, and multilingual radiance." This is all well and good, but is it also protected from the street?

The author of *Pyramids* and *The Epistle of the Destinys*, Gamal al-Ghitany, is literally swimming in censorship—first, because, as he says, he takes the risk of openly confronting censorship on a weekly basis

---

*With regard to France, it has had a foretaste of this with its own leagues of virtue and associations for defending the monolithic family, which complain with great hue and cry about novelists, who are always delighted to receive such unhoped-for attention.

with his literary magazine,[4] and second, because, as managing editor, he is officially invested with the duties of censor by the authorities. He is not the most devoted believer in Islam, but hanging on the wall facing him in his office there is a cheap but resplendent color print of Hussein, the son of Ali, which defies a double taboo. He thus dissects with an ambiguous tranquillity the way in which obscurantism weighs heavily upon Egypt: Corruption at every level of government, starting with the top (America floods the country with $2 billion a year to keep it out of regional disturbances), oils all the cogs of communication—one press administrator became so rich that he did nothing but the bare minimum to keep his sinecure, even holding back the growth of his own newspaper—and manipulates the common people in such a way as to organize a general climate of censorship.

In a text he submitted to a new work full of praise for this "exemplary success" (the new Alexandrian Library),[5] Ghitany discusses how this institution could help the country by the positive example it sets as an international institution open to all currents of thought, which will henceforth be protected from danger. His somewhat disarming optimism goes even further by observing the impossibility of anyone controlling the Internet, which, according to him, should kill censorship in ten years.

Should we be seeing a sign in this? The quarter that neighbors the new Alexandrian Library is called Rushdie.*

Now that it has moved from a Stalinist management to a more Florentine ambience, will the new Alexandrian Library go anywhere despite the infernal weights attached to its feet? A combination of circumstances has resulted in the appearance of a magnificent 200-million-euro building that, for the moment, seems little burdened by books or readers, which is no doubt natural for such a young establishment. But couldn't less money have been been spent this way and more used

---

*This Rushdie is Rushdy Basha (or Rochdi, depending on which language you speak), who was a former prime minister of Egypt. Just as the label *rashidun* describes the religious orthodoxy of the first four caliphs, this name comes from *rashada,* meaning "to be on the right path." Thus a peaceful neutrality lies at the root of the verb.

toward buying an abundant collection of books that would have been useful from the start? As with the BNF, it seems clear that a poorly defined cultural project always becomes a complex set of gears in which the only option becomes a constant flight forward.

The wife of the Egyptian head of state, who, incidentally, truly holds the ultimate authority over the library, seems to invest more of her energy in campaigns that encourage children to read and that aim to provide small libraries to ten thousand villages in the country, which has an illiteracy rate of 50 percent. If the Egyptians truly sought to remake the mythical assemblage of the Mouseion, it would not only require as a priority the stocking of its shelves rather than organizing concerts or exhibits, but also would determine specifically just what kind of researchers it wished to attract. It so happens that the majority of today's (and almost all of tomorrow's) scholars have no need to travel to conduct their investigations: Their screens tell them everything.

The fact remains that many philologists would be enchanted to spend a month or more at this elegant site with perfect lighting and acoustics* to study (the obvious subjects would seem to be) Egyptology, papyrology, Mediterranean civilizations, history of philosophy, religions such as Islam, and so forth.† Large quantities of documents dealing with these subjects are slumbering in the dust of monasteries and mosques, no doubt revealing manuscript treasures from all the dynasties. All we need is a Joseph II to hunt them down.

No farther away than the municipal library in Alexandria we can still find four hundred thousand printed volumes, including 55,490 in French (especially), English, Greek, and Italian, which come from the scholarly collections of the city's cosmopolitan era. They are all well ordered in their leather bindings up to the year 1950 and in moleskin

---

*Except, oddly enough, for the scraping of chairs (of which there are two thousand) on the floor, which echoes and intensifies in a way that quickly becomes intolerable, but remedies should exist to fix this.

†A high-level librarian should also be hired. The extraordinary prestige of the position would of course compel the recipient to abandon any hopes for a Western salary, which would be a thousand times higher than that of his Egyptian employees.

for the years that follow; they are all cataloged correctly. The famous *Description of Egypt* is there, for example, but not in the best condition. Since the government began financing the new mastodon, there is no money left over to modernize the municipal library, where the windows of eight storehouses remain permanently open for lack of any climate control. Its five thousand manuscripts have already been placed in a safer temperature and environment in the new library; all that remains is to move the rest, without forgetting a considerable collection of newspapers from the nineteenth and twentieth centuries in various languages. We should also remember that the building housing the municipal library is the former residence of the Jewish baron Elie de Menasce.

This city "near Egypt" was already once the navel of wisdom. Wouldn't it be the ideal place to feel the weight of history and get a sense of where life is heading? Thus we can only hope for the new Alexandrian Library to one day again be the beacon of the world's libraries and to survive the turbulence surrounding it. Yet in order for it to be taken seriously, it first must heed this echo from the *Letter of Aristeus,* which appeared in the second century B.C.E.: " 'I have heard it said that the books of the Jews are also worthy of being reproduced and forming part of your library,' the library's director said. 'And what is stopping you from doing that?' asked the head of state."

THE GREAT WRITERS ARE UNANIMOUS: *DELENDA EST BIBLIOTHECA!**

❧

The knowledge I have acquired
Is nought but dry tinder.
Come flames, devour
All these baubles.

FRIEDRICH GEORG JÜNGER

The biblioclastic attitude goes back to the dawn of writing and finds its defense from the author personally. After Plato, Seneca, and Lucian, who confessed their distrust from the first, we can find words against the collecting of books in the writing of Erasmus, Cornelius Agrippa, Rabelais, and even Montaigne. La Bruyère mocks the upstarts and fans of rich bindings, one of whom had compelled him to visit a "tannery that he calls his library."

Philosophically, the burning of the Great Library of Alexandria was applauded by quite a number of literary men—sometimes obscure ones, such as Louis Le Roy in 1575 *(De la Vicissitude ou varieté des choses . . .),* and sometimes distinguished ones, such as Thomas Browne

---

*The library must be destroyed.

in his *Pseudodoxia Epidemica* of 1646, which, translated in 1733 in Paris *(Essai sur les erreurs populaires),* * was a work full of charming and diverse ideas, including the following: "So large is the empire of Truth that it hath place within the walls of hell and the devils themselves are daily forced to practice it."

Depending on the degree of conviction, this survey can be organized into two parts: the igniters, such as Cervantes, who held an unshakable belief that the hero could fulfill himself only without books, and the hierophants, who pretend the same to a small degree and, in any case, are playing with fire.

THE IGNITERS

Never have a priest or a barber or a niece or a housekeeper; or else tremble for your freedom. And if by ill fortune you have all four at once, carefully hide the place where you house your books.

Four centuries after its first appearance, the sixth chapter of *Don Quixote* is still poignant torture for the reader. It is in this chapter that we see these four figures indulging themselves, pretending to be a tribunal by taking cowardly advantage of Hidalgo's well-earned rest. "They all went into [his library], the housekeeper with them, and found more than a hundred large volumes, very well bound, and some small ones as well." Master Nicholas hands each title to the priest, who analyzes, assesses, and decides while the niece shrieks that they should all be burned and the housekeeper acts as the secular arm, tossing the books out the window.

Of course, this is a vicious affair; just like the inquisitors, the priest removes and keeps the best works for himself. "Give it to me, my friend, for I had rather have found this than have the present of a Florentine serge cassock." Then, "that same night, the housekeeper set light to all the books in the yard and to all those in the house as well, and burned them. These latter were condemned without judgment, and their number

---

*[An Essay on Popular Errors. —*Trans.*]

is unknown, because 'the saint sometimes pays for the sinner.' " The next day the room was walled up as if the library had never existed, and the two wicked women told the gentle knight that an enchanter who had come on the back of a dragon had taken away everything—books and shelves. All the wandering knight could do was set off wandering.

> *If all the books have killed me,*
> *all it takes is one for me to live as a*
> *Ghost in this life and as a real being in death.*
>
> Alexandre Arnoux (1884–1973),
> *Chanson de la mort de Don Quichotte*

It was most likely Jean-Jacques Rousseau who set ears burning in the eighteenth century with his *Discourse on the Arts and Sciences* by praising the fire that struck the legendary Library of Alexandria, "considering the frightful disorders the printing press has already caused in Europe, and on seeing the progress the evil makes from one day to the next." His friend Denis Diderot followed his lead and also justified the actions of the "emperors of China."

Then the great dreamer Louis-Sébastien Mercier, who grasped better than any other the utopia of all this, marched into the breach they had thus opened. The author of stories and sixty works of the theater, he is best known today for his 1781 work *Tableau de Paris* [Portrait of Paris]. In it he resolves the fate of the king's collection of books: "The mind finds itself darkened within this multitide of insignificant books, which take up so much space and are good only for disturbing the memory of the librarian who can never finish arranging them. . . . So they are not arranged, and the catalog compiled thirty-five years ago only doubles the confusion of this dark chaos." But there is better: "The oyster in its shell, peaceful on its rock, appears superior to this doctor, who babbles for six thousand pages and still boasts of having encompassed *the universal science*. . . . We are tempted to take a *Montaigne* for an antidote and flee at top speed."

Ten years earlier, when he was not yet thirty, Mercier had already described in *L'An 2440** this princely archive reduced to "a small cabinet holding a few books that appear to me nothing short of voluminous." The librarians of the future necessarily explain to him that

> [w]e have gathered on a vast plain all the books we deemed frivolous, useless, or dangerous . . . It was definitely another tower of Babel . . . consisting of five or six hundred thousand dictionaries, one hundred thousand volumes of jurisprudence, one hundred thousand poems, sixteen hundred thousand travel books, and a billion novels. We set fire to this terrifying mass as if it were an expiatory sacrifice offered to truth, good sense, and true taste.

Consequently, the twenty-fifth century clearly will have to be satisfied with the handful of authors who are necessary, such as (at least), Homer, Plato, Virgil, Pliny, Sallust, Shakespeare, Torquato Tasso, and, of course, Montaigne. Rousseau will be among them, too—although much of his poeticized rubbish will be amputated.

A literary genre was born.

THE HIEROPHANTS

By coming down a notch regarding the absolute, we may consider that the philosophical advice to destroy the library can be reduced to the only true literary bliss.

Gaston Bachelard ventured this opinion for the good cause: "We should get rid of books and teachers so that we may rediscover poetic primitiveness." The symbolist poets or the first stirrings of the moral liberalization that feigned the application of this saying had all studied their humanities. The emotional power of the concept in the ambient fetishism of today, however, seems to be turned more and more to a profit—though success can turn a profitable image into a cliché and empty it of its meaning, as is the case with Montauban.

---

*[The Year 2440. —*Trans.*]

Alphabetically the most famous hierophants are Borges, Bradbury, Canetti, Cortázar, Eco, France, Gide, Hugo, Huxley, Orwell, Schwob, Shakespeare, and Shaw—listed, more or less, in chronological order of their appearance in history.

The dreamer of sound and fury who was Shakespeare was not insensitive to the rhetorical strength of the burned library. He decided that the sole means of knocking down Prospero's house was to annihilate his wall of paper. As Caliban says:

> Remember first to possess his books; for without them
> He's but a sot as I am, nor hath not
> One spirit to command: they all do hate him
> As rootedly as I. Burn but his books.

> (*The Tempest*, ACT III, SCENE 2)

The final novel by Victor Hugo, *Quatrevingt-treize (93),* was published in 1874, and its writing was permeated by family griefs (the loss of Adèle, his wife, and his two sons) and national mourning (*L'Année terrible;* The Terrible Year). This tumultuous and disjointed tale of the year 1793, in which the Vendée is a transposition of the Paris Commune, shows an increasingly convulsive author who writes only in slogans and scatters his incomparable vision throughout a simplified plot. This includes the cannon that breaks loose in the hold of the *Claymore;* the impossible conversation of Marat, Robespierre, and Danton in a bistro; and the long biblioclastic sequence by the three urchins locked up in a library, condemned to burn with it, who make a game out of massacring

> a magnificent and memorable folio. This *Saint Bartholomew* had been published in Cologne by the famous publisher of the 1682 Bible, Bloeuw, or, in Latin, Coesius. It had been manufactured on a press with movable type, and bound with thread made from ox tendons. It was printed not on Dutch paper, but on that Arab paper so admired

by Edrisi, which was made from silk and cotton and never grew yellow. The binding was of gilt leather and the clasps of silver.

We are tempted to think that an object of such poor taste was already deserving of condemnation, but this would be a betrayal of the author's intent. What especially caught the urchins' eyes in this folio lying open on a lectern was the image of the tortured saint carrying his skin over his arm. "The first page to be torn out is like the spilling of first blood—it decides the carnage." After receiving a solid kick from an urchin's foot, the old tome is eventually turned into confetti, "and the inexorable massacre of the old book absorbed them so entirely that a mouse ran past without their perceiving." Victor Hugo's conviction here is that despite the necessity to always defend "the fraction against the whole," the Vendée against the inhuman Republic, obscurantism should also be abolished. As a symbol of this, he chooses this bloody religious bauble, which will revolt Protestants—specifically the torture of St. Bartholomew.

The image then becomes a cloud of "butterflies" cast to the wind by the youngsters. Its destruction is the prologue to the destruction by means of a suicidal fire of the rest of the Tourgue Library. The books are henceforth "just things," because the place is abandoned and is merely a room in which the mantels hold busts of forgotten historical figures illustrating one day in the scholary research of lost works.[1] "Fire is recklessly prodigal with its treasures; its furnaces are filled with gems which it flings to the winds. . . . The hollow sound of cracking timbers rose above the roar of the flames. The panes of glass of the bookcases of the library cracked and fell with a crash. It was evident that the timberwork had given way. Human strength could do nothing." Like the children tearing apart the book on the life of the saint, the fire lit by the Chouans destroys a temple of knowledge serving no purpose, a library with no reader. After thereby hailing the new world he thinks is taking things in hand, Victor Hugo, "on the heights," draws away.

"And it was terrifying to look at all this through the keyhole! Ah, books there were—big ones, middle-sized ones, extremely small books in all forms and colors, books that from the plinth to the corniche [cornice] stocked the four walls, were piled over the fireplace, on tables, even covered the floor . . . !" And over the door of this library was written in large letters: ENTRY FORBIDDEN. This is because the library of L'Abbé Jules [Father Jules] is itself the garrison of a locked holy of holies in which can be found *the* trunk—and a chair. On his death, Jules leaves his fortune to the first priest who defrocks himself and enjoins that individual who inherits the library to burn the trunk. As nothing "supernatural and comic" takes place at the burial, the friends and relatives gather in a circle around the auto-da-fé. It is not known whether Father Jules had foreseen what would happen then.

Octave Mirbeau's novel *L'Abbé Jules* appeared in 1888, and despite the increasing rarity of cassocks, it has lost nothing of its punch.

While Borges eventually acknowledged late and in somewhat "muddled"[2] fashion that it was his reading of Marcel Schwob's *Imaginary Lives* that shaped his own career as a storyteller, André Gide, for his part, never confessed that he shamefully plagiarized the delicate *Book of Monelle* to pull out his own indigestible *Earthly Foods*.

Schwob's book appeared in 1894 and already committed the (female) reader to forget learning and constraints. For example: "Build your house yourself and burn it down yourself . . . offer your pages for tearing out exquisite pleasures. . . . You shall erase with your left foot the print of your right." Three years later, Gide's command stated specifically: "It is necessary, Nathaniel, for you to burn all the books within yourself" and, in the small print, "At present, throw away my book." In fact, potential buyers started there and he sold only five hundred copies in ten years of what was only a laborious *outing,** while the books of Marcel Schwob enjoyed great success. The situation then reversed—and could do so again.

In 1901, George Bernard Shaw shed light on the mystery of Alexandria by obtaining Julius Caesar's confession in his *Casear and Cleopatra*:

---

*[This term is in English in the original edition. —*Trans.*]

CAESAR: Theodotus, I am an author myself; and I tell you it is better that the Egyptians should live their lives than dream them away with the help of books.

THEODOTUS (to Pothinus): I must go to save the library. (He hurries out.)

In 1924, the surrealists wrote their first group text, *A Corpse,* in order to give a burning homage to Anatole France, who was recently deceased. What they condemned France for was not the aesthetic flabbiness of his commitment to the Center Left, but rather his style and erudition on subjects of a pinched imagination.

Born in a bookstore, the future Nobel Prize–winner could conceive of no existence other than that of a pure library offshoot. In fact, this formed the real protagonist of several of his books, from *The Crime of Sylvester Bonnard* to *The Revolt of the Angels,* and is especially at the heart of *At the Sign of the Reine Pedauque* (1893), in which the alchemist Astarac has gathered a collection next to which that of the king "is but a book peddler's lot." Astarac adds:

"If all the lines traced on these innumerable leaves of parchment and paper could enter into your brain in due order, monsieur, you would know all things, be capable of all things; you would be the master of nature, a worker in plasmic matter; you would hold the world between the two fingers of your hand as I hold these grains of snuff."

Whereupon he offered his box to my good master.

"You are very good," said Monsieur l'Abbé Coignard.

In addition, on the final page of this initiatory story, the hidden child who was Anatole France settled his account with the mother/wet nurse of his imagination:

A thick column of smoke rose above the château. A rain of sparks and cinders fell around me and I soon perceived that my clothes and hands were blackened with them. I thought with despair that this dust which filled the air was the remains of so many books and precious manuscripts which had been my master's joy. . . . I felt that a part of myself was destroyed at the same time. The wind which was rising added strength to the fire, and the flames roared like hungry throats. . . . Then I recognized with horror the tall black form of Monsieur d'Astarac running along the gutter. The alchemist cried in a ringing voice: "I rise on the wings of flame into the abode of divine life."

He spoke, and all at once the roof gave way with a horrible crash, and flames high as mountains enveloped the friend of the Salamanders.

It has been forgotten that though the exceptional *Auto-da-Fé* began to be recognized around 1970, it was written by a young man at the end of the 1930s under the title *Die Blendung* (The Blinding, or The Dazzling), a date and title that intensifies the expressionist light permeating the book. In the novel *Auto-da-Fé,* which is one of the most terrifying ever written, Elias Canetti recounts the downward spiral of Kien,* a Sinologist living in Vienna who surrounds himself with so many books that he walls up his windows in order to erect more shelves. At the same time his library closes in around him, the sordid and agonizing power of Therese, the housekeeper he married for no reason, is growing. At the end of this slow degradation into the grotesque, so compact that the author's icy humor often clutches it like a mirage, all we find is murder, madness, and fire.

Because the French [and English] title reveals the end of the book, I have no scruples about citing the last three lines of the novel: "He places the ladder in the middle of the floor, where it stood before. He climbs up to the sixth step, looks down on the fire, and waits. When the flames reached him at last, he laughed out loud, louder than he had ever laughed in his life."

---

*A name rhyming with Wien [Vienna] and which a meaningful slip of the pen by distracted reviewers and commentators becomes Klein [little].

Aldous Huxley said in 1946 of his *Brave New World,* published in 1932: "A book about the future can interest us only if its prophecies look as though they might conceivably come true." Other aspects of his novel remain unthinkable, such as the electric shocks inflicted on babies at the same time they are shown books, and the great British Massacre and its "two thousand culture fans gassed with dichlorethyl sulphide," and worse yet, the following:

> "But why is it prohibited?" asked the Savage. In the excitement of meeting a man who had read Shakespeare he had momentarily forgotten everything else.
>
> The Controller shrugged his shoulders. "Because it's old; that's the chief reason. We haven't any use for old things here."
>
> "Even when they're beautiful?"
>
> "Particularly when they're beautiful. Beauty's attractive and we don't want people to be attracted by old things. We want them to like the new ones."

One of Huxley's students at Eton, Blair, instead of continuing in teaching, became a policeman in Burma, was a hobo in Paris, fought in Teruel in Spain, then landed a job as a literary critic at a small leftist newspaper. Having chosen the name of a river he loved, Orwell, as his new name, he began to make money in 1944 with his satire of the communist state, *Animal Farm.* Five years later, *1984* was released and Orwell died of tuberculosis. This last book, inspired by the mental oppression of the Nazis and Stalinists, has so infused its successive readers that the terms "Big Brother" and *newspeak* have become common words in the English vocabulary.

The hero of *1984* lives in a world where "the hunting down and destruction of books had been done with the same thoroughness in the prole quarters as everywhere else. It was very unlikely that there existed anywhere in Oceania a copy of a book printed earlier than 1960." His mission is to update the archives based "on the needs of the moment. All history was a palimpsest, scraped clean and reinscribed exactly as often as necessary. . . . Books, also, were recalled and rewritten again and again, and were invariably reissued without any admission that any alteration had been made." It is extremely regrettable that George Orwell did not live into his nineties and provide a postface to his best seller, taking into account the exorbitant facilities that digitalization and the depositing of knowledge online give to the modern world.

"Today, people do not burn books," the writer of a preface to *Farenheit 451* imprudently starts singing—but of course they are still being burned all over the world, and the current state of our knowledge gives us every indication that the frequency of autos-da-fé is only increasing. This simple novel made Ray Bradbury famous and became a cultural paragon of 1953 as the inevitable fruit of the puritanical and reactionary climate of the United States at that time. The book starts off this way: "It was a pleasure to burn. It was a special pleasure to see things eaten, to see things blackened and *changed*." Why would the pyromaniac fireman Montag worry his mind about it? " 'Why should I read? What *for*?' Many people undoubtedly already know some passage of this book by heart: 'I am Plato's *Republic*. Like to read Marcus Aurelius? Mr. Simmons is Marcus.' 'How do you do?' said Mr. Simmons."

A vaguely Oulipo-like* exercise consists of talking about libraries without writing the name Borges one single time or citing even the shortest of his works. Again, it would require a joker to invent the double of the Argentine and indulge himself in some charming Quixote-esque activity.

An equally troubling phenomenon was produced with *La Biblioteca de Robinsón,* an unpublished manuscript that sold for three hundred thousand francs in 2001[3] and today graces a South American library. This text, dating from approximately 1930 according to the experts, is a fake according to the widow of the writer, but according to Jean-Pierre Barnes is absolutely authentic. In it, regarding the Qur'an, we can read that "the hell promised in its pages is less atro-

---

*Oulipo was a French avant-garde literary group of the '50s founded by Raymond Queneau and François Le Lionnais; its members included Georges Perec and Italo Calvino. Oulipo is an acronym for OUvroir du LIterature POtentielle [Workshop of Potential Literature —*Trans.*].

cious than a small island without any other library but a single copy of the Qur'an"—a scarcely subtle provocation by someone who claims Arab blood for want of being Jewish. Future Robinson Crusoes would do well to note that Borges's complete works, excellently published by La Pléiade, form a true library in two volumes that would perfectly fit the desert island hypothesis, except that its publisher is specifically forbidden to sell it by the current rights holder,* a situation that cannot help but be amusing . . . what is his name already?

If each of the phrases of the Borges story "The Library of Babel" seems to have been molded to serve as an epigraph to subsequent generations of hack writers, it is in the novella *The Congress* that the author comes to the essential point: The logic of an action as infinite as the universe is that it prepares for its own disappearance. Don Alejandro gives the order to burn the library of the World Congress: "There is a mysterious pleasure to be had in destruction; the flames crackled brightly. . . . Night, ashes, and the smell of burning linger on the patio." This novella, from 1955, is not one of Borges's best pieces of writing; nevertheless, the author swears in an insert that it is the only text from the collection in which it was published that he kept twenty years later because "it was the most autobiographical." In fact, he went one better in an interview with this fairly absurd and jarring analysis in which his familiar wink can be recognized: It is "the description of a mystical experience I never had but that I have tried to imagine."[4]

Soviet pulping of libraries was something Bohumil Hrabal had enough experience of in Prague in 1968 to write *Too Loud a Solitude,* finally published in 1976. He places this self-portrait of Hanta at a time during World War II. This worker is a slave to his hydraulic press, which destroys tons of beautiful and not so beautiful books poured to him through a basement window by invisible colleagues day after day, for thirty-five years.

---

*All book lovers, especially writers nearing the end of their lives, can read with amusement and terror the short study by Anatole de Monzie, *Les Veuves abusives* [The Domineering Widows], which must be republished. (It is available only on microfiche at the BNF; its 251 pages have also been digitalized, NUMM-84033, and are available online.)

In such circumstances, the protagonist quickly establishes a growing conversation with Jesus, Lao-tzu, Kant, and Van Gogh. "I can be by myself because I'm never lonely; I'm simply alone, living in my heavily populated solitude, a harum-scarum of infinity and eternity, and Infinity and Eternity seem to take a liking to the likes of me."

In 1997, when trying to feed a pigeon, this king of Czechoslovakian chitchat fell from his window on the fifth floor of the hospital he was scheduled to leave the next day. Hrabal had often mentioned his lifelong fear of falling or his wish to jump from the window of his fifth-floor apartment.

Fantomas against the Multinational Vampires is a graphic novel told in the first person by Julio Cortazar on his somewhat despondent exit from the second Russell Tribunal, which targeted South American dictatorships. (The first session, on the instigation of Bertrand Russell and Jean-Paul Sartre, sat in judgment of the United States on Vietnam—though today we cannot really see who would be capable of initiating a third Russell Tribunal.) This fairly rough first draft of a lampoon was not published in France until 1991.*

It first appeared in Mexico, and in it we see all the world's libraries suddenly emptied of their billions of books as a result of the mysterious action of a multinational superpower that seeks to dominate the world. Hence the appeal to the only force capable of fighting back (and attracting the attention of the ordinary Latin American reader): Fantomas. We do not know if the superman managed to restock the planet's bookshelves, but in the story the condemnation of Nixon and Kissinger by the Russell Tribunal was finally read on television, and it was likewise read by readers of the novel.

> "And is a library then an instrument for not distributing the truth, but rather for delaying its appearance?" I asked dumbfounded.
>
> "Definitely, my son, insofar as this is already the case for each

---

*[And has yet to be translated into English. —*Trans.*]

book, a deaf-mute who delays most cunningly its revelation, which must be tortured from it one page at a time."

When Umberto Eco wrote *The Name of the Rose* (it was released in Italy in 1980, followed by French and English editions two years later), the ultimate reference to the burned library, he had no idea that the success of this quite ordinary tale would be such that, twenty years later, people asked in the street would call it the *Romance of the Rose*. This popularity is perhaps the confession of a culturally adrift world that feels all its landmarks are disappearing and has lost a Latin that it never had. Later, it was written: It is precisely around the year 2000 that the burning of the library would haunt the mind most, like the myth of Frankenstein when gods were being swapped.

In the meantime, medievalists frustrated by such large royalty checks could not help but denounce the heresies of Eco's novel. For example, according to the author's description, there were eighty-seven thousand volumes in this improbable ancient fortress, whereas it was more the norm in the year 1327 for there to be twenty codexes here and three hundred manuscripts there; it would have required, at the very least, eight million calves and the work of all the world's known copyists during two generations to attain such a voluminous quantity.[5] Nevertheless, dream and fantasy laugh at accountants.

In 1995, Jon Thiem, professor of comparative literature at Colorado State University, explored the theme of global digitalization and predicted its future: In the year 2039, the Universal Library will be brought online; twenty years later it will have been raised to the status of myth. As Thiem says, it is "a sphere whose center is everywhere, whose circumference is nowhere."

The author then draws a parallel between a Ptolemaic archive, or the one known as "Babel," and its well-known *sui generis* curse. Toward 2060, it will be realized that "predictions of a deluge of repetitive, half-baked, fraudulent and plagiarized communications have come true" and that, furthermore, numerous cults and sects have appeared for whom the electronic entity is the new god or the beast to be struck down: anonymists, Apos (Apocrypha), Borgesians, Luddites, Nousers (or Newsers). Finally, in a fairly unexpected postscript, we learn that a virus released seventy years earlier by worshippers of the book has, in one blow, erased all the world's knowledge forever. A light euphoria then overcomes humanity.

In what could pass for a parody of apocalyptic sci-fi novels, Paul Auster describes a self-destructing city (*In the Country of Last Things,* 1987) that is so destitute that all its inhabitants have been transformed into carrion feeders. The narrator (a woman) manages by chance to find refuge in the National Library and, during a most dreadful winter, "with the sun tracing a puny arc across the sky in just a few short hours," its books are used to feed the fire.

> Perhaps it released some secret anger in me; perhaps it was simply a recognition of the fact that it did not matter what happened to them. The world they had belonged to was finished and at least now they were being used for some purpose. Most of them were not worth opening: sentimental novels, collections of political speeches, out-of-date textbooks.

The protagonist does manage to read a little before the books are burned for heat: "parts of Herodotus" and "the odd little book" of Cyrano de Bergerac—but seemingly with no great benefit (otherwise this novel would take a positive turn). "But in the end, everything made its way into the stove, everything went up in smoke."

Jean Roudaut (*Les Dents de Bérénice,* 1996) seems to believe that all these books sitting side by side and the love people hold for them are a decoy. For him "a library is a secret room; what offers itself hides, what can be grasped diverts, what is retained inspires pursuit. One enters a book-lined room with fascination; what is distressing is not the knowledge that one will never read all the books there but the understanding that every existing library forbids the existence of another absent library where nothing is offered that leaves desire intact."

"Phony diplomas, swinging professors, rigged competitions, revisionist neo-Nazis . . ." With his customary charitable intention for those lazy enough to read between the lines, Didier Daeninckx has written a Poulpe* detective novel somewhat inspired by the recipe for Lyonnaise salad† and especially by the burning of the university library of Lyon II during the year 2000. Given that the author has no fear about blending every seasoning within his reach (Caluire,‡ Algeirs, Phnom Penh), some guards of reasonable thought, if they indeed read him, criticized him for going overboard.

What all these writers agree upon: Collecting books makes the owner a victim of his passions, and if they speak of getting rid of them it is because they know it is impossible to do so.

The unspoken elements that permeate the Lyon affair, however, are far from being imaginary, and various new ingredients that appeared in 2003 could almost provide a sequel to this amusing book. Literature or not, the library really was burned down.

As Jean-Claude Biraben wrote in in the short story "Le Pique-feu," in 2003: "Henri-Mathieu opened the windows overlooking the boulevard, but it did no good. An acrid smoke filled the room every time he turned on the motor. Day after day, the blue cloud yellowed walls, ceiling, and woodwork." A change was necessary. "There was no question, though, about bringing a mechanic up to the third floor. Most irritating was that the gas from the exhaust was dirtying the books and covering the bindings with a sticky soot. Sooner or later, he really would have to choose between the library and the truck."

---

*[Le Poulpe (octopus) is the nickname of investigator Gabriel Lecouvreur of a popular series of French detective novels (numbering more than two hundred and twenty graphic novels and spawning a film starring Jean-Pierre Darrousin, released in 1988). He is a kind of leftist alternative to the traditional hard-boiled detective—half Robin Hood, half anarchist avenger. —*Trans.*]

†[Lyonnaise salad is a green salad with cubed bacon and soft-boiled eggs. It can and often does include herring, anchovies, sheep's feet, and chicken livers. —*Trans.*]

‡[Caluire-et-Cuire is a large suburb north of Lyon. —*Trans.*]

A SHORT HISTORY OF THE CENSUS OF LOST BOOKS

With a Legend to Bring It to a Close— The Hidden Library

———— ❧ ————

They placed sand inside the square box, and drew lines in it; they made their calculations with their parchment talismans, they made the mirror black with water mixed with smoke.

MARCEL SCHWOB

Based on what we currently know,* Athenaeus of Naucratis was the first to be fascinated by vanished literature. Around 228, in his *Deipnosophistai*, he tells of a literary banquet during which were cited eight hundred writers and fifteen hundred works, the majority about which we know little more than he tells us. To this I should add that the book by Athenaeus is obviously incomplete: Only ten volumes of the fifteen (some claim thirty) have come down to us. *Suda* or the *Lexicon of Suidas* is the nomenclature for lost texts and people, allegedly written by

---

*Nothing, however, forbids us from imagining that the first human being to have compiled an inventory of lost books was himself the victim of imminent injustice and was forgotten, with even the slightest trace of his labor irretrievably erased.

a Greek in the tenth or eleventh century in Constantinople. Effigies of Suidas and Athenaeus were enthroned in Hugo's useless (and eventually burned) library in 93.

Closer to our time, Charles Nodier also shared this desire to gather dead leaves. Yet he did not throw himself into the adventure without caution, for that would have presumed an excessive, restless idleness. It did inspire, however, a literary half-genre that smacked as much of arguing by the fireside as it did of a withering mental polarization. The first to illustrate it—the amateur William Blades, for example—deplored the loss of the *parchments* of Alexandria. He had found his inspiration and source in Disraeli.

Isaac d'Israeli, then known as Disraeli (1766–1848), was the despair of his father, who, son of a family of Venetian merchants, had made his fortune at eighteen and promptly retired to London. At the same age, alas, Isaac wrote a long poem against commerce and became an ardent disciple of Rousseau. Later, after a tiff with his synagogue, he decided to baptize his children, which, incidentally, allowed his son Benjamin to enter Parliament and pursue the career for which he is remembered in history. The most pleasant of Isaac's books to read today, although crammed with errors, is entitled *Curiosities of Literature,* three tomes of literary blends, anecdotes, critical pieces, and odd pieces of information. All of the first hundred notes in the book are devoted to libraries. The beginning of volume 1 also includes ten pages on the destruction of libraries.

There are, however, more professional researchers who did not shirk the fastidious task of performing a stocktaking of destroyed libraries. This is an almost futile task save for the researchers it grows upon and the readers who imagine that there may be in these rows of titles that can appear starkly obscure, one book that may have been invented out of whole cloth.

"But is it possible," readers will ask, "that individuals exist who are wicked enough or mad enough to commit such attacks against an object as precious, as eminently respectable as a book?" Bibliophile and collector Fernand Drujon pretends to take umbrage in his treatise *De la Bibliolytie.* Under this "more scholarly than harmonious name" he lists 278 books destroyed not as a result of ecclesiastical or legal actions or by accident, but rather in large part to the remorse of their authors or publishers inspired by various reasons—for example, because the wind had shifted (as was the case for an exhortation of nobles to join the invincible armada, and a heated plea to spare the head of Louis XVI, and so forth) or because age and honors gave birth to regret for having written verses that are too risqué, revolutionary, or idiotic (the most numerous are erotic). Some reasons are more thought provoking, however: *L'Expédition de Chine* (The Chinese Expedition), by the count de Hérisson, based on the confidential correspondence of General de Montauban, was massively bought up by the war ministry to conceal the sack of the Summer Palace. In 1893, following the *Essai bibliographique sur la destruction volontaire des livres ou Bibliolytie* (Paris, 1889),* the author published a list† of one hundred titles lost accidentally. This list, *Destructarum editionum centuria,* is available online at textesrares.com.

Fernand Drujon was merely imitating Paul Lacroix (the bibliophile Jacob), who compiled an inventory of 115 titles in 1880, and Gustave Brunet. Lost only if speaking relatively, finds of this kind of booklet primarily display the interest their rarity holds in the eyes of fans of curiosities and crafty collectors, and the research involves more a penchant for stock-market dabbling than for abused literature. We should note the limited reliability of these studies, sometimes accompanied by the openly ignorant and reactionary minds of some of the compilers stubbornly committed to this undertaking. We can take Brunet, for example: In another book he wrote, he classifies among literary madmen "Socrates, Walt Whitman, Michelet, and, naturally, Gérard de Nerval and the Marquis de Sade." This "naturally" did not fail to offend Raymond Queneau in the preface to his much more penetrating study on literary madmen, which almost failed to find a publisher.

---

*[Bibliographical Essay on the Intentional Destruction of Books or Bibliocide. —*Trans.*]

†Into which he slips this analysis in the form of a sigh: "The history of burned libraries and bookstores would provide material for an extensive work."

We could say that if these tens of thousands of lost books had not gone astray, there would be no one to analyze them today. Be that as it may, the curious will perhaps be interested in this supplement to the bibliography collected by Drujon:

Schelhorn, *Amoenitatis litterariae, passim*. Gabriel Peignot, *Dictionnaire des principaux livres condamnés au feu*, 1806. Gustave Brunet, Supplement to the book above, *Bibliophile belge*, 1848 and 1850. G. Brunet, *Dictionnaire de bibliologie*, col. 1087 to 1090. Cornelius Walford, *Destruction of Libraries by Fire, etc.*, London, 1880, "which I regret knowing only by its title." Octave Delepierre, *Bibliophagie*. Maurice Tourneux, "Les livres détruits par leurs auteurs," *Bibliophile français*, year 1873, vol. 7, 246 to 250. Oelrichs, *Dissertatio de Bibliothecarum ac librorum fatis, imprimis libris comestis*, Berolini, 1756. A. A. Renouard, *Catalogue*, vol. I, 286 to 291. Joseph-Marie Quérard, *Livres perdues et exemplaires uniques*, Bordeaux, 1872.

This last study is actually entitled *Books Nowhere to Be Found* in the author's files; it is intriguing that the 1984 facsimile edition changed the name to *Lost Books* whereas, strictly speaking, current reproductions have made what was nowhere to be found also no longer lost. (No doubt it has had the reciprocal effect as well.)

As a throw-in, as auctioneers say, we have the catalogs of what was destroyed in Paris on May 23, 1871, the first two of which are directly available online on the gallica.fr site:

Louis Paris, *Les Manuscrits de la Bibliothèque du Louvre brulé dans la nuit du 23 au 24 mai 1871*, Paris 1872. Henri Baudrillart, *Rapport sur les pertes éprouvées par les bibliothèques publiques de Paris en 1870–1871*, Paris, 1872. Patrice Salin, *Un Coin de tableau, mai 1871. Catalogue raisonné d'une collection d'ouvrages rares et curieux, anciens et modernes, détruites au palais du Conseil d'État du 23 au 24 mai 1871*, Paris, 1872.

THE HIDDEN LIBRARY

This extravagant legend has such a real foundation that many people have exhausted their health, fortunes, and reputations searching for it. It was recorded by the historian David Arans and has not yet appeared in published form outside scholarly journals.[1]

The affair seems to have its origin at the turn of the sixteenth century, when the grand duke of Moscow, Basil III (1505–1533), sent Greek scholars to correct translations of old manuscripts he owned, with an eye to modernizing local cultural life and strengthening his power. Mikhail Trivolis, known as Maximus the Greek and also nicknamed the Philosopher, came to the prince to express his stupefaction; for his entire life he had never seen such ancient manuscripts.

There matters rested for a time. At the end of the century, Johannes Wetterman, a learned German Protestant pastor, was summoned by Czar Ivan the Terrible to examine some old books that had been shut away too long. In the presence of a number of other experts, the czar ordered several piles of books brought in. Wetterman discovered that these codices were known by frequent references made to them in ancient times but that no copies remained in existence anymore because of fires and wars. Some of them even went back to the time of the Ptolemies. Wetterman said that he was poor but would even trade his children for them. The Russian scholars smiled in response and suggested he translate at least one of them first, but he refused because he did not want to end his days there.

Two centuries passed. Professor Dabelov discovered a document in the Piarnu city archives entitled *Manuscripts Owned by the Czar.* He copied one of its pages and brought it to a Professor Claudius, who could identify it at its true worth. This professor immediately rushed to Piarnu to see the rest of the document, but he was too late; everything had disappeared. Dabelov could remember only that this page was the work of a Protestant pastor who had said that the czar owned eight hundred manuscripts, "some purchased, others presents from the emperor of Byzantium."

Oblivion again swallowed everything, but a renewed search got off to a good start when a Professor Thraemer found in Strasbourg a portion of a Homer that he thought came from Moscow. In his opinion, this manuscript formed part of the dowry of Princess Sophia Paleologe when she married Ivan III, grand duke of Moscow. He then went straight to Russia and inventoried all the Muscovite libraries and eventually concluded that he needed to conduct an excavation in an underground space beneath the Kremlin. Two years later, Dr. Zabelin published "The Underground Chambers of the Kremlin," an article in which he declared that the mythical library had actually existed but had been destroyed when the Polish invasion engulfed the city in fire and blood during the seventeenth century. One document states, however, that a certain Konon Osipov saw the secret rooms in 1724. It seems the precious Byzantine manuscripts were there, packed in trunks. A huge skirmish then broke out between experts both pro and con. Words flew: liar, forger, sellout. Then diggings were conducted, soundings taken, demolitions begun: underground rooms turned out actually to have existed, but they were empty.

Next, in 1891 a book appeared by A. Belokurov, *O bibliteke moskovskikh gosudarei v XVI stoletii*, which refuted the whole existence and showed that Dabelov's list was a fake. Then, however, another study emerged, contradicting Belokurov. The 1920s went by, as did the 1930s, and eventually the 1960s. Several more articles were published, attempting to prove that these manuscripts were there, or trying to prove the opposite.

The search has abated a bit at present, the general conviction being that this tremendous library did truly exist, but that it was unable to withstand all those centuries of waiting, perhaps in a damp environment. If it consisted of manuscripts going back if not to Alexandria, then at least to Byzantium, some of them would already have been four centuries old when they were last seen and their existence was confirmed, although in Dunhuang, China, texts on paper have been discovered that are at least as old, and they remain perfectly legible. So . . .

So, the manuscripts of the czar are, today, like the Grail or the Templar treasure. Even if they were to be found, people would continue to hunt for them.

APPENDIX 3

A SELECTIVE CHRONOLOGY

————— ✺ —————

1358 B.C.E.	The libraries of Thebes are destroyed.
1336	Akhnaten's library (Amarna) is destroyed.
525	The Egyptian libraries are destroyed by the Persians.
450–410	The founder of the Saba empire has written a "treatise of victory" over the Ousan tribe. In it he says: "I, Karib'il Wattar, have slain my enemies, humiliated their gods, and demolished all trace of their writings." He calls himself *mukkarrib,* "unifier."
411	All copies of the books of the sophist Protagoras are burned in the Athens agora because he stated, "As for the gods, we can neither confirm that they exist, nor if they do not exist. Many things prevent us from understanding this. The first is the obscurity of the subject, the second is the brevity of human life."
330	Alexander the Great destroys the palace of Persepolis and most likely the books it contained, which include, perhaps, the originals of Zoroaster.
213	The unifier of China decrees the annihilation of all writings.
207	The Chinese capital is burned and the imperial collection is lost.
186	Titus-Livy says on several occasions that the Roman senate collected and burned all the *vaticini libri.*
181	Numa's library, which had been buried in a chest, is discovered in Rome and is burned for the Greek philosophy books it contains.

167   Antiochos Epiphanes has all the Hebrew manuscripts of Palestine cast into the flames.

146   Carthage and its libraries are lost.

83   Rome burns in the great fire and the sibylline books are lost.

48   Alexandria is burned. This is the date on which Caesar is said to have destroyed the Great Library.

12   Augustus, now pontiff, has two thousand "superstitious" books burned.

23 C.E.   Chang'an burns in a great fire and the imperial library is lost.

57   The books of Ephesus are destroyed.

64   Rome burns again in a great fire attributed to Nero.

79   Vesuvius erupts and buries the villa of the papyri.

80   The libraries of Octavio's portico burn in Rome.

188   The library of the temple of Jupiter burns in Rome.

190   In China, Luoyang and the imperial library are pillaged.

191   Several libraries in Rome are burned.

208   During the disorders in Chang'an, the library is burned.

212   Caracalla decides to have all the books of the Peripateticians tossed into the fire. Dio Cassius, who reports this, does not say if he actually went through with it.

213   There is possible partial destruction of the Alexandrian Library by Caracalla.

273   There is possible partial destruction of the Alexandrian Library by Aurelian.

296, 297, or 298   There is possible partial destruction of the Alexandrian Library by Diocletian.

Beginning of 4th century   The bishop Macedonius burns the books of the bishop Paulinus.

303   Diocletian decrees the burning of the scriptures.

311   Luoyang is sacked.

363 or 364   The emperor Jovian burns the Antioch Library, founded by Julian.

371	Valens has the inhabitants of Antioch empty their libraries and condemns to fire or burial all non-Christian books. Ammianus Marcellinus says that the people of the province are so scared of being harassed that they do so spontaneously.
391	The second Alexandrian Library is destroyed by the bishop Theophilus.
398	Arcadius casts into the flames the writings of Eunomius and his emulators.
5th century	Taxila in the Gandhara is destroyed by the white Huns.
416	The Pelagians burn down the monastery of Bethlehem, where Jerome had settled with his large library in 385.
435 and 448	Theodosius and Valentinian condemn to the fire the works of the Nestorians as well as those of the Neoplatonic philosopher Porphyry.
455	Marcian, successor to Theodosus, decrees the burning of several authors declared heretical.
475	There is a coup d'état in Constantinople, accompanied by the loss of the imperial library.
546	Rome is sacked by the Ostrogoths and its libraries are destroyed.
554	The emperor Yuan burns his library.
Circa 590	Pope Gregory I burns all the remaining books of ancient Rome.
614	The Jerusalem library is destroyed by the Persians.
637	The Ctesiphon library is destroyed by the Arabs.
638	The Gondeshapur library is destroyed by the Arabs.
640	The Caesarea library is destroyed by the Arabs.
642	The Arabs allegedly destroy the Alexandrian Library.
644–656	All Qur'ans are destroyed by 'Uthman.
726	The iconoclast campaigns in Constantinople begin, including the destruction of numerous book collections (for example, that of the Academy).
814	Charlemagne's library is annihilated.
867	The library of Photius is burned.

905   The abbatial library of St. Martin of Tours is burned, to cite but one example.

960   Emperor Houzhu sets fire to his library.

Circa 980   The library of the caliphs of Córdoba is burned by Almanzor.

1059   The dar al-'ilm of Baghdad is annihilated.

1068   The libraries of the caliphs of Cairo are pillaged.

1109   The dar al-'ilm of Tripoli is destroyed by the Crusaders.

1174   The Fatimid library in Cairo is dispersed by Saladin.

1199   Nalanda in India is annihilated.

1204   The Bibliotheca Byzantina is destroyed by the Crusaders.

1233   There is an auto-da-fé of Jewish books in Montpellier.

1242 and
1244   The Talmuds are burned in Paris.

1255   The library of the Assassins is destroyed by the Mongols.

1258   Baghdad's thirty-six libraries are destroyed by the Mongols.

1281   The Taoist libraries are burned by Kublai Khan.

1294   The al-Fadil library in Cairo disappears.

1298   Edward I destroys Scottish books.

1309   The Jewish libraries of Paris are burned.

1453   Constantinople is captured by the Turks and its libraries are annihilated.

1490   Torquemada engages in book burning in Salamanca.

1494   The Medici library is pillaged.

1497–1498   Savonarola runs autos-da-fé.

1499   In Grenada there is an immense auto-da-fé of Muslim books.

1515   The Lateran Council ratifies the burning of all erroneous books.

1520   Luther is placed on the index.

1524–1525   Hundreds of libraries are lost in Germany during the Bauernkrieg.

1526   Budapest is devastated by Suleiman and the Corviniana is destroyed.

1527   Rome is pillaged by Charles V.

1529   All Aztec books in Mexico are destroyed.

1534   All the books of Münster are burned.

1535   Tunis is captured by Charles V and its libraries are destroyed.

1536–1550   Hundreds of thousands of books are destroyed during the ecclesiastical upheaval initiated by Henry VIII and continued by Edward VI.

1559–1560   There is an auto-da-fé of Protestant books.

1561   All the Mayan books in the Yucatán are destroyed.

1562   Iconoclasm reaches new heights with the burning of numerous libraries by the reformers.

1568   Hebraica is burned in Venice.

1583   The quipus archives are destroyed by the Council of Lima.

1666   London burns in the Great Fire.

1671   The Escorial near Madrid burns.

1727   Copenhagen burns in a great fire.

1731   Ashburnham House in Westminster burns.

1757   All the books in Podalia are burned by millenniarists.

1759–1773   Huge quantities of books deteriorate due to the seizure of Jesuit libraries throughout the world.

1782   The Austrian congregations seize libraries.

1789   The Bastille library is captured and a book massacre begins.

1814   The Library of Congress is burned by the British.

1837   Constantine, Algeria, is captured.

1860   The Summer Palace in China (now in Beijing) is sacked.

1870   The Strasbourg Library is destroyed by bombardment.

1871   Three large Parisian libraries are lost during Bloody Week.

1881   The Chilean occupation army is installed in the National Library of Peru.

1900   The Hanlin Library is burned in Peking (later Beijing).

1914   The Louvain Library is burned by German soldiers.

1923   Japan experiences its great earthquake.

1932   The Dongfang of Shanghai and the Hanfenlou are bombed and subsequently lost.

1933   The Nazis burn books in Berlin, followed by several other sites.

1939   Germany begins plundering and destroying the public and private libraries in the countries it occupies.

1940   The new Louvain Library is destroyed by German bombs.

1940–1944   Several hundred European libraries are destroyed or damaged by bombing.

1943   The Royal Society Library in Naples is burned.

1945   The Soviet booty taken in Germany is estimated to include twelve million books, the majority of which are French. Many of these disappear during the Soviet purges of the 1950s.

1962   The University Library of Algiers is bombed.

1966   The Cultural Revolution in China begins.

1975   The Khmer Rouge gains a stranglehold in Cambodia.

1981   The Jaffna Library in Sri Lanka is burned.

1986   The Los Angeles Public Library is destroyed by fire.

1988   The library of the Academy of Sciences in Leningrad burns.

1992   The Sarajevo Library is burned by the Serbs.

1998   The Pul-i-Khumri Library is destroyed by the Taliban in Afghanistan.

1999   The Lyon II library is destroyed by fire.

2003   Fire, pillage, and simple destruction claim almost all of the Iraqi libraries following the American "libervasion."

NOTES

PREFACE

1. Ernest Richardson, *The Beginnings of Libraries* (Princeton, N.J.: Princeton University Press, 1914). To learn more about Pierre Brisset, see Raymond Queneau, *Aux confins des ténèbres. Les fous littéraires français du XIXe siècle* (Paris: Gallimard, 2002).

CHAPTER 1. IN THE CRADLE OF LIBRARIES

1. For Uruk (Warka) as well as Ebla (Tell Mardikh) and its gummed shelves, see Daniel T. Potts, *Mesopotamian Civilization: The Material Foundations* (Ithaca, N.Y.: Cornell University Press, 1997).
2. Joachim Menant, *La Bibliothèque de palais de Ninive* (Paris: n.p., 1880) (this book is available online at http://gallica.bnf.fr).

CHAPTER 2. THE PAPYRUS REGION

1. Mariette, cited in Pierre Montet, *L'Egypte au temps des Ramsès, 1300–1100 avant J.-C.* (Paris: Hatchette, 1946).
2. Charles L. Nichols, *The Library of Rameses the Great* (Berkeley: University of Califormia Press, 1964).
3. As reported by Guillemette Andreu, *L'Egypte au temps des pyramides* (Paris: Hatchette, 1994).
4. According to P. W. Pestman's study of the Chester Beatty papyrus; cited by Richard Parkinson and Stephen Quirke, *Papyrus* (London: British Museum Press, 1995).
5. Cf. David Roxburgh, *The Persian Album, 1400–1600: From Dispersal to Collection* (New Haven, Conn.: Yale University Press, 2004).
6. Luciano Canfora, *La Véritable Histoire de la bibliothèque d'Alexandrie* (Paris: Desjonquères, 1988).
7. Guglielmo Cavallo and Roger Chartier, *Histoire de la lecture dans le monde occidental* (Paris: Seuil, 2001).
8. Mostafa El-Abbadi, *Vie et destin de l'ancienne Bibliothèque d'Alexandrie* (Paris: UNESCO, 1992).

9. Giuseppe Botti, in whom we also find Aphthonius's account, *L'Acropole d'Alexandrie et le Serapeum d'après Aphthonius et les fouilles* (Alexandria, Egypt: Imprimerie general L. Carrière, 1895).

10. As E. M. Forster was pleased to relate in *Alexandria* (Oxford: Oxford University Press, 1986).

11. According to Paul Casanova, *L'Incendie de la bibliothèque d'Alexandrie par les Arabes* (Paris: n.p., 1923). He is followed on this path by El Abbadi.

12. Diogenes Laertes, cited by H. J. Drossaart Lulofs, "Neleus of Scepsis and the Fate of the Library of the Peripatos," *Tradition et Traduction: Les textes philosophiques et scientifiques grecs au Moyen Âge latin*. Homage to Fernand Bossier. Edited by Rita Beyers (Louvain: Louvain University Press, 1999).

13. Cf. Canfora, *La Véritable Histoire de la bibliothèque d'Alexandrie* or Edward Edwards, *Libraries and Founders of Libraries* (New York: Burt Franklin, 1968).

14. Aulus Gellius, *Noctium Atticarum* (Attic Nights) 7, 17, 1–2 (Cumberland, R.I.: Harvard University Press, 1982).

15. St. Augustine, cited by M. H. Fantar, *Carthage, approche d'une civilization* (Tunis: ALIF, 1993).

16. Clarence Forbes, "Books for the Burning," *Transactions of the American Philological Association* 67 (1936).

17. As detected by Catherine Salles, *Lire à Rome* (Paris: Les Belles Lettres, 1992), when reading the *Satyricon*.

18. Robert Sablayrolles made a determined effort to raise it for his magnificent survey in *Libertinus Miles. Les Cohortes de vigils* (Rome: École Française de Rome, 1996).

19. Titles mentioned by G. Hacquard, *Guide roman antique* (Paris: Hachette, 1952), or G. Cavallo and R. Chartier, *Histoire de la lecture dans le monde occidental*.

20. *Didascalia Apostolorum,* cited by Thomas N. Tanner, "A History of Early Christian Libraries from Jesus to Jerome," *Journal of Library History* 14, no. 4 (Autumn 1979).

21. Edward Gibbon, *The Decline and Fall of the Roman Empire,* vol. 1 (London: Penguin, 1983).

22. Procopius of Caesarea, *The Secret History* (New York: Covici Friede, 1927).

23. Warren Treadgold, *The Nature of the Bibliotheca of Photius* (Washington, D.C.: Dumbarton Oaks, 1980).

24. Leighton D. Reynolds and Nigel G. Wilson, *Scribes and Scholars: A Guide to the Transmission of Greek and Latin Literature*. Oxford: Clarendon Press, 1974.

25. Jean Irigoin, "Survie et renouveau de la literature antique à Constantinople (9th siècle)," *Griechische Kodikologie und Textüberlieferung* (Darmstadt: Wissenschaftliche Buchgesellschaft [Abt. Verlag], 1980), and also Luciano Canfora, *La Bibliothèque du patriarche: Photius censure dans la France de Mazarin* (Paris: Les Belles Lettres, 2003).

26. Gibbon, *The Decline and Fall of the Roman Empire*.

27. Pero Tafur, *Andanças e viajes de pero Tafur por diversas partes del mundo avidos (1435–1439)* (Madrid, 1874).

28. Gustave Schlumberger, *Le Siège, la prise et le sac de Constantinople par les Turcs en 1453* (Paris: Plon, 1914).

CHAPTER 3. ISLAM OF THE FIRST DAYS

1. Cf. the exposition and catalog *La Splendeur des Omeyyades* (Paris: IMA, 2000).

2. This is the theory developed by David Wasserstein in "The Library of al-Hakam al-Mustansir and the Culture of Islamic Spain," in *Manuscripts of the Middle East, 1990–1991,* vol. 5 (Leiden: Ter Lugt Press, 1993).

3. Mohamed Makki Sibai, *Mosque Libraries: A Historical Study* (London: Mansell, 1987).

4. Richard Erdoes, *AD 1000: A World on the Brink of Apocalypse* (Berkeley: Ulysses Press, 1998).

5. The expression belongs to Gabriel Martinez Gros, *L'Idéologie omeyyade: la construction de la légitimité du califat de Cordoue: X–Xie siècles* (Madrid: Casa de Velazquez, 1992).

6. For example, J. Ribera Tarrago, *Bibliófilos y bibliotecas en la España musulmana* (Saragossa, Aragon, Spain, 1896).

7. Pierre Guichard, *De la Conquête arabe à la Reconquête: grandeur et fragilité d'al-Andalus* (Grenada: Legado Andalusi, 2003).

8. Évariste Lévi-Provençal, *Histoire de l'Espagne musulmane* (Paris: G. P. Maisonneuve, 1950). This scholar preferred to imagine Almanzor's sorting and destruction of the library as a daily process spanning a period of six months.

9. Maribel Fierro Bello and M. Isabel, *La Heterodoxia en al-Andalus durante el periodo omeya* (Madrid: Instituto Hispano-Arabe de Cultura, 1987).

10. Ibn Sa'id al-Andausî, *Kitab tabakât al-umam* (Book of the Categories of Nations) (Paris: n.p., 1935).

11. Takriti (1972) cited by Marie-Geneviève Balty-Guesdon, "Le Bayt el-hikma de Bagdad," *Arabica,* no. 39 (1992), 131–50.

12. In his *Ikhtilaaf al-fuqaha* [Divergences Among the Jurists], cited by M.-G. Balty-Guesdon, "Le Bayt el-hikma de Bagdad."

13. Al-Qadi al Nu'man, cited by Heinz Halm, *The Fatimids and Their Traditions of Learning* (London: I. B. Yauris, 1997).

14. Al-Maqrizi, stroller of Cairo, cited by R. G. Khoury, "Une description fantastique des fonds de la bibliothèque royal khizanat al-kutub au Caire, sous le régime du calife fatimide al'Aziz bi-llah," *Proceedings of the Ninth Congress of the Union européene des arabisants et islamisants,* Amsterdam, September 1978 (Leiden: E. J. Brill, 1981).

15. André Raymond, *Le Caire* (Paris: Arthème Fayard, 1993).

16. Al-Maqrizi, cited by Fu'ad Sayyid, "Que reste-t-il de la bibliothèque des Fatimides?" In *Des Alezandries II. Les metamorphoses du lecteur* (Paris: BNF, 2003).

17. Khitat el-Sham, cited by Yusef Eche, *Bibliothèques arabes publiques et semi-*

publiques en Mésopotamie, en Syrie at en Égypte au Moyen Âge (Damascus: n.p., 1967).

18. P. K. Hitti, *The Arabs* (London: Macmillan, 1948).
19. 'Ala-ad-Din 'Ata-Malik Juvaini, *Ghengis Khan: The History of the World Conqueror,* J. A. Boyle, trans. (Manchester: Manchester University Press, 1997).
20. Etan Kohlberg, *A Medieval Muslim Scholar at Work: Ibn Tâwûs and His Library* (Leiden: E. J. Brill, 1992).

CHAPTER 4. PEOPLE OF THE BOOK

1. S. K. Padover, chapter 11, in James W. Thompson, *The Medieval Library* (New York: Hafner, 1957).
2. Henri-Charles Lea, *Histoire de l'Inquisition au Moyen Âge* (Paris: Société nouvelle de librarie, 1901; reprint, Grenoble: Millon, 1990). Also Gilbert Dahan, ed., *Le Brûlement du Talmud à Paris, 1242–1244* (Paris: Cerf, 1999).
3. Paul Grendler provides extremely precise information concerning the titles and their print runs: "The Destruction of Hebrew Books in Venice, 1568," *Proceedings of the American Academy for Jewish Research,* vol. 45 (1978).
4. Edward Edwards, *Libraries and Founders of Libraries* (1864; reprint, Amsterdam: Gerard th. Van Heusden, 1968).
5. As recalled by Gérard Haddad in the new edition of his book *Les Folies millénaristes Biblioclastes* (Paris: Le Livre de Poche, 2002).

CHAPTER 5. ASIA BEFORE THE TWENTIETH CENTURY

1. Oliver Moore, *Reading the Past: Chinese* (Berkeley: University of California Press, 2000); David Keightly, *Sources of Shang History: The Oracle-bone Chinese Inscriptions of Bronze Age China* (Berkeley: University of California Press, 1978); and Édouard Chavannes, who provides an account of the first publication of Luo Zhengyu in Peking less than a year later, in *Revue Asiatique: La Divination par l'écaille de tortue dans la haute Antiquité chinoise (d'après un livre de M. Lo Tchen-Yu)* (Paris: Imprimerie nationale, 1911).
2. Jessica Rawson, ed., *Mysteries of Ancient China* (London: British Museum Press, 1996).
3. The *Yili,* cited by Chavannes, *Les livres chinois avant l'invention du papier* (Paris: 1905). In Pinyin, *ts'o* is written *ce*.
4. Qian Cunxun, *Written on Bamboo and Silk: The Beginnings of Chinese Books and Inscriptions* (Chicago: University of Chicago Press, 1962).
5. Primary reading is found in Twitchett-Fairbank, Bodde, Wu Guangqing, and, of course, Sima Qian.
6. Qian Cunxun, *Written on Bamboo and Silk.*
7. See K. Schiffer, "Xunsi," and "Yang Zhu," *Dictionnaire de la civilisation chinoise* (Paris: Albin Michel, 1998).
8. Wei Heng, cited by Chevannes, *Les livres chinois avant l'invention du papier.*
9. Wu Guangqing, "Libraries and Book-collecting in China before the Invention of Printing," *T'ien hsia Monthly* 5, no. 3 (October 1937).

10. Paul Demiéville and Yves Hervouet, on Taoism, "Littérature," *Dictionnaire de la civilisation chinoise* (Paris: Albin Michel, 1998).

11. Cf. Robin Yates, *Five Lost Classics: Tao, Huang-Lao, and Yin-Yang in Han China* (New York: Ballantine Books, 1997).

12. Description of Sima Guang (1019–1086), translated in Jean-Pierre Drège's important study of Chinese libraries in the tenth century: *The Bibliothèques en Chine au temps des manuscripts: jusqu'a Xe siècle* (Paris: École française d'Extrême-Orient, 1991).

13. Cf. Dennis Twitchett, *Printing and Publishing in Medieval China* (New York: Frederic C. Beil, 1983).

14. Cf. Jiang Fucong, "A Historical Sketch of Chinese Libraries," *Philobiblon* vol. 2, no. 2 (March 1948).

15. Cf. Nancy Swann, "Seven Intimate Library Owners," *Harvard Journal of Asiatic Studies* 1, no. 3–4 (November 1936).

16. Based on what Ma Mongchuan reports, cited by Chen Dengyuan in *Gujindianji-jusankao* [Considerations on the Collecting and Destruction of Books in Chinese History] (Shanghai: n.p., 1936). Also worth reading is S. Edgren, "Cangshu: The Tradition of Collecting Books in China," *Biblis: The Georg Svensson Lectures Yearbook* (Stockholm, 1996), and Yu Qiuyu, "The Vicissitudes of Tianyi Pavilion," *Chinese Literature* (Autumn 1998).

17. Cited by Tan Zhuoyuan (Cho-Yüan Tan), *The Development of Chinese Libraries under the Ch'ing Dynasty, 1644–1911* (Shanghai: Commercial Press Limited, 1935).

18. Ibid.

19. Cf. Jean-François Billeter, *Li Zhi philosophe maudit (1527–1602)* (Geneva: Droz, 1979). The book examines, alas, only the first part of Li Zhi's life. With respect to the subsequent part and end, the author wrote to me: "All the materials, all the translations have been left in a drawer for more than twenty years. I will get back to it, perhaps—but when?"

20. Reported by L. C. Goodrich, *The Literary Inquisition of Ch'ien-Lung* (Baltimore: Waverly Press, 1935).

21. In the *Banli siku quanshu tang'an,* cited by R. K. Guy, *The Emperor's Four Treasuries: Scholars and the State in the late Ch'ienlung Era* (Cambridge, Mass.: Harvard University Press, 1987).

22. Cf. Fernand Drujon, *Essai bibliographique sur la destruction volontaire des livres or bibliolytie* (Paris: Maison Quantin, 1889), which is featured in appendix 2.

23. Cf. E. Wilkinson, *Chinese History: A Manual* (Cambridge, Mass.: Harvard University Press, 2000). Furthermore, a reprinting, or rather a sequel *(xixiu),* of the *Siku Quanshu* was recently published (*Shanghai guji chubanshe,* eighteen hundred volumes of seven hundred pages each, on average, $55,000). It brings together more than eighty-five hundred books and reintegrates the forbidden books it was possible to find as well as those that the editors of Qianlong had scorned, such as the popular classics *(Water Margin,* also known as *Outlaws of the Marsh; The Dream of the Red Chamber; The Journey to the West;* and

Romance of the Three Kingdoms). Several authors who had become prominent in the period between Qianlong and 1911 were also included. One of the two lead editors was the famous philologist and librarian of Shanghai, Gu Tinglove, who undoubtedly felt he was going out in a blaze of glory: he died at the age of ninety-four at the very time this monument had come back from the printer.

24. This exclamation is Peter Fleming's from his book *The Siege at Peking* (Cary, N.C.: Oxford University Press, 1983).

25. Testimony of Roland Allen, *The Siege of the Peking Legations* (London: Smith, Elder, and Co., 1901).

26. Cf. http://www.museum-security.org/of January 29, 2003.

27. Wilkinson, *Chinese History: A Manual.*

28. Ibid. Wilkinson retells this episode. See also Tan Zhuoyuan, *The Development of Chinese Libraries under the Ch'ing Dynasty, 1644–1911.*

29. Simon Leys, *L'Humeur, l'honneur, l'horreur. Essais sur la culture et la politique chinoises* (Paris: Robert Laffont, 1991).

30. Cited by Joseph Kitigawa, *Religions in Japanese History* (New York: Columbia University Press, 1966).

31. In Donald Keene, *Les Journaux intimes au Japon,* translation by Jean-Noël Robert (Paris: Institute of High Japanese Studies of the Collège de France, 2003).

32. Cf. Hiroshi Ichikawa, "Pensée, grands traits de la . . . ," in *Dictionnaire de la civilisation japonaise* (Paris: Hazan, 1994).

CHAPTER 6. THE CHRISTIAN WEST

1. Cf. among others Julián Ribera Tarrago, *Bibliófilos y bibliotecas en España musulmana,* or Henry Kamen, *The Spanish Inquisition* (New York: New American Library, 1975).

2. Malón de Chaide, *La Conversión de la Magdalena* (n.l., n.p., 1588).

3. See Francisco Olmos, *Cervantes en su época* (Madrid: Ricardo Aguilera, 1968).

4. José Pardo Tomás has studied this aspect of the expurgation of libraries and the organized as well as unorganized disappearance of scientific works, *Ciencia y censura. La Inquisición española y los libros científicos en los siglos XVI y XVII* (Madrid: CSIC, 1991).

5. See Bartolomé Bennassar, *L'Inquisition espagnole, XVe–XIXe siècles* (Paris: Hachette, 1979).

6. Cf. Henry Kamen, *The Spanish Inquisition.*

7. Cf. Latifa Benjelloun-Laroui, *Les Bibliothèques au Maroc* (Paris: Maisonneuve and Larose, 1990).

8. P. Julián Zarco Cuevas, *Catálogo de manuscritos castellanos de la Real Biblioteca de El Escorial,* vol. 3 (San Lorenzo de El Escorial: Tip. del Archivos, 1929).

9. P. Francisco de los Santos, *Descripción del real monasterio de S. Lorenzo del Escorial, única maravilla del mundo . . .* (Madrid: Juan Garcia Infancion, 1681).

10. James W. Thompson, *The Medieval Library* (New York: Hafner, 1957).

11. Guillaume de Montoiche (or Montoche), "Voyage et expedition de Charles Quint au pays de Tunis de 1535," Gachard and Piot, eds., *Collection des voyages des souverains des Pays-Bas* (Brussels: Commission Royale d'Histoire, 1881).

12. Henri-Charles Lea, *Histoire de l'Inquisition au Moyen Âge*.

13. Michel de Montaigne, *Essays,* vol. 3, chapter 6 (Paris: Garnier Flammarion, 1998).

14. Louis Baudin, *L'Empire socialiste des Inka* (Paris: Institut d'Ethnologie, 1928).

15. Cf. Victor Wolfgang von Hagen, *The Aztec and Mayan Papermakers* (New York: J. J. Augustin, 1944).

16. William Prescott, *History of the Conquest of Mexico* (New York: Harper & Brothers, 1843).

17. Gonzalo Fernández de Oviedo y Valdés, *Singularités du Nicaragua* (Paris: Presses Universitaires de Marne-la-Vallée, 2002).

18. Diego de Landa Calderón, *Relation des choses de Yucatán* (Paris: Les Éditions Genet, 1928). See also Alfred M. Tozzer, ed., *Landa's Relación de las cosas de Yucatán* (Cambridge, Mass.: Harvard University Press, 1941).

19. Cf. V. W. von Hagen, *The Aztec and Mayan Papermakers*.

20. Cf. Frans Blom, *Conquest of Yucatán* (New York: Houghton Mifflin, 1936).

21. *Popol-Vuh. Les Dieux, les héros et les hommes de l'ancien Guatemala d'après le "Livre de Conseil,"* trans. Georges Raynaud (Paris: Librairie d'Amerique et d'Orient, 1975).

22. José de Acosta, *Historia natural y moral de las Indias* [Natural and Moral History of the West Indies], trans. Jacques Rémy-Zephir (Paris: Payot, 1979).

23. Serafim Leite, author of a history of the Company in Brazil in ten volumes, cited by M. L. Grover, "The Book and the Conquest: Jesuit Libraries in Colonial Brazil," *Libraries and Culture* vol. 28, no. 3 (Summer 1993). Read more at length in R. Moraes, *Livros e Bibliotecas no Brasil Colonial* (Rio de Janeiro: LTC, 1979).

24. Cf. Laurence Hallewell, "Rare Books in Latin American Libraries," *IFLA Journal* vol. 21, no. 1 (1995).

25. Commentary on the Rule of the Brothers of the Holy Cross, cited by Alfred Franklin, *Les Anciennes Bibliothèques de Paris* (Paris: Imprimerie Royale, 1873).

26. Ibid.

27. Edward Edwards, *Libraries and Founders of Libraries*.

28. Cited by C. R. Gillett, *Burned Books: Neglected Chapters in British History and Literature* (New York: Columbia University Press, 1932).

29. Reported by Isaac Disraeli, *Curiosities of Literature,* 3rd edition (London, 1793).

30. Collier's *Ecclesiastical History,* cited by F. S. Merryweather, *Bibliomania in the Middle Ages* (London: n.p., 1849).

31. From Elmer D. Johnson and Michael H. Harris, *History of Libraries in the Western World* (Metuchen, N.J.: Scarecrow Press, 1976).

32. Charles Ripley Gillett compiled a nomenclature of 750 densely packed pages in 1932, *Burned Books: Neglected Chapters in British History and Literature* (New York: Columbia University Press, 1932).

33. Cf. Johnson and Harris, *History of Libraries in the Western World*.

34. Reynolds and Wilson, *Scribes and Scholars: A Guide to the Transmission of Greek and Latin Literature* (New York: Oxford University Press, 1991).

35. George Young, *Les Médicis* (Paris: Robert Laffont, 1969).

36. Walter Scaife, *Florentine Life During the Renaissance* (Baltimore: Johns Hopkins University Press, 1893).

37. E.-P. Rodocanachi, *Histoire de Rome, le pontificat de Léon X* (Paris: Hachette, 1931).

38. Brassicanus, cited by C. Csapodi in an admirable album devoted to several saved manuscripts, *Bibliotheca corviniana* (Budapest: Magyar Helikon, 1967; French translation, Budapest: n.p., 1982).

39. Nicolas Oláh, then Martin Brenner, both also in Csapodi, *Bibliotheca corviniana*.

40. Sebastian Schertlin, *Leben und Thaten des . . . Herrn Sebastian Schertlin von Burtehbach durch ihn selbst deutsch beschrieben . . . herausgegeben von Ottmar F. H. Schönhuth . . .* (Münster: Aschendorff, 1858).

41. Pierre Barret and Jean-Noël Gurgand, *Le Roi des derniers jours* (Paris: Hachette, 1981).

42. Norman Cohn, *Les Fanatiques de l'apocalypse* (Paris: Julliard, 1983). Translation of *The Pursuit of the Millennium* (London: Secker and Warburg, 1957).

43. As we are reminded by Louis Réau, who has minutely dissected the vandalism in the architecture and works of art on France across the ages in a singular and incontestably useful book, albeit one best read with a certain distance: *Histoire du vandalism* (Paris: Robert Laffont, 1994).

44. Or *Bildergalerie klösterliche Misbraüche*, Joseph Richter, 1784, represented in Jeffrey Garrett, *The Fate of Monastic Libraries in Central Europe, 1780–1810*, Northwestern University presentation at a conference in Hungary, October 3, 1997, at www.library.northwestern.edu/collections/garrett/kloster/index.htm.

45. Cf. Paul Mech, "Les bibliothèques jésuites," *Histoire des bibliothèques françaises. Les bibliothèques sous l'Ancien Régime: 1530–1789* (Paris: Éditions du Cercle de la Librairie, 1988).

46. Ibid.

47. Cf. Garrett, *The Fate of Monastic Libraries in Central Europe, 1780–1810*.

48. Cf. François Fejtö, *Joseph II* (Paris: Plon, 1953).

49. Donatien A. F. de Sade, "Français, encore un effort si vous voulez être républicains," in *La Philosophie dans le boudoir* (London: Compagnie, 1795).

50. Cited by B. Deloche and J. M. Leniaud in their anthology of some of the less senseless reports and speeches of the era, *La Culture des sans-culottes* (Paris: Presses du Languedoc, 1989).

51. Cf. *1789, Le patrimoine libéré* (exhibition catalog) (Paris: BNF, 1989).

52. Cited by Pierre Riberette, *Les Bibliothèques françaises pendant la Révolution (1789–1795), recherches sur un essai de catalogue collectif* (Paris: BNF, 1970).

53. His two discourses on the subject, "Rapport sur la bibliographie, 22 germinal an II" and "Rapport sur les destructions opérées par le vandalisme, 14 fructidor an II," are reprinted in Deloche and Leniaud, *La Culture des sans-culottes.*

54. Ibid.

55. For more on the breathless quest for raw materials by papermakers of the eighteenth century and no doubt forever, see L. X. Polastron, *Le Papier, 2000 ans d'histoire et de savoir-faire* (Paris: Imprimerie Nationale, 1999).

56. Cited by Dominique Varry, "Le livre, otage de la revolution: consequences bibliographiques des saisies politiques," *Le Livre voyageur*. Proceedings of the international seminar organized by ENSSIB and the CERL, May 23–24, 1997 (Paris, 2000).

57. Cf. Jean-Baptiste Labiche, *Notice sur les depots littéraires et la revolution bibliographique de la fin du siècle dernier* (Paris: A. Parent, 1880).

58. The figures are those reported by Alfred Hessel, *A History of Libraries,* trans. Reuben Peiss (Metuchen, N.J.: The Scarecrow Press, 1965), but he also says that ten thousand manuscripts were saved from the water of the pumps and brought to the National Library.

59. Dominique Varry, "Le livre, otage de la revolution: consequences bibliographiques des saisies politiques," *Le Livre voyageur.*

60. This was the hypothesis ventured by, among others, Bernard Deloche and Jean-Michel Leniaud, *La Culture des sans-culottes.*

61. According to the testimony of his great-grand-nephew and biographer Erwein von Aretin, cited by Jeffrey Garrett, *The Fate of Monastic Libraries in Central Europe, 1780–1810.* See also E. H. Dummer, "Johann Christoph von Aretin: A Reevaluation," *Library Quarterly* vol. 16, no. 2 (April 1946).

62. Jules Cousin, librarian of the Hotel-de-Ville, cited in *Constitution d'un patrimoine parisien: la Bibliothèque historique depuis l'incendie de 1871,* exhibition catalog, Hôtel de Lamoignon (Paris, June 12–July 31, 1980).

63. Prosper-Olivier Lissagaray, *Histoire de la Commune de 1871* (Paris: 1896).

64. Georges Bell, who described himself as a relentless reader of this archive, *Paris incendié. Histoire de la Commune de 1871* (Paris: Imprimerie Martinet, 1872).

65. Extract from *Le Contemporain.*

66. Jules Cousin, correspondence, cited in *Constitution d'un patrimoine parisien: la Bibliothèque historique depuis l'incendie de 1871.*

67. Cited by Georges Bell, *Paris incendié. Histoire de la Commune de 1871.*

68. Taine, cited by Paul Lidsky, in his very gripping study that I have profited greatly from here, *Les Écrivains contre la Commune* (Paris: La Découverte, 1999).

CHAPTER 7. THE NEW BIBLIOCLASTS

1. Tomi Ungerer, *À la Guerre comme à la guerre: dessins et souvenirs d'enfance* (Paris: École des Loisirs, 2002).

2. Reporting by Paul Rincon on BBC News, July 7, 2003, http://news.bbc.co.uk/1/hi/sci/tech/3038368.stm.

3. Cf. Hilda Urén Stubbings, *Blitzkrieg and Books: British and European Libraries as Casualties of World War II* (Bloomington: University of Indiana Press, 1993). On the other hand, Hans van der Hoeven drew up an inventory of this devastation for UNESCO: *Mémoire du Monde: Mémoire perdue. Bibliothèques et archives détruites au XXe siècle* (Paris: UNESCO, 1996).

4. The information contained in this paragraph comes from W. G. Sebald, *On the Natural History of Destruction: With Essays on Alfred Anderson, Jean Améry, and Peter Weiss,* trans. Anthea Bell (New York: Random House, 2003).

5. Walter Mehring, *The Lost Library,* trans. Richard and Clara Winston (New York: Bobbs and Merrill, 1951).

6. Ernst Jünger, *Second journal parisien,* Journal 3, 1945 (Paris: Christian Bourgeois, 1980).

7. Cf. Theodore Welch, *Libraries and Librarianship in Japan* (Westport, Conn.: Greenwood, 1997).

8. Reprinted in Hans van der Hoeven *Mémoire du Monde: Mémoire perdue. Bibliothèques et archives détruites au XXe siècle.*

9. As recalled by Lionel Richard in his rich and impassioned study on this subject, *Le Nazisme et la culture* (Brussels: Complexe, 1988).

10. *Le Temps* (May 12, 1933).

11. Cf. Lionel Richard, *Le Nazisme et la culture.*

12. Confided to Dr. Grayson N. Kefauver and cited in "Library Pillaging by Nazis Surveyed," the *New York Times,* April 4, 1945, page 12, column 1.

13. For more on this subject, read Margaret Stieg, *Public Libraries in Nazi Germany* (Tuscaloosa: University of Alabama Press, 1992).

14. Leo Löwenthal, "Calibans Erbe," in *Schriften* (1984).

15. Einsatzstab Reischsleiter Rosenberg für die besetzten Gebiete, or ERR, Rosenberg Commission for the Occupied Territories, translated by the Vichy government, *Commission Rosenberg pour les territoires occupés.*

16. April 1941, letter cited by Counselor Raginsky. For more on the ERR, see, among others, his report at the Nuremberg trial, February 21, 1946, International Military Tribunal, *Trial of the Great War Criminals Before the International Military Tribunal,* vol. 8 (Nuremberg, 1947–1949).

17. Cf. Barbara Bienkowska, *Books in Poland: Past and Present* (Wiesbaden: O. Harrassowitz, 1990), and "Report on the Losses of Polish Libraries in the Second World War," *Polish Libraries Today* 3 (1995), 25–33.

18. Testimony by Dr. Forster at the Nuremberg trial, International Military Tribunal, *Trial of the Great War Criminals Before the International Military Tribunal,* vol. 8 (Nuremberg, 1947–1949).

19. Cf. Patricia Grimsted, "The Odyssey of the Petliura Library during World War II," *Harvard Ukrainian Studies* 22 (1999).

20. Cf. Leonidas E. Hill, in Jonathan Rose, ed., *The Holocaust and the Book* (Amherst: University of Massachusetts Press, 2001).

21. Cited by Stanislao G. Pugliese, "Bloodless Torture," in Jonathan Rose, ed., *The Holocaust and the Book* (Amherst: University of Massachusetts Press, 2001).

22. From an article appearing in the *Frankfurter Zeitung,* March 28, 1941, and

cited by Jacqueline Borin in "Embers of the Soul: The Destruction of Jewish Books and Libraries in Poland during World War II," *Libraries and Culture* 28, no. 4 (Autumn 1993). A "tentative list" of the contents of 704 plundered Jewish archives in Europe was established in New York in 1946.

23. Cf. Stanislao G. Pugliese, "Bloodless Torture," in Jonathan Rose, ed., *The Holocaust and the Book*.

24. Giacomo Debenedetti, *October 16, 1943/Eight Jews*, trans. Estelle Gilson (South Bend, Ind.: University of Notre Dame Press, 2001).

25. Cf. AP wire report of November 17, 2003.

26. See Pohl's inventory note of July 1943 for the "current compositions" of the research library on the Jewish question, made "almost exclusively from volumes collected by the Einsatzstab" in Jean Cassou, *Le Pillage par les Allemands des oeuvres d'art et des bibliothèques appartenant à des Juifs en France* (Paris: Éditions du Centre, 1947). See also Nicolas Reymes, "Les livres dans la tormente. Le pillage des bibliothèques appartenant à des Juifs pendant l'Occupation," *Revue d'histoire de la Shoah–Le Monde juif* 168, no. 31 (January–April 2000).

27. "Review of Principles" of the ERR, November 23, 1941, signed by Utikal in response to the Vichy representation of July 5, cf. Jean Cassou, *Le Pillage par les Allemands des oeuvres d'art et des bibliothèques appartenant à des Juifs en France.*

28. Marcel Thiébaut, cited by Reymes, "Les livres dans la tormente. Le pillage des bibliothèques appartenant à des Juifs pendant l'Occupation," *Revue d'histoire de la Shoah–Le Monde juif.*

29. OMGUS (Office of Military Government of the United States), narrated by Robert G. Waite, "Returning Jewish Cultural Property: The Handling of Books Looted by the Nazis in the American Zone of Occupation, 1945–1952," *Libraries and Culture* 37, no. 3 (Summer 2002).

30. Testimony of Jacqueline Jacob-Delmas, mistakenly illustrated with a photo of the neighboring refrigerated warehouse, a building that still exists. "Austerlitz-Lévitan-Bassano," *Le Monde juif* 146, no. 34 (March 1, 1993).

31. According to Jennifer Allen, in her preface to Walter Benjamin, *Je déballe ma Bibliothéque.*

32. From the unpublished letters of Robert Manuel and Marcel Lob to Madame J. Delsaux, delegate of the subcommission of the book, National Archives, file AJ/38/5937.

33. Cf. Reymes, "Les livres dans la tormente. Le pillage des bibliothèques appartenant à des Juifs pendant l'Occupation," in *Revue d'histoire de la Shoah–Le Monde juif.*

34. Per Marie Guastalla, a painter who had her studio in the neighboring "Frigos."

35. Cf. Timothy W. Ryback, "Hitler's Forgotten Library," the *Atlantic Monthly* (2003), online at www.theatlantic.com/issues/2003/05/ryback.htm.

36. Cf. Francine-Dominique Liechtenhan, *Le Grand Pillage: du butin des nazis aux trophées des Soviétiques* (Rennes: Éditions Ouest-France, 1998).

37. This nebulous and misunderstood period was only redrawn for the first time in

1996 by Arlen Blium: "'The Jewish Question' and Censorship in the USSR," in Jonathan Rose, ed., *The Holocaust and the Book*.

38. Jiang Fucong, "Habent sua fata libelli," *Philobiblon* 1, no. 2 (September 1946).

39. Ibid. Also read Roger Pélissier, *Les Bibliothèques en Chine pendant la première moitié du XXe siècle* (Paris: Mouton, 1971).

40. Opened in September 1936, the National Library of Peiping (Peking) still operates and offers five hundred thousand books in Chinese and 117,000 in other languages.

41. Cf. Zhou Yuan and Calvin Elliker, also for the figures of the losses, "From the People of the United States of America: The Books for China Programs during World War II," *Libraries and Culture* vol. 32, no. 2 (Spring 1997).

42. See John Barclay, *The Seventy-year Ebb and Flow of Chinese Library and Information Services: May 4, 1919, to the Late 1980s* (Lanham, Md.: Scarecrow Press, 1995).

43. Ding Lixia Xu, "Library Services in the People's Republic of China: A Historical Overview," *Library Quarterly* 53, no. 2 (1983), 148.

44. John Barclay, *The Seventy-year Ebb and Flow of Chinese Library and Information Services*.

45. *Zhongguo tushuguan shiye jishi* [Chronology of China's Libraries] (Peking: n.p., n.d.).

46. Ken Ling, *The Revenge of Heaven: Journal of a Young Chinese* (New York: Putnam, 1972), 52, 54.

47. Li Zhensheng, *Le Petit Livre rouge d'un photographe chinois* (Paris: Phaidon, 2003).

48. Gail King, *The Xujiahui (Zikawei) Library of Shanghai,* at www.gslis.utexas .edu/landc/fulltext/LandC-32-4-Fking.pdf.

49. Cited by John Barclay, *The Seventy-year Ebb and Flow of Chinese Library and Information Services*.

50. *Zhongguo tushuguan shiye jishi* [Chronology of China's Libraries] (Peking: n.p., n.d.).

51. *China Daily News,* December 17, 1979, cited by Ding Lixia Xu, "Library Services in the People's Republic of China: A Historical Overview."

52. Bernard Hamel, *De Sang et de larmes, la grande déportation de Cambodge* (Paris: Albin Michel, 1977).

53. Cited by Mohan Lal Koul, *Kashmir, Wail of a Valley* (Delhi: Gyan Sagar Publications, 1999).

54. Cf. the extremely committed Mohan Lal Koul. For daily information, the journalist has given his support and argues for the Hindus. His writings can be read in the *Kashmir Herald.* In support of the other side, there is the *Milli Gazette.*

55. Cf. the article from the *Jeune Independent,* June 7, 2003, reprinted on the gecos Web site, http://gecos.dz/modules.asp?page=afactualite&articles=3119.

56. Catherine Canazzi, "Orange, la bibliothèque pervertie," www.enssib.fr/bbf/ bbf-97-4/04-canazzi.pdf.

57. Gilles Lacroix, "Censure et bibliothèques," in *Fatwa pour Schéhérazade et*

authes recits de la censure ordinaire (Saint-Julien-Molin-Molette: Jean-Pierre Huguet, 1997).

58. Gilles Eboli, report to Free Access to Information and Freedom of Expression (FAIFE), July 2002. See also Laurence Santantonios, "Biblothèques: 7 ans avec l'extreme droite," *Libres Hebdo,* no. 483 (September 27, 2002).

59. Azo Vauguy and Didier Depry, "Le temple du savoir en souffrance," *Notre voix,* no. 718 (October 5, 2000).

60. Kemal Bakarsic, *The Libraries of Sarajevo and the Book That Saved Our Lives,* www.540.com/bosnia/briefings/article.html.

61. We owe this to Vesna Blazina of the University of Montreal, "Mémoricide ou la purification culturelle: la guerre contre les bibliothéques de Croatie et de Bosnie-Herzégovine," www.kakarigi.net/manu/blazina.htm.

62. For this subject see Andras Riedlmayer, *Libraries and Archives in Kosovo: A Postwar Report,* www.bosnia.prg.uk/bosrep/decfeb00/libraries.htm.

63. Interview with Latif Pedram, *Afghanistan. La Mémoire assassinée* (Paris: Éditions Mille et une Nuits, 2001), and "Afghanistan: la bibliothèque est en feu," *Autodafé,* no. 1 (2001).

64. Olivier Weber, *Le Faucon afghan, un voyage au pays des Taliban* (Paris: Robert Laffont, 2001).

65. For more on this subject, read the investigation by Philippe Flandrin, *Le Trésor perdu des rois d'Afghanistan* (Paris: Éditions du Rocher, 2001).

66. Patrick Healy, "Library's Volumes Safely Hidden," *Boston Globe,* May 13, 2003. This report was confirmed by a team of historians who arrived from Damascus five weeks later, then by J. M. Arnoult.

67. Robert Fisk, "Islamic Library Burned to the Ground," the *Independent,* April 15, 2003.

68. Cf. Zainab Bahrani, "Conjuring Mesopotamia: Imaginative Geography and a World Past," in Lynn Meskell, ed., *Archaeology Under Fire* (London: Routledge, 1998).

69. Declaration by American Secretary of Defense Donald Rumsfeld, *Le Monde* (July 2, 2003), 4. Meanwhile, the relevant clause of the Patriot Act of October 2001 did prompt a court challenge from the powerful American Library Association (ALA) against the U.S. government.

CHAPTER 8. PEACE DAMAGES

1. Cf. www.amnistia.net, which is particularly active, if not activist, on the chapter of revisionist history as well as the local and national press coverage at this time of the event and its consequences (and lack of consequences).

2. *Le Monde,* July 22, 1999.

3. *Le Progrès,* August 2, 2000.

4. Claude Burgelin, professor emeritus at Lyon II, in *Lyon capitale,* December 12, 2001.

5. Harry Skallerup, *Books Afloat and Ashore* (Hamden: Archon Books, 1974).

6. Cf. Harold Otness, "Passenger Ship Libraries," in *Journal of Library History* 14, no. 4 (Autumn 1979).

7. The information for this chapter was provided by recent editions of *Le Monde*, the *Detroit News* (in particular, Jennifer Brooks, "Thieves Plunder Libraries for Profit," January 21, 2001), the *Guardian*, and the *Asahi Shimbun*, as well as the *Dernières Nouvelles d'Alsace*. Also referred to were the studies by Ralph Munn, "The Problems of Theft and Mutilation," *Library Journal* 60 (August 1935), and John Burrows and Diane Cooper, *Theft and Loss from UK Libraries: A National Survey*, Police Research Group, Crime Prevention Unit Series, paper no. 37 (London: n.p., 1992).

8. Cf. Nicholas A. Basbanes, *A Gentle Madness* (New York: Henry Holt, 1995).

9. *La Nación*, relayed by *Ex Libris*, July 7, 2003.

10. Miles Harvey, *The Island of Lost Maps: A True Story of Cartographic Crimes* (New York: Random House, 2000).

11. Gaston Bachelard, in his introduction to *La Poétique de la reverie* (Paris: José Corti, 1960). Translated by Daniel Russell as *The Poetics of Reverie* (Boston: Beacon Press, 1971).

12. Cf. Bashkim Shehu, for "Enver Hoxha: La bibliothèque du dictateur," in *Autodafé*, no. 2 (Autumn 2001).

13. Cf. Aby Warburg, *Le Rituel de serpent* (Paris: Macula, 2003).

14. Fritz Saxl, quoted by Salvatore Settis, "Warburg continuatis. Description d'une bibliothèque," in *Le Pouvoir des bibliothèques* (Paris: Albin Michel, 1996). The entire history of the Warburg Library (in English) with photos and information about the London-based research center can be found at http://warburg.sas .ac.uk.

15. Cf. Marc Bergé, *Pour un Humanisme vécu. Abu Hayyan al-Tawhidi* (Damascus: Institut français de Damas, 1979).

CHAPTER 9. AN EMBARRASSMENT OF MODERNITY

1. Jean-Marc Mandosio, *L'Effondrement de la très grande bibliothèque nationale de France. Ses causes, ses consequences* (Paris: Encyclopédie des nuisances, 1999), and François Stasse, *La Véritable Histoire de la grande bibliothèque* (Paris: Seuil, 2002).

2. Read Nicholas Basbanes, *Patience and Fortitude* (New York: Harper, 2001), and Nicholson Baker, *Double Fold: Libraries and the Assault on Paper* (New York: Random House, 2001).

3. Cf. Basbanes, *Patience and Fortitude*.

4. *Shui xiedule Ba Jin?* [Who Vandalized Ba Jin], in *Nanfang Ribao*, December 19, 2002.

5. This report can be read online at www.education.gouv.fr/syst/igb/dochtm/ rapport2000htm. The details of the Grenoble sale were kindly furnished by Catherine Pouyet.

6. Cf. Lewis Coser et al., *Books: The Culture and Commerce of Publishing* (New York: Basic Books, 1982).

7. Cf. a dozen articles in *The Guardian* between August 14, 2000, and March 18, 2003, available online.

CHAPTER 10. FLAMEPROOF KNOWLEDGE

1. Message signed Jerry Randall and posted on the discussion list of *Ex Libris,* August 19, 2002.
2. Cf. Daniel Renoult, "Les Bibliothèques numériques," in Christian Jacob, *Des Alexandries I. Du livre au texte* (Paris: BNF, 2001).
3. In this instance, Omnipage 12.
4. Cited by Jenö Platthy, *Sources on the Earliest Greek Libraries, with the Testimonia* (Amsterdam: n.p., 1968).
5. Otto Pächt, *L'Enluminure médiévale* (Paris: Macula, 1997).

CHAPTER 11. EPILOGUE: RETURN TO ALEXANDRIA

1. Alexandre Buccianti mentions the matter in "Politique et polémiques autour d'une construction," in *Le Monde* (June 14, 2002). Contemporary accounts of the event that can be cited are Carol Berger, "Ancient History Is Bulldozed Away," in the *Daily Telegraph,* Monday, June 14, 1993, and Susanna Beaumont, "New Alexandria Library to Entomb the Ancient," in *Al-Ahram Weekly,* June 10–16, 1993.
2. Mustapha al-Ahnaf, ed., "Cedej Égypte/Monde arabe," in *La censure ou comment la contourner* (Brussels: Complexe, 2001).
3. In his inaugural speech at the seminar on freedom of expression held in Alexandria on May 19, 2003. Cf., in addition, the Norwegian database www.beaconforfreedom.org.
4. *Akhbar al-adab* [Literary News], sponsored by a weekly paper belonging to the state, *Akhbar el-yom.*
5. Gérard Grunberg, current director of the BPI of Beaubourg, was the first organizer of the Egyptian library. Cf. Fabrice Pataut, ed., *La Nouvelle Bibliothèque d'Alexandrie* (Paris: Buchet Chastel, 2003).

APPENDIX 1. THE GREAT WRITERS ARE UNANIMOUS: *DELENDA EST BIBLIOTHECA!*

1. Cf. the footnotes of Bernard Leuilliot in *Quatre-vingt-Treize* (Paris: Livre de Poche, 2001), and also Pierre Nicq, "Bastille et bibliothèque ou l'impossible accouplement," at *Le Français dans tous ses états,* www.crdp-montpellier.fr/ressources/frdtse/F044009A.html.
2. Only in 1970, says Jean-Pierre Bernès in Borges, *Oeuvres complètes,* vol. 1 (Paris: Gallimard, 1993).
3. Beaussant-Lefèvre, "Study in Paris," no. 8, December 3, 2001, session.
4. Jorge Luis Borges, *Oeuvres complètes,* vol. 2.
5. Cf. J. O. Ward, "Alexandria and Its Medieval Legacy: The Book, the Monk, and the Rose," in *The Library of Alexandria* (London: Tauris, 2000).

APPENDIX 2. A SHORT HISTORY OF THE CENSUS OF LOST BOOKS, WITH A LEGEND TO BRING IT TO A CLOSE—THE HIDDEN LIBRARY

1. David Arans, "A Note on the Lost Library of the Moscow Tsars," in *Journal of Library History* 18, no. 3 (Summer 1983).

BIBLIOGRAPHY

———— ꙮ ————

GENERAL WORKS

Cavallo, Guglielmo, and Roger Chartier. *Histoire de la lecture dans le monde occidental.* Paris: Seuil, 2001.

Delon, Michel. *La Bibliothèque est en feu.* Nanterre: Centre de recherches du Département de français de Paris-Nanterre, 1991.

Disraeli (d'Israeli), Isaac. *Curiosities of Literature,* 3rd edition. London: n.p., 1793.

Drogin, Marc. *Biblioclasm: The Mythical Origins, Magic Powers, and Perishability of the Written Word.* Savage, Md.: Bowman and Littlefield, 1989.

Edwards, Edward. *Libraries and Founders of Libraries.* 1864; reprint, New York: Burt Franklin, 1968.

———. *Memoirs of Libraries.* 1859; reprint, New York: Burt Franklin, 1964.

Franklin, Alfred. *Les Anciennes Bibliothèques de Paris.* Paris: Imprimerie nationale, 1873.

Hessel, Alfred. *A History of Libraries.* Translated and with supplementary material by Reuben Peiss. Metuchen, N.J.: Scarecrow Press, 1965.

Hoeven, Hans van der, ed. *Mémoire de Monde: Mémoire perdue. Bibliothèques et archives détruites au XXe siecle.* Paris: UNESCO, 1996.

Johnson, Elmer D., and Michael H. Harris. *History of Libraries in the Western World.* Metuchen, N.J.: Scarecrow Press, 1976.

Löwenthal, Leo. "Calibans Erbe." In *Schriften* Band 4, Seite 136–150. Frankfurt: n.p., 1984.

"L'universe des bibliothèques d'Alexandrie à Internet," *Magazine littéraire,* no. 349 (December 1996).

Poulain, Martine, ed. *Histoire des bibliothèques françaises.* Paris: Promidis-Cercle de la Librairie, 1992.

Wiegand, Wayne A., and G. Davis Donald Jr., eds. *Encyclopedia of Library History.* New York: Garland, 1994.

INTERNET SITES

For the advanced bibliography and for research on books and libraries from all periods of history, I widely consulted the following sites:

American Library Association (ALA). www.ala.org/bbooks/bookburning21.html. (Source for current world news involving book-burning.)

Bulletin des Bibliothèques de France. http://bbf.enssib.fr.

Exlibris. http://palimpsest.stanford.edu/byform/mailing-lists/exlibris.

International Federation of Library Associations (IFLA). www.ifla.org/search/search.htm. (Source for archived conferences.)

Librarian. www.librarian.net.

PREFACE

Richardson, Ernest C. *The Beginnings of Libraries*. Princeton: Princeton University Press, 1914.

CHAPTER 1. IN THE CRADLE OF LIBRARIES

Mesopotamia

Cameron, George Glenn. *Persepolis Treaty Tablets*. Chicago: University of Chicago Press, 1948.

Fergusson, James. *The Palaces of Niniveh and Persepolis Restored: An Essay on Ancient Assyrian and Persian Architecture*. London: John Murray, 1851.

Layard, Henri Austen. *Les Ruines de Ninive*. Paris: Errance, 1999.

Maul, Stefan M. *Tracing Assyrian Scholarship,* http://prelecture.Stanford.edu/lecturers/maul/tracing.html.

Menant, Joachim. *La Bibliothèque du palais de Ninive*. Paris: E. Leroux, 1880. (This book is available online at http://gallica.bnf.fr.)

Meskell, Lynn, ed. *Archaeology under Fire*. London: Routledge, 1998.

Potts, Daniel T. *Mesopotamian Civilization: The Material Foundations*. Ithaca, N.Y.: Cornell University Press, 1997.

Schmidt, Erich F. *Persepolis . . . 2, Contents of the Treasury and Other Discoveries*. Chicago: University of Chicago Press Oriental Institute, 1957.

CHAPTER 2. THE PAPYRUS REGION

Egypt

Andreu, Guillemette. *L'Égypte au temps des pyramides*. Paris: Hachette, 1994.

Cerny, Jaroslav. *Paper and Books in Ancient Egypt*. London: H. K. Murray, 1952.

Hussein, Mohamed A. *Origins of the Book: Egypt's Contribution to the Development of the Book from Papyrus to Codex*. New York: New York Graphic Society, 1972.

Lichtheim, Miriam. *Ancient Egyptian Literature*. Berkeley: University of California Press, 1980.

Montet, Pierre. *L'Égypte au temps des Ramsès, 1300–1100 avant J.-C.* Paris: Hachette, 1946.

Nichols, Charles L. *The Library of Rameses the Great*. Berkeley: University of California Press, 1964.

Parkinson, Richard, and Stephen Quirke. *Papyrus*. London: British Museum Press, 1995.

Putnam, George Haven. *Authors and Their Public in Ancient Times*. New York: G. P. Putnam, 1894.

Richardson, Ernest C. *Some Old Egyptian Librarians*. Berkeley: University of California Press, 1964.

Turner, Eric Gardner. *Greek Papyri, An Introduction*. Oxford: Oxford University Press, 1968.

Alexandria

El-Abbadi, Mostafa. *Vie et destin de l'ancienne Bibliothèque d'Alexandrie*. Paris: UNESCO, 1992.

Bernard, André. *Alexandrie la Grande*. Paris: Hachette, 1998.

Blum, Rudolf Kallimachos. *The Alexandrian Library and the Origins of Bibliography*. Madison: University of Wisconsin Press, 1991.

Botti, Giuseppe. *L'Acropole d'Alexandrie et le Serapeum d'après Aphtonius et les fouilles*. Alexandria: Imprimerie general L. Carrière, 1895.

Canfora, Luciano. *La Veritable Histoire de la bibliothèque d'Alexandrie*. Paris: Desjonquères, 1988. Translated by Martin Ryle as *The Vanished Library: A Wonder of the Ancient World*. Berkeley: University of California Press, 1990.

Casanova, Paul. *L'Incendie de la bibliothèque d'Alexandrie par les Arabes*. Paris: n.p., 1923.

Caesar, Julius. *The Civil War*. London: Penguin, 1976.

Diringer, David. *The Book Before Printing: Ancient, Medieval, and Oriental*. New York: Dover, 1982.

Empereur, Jean-Yves. *Alexandrie, redécouverte*. Paris: Fayard, 1998. Translated as *Discoveries: Alexandria: Jewel of Egypt*. New York: Harry N. Abrams, 2002; and *Alexandria: Past, Present and Future*. London: Thames and Hudson, 2002.

Forster, Edward M. *Alexandria: A History and a Guide*. Oxford: Oxford University Press, 1986.

Fraser, Peter Marshall. *Ptolemaic Alexandria*. Oxford: Oxford University Press, 1972.

Georgiadès, Patrice. *L'Étrange destin de la bibliothèque d'Alexandrie*. Alexandria, Egypt: n.p., 1982.

Jochum, Uwe. "The Alexandrian Library and Its Aftermath." In *Library History* vol. 15, no. 1 (1999).

Parsons, E. A. *The Alexandrian Library: Glory of the Hellenistic World*. New York: Elsevier, 1952.

Athens

Drossaart Lulofs, Henrik Joan. "Neleus of Scepsis and the Fate of the Library of the Peripatos." In *Tradition et traduction: Les texts philosophiques et scientifiques grecs au Moyen Âge latin. Hommage to Fernand Bossier*. Edited by Rita Beyers. Louvain: Louvain University Press, 1999.

Irigoin, Jean. *Le Livre grec des origins à la Renaissance*. In the Léopold Delisle Conferences. Paris: BNF, 2001.

Pfeiffer, Rudolf. *History of Classical Scholarship*. Oxford: Oxford University Press, 1968.

Platthy, Jenö. *Sources on the Earliest Greek Libraries, with the Testimonia*. Amsterdam: Adolf M. Hakkert, 1968.

Reynolds, Leighton D., and Nigel G. Wilson. *Scribes and Scholars: A Guide to the Transmission of Greek and Latin Literature*. Oxford: Clarendon Press, 1974.

Rome

Aulus-Gellius. *Noctium Atticarum* VII, XVII, 1–2 [*Attic Nights,* 2]. Cumberland, R.I.: Harvard University Press, 1982.

Beaujeu, Jean. *L'Incendie de Rome en 64 et les Chrétiens*. Brussels: n.p., 1960.

Berthaud (Abbé). *L'Incendie de Rome sous Néron et la critique contemporaine*. Toulouse: n.p., 1901.

Delarue, Jacques. *La Mort comme spectacle*. Followed by: *Les chrétiens ont-ils été les victims expiatoires de l'incendie de Rome?* n.l.: n.p., 1957.

Fantar, M'hamed Hassine. *Carthage, approche d'une civilization*. Tunis: ALIF, 1993.

Forbes, Clarence A. "Books for the Burning." In *Transactions of the American Philological Association* 67 (1936).

Gibbon, Edward. *The Decline and Fall of the Roman Empire*, vol. 1. London: Penguin, 1983.

Gigante, Marcello. *Philodemus in Italy, the Books from Herculaneum*. Ann Arbor: University of Michigan Press, 1995.

Gilberg, Mark. "Antonio Piaggio and the Conservation of the Herculaneum Papyri." In Daniels, V. *Early Advances in Conservation*. London: British Museum, 1988.

Gregorovius, Ferdinando. *Storia della città di Roma nel Medio evo*. Rome: Unione Arte Grafiche, 1990.

Hacquard, Georges. *Guide roman antique*. Paris: Hachette, 1952.

Homo, Léon. *Vespasien, l'empereur du bon sens*. Paris: Albin Michel, 1949.

Petronius. *The Satyricon*. Translated by William Arrowsmith. New York: Plume, 1983.

Sablayrolles, Robert. *Libertinus Miles. Les Cohortes de vigils*. Rome: École Française de Rome, 1996.

Salles, Catherine. *Lire à Rome*. Paris: Les Belles Lettres, 1992.

Suetonius. *The Twelve Caesars*. Translated by Robert Graves. London: Penguin, 2003.

Tanner, Thomas N. "A History of Early Christian Libraries from Jesus to Jerome." In *Journal of Library History*, vol. 14, no. 4 (Autumn 1979).

Vitruvius. *Les Dix Livres d'architecture de Vitruve corrigés et traduits en 1684 par Claude Perrault*. Liège: n.p., 1986. Translated by Morris Hicky Morgan as *The Ten Books of Architecture*. Dover, N.Y.: Dover, 1960.

Byzantium

Canfora, Luciano. *La Bibliothèque du patriarche: Photius censure dans la France de Mazarin*. Paris: Les Belles Lettres, 2003.

Ducas, Michael (or Doukas, Michel). *Historia Byzantina*. Bonn: Webieri, 1834. Translation by Harry J. Magoulias as *Decline and Fall of Byzantium to the Ottoman Turks*. Detroit: Wayne State University, 1975.

Gibbon, Edward. *The Decline and Fall of the Roman Empire*, vol. 2. London: Penguin, 1983.

Irigoin, Jean. "Survie et renouveau de la literature antique à Constantinople (9th siècle)." In *Griechische Kodikologie und Textüberlieferung*. Darmstadt: Wissenschaftliche Buchgesellschaft (Abt. Verlag), 1980.

Procopius of Caesarea. *The Secret History*. Translated by Richard Atwater. New York: Covici Friede, 1927.

Reynolds, Leighton D., and Nigel G. Wilson. *Scribes and Scholars: A Guide to the Transmission of Greek and Latin Literature*. Oxford: Clarendon Press, 1974.

Schlumberger, Gustave. *Le Siège, la prise et le sac de Constantinople par les Turcs en 1453*. Paris: Plon, 1914.

Tafur, Pero. *Andanças e viajes de Pero Tafur por diversas partes del mundo avidos (1435–1439)*. Madrid: Hernando, 1974. Translated by Malcolm Letts as *Pero Tafur: Travels and Adventures 1435–1439*. New York: Harper & Brothers, 1926.

Thompson, James W. *The Medieval Library*. New York: Hafner, 1957.

Treadgold, Warren T. *The Nature of the Bibliotheca of Photius*. Washington, D.C.: Dumbarton Oaks, 1980.

Vast, Henri. *Le Siège et la prise de Constantinople par les Turcs d'après des documents nouveaux*. Paris: n.p., 1880.

Villehardouin, Geoffrey de. *La Conquête de Constantinople*. Paris: Garnier Flammarion, 1969.

Wilson, Nigel G. "The Libraries of the Byzantine World." In *Griechische Kodikologie und Textüberlieferung*. Darmstadt: Wissenschaftliche Buchgesellschaft (Abt. Verlag), 1980.

CHAPTER 3. ISLAM OF THE FIRST DAYS

Islamic Andalusia

Dozy, Reinhart. *Histoire des Musulmans d'Espagne*. Leiden: E. J. Brill, 1932. Translated by Francis Griffin Stokes as *Spanish Islam: A History of the Muslims in Spain*. Kita, Mont.: Kessinger, 2003.

Erdoes, Richard. *AD 1000*. Berkeley, Calif.: Ulysses Press, 1998.

Fierro Bello, Maribel, and M. Isabel. *La Heterodoxia en al-Andalus durante el periodo omeya*. Madrid: Instituto Hispano-Arabe de Cultura, 1987.

Guichard, Pierre. *De la Conquête arabe à la Reconquête: grandeur et fragilité d'al-Andalus*. Grenada: Legado Andalusi, 2003.

Ibn Sa'id al-Andalusî. *Kitâb tabakât al-umam* (Book of the Categories of Nations). Translated by R. Blachère. Paris: n.p., 1935.

Lévi-Provençal, Évariste. *Histoire de l'Espagne musulmane*. Paris: G. P. Maisonneuve, 1950.

Martinez Gros, Gabriel. *L'Idéologie omeyyade: la construction de la légitimité du califat de Cordoue: Xe–XIe siècles*. Madrid: Casa de Velazquez, 1992.

Polastron, Lucien X. *Le Papier, 2,000 ans d'histoire et de savoir-faire*. Paris: Imprimerie Nationale, 1999.

Ribera Tarrago, Julián. *Bibliófilos y bibliotecas en la España musulmana*. Saragossa: n.p., 1896.

Sibai, Mohamed Makki. *Mosque Libraries: A Historical Study*. London: Mansell, 1987.

Viguera Molins, Maria Jésus. "Imágenes de Almanzor." In *Codex Aquilarensis* no. 14. La Península ibérica y el Mediterráneo entre los siglos XI y XLL, actas II, Palencia, 1999.

Wasserstein, David J. "The Library of al-Hakam al-Mustansir and the Culture of Islamic Spain." In *Manuscripts of the Middle East, 1990–1991*, vol. 5. Leiden: Ter Lugt Press, 1993.

Medieval Islam in the East and Middle East

Balty-Guesdon, Marie-Geneviève. "Le Bayt el-hikma de Bagdad." In *Arabica*, no. 39 (1992).

Benjelloun-Laroui, Latifa. *Les Bibliothèques au Maroc*. Paris: Maisoneuve et Larose, 1990.

Bartol, Vladimir. *Alamut*. Seattle: Scala House, 2005.

Bergé, Marc. *Pour un Humanisme vécu: Abu Hayyân al-Tawhîdî*. Damascus: Institut français de Damas, 1979.

Berkey, Jonathan P. *The Transmission of Knowledge in Medieval Cairo: A Social History of Islamic Education*. Princeton, N.J.: Princeton University Press, 1992.

Bulliet, Richard W. *The Camel and the Wheel*. Cambridge: Harvard University Press, 1975.

Chauvin, Victor. *Le Livre dans le monde arabe*. Brussels: Goosens, 1911.

Eche, Yusef. *Bibliothèques arabes publiques et semi-publiques en Mésopotamie, en Syrie et en Égypte au Moyen Âge*. Damascus: n.p., 1967.

Fu'ad Sayyid, Ayman. "Que reste-t-il de la bibliothèque des Fatimides?" In *Des Alexandries II. Les metamorphoses du lecteur*. Paris: BNF, 2003.

Halm, Heinz. *The Fatimids and Their Tradition of Learning*. London: I. B. Tauris, 1997.

Hitti, Philip K. *The Arabs*. London: Macmillan and Co., 1948.

Ibn Khaldun. *Discours sur l'Histoire universelle (al-Muqaddima)*. Beirut: Commission internationale pour la traduction des chefs-d'oeuvre, 1967–1968.

Juvaini, 'Ala-ad-Din 'Ata-Malik. *Genghis Khan: The History of the World Conqueror*. Translated by J. A. Boyle. Manchester, England: Manchester University Press, 1997.

Kohlberg, Etan. *A Medieval Muslim Scholar at Work: Ibn Tâwûs and His Library*. Leiden: E. J. Brill, 1992.

Khoury, R. G. "Une Description fantastique des fonds de la Bibliothèque royale khizanat al-kutub au Caire, sous le régime du calife fatimide al'Aziz bi-llah." In *Proceedings of the Ninth Congress of the Union européene des arabisants et islamisants*, Amsterdam, September 1 to 7, 1978. Leiden: E. J. Brill, 1981.

Lewis, Bernard. *The Assassins: A Radical Sect in Islam*. New York: Basic Books, 2002.

Mutahhari, Murtadha. *The Burning of Libraries in Iran and Alexandria*. Tehran Islamic Propagation Organization, 1983.

Raymond, André. *Le Caire*. Paris: Arthème Fayard, 1993. Translated by Willard Wood as *Cairo*. Cambridge: Harvard University Press, 2000.

Ringel, Joseph. *Césarée de Palestine, étude historique et archéologique*. Paris: Éditions Ophrys, 1975.

Roxborough, David. *The Persian Album, 1400–1600: From Dispersal to Collection.* New Haven, Conn.: Yale University Press, 2004.

Trésors fatimides du Caire, exhibition catalog from the Institute of the Arab World. Paris: Institut du monde arabe, 1998.

Wiet, Gaston. "Recherches sur les bibliothéques égyptiennes au Xe et au XIe siècle." In *Cahiers de civilization médiévale,* no. 6 (1963).

CHAPTER 4. PEOPLE OF THE BOOK

The Jewish World

Dahan, Gilbert, ed. *Le Brûlement du Talmud à Paris, 1242–1244.* Paris: Cerf 1999.

Grendler, Paul. "The Destruction of Hebrew Books in Venice, 1568." In *Proceedings of the American Academy for Jewish Research,* vol. 45. Jerusalem: American Academy for Jewish Research, 1978.

Haddad, Gérard. *Les Biblioclastes: le Messie et l'autodafé.* Paris: Grasset, 1990.

Kahle, Paul E. *The Cairo Geniza.* London: British Academy, 1947.

Lea, Henri-Charles. *Histoire de l'Inquisition au Moyen Âge.* Paris: Société nouvelle de librarie, 1901. Reprint, Grenoble: Millon, 1990.

Roth, Cecil. *A History of the Marranos.* Philadelphia: Jewish Publications Society, 1947. Reprint, New York: Schocken, 1975.

Reuchlin, Johannes. *Recommendation Whether to Confiscate, Destroy, and Burn All Jewish Books: A Classic Treatise against Anti-semitism.* Translated, edited, and with a foreword by Peter Wortman. New York: Paulist Press, 2000.

CHAPTER 5. ASIA BEFORE THE TWENTIETH CENTURY

China before 1911

Allen, Roland. *The Siege of the Peking Legations.* London: Smith, Elder, and Co., 1901.

Alleton, Viviane. *L'Écriture chinoise.* Paris: PUF, 1970.

Billeter, Jean-François. *Li Zhi philosophe maudit (1527–1602).* Geneva: Droz, 1979.

Bodde, Derk. *China's First Unifier: A Study of the Ch'in Dynasty as Seen in the Life of Li Ssù . . . (280?–208 BC).* Leiden: E. J. Brill, 1938. Reprinted in Hong Kong: Hong Kong University Press, 1967.

Bourgerie, Raymond, and Pierre Lesouef. *Palikao (1860). Le Sac du palais d'été et la prise de Pekin.* Paris: Economica, 1995.

Chavannes, Édouard. *Les livres chinois avant l'invention du papier.* Paris: n.p., 1905.

———. *Revue Asiatique: La Divination par l'écaille de tortue dans la haute Antiquité chinoise (d'après un livre de M. Lo Tchen-Yu).* Paris: Imprimerie nationale, 1911.

Chen Dengyuan (Ch'en Teng-yüan). *Gujindianjijusankao* (Considerations on the Collection and Destruction of Books in Chinese History). Shanghai: n.p., 1936.

Cheng, Anne, *Histoire de la pensée chinoise.* Paris: Seuil, 1997.

Cheng Huanwen. "The Destruction of Chinese Books in the Peking Siege of 1900." In *Proceedings of the 62nd IFLA General Conference.* August 25–31, 1996.

―――. "The Destruction of a Great Library: China's Loss Belongs to the World." In *American Libraries Magazine* 28 (1997).

Demiéville, Paul, and Yves Hervouet. "Littérature." In *Dictionnaire de la civilisation chinoise*. Paris: Albin Michel, 1998.

Drège, Jean-Pierre. *Les Bibliothèques en Chine au temps des manuscripts: jusqu'au Xe siècle*. Paris: École française d'Extrême-Orient, 1991.

Dudbridge, Glen. *Lost Books in Medieval China*. London: British Library, 2000.

Edgren, Sören, "Cangshu: The Tradition of Collecting Books in China." In *Biblis: The Georg Svensson Lectures Yearbook, 1995–1996*. Stockholm: n.p., 1996.

Fleming, Peter. *The Siege at Peking*. Cary, N.C.: Oxford University Press, 1983.

Giles, Lancelot. *The Siege of the Peking Legations: A Diary*. Perth: Western Australia University Press, 1970.

Goodrich, Luther Carrington. *The Literary Inquisition of Ch'ien Lung*. Baltimore: Waverly Press, 1935.

Granet, Marcel. *La Pensée chinoise*. Paris: Albin Michel, 1990.

Guy, R. Kent. *The Emperor's Four Treasuries: Scholars and the State in the Late Ch'ien-lung Era*. Cambridge: Harvard University Press, 1987.

Hérisson, Comte d' (also Irisson or d'Irisson, Maurice). *Journal d'un interprète en Chine*. Paris: Paul Ollendorf, 1886.

Huang Weilian (also Wong, V. L.). "Libraries and Book-collecting in China from the Epoch of the Five Dynasties to the End of Ch'ing." In *T'ien hsia Monthly* 8, no. 4 (April 1939).

Hugo, Victor. "Au Capitaine Butler." In *Actes et Paroles II*. Paris: n.p., 1875, and in *Oeuvres complètes. Politique*. Paris: Robert Laffont, 1985.

Jiang Fucong (also Chiang Fu-Ts'ung). "A Historical Sketch of Chinese Libraries." In *Philobiblon* 2, no. 2 (March 1948).

Keightley, David N. *Sources of Shang History: The Oracle-bone Chinese Inscriptions of Bronze Age China*. Los Angeles: University of California Press, 1978.

Leys, Simon. *L'Humeur, l'honneur, l'horreur. Essais sur la culture et la politique chinoises*. Paris: Robert Laffont, 1991.

Li Xuequin. *Eastern Zhou and Qin Civilizations*. New Haven, Conn.: Yale University Press, 1985.

Loewe, Michael, et al. "The Classical Philosophical Writings." In *The Cambridge History of Ancient China*. Cambridge: Cambridge University Press, 1999.

Moore, Oliver. *Reading the Past: Chinese*. Berkeley: University of California Press, 2000.

Qian Cunxun (also Tsien Tsuen-hsuin). *Written on Bamboo and Silk: The Beginnings of Chinese Books and Inscriptions*. Chicago: University of Chicago Press, 1962.

Rawson, Jessica, ed. *Mysteries of Ancient China*. London: British Museum Press, 1996.

Ren Jinyu. *Zhongguo cangshulou* (Book Collections in China). Shenyang: n.p., 2001.

Schiffer, Kristofer. "Xunsi" and "Yang Zhu." In *Dictionnaire de la civilisation chinoise*. Paris: Albin Michel, 1998.

Sima Qian. *Les Mémoires historiques (Shiji)*. Partial translation by Édouard Chavannes. Paris: Librairie d'Amerique et d'Orient, 1969.

———. *Records of the Grand Historian: Qin Dynasty*. Translated by Burton Watson. New York: Columbia University Press, 1995.

Swann, Nancy Lee. "Seven Intimate Library Owners." In *Harvard Journal of Asiatic
Studies* 1, no. 3–4 (November 1936).

Tan Zhuoyuan (also Cho-yüan Tan and Cheuk-woon Taam). *The Development
of Chinese Libraries under the Ch'ing Dynasty, 1644–1911*. Shanghai: China
Commercial Press, 1935.

Twitchett, Denis. *Printing and Publishing in Medieval China*. New York: Frederic
C. Beil, 1983.

Twitchett, Denis, and John K. Fairbank. *The Cambridge History of Ancient China*.
Cambridge: Cambridge University Press, 1986.

Watson, Burton. *Early Chinese Literature*. New York: Columbia University Press,
1962.

Wilkinson, Endymion. *Chinese History: A Manual*. Cambridge: Harvard University
Press, 2000.

Wu Guangqing (also Wu Kuang-ts'ing). "Libraries and Book-collecting in China before
the Invention of Printing." In *T'ien hsia Monthly* 5, no. 3 (October 1937).

Yates, Robin D. S. *Five Lost Classics: Tao, Huang-Lao, and Yin-Yang in Han China*.
New York: Ballantine Books, 1997.

Yu Qiuyu. "The Vicissitudes of Tianyi Pavilion." In *Chinese Literature* (Autumn
1998).

India

Coppieters, Jean-Christian. "Xuanzang." In *Dictionnaire du bouddhisme*. Paris:
Encyclopedia Universalis, 1999.

Keay, F. E. *Ancient Indian Education: An Inquiry into Its Origin, Development and
Ideals*. London: Oxford University Press, 1918.

Marshall, John. *A Guide to Taxila*. Cambridge: Harvard University Press, 1960.

Mukerji, Radha Kumud. *Ancient Indian Education, Brahmanical and Buddhist*.
London: Macmillan, 1947.

Prakash, Buddha. "Aspects of Indian History and Civilization." In *Agra* (1965).

Régnier, Rita. "Nalanda." In *Dictionnaire du bouddhisme*. Paris: Encyclopedia Universalis, 1999.

Japan

Ichikawa, Hiroshi. "Pensée, grands traits de la . . ." *Dictionnaire de la civilisation
japonaise*. Paris: Hazen, 1994.

Keene, Donald. *Les Journaux intimes au Japon*. Paris: Institute of Advanced Japanese Studies of the Collège de France, 2003. In English as *Modern Japanese
Diaries*. New York: Henry Holt, 1995.

Kitagawa, Joseph M. *Religions in Japanese History*. New York: Columbia University
Press, 1966.

CHAPTER 6. THE CHRISTIAN WEST

The Inquisition in Catholic Spain

Bennassar, Bartolomé, *L'Inquisition espagnole, XVe–XIXe siècles*. Paris: Hachette, 1979.

Chaide, Malón de. *La Conversión de la Magdalena*. n.l.: n.p., 1588.

Desfourneaux, Marcellin. *L'Inquisition espagnole et les livres français au XVIIIe siècle*. Paris: P.U.F., 1963.

Justel Calabozo, Braulio. *La real Biblioteca de El Escorial y sus Manuscritos arabes*. Madrid: Instituto. Hispano-Arabe de Cultura, 1987.

Kamen, Henry. *The Spanish Inquisition*. New York: New American Library, 1975.

Lea, Henri-Charles. *Histoire de l'Inquisition au Moyen Âge*. Paris: Société nouvelle de librarie, 1901. Reprint, Grenoble: Millon, 1991.

Liebman, Seymour B. *The inquisitors and the Jews in the New World*. Coral Gables, Fla.: University of Miami Press, 1974.

Montoiche (or Montoche), Guillaume de. "Voyage et expedition de Charles Quint au pays de Tunis de 1535." In Gachard et Piot, eds. *Collection des voyages des souverains des Pays-Bas*. Brussels: Commission Royale d'Histoire, 1881.

Olmos, Francisco. *Cervantes en su época*. Madrid: Ricardo Aguilera, 1968.

Pardo Tomás, José. *Ciencia y censura. La Inquisicíon española y los libros cientificos en los siglos XVI y XVII*. Madrid: CSIC, 1991.

Ribera Tarrago, Julián. *Bibliófilos y bibliotecas en la España musulmana*. Saragossa: n.p., 1896.

Santos, Francisco de los. *Descripcíon del real monasterio de S. Lorenzo de El Escorial, única maravilla del mundo. . . .* Madrid: Juan Garcia Infancion, 1681.

Sigüenza, José de. *Historia primitiva y exacta del monasterio del Escorial, escrita en el siglo XVI*. Madrid: M. Tello, 1881.

Zarco Cuevas, P. Julián. *Catálogo de manuscritos castellanos de la Real Bibloteca de El Escorial*, vol. 3. San Lorenzo de El Escorial: Tip. del Archivos, 1929.

The New World

Acosta, José de. *Historia natural y moral de las Indias* (Natural and Moral History of the Indies). Durham, N.C.: Duke University Press, 2002.

Baudin, Louis. *L'Empire socialiste des Inka*. Paris: Institut d'Ethnologie, 1928. Translated as *A Socialist Empire: The Incas of Peru*. Princeton, N.J.: Van Nostrand, 1961.

Bollaert, William. *Sur les Signes graphiques des anciens Péruviens*. n.l.: n.p., 1874.

Blom, Frans. *Conquest of Yucatán*. New York: Houghton Mifflin, 1936.

Calderón, Diego de Landa. *Relation des choses de Yucatán*. Paris: Les Editions Genet, 1928.

Diaz del Castillo, Bernal. *The True Story of the Conquest of Mexico*. New York: Robert McBride and Co., 1927.

Fernández de Oviedo y Valdés Gonzalo. *Historia general y natural de las Indias*. n.l.: n.p., 1529. Translated by Earl Raymond Hewitt as *General and Natural History of the Indies*. Berkeley: University of California Press, 1941.

Grover, Mark L. "The Book and the Conquest: Jesuit Libraries in Colonial Brazil." In *Libraries and Culture* 28, no. 3 (Summer 1993).

Hallewell, Laurence. "Rare Books in Latin American Libraries." In *IFLA Journal* 21, no. 1 (1995). At www.ifla.org.

Las Casas, Bartolomé de. *Tyrannies et crautez des Espagnols commises es Indes occidentals, qu'on dit le Nouveau Monde.* Rouen: Chez Jacques Caillous', 1630.

———. *Short Account of the Destruction of the Indies.* New York: Penguin, 1999.

Lea, Henri-Charles. *Histoire de l'Inquisition au Moyen Âge.* Paris: Société nouvelle de librarie, 1901. Reprint, Grenoble: Millon, 1991.

Montaigne, Michel de. *Essais,* volume 3. Paris: Garnier Flammarion, 1998. Translated by M. A. Screech as *The Complete Essays.* New York: Penguin, 1993.

Moraes, Rubens Borba de. *Livros e Biblotecas no Brasil Colonial.* Rio de Janeiro: LTC, 1979.

Popol-Vuh. Les Dieux, les héros et les hommes de l'ancien Guatemala d'après le "Livre de Conseil." Translated by Georges Raynaud. Paris: Librairie d'Amerique et d'Orient, 1975.

Prescott, William Hickling. *History of the Conquest of Mexico.* New York: Harper & Brothers, 1843.

Sarmiento de Gamboa, Pedro. *History of the Incas.* Cambridge: Hakluyt Society, 1907.

Tozzer, Alfred M., ed. *Landa's Relacíon de las cosas de Yucatán.* Cambridge, Mass.: Harvard University Press, 1941.

Von Hagen, Victor Wolfgang. *The Aztec and Mayan Papermakers.* New York: J. J. Augustin, 1944.

The Middle Ages and the Renaissance

Barret, Pierre, and Jean-Noël Gurgand. *Le Roi des derniers jours.* Paris: Hachette, 1981.

Brisac, Catherine. "Les grands bibles romanes dans la France du sud." In *Les Dossiers de l'archéologie* no. 14 (1976).

Chartier, Roger. *L'Ordre des livres: lecteurs, auteurs, bibliothèques en Europe entre XIVe et XVIIIe siècle.* Aix-en-Provence: Éditions Alinéa, 1992.

Cohn, Norman. *The Pursuit of the Millennium.* London: Secker and Warburg, 1957.

Csapodi, Csaba. *Bibliotheca Corviniana.* Budapest: Magyar Helikon, 1967.

Edwards, Edward. *Libraries and Founders of Libraries.* 1864; reprint, New York: Burt Franklin, 1968.

Franklin, Alfred. *Les Anciennes Bibliothèques de Paris.* Paris: Imprimerie Royale, 1873.

Gillett, Charles Ripley. *Burned Books: Neglected Chapters in British History and Literature.* New York: Columbia University Press, 1932.

Johnson, Elmer D., and Michael H. Harris. *History of Libraries in the Western World.* Metuchen, N.J.: Scarecrow Press, 1976.

Merryweather, F. Somner. *Biblomania in the Middle Ages.* London: n.p., 1849.

Pellegrin, Élisabeth. *Bibliothèques retrouvées: manuscripts, bibliothèques et bibliophiles du Moyen Âge et de la Renaissance.* Paris: IRHS, 1988.

Perrens, François-Tommy. *Jérôme Savonarole, sa vie, ses predications, ses écrits. . . .* Paris: n.p., 1853.

Réau, Louis. *Histoire du vandalisme.* Paris: Robert Laffont, 1994.

Reynolds, Leighton D., and Nigel G. Wilson. *Scribes and Scholars: A Guide to the Transmission of Greek and Latin Literature.* New York: Oxford University Press, 1991.

Rodocanachi, Emmanuel-Pierre. *Histoire de Rome, le pontificat de Léon X.* Paris: Hachette, 1931.

Scaife, Walter Bell. *Florentine Life During the Renaissance.* Baltimore: Johns Hopkins University Press, 1893.

Schertlin, Sebastian. *Leben und Thaten des . . . Herrn Sebastian Schertlin von Burtenbach durch ihn selbst deutsch beschrieben . . . herausgegeben von Ottmar F. H. Schönhuth. . . .* Münster: Aschendorff, 1858.

Thompson, James W. *The Medieval Library.* New York: Hafner, 1957.

Wilson, Robert Middlewood. *The Lost Literature of Medieval England.* London: Methuen, 1952.

Young, George. *Les Médicis.* Paris: Robert Laffont, 1969.

Zeller, Jules-Sylvain. *Italie et Renaissance.* Paris: Didier et cie., 1883.

Zorzi, Mariano. "Le Biblioteche a Venezia nell'età di Galileo." In *Galileo Galilei e la cultura veneziana.* Venice: Instituto veneto di scienza, lettere ed arti, 1995.

Revolutions

Bacha, Myriam, and Christian Hottin, eds. *Les Bibliothèques parisiennes. Architectures et décor.* Paris: Action artistique de la ville de Paris, 2002.

Baudrillart, Henri. *Rapport sur les pertes épouvées par les bibliothèques publiques de Paris en 1870–1871, adressé à M. le minister de l'Instruction publique.* Paris: P. Dupont, 1871.

Bell, Georges. *Paris incendié. Histoire de la Commune de 1871.* Paris: Imp. Martinet, 1872.

Constitution d'un patrimoine parisien: la Bibliothèque historique depuis l'incendie de 1871. Exhibition catalog, Hôtel de Lamoignon, Paris, June 12–July 31, 1980.

Deloche, Bernard, and Jean-Michel Leniaud. *La Culture des sans-culottes.* Paris: Presses du Languedoc, 1989.

Dummer, Edwin Heyse. "Johann Christoph von Aretin: A Reevaluation." In *Library Quarterly* 16, no. 2 (April 1946).

Fejtö, François. *Joseph II.* Paris: Plon, 1953.

Garrett, Jeffrey. *The Fate of Monastic Libraries in Central Europe, 1780–1810.* Northwestern University presentation at a conference in Hungary, October 3, 1997. At www.library.northwestern.edu/collections/garrett/kloster.

Heine, Heinrich. *Lutece: letters sur la vie politique, artistique et sociale de la France.* Paris: Michel Levy frères, 1855.

Hugo, Victor. "A qui la faute?" In *L'Année terrible.* Paris: Librairie de Victor Hugo illustré, 1872.

Labiche, Jean-Baptiste. *Notice sur les depots littéraires et la revolution bibliographique de la fin du siècle dernier.* Paris: A. Parent, 1880.

Lacroix, Abbé E. *La semaine sanglante.* Abbeville: n.p., n.d.

Lebendiges Büchererbe Säkularisation, Mediatisierung und die Bayerische Staats-bibliothek. Munich: Bayerische Staatsbibliothek, 2003.

Le Roy Ladurie, Emmanuel. *1789 Le Patrimoine libéré*. Paris: BNF, 1989.

Lidsky, Paul. *Les Écrivains contre la Commune*. Paris: La Découverte, 1999.

Lissagaray, Prosper-Olivier. *Histoire de la Commune de 1871*. Paris: 1896; reprint, Paris: La Découverte, 2005.

Mech, Paul. "Les bibliothèques jésuites." In *Histoire des bibliothèques françaises. Les bibliothèques sous l'Ancien Régime: 1530–1789*. Paris: Promodis—Éditions du Cercle de la Librairie, 1988.

Mercier, Louis-Sébastien. *Tableau de Paris*. Hamburg: n.p., 1781.

Paris, Louis. *Les Manuscrits de la bibliothèque du Louvre brulés dans la nuit du 23 au 24 mai 1871*. Paris: Bureau du Cabinet historique, 1872.

Polastron, Lucien X. *Le Papier, 2000 ans d'histoire et de savoir-faire*. Paris: Imprimerie Nationale, 1999.

Réau, Louis. *Histoire du vandalisme*. Paris: Robert Laffont, 1994.

Reclus, Élie. *La Commune de Paris au jour le jour, 19 mars–28 mai 1871*. Paris: Séguier, 2000.

Riberette, Pierre. *Les Bibliothèques françaises pendant la Révolution (1789–1795), recherches sur un essai de catalogue collectif*. Paris: BNF, 1970.

Rocquain, Félix. *L'Esprit révolutionnaire avant la Révolution, 1715–1789*. Paris: Plon, 1878. Translated as *The Revolutionary Spirit Preceeding the French Revolution*. London: Swan Sonnenschein and Co., 1891.

Sade, Donatien A. F. de. "Français, encore un effort si vous-voulez être républicains." In *La Philosophie dans le boudoir*. London: Compagnie, 1795. Translated by Richard Seaver and Austryn Wainhouse as *The Complete Justine, Philosophy in the Bedroom and Other Writings*. New York, Grove Press, 1965.

Salin, Patrice. *Un coin de tableau, mai 1871. Catalogue raisonné d'une collection d'ouvrages rares et curieux, anciens et modernes, détruite au palais du Conseil d'État du 23 au 24 mai 1871*. Paris: J. Leclere, 1872.

Varry, Dominique. "Le livre, otage de la révolution: consequences bibliographiques des saisies politiques." In *Le Livre voyageur*. Records of the International Seminar organized by the ENSSIB and the CERL on May 23–24, 1997, Paris, 2000.

CHAPTER 7. THE NEW BIBIOCLASTS

World Wars

Fischbach, Gustave. *Guerre de 1870. Le siege et le bombardement de Strasbourg*. Strasbourg: Maurice Schauenburg, 1871.

Guibal, Georges. *Le Siege et le bombardement de Strasbourg*. Conference given at Castres and at Montauban, October 15 and 22, 1870, Toulouse, 1870.

Jünger, Ernst. *Jardins et Routes*, Journal 1, 1939–1940. Paris: Christian Bourgeois, 1979.

———. *Second journal parisien*, Journal 3, 1943–1945. Paris: Christian Bourgeois, 1980.

Lamy, Étienne. *La Bibliothèque de Louvain*. Commemorative session of the fourth anniversary of the fire. Paris: Perrin, 1919.

Library of the Catholic University of Louvain. *Les Crimes de guerre commis lors de l'invasion du territoire national, mai 1940: la destruction de la bibliothèque de l'université de Louvain.* Liège: Georges Thone, 1946.

Mehring, Walter. *Die verlorene Bibliothek: Autobiographie einer Kultur.* Hamburg: Rowohlt, 1952. Translated by Richard and Clara Winston as *The Lost Library.* New York: Bobbs and Merrill, 1951.

Sebald, Winifred Georg. *Luftkrieg und Literatur: mit einem Essay zu Alfred Andersch.* Munich: C. Hanser, 1999. Translation by Anthea Bell as *On the Natural History of Destruction: With Essays on Alfred Anderson, Jean Améry, and Peter Weiss.* New York: Random House, 2003.

Simon, Claude. *La Route des Flandres.* Paris: Éditions de Minuit, 1960. Translated by Richard Howard as *The Flanders Road.* New York: Riverrun Press, 1985.

Stubbings, Hilda Urén. *Blitzkrieg and Books: British and European Libraries as Casualties of World War II.* Bloomington: University of Indiana Press, 1993.

Ungerer, Tomi. *À la Guerre comme à la guerre: dessins et souvenirs d'enfance.* Paris: École des Loisirs, 2002. Translation as *A Childhood Under the Nazis.* Boulder, Colo.: Robert Rinehart, 1998.

Welch, Theodore. *Libraries and Librarianship in Japan.* Westport, Conn.: Greenwood Press, 1997.

Nazism and Holocaust

Badia, Gilbert, et al. *Les Bannis de Hitler: accueil et lutte des exiles allemands en France, 1933–1939.* Paris: Presses universitaires de Vincennes, 1984.

Benjamin, Walter. *Je déballe ma Bibliothéque.* Paris: Payot et Rivages, 2000. Translated by Harry Zohn as "Unpacking My Library." In *Illuminations.* New York: Schocken, 1969.

Bienkowska, Barbara. *Books in Poland: Past and Present.* Wiesbaden: O. Harrassowitz, 1990.

———. "Report on the Losses of Polish Libraries in the Second World War." In *Polish Libraries Today* 3 (1995).

Borin, Jacqueline. "Embers of the Soul: The Destruction of Jewish Books and Libraries in Poland during World War II." In *Libraries and Culture* 28, no. 4 (Autumn 1993).

Cassou, Jean, ed. *Le Pillage par les Allemands des oeuvres d'art et des bibliothèques appartenant à des Juifs en France.* Paris: Éditions du Centre, 1947.

Chevreuse, Irene. "Quels furent les livres brulés à Berlin?" In *L'Illustration,* no. 4713 (July 1, 1933).

Collins, Donald E., and Herbert P. Rothfeder. "The Einsatzstab Reichsleiter Rosenberg and the Looting of Jewish and Masonic Libraries during World War II." In *Journal of Library History* 18, no. 1 (Winter 1983).

Corti, José. *Souvenirs désordonnés.* Paris: José Corti, 1983.

Debenedetti, Giacomo. *October 16, 1943/Eight Jews.* Translated by Estelle Gilson. South Bend, Ind.: University of Notre Dame Press, 2001.

Feliciano, Hector. *Le Musée disparu. Enquête sur le pillage des oeuvres d'art en France par les Nazis.* Paris: Austral Documents, 1995.

Friedmann, Philip. "The Fate of the Jewish Book During the Nazi Era." In *Jewish Book Annual* 15 (1957).

Grimsted, Patricia Kennedy. "The Odyssey of the Petliura Library during World War II." In *Harvard Ukrainian Studies,* 22 (1999).

——. *Trophies of War and Empire: The Archival Heritage of Ukraine, World War II, and the International Politics of Restitution.* Cambridge: Harvard University Press, 2001.

——. "Twice Plundered, but Still Not Home from War: The Fate of Three Slavic Libraries Confiscated by the Nazis from Paris." In *Solanus,* no. 16 (2002).

Hacken, Richard. *The Jewish Community Library in Vienna: from Dispersion and Destruction to Partial Restoration.* At www.lib.virginia.edu/wess/LB147-10-Hacken.pdf.

International Military Tribunal. *Trial of the Major War Criminals before the International Military Tribunal,* vol. 8. Nuremburg: n.p., 1947–1949.

Jacob-Delmas, Jacqueline, and Lucien Steinberg. "Austerlitz-Lévitan-Bassano." In *Le Monde juif,* no. 146 (March 1, 1993).

Krockow, Christian, Graf von. *Scheiterhaufen: Grösse und Elend des deutschen Geistes.* Hamburg: n.p., 1993.

L'Illustration, no. 4713 (July 1, 1933).

"Library Pillaging by Nazis Surveyed," *New York Times,* April 4, 1945, page 12, column 1.

Reymes, Nicolas. "Les Livres dans la tormente. Le pillage des bibliothèques appartenant à des Juifs pendant l'Occupation." In *Revue d'histoire de la Shoah–Le Monde juif,* no. 168 (January–April 2000).

Richard, Lionel. *Le Nazisme et la culture.* Brussels: Complexe, 1988.

Rose, Jonathan, ed. *The Holocaust and the Book.* Amherst: University of Massachusetts Press, 2001.

Roth, Joseph. "L'Auto-da-fé de l'Esprit." In *L'Apport des Juifs d'Allemagne à la civilization allemande,* vol. 2. Paris: Cahiers juifs, 1933.

Ryback, Timothy W. "Hitler's Forgotten Library." In *Atlantic Monthly,* Boston, 2003. At www.theatlantic.com/issues/2003/05/ryback.htm.

Sebald, Winifred Georg. *Austerlitz.* Actes: Sud, 2002. Translated by Anthea Bell as *Austerlitz.* New York: Random House, 2001.

Steig, Margaret F. *Public Libraries in Nazi Germany.* Tuscaloosa: University of Alabama Press, 1992.

"Tentative List of Jewish Cultural Treasures in Axis-occupied Countries." In *Jewish Social Studies* 8, no. S1 (1946).

Waite, Robert G. "Returning Jewish Cultural Property: The Handling of Books Looted by the Nazis in the American Zone of Occupation, 1945–1952." In *Libraries and Culture* 37, no. 3 (Summer 2002).

The End of the Twentieth Century

Assia, Issak. "Public Libraries in Africa: A report and Annotated Bibliography." Oxford: International Network for the Availability of Scientific Publications, 2000. At www.inasp.org.uk/lsp/libraries/PublicLibrariesInAfrica.pdf.

Ba Jin (Pa Kin). *Random Thoughts.* Hong Kong: Joint Pub., 1985.

Bahrani, Zainab. "Conjuring Mesopotamia: Imaginative Geography and a World Past." In Lynn Meskell, ed., *Archaeology Under Fire*. London: Routledge, 1998.

Bakarsic, Kemal. *The Libraries of Sarajevo and the Book That Saved Our Lives*. At www.540.com/bosnia/briefings/article.html.

Barclay, John. *The Seventy-year Ebb and Flow of Chinese Library and Information Services, May 4, 1919, to the Late 1980s*. Lanham, Md.: Scarecrow Press, 1995.

Barnouin, Barbara, and Changgen Yu. *Ten Years of Turbulence: The Chinese Cultural Revolution*. London: Kegan Paul, 1993.

Barry, Ellen. *How the Vijecnica Was Lost*. At www.metropolis-mag.com/html/content/5F0699/ju99/howt.htm.

Blazina, Vesna. "Mémoricide ou la purification culturelle: la guerre contre les bibliothéques de Croatie et de Bosnie-Herzégovine." At www.kakarigi.net/manu/blazina.htm.

Blium, Arlen Viktorovich. "'The Jewish Question' and Censorship in the USSR." In Jonathan Rose, ed., *The Holocaust and the Book*. Amherst: University of Massachusetts Press, 2001.

Canazzi, Catherine. "Orange, la bibliothèque pervertie." At www.enssib.fr/bbf/bbf-97-4/04-canazzi.pdf.

"Chinese Communist Leader Burns the Books," *New York Times,* August 25, 1950. In *Library Journal 75*, no. 1609 (October 1950).

Ding Lixia Xu (Lee-hsia Hsu Ting). "Library Services in the People's Republic of China: A Historical Overview." In *Library Quarterly 53*, no. 2 (1983).

Flandrin, Philippe. *Le Trésor perdu des rois d'Afghanistan*. Paris: Éditions du Rocher, 2001.

Gautier, François. *Un autre Regard sur l'Inde*. Geneva: Tricorne, 1999.

Hamel, Bernard. *De Sang et de larmes, la grande déportation de Cambodge*. Paris: Albin Michel, 1977.

Hu Daojing. *Shanghai tushuguan shi* (History of the Library of Shanghai). Shanghai: n.p., 1935.

Jiang Fucong (Chiang Fu-Ts'ung). "Habent sua fata libelli" (Books Make Their Own Fate). In *Philobiblon* 1, no. 2 (September 1946).

King, Gail. *The Xujiahui (Zikawei) Library of Shanghai*. At www.gslis.utexas.edu/landc/fulltext/LandC-32-4-Fking.pdf.

Koul, Mohan Lal. *Kashmir, Wail of a Valley*. New Delhi: Gyan Sagar Publications, 1999.

Lacroix, Gilles. "Censure et bibliothèques." In *Fatwa pour Schéhérazade et autres recits de la censure ordinaire*. Saint-Julien-Molin-Molette: Jean-Pierre Huguet, 1997.

Li Zhensheng. *Le Petit Livre rouge d'un photographe chinois*. Paris: Phaidon, 2003.

Liechtenhan, Francine-Dominique. *Le Grand Pillage: du butin des nazis aux trophées des Soviétiques*. Rennes: Éditions Ouest-France, 1998.

Ling, Ken. *La Vengeance du ciel: une jeune Chinois dans la Révolution culturelle*. Paris: Robert Laffont, 1981. Translated by Miriam London and Ta-ling Lee as *The Revenge of Heaven: Journal of a Young Chinese*. New York: Putnam, 1972.

Pedram, Latif. *Afghanistan. La Mémoire assassinée.* Paris: Édition Milles et une nuits, 2001.

———. "Afghanistan: la bibliothèque est en feu." In *Autodafé,* no. 1 (2001).

Pélissier, Roger. *Les Bibliothèques en Chine pendant la première moitié du XXe siècle.* Paris: Mouton, 1971.

Riedlmayer, Andras. *Libraries and Archives in Kosovo: A Postwar Report.* At www .bosnia.prg.uk/bosrep/decfeb00/libraries.htm.

Santantonios, Laurence. "Biblothèques: 7 ans avec l'extreme droite." In *Libres Hebdo,* no. 483 (September 27, 2002).

Stipcevic, Alecsandar. "The Oriental Books and Libraries in Bosnia During the War, 1992–1994." In *Libraries and Culture* 33, no. 3 (Summer 1998).

Thurston, Anne F. *Enemies of the People: The Ordeal of the Intellectuals in China.* Cambridge: Harvard University Press, 1988.

Wang, Youmei, and A. R. Rogers. "Thirty Years of Library Development in the People's Republic of China." In *International Library Review* 14, no. 4 (October 1982).

Weber, Olivier. *Le Faucon afghan, un voyage au pays des Taliban.* Paris: Robert Laffont, 2001.

Yan Jiaqi, Gao Gao, *Turbulent Decade: A History of the Cultural Revolution.* Honolulu: University of Hawaii Press, 1996.

Zhongguo tushuguan shiye jishi (Chronology of China's Libraries). Peking: n.p., n.d.

Zhou, Yuan, and Calvin Elliker. "From the People of the United States of America: The Books for China Programs during World War II." In *Libraries and Culture* 32, no. 2 (Spring 1997).

CHAPTER 8. PEACE DAMAGES

Basbanes, Nicholas A. *A Gentle Madness.* New York: Henry Holt, 1995.

Bekker-Nielson, Hans, and Ole Widding. *Arne Magnusson: The Manuscripts Collector.* Odense: Odense University Press, 1972.

Benjamin, Walter. *Je déballe ma Bibliothéque.* Paris: Payot et Rivages, 2000. Translated by Harry Zohn as "Unpacking My Library." In *Illuminations.* New York: Schocken, 1969.

Bergé, Marc. *Pour un Humanism vécu. Abu Hayyan al-Tawhidi.* Damascus: Institut français de Damas, 1979.

Bourgin, Georges. "L'Incendie de la Bibliothèque nationale et universitaire de Turin." In *Bibliothèque de l'École des chartes* (1904).

Burgess, Dean. "The Library Has Blown Up!" In *Library Journal* (October 1, 1989).

Burrows, John, and Diane Cooper. *Theft and Loss from UK Libraries: A National Survey.* Police Research Group, Crime Prevention Unit Series, paper no. 37, London, n.p., 1992.

Butler, Randall. "The Los Angeles Central Library Fire." In *Conservation Administration News* (1986).

Dorez, Léon. *L'Incendie de la Bibliothèque nationale de Turin.* Paris: R. Streglio & Cia., 1904.

Goetz, Arthur H. "A History of Horrid Catastrophes." In *Wilson Library Bulletin* (January 1973).

Gorrini, Giovanni. *L'Incendie de la Bibliothèque nationale de Turin.* Turin-Genoa: n.p., 1904.

Gracq, Julien. *Liberté grande.* Paris: José Corti, 1946.

Hamlin, Arthur T. "Libraries in Florence." In *Encyclopedia of Library and Information Science* 8 (1968).

Harvey, Miles. *The Island of Lost Maps: A True Story of Cartographic Crimes.* New York: Random House, 2000.

"Leningrad Library Fire." In *Abbey Newsletter* 12, no. 4 (June 1988).

Morrow, Lance. "A Holocaust of Words." In *TIME* magazine, May 2002.

Munn, Ralph. "The Problems of Theft and Mutilation." In *Library Journal* 60 (August 1935).

Otness, Harold. "Passenger Ship Libraries." In *Journal of Library History* 14, no. 4 (Autumn 1979).

Settis, Salvatore. "Warburg continuatis. Description d'une bibliothèque." In *Le Pouvoir des bibliothèques.* Paris: Albin Michel, 1996.

Shehu, Bashkim. "Enver Hoxha: La bibliothèque du dictateur." In *Autodafé,* no. 2 (Autumn 2001).

Skallerup, Harry. *Books Afloat and Ashore.* Hamden: Archon Books, 1974.

"Special Report: Fire at the USSR Academy of Sciences Library." In *Library Journal* (June 15, 1988).

Walford, Cornelius. "The Destruction of Libraries by Fire Considered Practically and Historically." In *Transactions and Proceedings of the Second Annual Meeting of the Library Association of the United Kingdom Held at Manchester, September 23, 24, and 25, 1879.* London: Chiswick Press, 1880.

Warburg, Aby. *Le Rituel de serpent, Art et anthropologie.* Paris: Macula, 2003. Translated by Michael P. Steinberg as *Images from the Regions of the Pueblo Indians of North America.* Ithaca, N.Y.: Cornell University Press, 1995.

Watson, Tom. "Out of the Ashes: The Los Angeles Public Library." In *Wilson Library Bulletin* (December 1989).

Welch, Theodore F. *Libraries and Librarianship in Japan.* Westport, Conn.: Greenwood Press, 1997.

Winter, Calvin. "The Libraries on the Trans-Atlantic Liners." In *The Bookman,* no. 31 (June 1911).

CHAPTER 9. AN EMBARRASSMENT OF MODERNITY

Burton, Margaret. *Famous Libraries of the World.* London: Grafton and Co., 1997.

Chandler, Georges. *Libraries in the East: An International and Comparative Study.* London: Seminar Press Ltd., 1971.

Coser, Lewis A., C. Kadushin, and W. W. Powell. *Books: The Culture and Commerce of Publishing.* New York: Basic Books, 1982.

Eco, Umberto. *De bibliotheca.* Presentation at a conference on March 10, 1981, given to celebrate the twenty-fifth anniversary of the installation of the public library of Milan in the Sormani Palace, Caen, 1986.

Esdaile, Arundell. *National Libraries of the World: Their History, Administration, and Public Services.* London: Grafton, 1957.

Kühlmann, Marie. *Censure et bibliothèques au XXe siècle.* Paris: Cercle de la Librairie, 1989.

Mandosio, Jean-Marc. *L'Effondrement de la très grande bibliothèque nationale de France. Ses causes, ses consequences.* Paris: Encyclopédie des nuisances, 1999.

Mercier, Louis-Sébastien. *Tableau de Paris,* vol. 1. Hamburg: n.p., 1781; reprint, Paris: Mercure de France, 1998.

Stasse, François. *La Véritable Histoire de la grande bibliothèque.* Paris: Seuil, 2002.

CHAPTER 10. FLAMEPROOF KNOWLEDGE

Baker, Nicholson. *Double Fold. Libraries and the Assault on Paper.* New York: Random House, 2001.

Basbanes, Nicholas. *Patience and Fortitude.* New York: Harper, 2001.

Gaspardone, Émile. "Bibliographical annamite." In *Bulletin de l'EFEO,* no. 34 (1935).

Pächt, Otto. *L'Enluminure médiévale.* Paris: Macula, 1997.

Renoult, Daniel. "Les Bibliothèques numériques." In Christian Jacob, *Des Alexandries I. Du livre au texte.* Paris: BNF, 2001.

Text-e: le texte à l'heure de l'Internet. Paris: Bibliothèque publique d'information, 2003.

CHAPTER 11. RETURN TO ALEXANDRIA

Al-Ahnaf, Mustapha, ed. "Cedej Égypte/Monde arabe." In *La censure ou comment la contourner.* Brussels: Complexe, 2001.

Pataut, Fabrice, ed. *La Nouvelle Bibliothèque d'Alexandrie.* Paris: Buchet Chastel, 2003.

APPENDIX 1. THE GREAT WRITERS ARE UNANIMOUS: *DELENDA EST BIBLIOTHECA!*

Auster, Paul. *In the Country of Last Things.* New York: Viking, 1987.

Bachelard, Gaston. *Lautréamont.* Paris: José Corti, 1939.

Biraben, Jean-Claude. *Le Pique-feu,* no. 8 (July 2003).

Borges, Jorge Luis. "The Congress." In *The Book of Sand.* New York: Plume, 1979.

Bradbury, Ray. *Fahrenheit 451.* New York: Del Ray, 1987.

Canetti, Elias. *Auto-da-fé.* New York: Farrar, Strauss, and Giroux, 1984.

Cervantes, Miguel de. *Don Quixote.* London: Penguin, 1951.

Chaintreau, Anne-Marie, and Renée Lemaître. *Drôles de bibliothèques: le theme de la bibliothèque dans la literature et le cinema.* Paris: Cercle de la Librairie, 1993.

Cortázar, Julio. *Fantômas contre les vampires des multinationals.* Paris: La Différence, 1998.

Eco, Umberto. *The Name of the Rose.* New York: Harcourt, Brace, Jovanovich, 1980.

France, Anatole. *La rotisserie de la Reine Pédauque.* Paris: Calmann-Levy, 1962. Translated by Wilfred Jackson as *At the Sign of the Queen Pedauque.* London: Bodley Head, 1925.

Hrabal, Bohumil. *Too Loud a Solitude.* Translated by Michael Henry Heim. New York: Harcourt, Brace, Jovanovich, 1992.

Hugo, Victor. *Quatrevingt-Treize*. Paris: Gallimard, 2001. Translation by Frank Lee Benedict as *93*. Amsterdam: Fredonia Books, 2001.

Huxley, Aldous. *Brave New World*. New York: Harper and Row, 1945.

Mercier, Louis-Sébastien. *L'An 2440, rêve s'il en fut jamais*. Paris: La Découverte, 1999.

Mirbeau, Octave. *L'Abbé Jules*. Paris: Albin Michel, 1949.

Orwell, George. *1984*. London: Penguin Books, 1954.

Roudaut, Jean. *Les dents de Bérénice: essai sur la representation et l'évocation de la bibliothèque*. Cahors: Deyrolle, 1996.

Rousseau, Jean-Jacques. *Discourse sur les sciences et les arts*. Paris: Gallimard 1987. Translated by Roger D. and Judith R. Masters as *The First and Second Discourses*. New York: St. Martin's Press, 1964.

Shaw, George Bernard. *Caesar and Cleopatra: A History*. Baltimore: Penguin Books, 1960.

Shehu, Bashkim. "La Bibliothèque du dictateur." In *Autodafé*, no. 2 (Autumn 2001). At www.autodafe.org.

Thiem, Jon. "Myths of the Universal Library: From Alexandria to the Postmodern Age." In *Serials Librarian* 26, no. 1 (1995).

Ward, J. O. "Alexandria and Its Medieval Legacy: The Book, the Monk, and the Rose." In *The Library of Alexandria*. London: Tauris, 2000.

APPENDIX 2. A SHORT HISTORY OF THE CENSUS OF LOST BOOKS, WITH A LEGEND TO BRING IT TO A CLOSE—THE HIDDEN LIBRARY

Arans, David. "A Note on the Lost Library of the Moscow Tsars." In *Journal of Library History* 18, no. 3 (Summer 1983).

Blades, William. *The Enemies of Books*. London: Elliot Stock, 1880.

Brunet, Pierre-Gustave. *Livres perdus. Essai bibliographique sur les livres devenues introuvables, par Philomneste junior*. Brussels: Gay and Doucé, 1882.

Drujon, Fernand. *Essai bibliographique sur la destruction volontaire des livres or bibliolytie*. Paris: Maison Quantin, 1889.

Lacroix, Paul. *Recherches bibliographiques sur des livres rares et curieux*. Paris: Édouard Rouveyre, 1880.

Queneau, Raymond. *Aux Confines des ténèbres. Les fous littéraires français du XIXe siècle*. Paris: Gallimard, 2002.

INDEX

Abelard, Peter, 131
Abu Hayyan al-Tawhidi, 266
Aeschylus, 13
Afghanistan, 228–31
Africa, 223–24
Agapitus I, 36
Aix-la-Chapelle, 130
Alamut, 67–68
Al-Andalus, 48–54
Albion, 253–54
Alcuin, 130
Alembert, Jean le Rond d', 263
Alexander the Great, 5
Alexander V, 74
Alexandria, 292–99
   buildings of, 10–16
   destruction of, 16–23
Almanzor, 51–54
Amenhotep IV, 9
American Library Association, 271
Ames, Joseph, 256
Amir, 63
Andalusia, 52–53
Anderson, David G., 271
Andronicus of Rhodes, 24
Anghiera, Peter Martyr d', 125
Antiochos, 73–74
Antonius, Marcus, 18–19, 27
Apellicon of Teos, 24
Aphthonius, 18
Arabic language, 55–56
Aragon, Enrique d', 121–22
Arans, David, 320
Archimedes, 11

architecture, 267–70
Arendt, Hannah, 196
Aretin, Johann Christoph von, 161–62
Argentine National Library, 260–61
Aristotle, 13–14, 23–24, 75–76
Arnoult, Jean-Marie, 234
Art of Typography, The, 256
Ashburnham House, 242
Ashurbanipal, 3–4
Asia
   book collecting in, 87–91
   destruction of books in, 86–89,
      92–93, 99–100
   early writing in China, 80–82
   inventories in, 90–96
   private collections in, 93–98
   selling of books, 103–5
Asoka, King, 13
Assassins, 66, 67, 68
astronomy, 70–71
Ata Malik Juvaini, 67, 69
Athens, 23–26
Atrium Libertatis, 27
Attalids, 19
Attavanti, Attavente degli, 140–41
Aucher, Anthony, 133
Aucour, Jean Barbier d', 147–48
Augustine, 35, 37
Augustus, 12, 27–28
Aurelian, 19
Austerlitz, 198, 200–201
Avicenna, 65
Awad, Muhammad, 293
Aztecs. *See* New World

Ba Jin, 271–72
Bagford, John, 256
Baghdad, 71–72
Bakarsic, Kemal, 228
Baker, Nicholson, 276, 278
Balkan Bosnia, 224–28
bamboo, 82
Bamboo Annals, 84
Barbarossa, Chairadin, 120–21
Basil I, Emperor, 38
Basiliscus, 38
Basra, 65
Baudrillart, Henri, 164
bayt al-hikma, 56, 57
Bayt al-Hikma, 234
Behr, Kurt von, 197
Belgium, 173
Bellwood, Peter, 261
Belokurov, A., 321
Benjamin, Walter, 262
Bergson, Henri, 172
Bernard, Charles, 109
Bernard, Claude, 251
Bèze, Theodore de, 146
Bible, 34–35
Biblioteca Nazionale ed Universitaria, 244–45
Bibliotheca Alexandrina, 292–99
Bibliothèque de Poitiers, 273–74
Billeter, Jean François, 98
Biraben, Jean-Claude, 315
Bland, Gilbert, 261
Bloch, Camille, 199–200
Blondel, Jacques-François, 269
Blumberg, Stephen, 260
Bomberg, Daniel, 77, 192
Bonaparte, Joseph, 120
bones, 80–81
Book of Changes, 82, 86
Book of Documents, 81–82, 87
Book of Dreams, 9
Book of Songs, 81–82
Boonen, Jacques, 171
Bosnia, 224–28
Boston Library, 248–49

Botta, Paul-Émile, 2
Bougre, Robert le, 112
Bourgin, Georges, 245
Bradbury, Richard, 276
Breton, André, 264
Brisac, Catherine, 146
British Library, 275–76, 289–90
Browne, Thomas, 300–301
Brunet, Jacques-Charles, 263
Buddha and Buddhism, 105–6, 108–9, 110
Budé Collection, 249
burial, 9–10
Burma, 108
Burtenbach, Sebastian Schertlin von, 142
Bury, Richard Aungerville de, 132
Buturline, Dimitri, 169–70
Byzantium, library of, 37–38

Caesar, Julius, 17–18, 27, 32–33
Cairo, 64
Calcutta Book Fair, 150
Callimachus, 15
Cambodia, 216–17
Cambysus, 9–10
Cameron, George, 5
Canfora, Luciano, 15
Caracalla, 19
card catalogs, 150–51, 154–55
Carlyle, Thomas, 258–59
Carthage, 26–27
Casamassima, Emmanuele, 247
Cassiodorus, 36
Cassirer, Ernst, 263–64
Cassius, Dio, 30
Cassou, Jean, 197
Catherine the Great, 148
Cecil, William, 134
censorship, 28, 295–97
census, of lost books, 315–21
Champollion, 7
Char, René, 265
Charles V, 142, 239
Chateaubriand, 11
Chevreuse, Irene, 182

Chicago Tribune, 277
China, 80–82, 207–16, 271–72
Christians and Christianity, 20, 34, 78, 117–18, 285–86. *See also* New World
Churchill, Winston, 176
Cicero, 29, 36
Cisneros, 113, 115
Clement IV, 74
Clement VII, Pope, 139–40
Clement XIV, Pope, 148
Cleopatra, 17
Clodius, 30–31
Codex Manesse, 145
Codex Sinaiticus, 45
collecting of books, 300–301
    hierophants of, 303–15
    igniters of, 301–3
Commission of Artistic Recovery (SCL), 198–99
Commodus, Emperor, 30
Company of Jesus, 148
Compt, Jean Marie, 274
Conde, José Antonio, 120
Confucius, 82
Constantine the Great, 37–38, 45
Constantinople, 37–41
Cordoba, 48–54
Cornudet, Michel, 165
Corvinus, Matthias, 140–41, 262
Corvinian Library, 141
Cotton, Henry, 242
Cousin, Jules, 165–66
Crimea, 204
Crusaders, 66
Cuba, 219–20
cuneiform, 1–2
Cyril, 21
Czechoslovakia, 185

Damalan, Henri-César Sama, 223
Darius I, 5
deaccession, 270–74
deacidification, 277–78
death, 261–66

Degrelle, Léon, 173
Delaigue, Serge, 251
Demetrios of Phalera, 12–13, 14–15
Dewey, Melville, 263
Dewidar, Lotfi, 292
Dharmaganja, 106
digitalization, 288
Din, Rashid al-, 10
Diocletian, 19–20, 35
Diodorus, 7
Disraeli, Isaac, 37
divination, 81
Domergue, Urbain, 156
Don Quixote, 301–2
Dong Fuxiang, 102–3
Donin, Nicolas, 73–74
Dowlin, Kenneth E., 270
Drujon, Fernand, 238–39, 317–19
Druzes, 67

Ebolli, Gilles, 222
Eche, Yusef, 48
Eco, Umberto, 313
Edward VI, 133
Egypt, 292–99
    building of Alexandria, 10–16
    destruction of Alexandria, 16–23
    libraries in, 6–10
Egyptian National Library, 265
Eichmann, Adolf, 193
Electronic Library, The, 270
elements, the, 241–52
elginism, 101
Aemilius, Scipio, 26
Aemilius, Paulus, 26
England, 100–101, 132–34
Epic of Gilgamesh, The, 3
Epiphanes, 77
Erosthenes, 11
Erskine, William, 166
Estonia, 204–5
ethnic cleansing, 113–14
Euclid, 11
Eumenes II, 19
Euripides, 13

Europe, 73
Eusebius, 45
executors against blasphemy, 76–77

Fabre-Luce, Robert, 182
Fan Dachong, 96
Fan Qin, 95–96
Fatih, Mehmed II al-, 41
Fatimids, 67, 70
faylasuf, 54
Ferdinand, Francis, 224
Ferdinand of Spain, 112–13
Fernando VII, 120
Ficino, Marsilio, 136
Field of Mars, 30
Filov, Vladimir, 206–7
Finland, 243–44
fire, 2, 29–30
Flanders Road, The, 177–78
Foa, Ugo, 192–93
Forbes, Clarence, 28
Fortress of Writings, 5
Foster, Norman, 269
Four Classics of the Yellow Emperor, 89
France, 74, 100–101, 174–75, 198–99,
    220–22, 272
Franco-Prussian War, 170–71
Frank, Jacob, 78
Franks, 39, 66
French National Assembly, 246
French Revolution, 151–68
Friedrich, Jörg, 178
Fu Shing, 87
Fucong, Jiang, 207–8
Fugger, Ulrich, 145

Galen, 13, 30
Galeotto, Marzio, 140
Gamboa, Sarmiento de, 123
Gao Yuan, 97
Gaspardone, Émile, 286
Gellius, Aulus, 17, 27
General Inspection of Libraries,
    272–73
Gentilis, Robert, 256

Germany, 176–78
Ghitany, Gamal al-, 295–97
ghiyar, 58
Gibbon, Edward, 19–20, 25, 41
Giles, Lancelot, 103
Giza, 9
Gorrini, Giovanni, 245
Goths, 25
Grand Canon of Yongle, 102–3
Greece, 23–26
Gregory I, 36
Grimstead, Patricia, 203
Gu Tinglong, 215
Guadalajara, Marcos de, 115
Gui, Bernardo, 74
Guichard, Pierre, 51

Hafsa, 47
Hakam II, al-, 48–50
Hall of Dreams, 109
Hall of Writings, 91–92
Hamlin, Arthur T., 247
hammans, 22
Hammer, Armand, 207
Han Gaozu, 88
Hanlin Yuan, 102
Harvard University Library, 258
Harvey, Miles, 261
Hassan-i Sabbah, 67–68
Heine, Heinrich, 168, 190
Helmy, Fouas, 292–93
Henry V, 134
Henry VIII, 132–33
Hernández, Francisco, 118
Herod the Great, 77
Herodian, 30
Herodotus, 7–8, 9, 39
Herophilus, 11
Hibiya Public Library, 178
hidden libraries, 320–21
hierophants, 303–15
Hirsch, Abraham, 251
Hisham, 49, 52
History of the Scholars, 22
Hitler, Adolf, 175–76, 179–80

Holocaust, 179–202
Homer, 14
Houzhu, 93
Hoxha, Enver, 262
Hugo, Victor, 101, 167, 304–5
Hulugu, 68–69, 70–71
humanism, 115
Hungary, 139–43
Hussein, Saddam, 293
Hypatia, 21

Iamblicus of Syria, 7
Ibn al-Khattab, Umar, 42–43
Ibn Khaldun, 43–44, 71
Ibn Killis, 59, 64
Ibn Mas'ud, Abdullah, 47
ignorance, 8–9
Illustration, 181–82
India, 105–9
Inquisition, 112–13
    New World and, 122–29
    Spain and, 113–22
Inquisition of Cologne, 76
Iraq, 71–72, 231–37
Islam
    founding of, 42–43
    libraries and, 43–48
Ismaili, 67
Italy, 175, 244–45

Jacob, Christian, 18
Janos, 141
Japan, 109–11, 172, 178–79, 207–8
Jefferson, Thomas, 243
Jerome, Saint, 37, 45, 75–76
Jesuits, 127–29
Jews and Judaism, 73–79, 112–13, 190,
    205–6
    Spanish Inquisition and, 114, 115–16
    See also Nazism
John II, King, 122
John of Antioch, 19–20
John the Grammarian, 21–22
John XXII, 74
Johnston, Mary, 255

Joseph II, 150, 151
Josephus, Flavius, 44
Jovian, 35
Julian III, 74
Jünger, Ernst, 174–75, 178

Kaneyoshi, 110–11
Kaplan, Chäim Aron, 190
Karadzic, Radovan, 225
Kashmir, 218–19
Kircher, Athanasius, 127
Koffi, Tiburce, 223
Kong Fu, 87
Kublai Khan, 92

La Mirandola, Pico de, 137
La Plume Noire, 251
Lacroix, Abbé, 165
Laeta, 37
Laisné, Blaney, 158
Landa Calderón, Diego de, 126
Lao-tzu, 82
Lascaris, Jean, 137
Lateran Council, 113, 137, 138
Laurentian Library, 139–40
Layard, Henry Austen, 2–3, 4
Le Ray, Louis, 300–301
Leland, John, 133
Lenoble, Michel, 246
Leo the Isaurian, 38
Leo X, Pope, 138
Les Belles Lettres, 249–50
Les Martyrs, 11
Letter of Aristeus, The, 12
Louvain (Brabant), 171–73
Li Cang, 89
Li Hui, 272
Li Si, 84–85
Li Zhensheng, 212
Li Zhi, 98
Libraries of Burned Books, 182
Library of Alexandria. *See* Alexandria
Library of Congress, 243, 260, 278–79
Library of Sippar, 232
Lindisfarne Gospels, 242

Lithuania, 205
Liu Bang, 88
Lloyd-Jones, Hugh, 43
Lob, Marcel, 198
Lombards, 36
Lorenzo the Magnificent, 136–37
Louis I, 130
Loyola, Ignatius, 148–49
Lü Buwei, 84–85
Lucan, 16–17
Lucian, 29
Lucretius, 32, 33
Lucullus, 26
Luo Zhengyu, 80, 104–5
Luther, Martin, 76
Lyon Affair, 250–52

Magnusson, Arne, 241–42
Maimonides, 78
Mandosio, Jean-Marc, 268–69
Manuel, Robert, 197–98
Mao Tse-tung, 90, 210–11
Marburg, Conrad de, 112
Marcellinus, Ammianus, 20, 35
Marx, Carl, 190
Matthys, Jean, 143–44
Maxims of Ptahhotep, 8
Mayans. *See* New World
Medici, Cosimo de, 135, 136
Menant, Joachim, 4
Mendoza Codex, 124
Mercier, Louis-Sébastien, 167–68, 173, 281, 288, 302–3
Mesopotamia, 2
Michael, James, 196
Michael VIII Paleologus, 40
Michigan State University, 246–47
microfilm, 277–81
Middle Ages, 129–34
Mindon, King, 108–9
Mithradates, king of Pontus, 26
Molotov cocktails, 247
monastic libraries, 129–34, 147–51
Mongols, 68, 71, 72
Montezuma II, 124

Moors, 114–15
Morgan Library, 248
Moroccan Library, 118
Muhammad, 42, 66–67
Mukhtasar, 50–51
multispectral imaging, 33
Munn, Ralph, 257
Muntzer, Thoman, 143
Museum of Modern Literature, 271–72
Museum of the Muses, 11, 12–13

Nachman, Hasid, 78–79
Naderi, Saïd Mansour, 229–30
National Front, 221
National Library in Beijing, 271–72
National Library of France, 171–72, 189, 256, 266–67, 284–85
National Library of Iraq, 233–34
National Library of the Ivory Coast, 223
Naudé, Gabriel de, 263
Nazism, 179–202
Needham, Joseph, 90
Neffer, Elisabeth, 231–32
Neleus of Skepsis, 23–24
Nero, 31
Netherlands, 186
New World, Inquisition and, 122–29
newspapers, 277
Nicetas, 39–40
Nineveh, 2–4
Niu Hong, 90–91
Nizar, 62–63
Nizarites, 67
Nobrega, Manuel de, 127–28

Octavian Library, 28, 30
Octavius, 19
Oda Nobunaga, 110
Odyssey, 14
Omar, 42–43
"On the Destruction of Libraries by Fire Considered Practically and Historically," 238–39
optical character recognition (OCR) scanning, 284–85

Orchid Pavilion Preface, 10
Origen, 44–45
Orosius, Paulus, 20–21, 30
Osman, 46–47
Ottheinrich, 144
Ouyang Xiu, 97
Oxyrhynchos (Greece), 26

Pachahutec, 123
paganism, 20
Palatina Library, 144–45
Palatine Library, 28, 30, 31, 36
Palestine, 45–46
Panckoucke, Charles, 246
paper, 82–83
papyrus, 7–8
parchment, 19
Paris, Louis, 164
Parker, Matthew, 134
Pascal, Blaise, 149
Paul, 34–35
peace damages, libraries
    death, 261–66
    elements and, 241–52
    sea and, 252–55
    theft, 255–61
Peasants War, 142–45
Pedram, Latif, 230
People of the Book, 77–79
Pepys, Samuel, 134
Pergamum, 18–19
Persepolis, 5
Perseus, 26
Persians, 9
Petricevic, Jozo, 228
Philip II, King, 117–18, 120–21
Philip the Fair, 74
Philodemus, 32, 33
Philoponus, John, 24
Photius, 38–39
Piaggio, Antonio, 33
Pichun, 83–84
Pinelli, Gian Vincenzo, 253
Pisistrarus 1, 25
Pius VII, 149

Plantin Affair, 251
Plato, 6, 14, 23
Pliny, 26–27, 32
Plutarch, 17, 26
Poggio Bracciolini, Gian Francesco, 135–36, 140
Pohl, Johannes, 195–96
Poland, 185–86, 190–91
Pollio, Asinius, 27
Polo, Marco, 68
Polybius, 14
Pomrenze, Seymour J., 196
ponentine, 76
popery, 242–43
Popol Vuh, 127
power, 143–44
printing presses, 76–77
Prisse Papyrus, 8
Proust, Marcel, 262
Ptolemy I, 11, 13–15
Ptolemy II Philadelphus, 11–14
Ptolemy III, 13
Ptolemy V, 19
public baths, 28–29
public libraries, 240–41
publishing industry, 274–75
Pul-e-Khumri, 230
Pythagoras, 6

Qin, 84
Qing, Jiang, 210–11
Quianlong, Emperor, 98–99
Quint, Charles, 120–21
quipus, 123–24
Qur'an, 46–48, 64, 66

Rahnab, Abd al-, 49
Ramesses II, 7, 8–9
Ramesseum of Thebes, 7
Rapperswil Collection, 186, 190–91
Ratnodadhi Tower, 106–7
Rawlinson, Henry, 4
Reclus, Elie, 166–67
Reformation, 134–35
Regia Laurentina, 118–20

religion, 237
Renaissance, 134–46
Renan, Ernest, 166–67
Republic, 14
Resources Liberté, 222
Reuchlin report, 75–76
Ricard, Robert, 124
Rizzi, Lorenzo, 148
Roman Empire, 19
Rome, 26–37, 145
Rosenberg, Alfred, 193–94, 202
Roth, Joseph, 182
Roudaut, Jean, 314–15
Rousseau, Jean-Jacques, 302
Rudomino, Margarita, 203
Russell Tribunal, 312–13
Russia, 169–70, 179, 186–88, 202–7
Russo, Baruchiah, 78

Saddam House of Manuscripts, 234–35
Saladin, 22, 40, 63–64, 264
Salin, Patrice, 164–65
San Francisco Library, 269–70
Sand, George, 167
Sarageldin, Ismael, 295–96
Saudi Arabia, 294
Savonarola, 137, 138
Sayyinda, 68
Schrettinger, Martin, 162
Scientific Study of the Classics, 97–98
scrolls, 14–15
sea, libraries at, 252–55
Sebald, Winifred Georg, 178
Seleucos Nicator, 25
Seljuks, 57, 58
Seneca, 17, 29
Serapeum, 15–16
Seville, 117
Shang Dynasty, 81
Shanghai Library, 271–72
Sharif, Mazare, 229–30
Shiites, 58
ship collections, 13
Sibyl of Cumae, 28
Siculus, Diodorus, 41

Sigismund of Luxembourg, 140
Siku Quanshu, 95, 100
Sima Qian, 84
Simon, Claude, 177
Sinology, 103–4
Siu Dynasty, 91–92
Slovenia, 186
Sophocles, 13
South America. *See* New World
Soviet Union, 169–70, 179, 186–88, 202–7
Spain, Inquisition and, 113–22
spirituality, 237
Sri Lanka, 217–18
Stephens, John Lloyd, 125
storage, 15–16
Strabo, 12, 15, 17, 23–24
Stubbings, Hilda, 176
Subh the Basque, 48–49, 52
Suetonius, 27–28
Suleiman the Magnificent, 121, 141
Sulla, 26, 30
Sumerians, 2–3
sunna, 57
Swieten, Gottfried van, 150–51

Tabularium, 30–31
Tafur, Pero, 40
Taizong, 10
Talmud, 73–74
Tan Xianjin, 214
Tao te Ching, 89, 92
Taoists, 86–87
Tarasicodissa, 38
Tarasius, 38–39
technology, 280–81, 282–91
Telephus of Pergamum, 32
Temple of Horus, 7
Temple of Peace, 30
Temple of the Nymphs, 30–31
Teo-Amoxtli, 125, 127
theft, 13, 255–61
Theodora, Empress, 38
Theodosius, 20
Theophilus, 20

Theophrastus, 23
Thiem, Jon, 313–14
Tibet, 209
Timon of Philus, 12
Tiraboschi, 253
Titus-Livy, 36
Totality of Books, Quanshu, 98–99, 100
Tripoli, 66
Turgenev Collection, 203–4
tushuguan, 89–90
Tyrannion the Grammarian, 24

Ukraine, 188–89
uncial, 37
Ungerer, Tomi, 171
United States, 169, 172–73, 248, 270–71, 277
Universal History, 41
University of Stanford, 245
Usaibi'a, 64
Uthman, 64

Varro, 27, 37
Vatican, 145
Verne, Jules, 253
Veronese, Guarino, 253
Vesalius, 171, 172
Videla, Luis Alberto, 260–61
Vijecnica, 224–26
virtual books, 282–83
Vivarium of Cassidorus, 36–37, 131
volcanoes, 32–33

waaf, 55
Wade, Thomas Francis, 101
Walford, Cornelius, 238, 239, 253
Wang Xian, 94–95
Wang Xizhi, 10
war
    books in, 170–79, 235–37
    See also Holocaust; world tour, end-of-the-century
Warburg, Aby, 262–64

Warburg Library, 262
Warsaw Uprising, 186
weeding, 272–74, 276
Welch, Theodore, 245
Wen, Emperor, 91
Wetterman, Johannes, 320
Wilhelm II, 172
William III, King, 242
wooden boards, 82
world tour, end-of-the-century
    Afghanistan, 228–31
    Africa, 223–24
    Bosnia, 224–28
    Cambodia, 216–17
    China, 207–16
    Cuba, 219–20
    France, 220–22
    Iraq, 231–37
    Kashmir, 218–19
    Soviet Union, 202–7
World War II, 174–79. *See also* Nazism
Wu, Emperor, 88–89
Wylie, Andrew, 244

Xerxes, 5, 25
Xiang Yu, 88
Xuanzang, 106–7
Xuanzong, 92
Xunxi, 86

Yuan Di, 92–93

Zacuto, 71
Zahran, Mohsen, 293
Zebi, Shabbethai, 78
Zenodotus, 11, 14
Zeno, 38
Zhang Yuanji, 96
Zhao Yu, 94–95
Zheng, 84–86, 87
Zhuangsu, 97
Zhuangzi, 92–93
Zidan, Moulay, 118
Zoroaster, 5